THE ROARING STREAM

THE
ROARING STREAM

A New Zen Reader

EDITED BY

Nelson Foster and
Jack Shoemaker

FOREWORD BY
ROBERT AITKEN

THE ECCO PRESS

THE ECCO PRESS
100 West Broad Street
Hopewell, New Jersey 08525

Published simultaneously in Canada by
Penguin Books Canada Ltd., Ontario
Printed in the United States of America

Library of Congress Cataloging-in-Publication Data

The roaring stream : a new Zen reader / edited by Nelson Foster and
Jack Shoemaker ; foreword by Robert Aitken.—1st. ed.
p.   cm.—(Ecco companions)
Includes bibliographical references and index.
ISBN 0-88001-344-3 (case).—ISBN 0-88001-511-X (pbk.)
1. Zen literature—Translations into English.   2. Zen Buddhism.
I. Foster, Nelson, 1951–   .   II. Shoemaker, Jack, 1946–   .
III. Series.
BQ 9264.R63   1996
294.3'927—dc20   96-5151

Pages 369 to 374 constitute an extension of this copyright page
Designed by Mina Greenstein
The text of this book is set in 10 point Simoncini Garamond

9   8   7   6   5   4   3   2   1

FIRST EDITION

In memory of

Anne Hopkins Aitken and Kenneth Rexroth

A monk introduced himself to the teacher Hsüan-sha, saying. "I have just entered this monastery. Please show me where to enter the Way."

"Do you hear the sound of the valley stream?" asked Hsüan-sha.

"Yes," said the monk.

"Enter there!"

Contents

JAPAN

Foreword

ON BOOKS AND READING FOR THE ZEN STUDENT

My life as a Zen Buddhist began with a good book, in a civilian internment camp in Kobe, Japan. One evening during the second winter of the Pacific War, a guard entered my dorm, waving a book, and mumbling drunkenly, "This book, my English teacher, . . . " Rising involuntarily from my bed, I boldly took it from his hand—and never gave it back. It was R. H. Blyth's *Zen in English Literature and Oriental Classics,* then recently published.

The world had been readying me for a long time. Until then, my preferred camp reading had been Miyamori's *Haiku, Ancient and Modern,* but the path of my preparation ran all the way back through my young adulthood in Honolulu to evenings as a small child, sitting on the carpet at my grandfather's feet with my brother and little cousins, absorbing a range of poems by Heine, Goethe, Burns, Longfellow, and Walter de la Mare.

I was probably also readied by the state of the world at war and by my own health—freezing cold had exacerbated my chronic asthma. In any case, when I got back in my bunk, opened the plain cover of Blyth's book, I had been searching for it all my life without knowing its title, its author, or its subject. As I read Blyth's words over and over, new and marvelous vistas of culture and thought opened for me. I felt that I was uncovering primordial configurations of myself. Now as I look at the book, its flaws and mistakes jump out at me, but at the time it was the communiqué I was unconsciously awaiting.

The great mystery of that encounter with Mr. Blyth's words has recurred many times in the ensuing half-century. Again and again, books have opened my eyes to the Dharma, shaken me out of superficial views and commonplace understanding, and even led me to good teachers. These experiences put the lie to the commonly heard notion that reading and study are at odds with Zen practice and with religious life generally.

Among the sources of this misunderstanding are the warnings given by Ch'an and Zen teachers themselves, past and present. Musō Soseki, the early Japanese master whose work has an honored place in this volume, declared in his Admonitions:

> I have three sorts of disciples. The best are those who resolutely give up all worldly relationships and devote themselves wholly to seeking and realizing their own true natures. The middle sort are not really earnest in Zen practice, and in

order to find distraction from it prefer to read about it in books. The lowest are
those who eclipse the light of their self-nature and do nothing but lick up the
Buddha's spit.

Regrettably, Zen Buddhist teachers in Asia—and in the Americas and Europe as
well—consider that books *as such* encourage a preoccupation with "the Buddha's spit." They advise their students to be single-minded in their practice and
not read anything at all. This is an egregious corruption of Musō's message and
an abuse of his eminent teachers, colleagues, and successors, all of whom, as we
know from their writings, were readers and writers at a high level, thoroughly
immersed in their religious, and indeed their literary tradition.

Admittedly, there may come a point in Zen study when reading should be indeed set aside. The classic case is Hsiang-yen, a former student of Pai-chang,
who was confronted with a tough question by his new teacher, Kuei-shan. He
ransacked all the notes he had made of Pai-chang's talks, but couldn't come up
with anything remotely suitable. Finally, with Kuei-shan's help, he realized that a
secondhand understanding would never satisfy his hunger for realization. Exclaiming "A painting of cakes won't fill the belly!" he went off to face his question in solitude.

Except for such crucial, usually quite brief intervals, it is generally very important for Zen students to read. Since our needs as readers vary widely from individual to individual and from one point in life to another, when students ask
me what to read, I give them a current bibliography, but I also tell them, "Follow
your nose." Go to the library or bookstore, pull down books and look at them.
Trust yourself to discover the right one. Perhaps it will be a book that will
awaken you to *bodhichitta*, the imperative for realization and compassion. But
next year, when you revisit the same library or bookstore, you will discover
books that you passed over the first time.

In the years when I was establishing my Zen practice, the need for a portable
compendium of Ch'an and Zen literature was met by D. T. Suzuki's *Manual of
Zen Buddhism,* which I read in my internment-camp days. Though it included
relatively few translations and was even then quite archaic in its English style, it
served us well, and it was an important resource for thinkers of that period. Al-
dous Huxley placed it on his list of ten books he would take to a desert island.

Today, however, the *Manual* and books of its era are quite dated. In the past
thirty years, translators, historians, and Zen teachers and students have rendered
an astonishingly large portion of the original literature into English. Back in the
early 1950s, even those bookshops that specialized in Asian books offered only
half a shelf of Mahāyāna Buddhist titles, with important traditions not represented at all. Now the situation is reversed, and we find a formidable array, more
books, it seems, than we can possibly read. This great corpus gives us variety and

detail, as well as important perspectives that were not evident earlier. For example, such key figures as Bodhidharma and Hui-neng shift to some degree from history to the edges of misty folklore, and yet at the same time their teachings become clarified, and we learn the importance of folklore itself—to our practice and to our spiritual maturity.

The Roaring Stream puts the fruits of these great labors in our hands. It brings together a wealth of material already published, but never before available in a single volume, plus a few translations appearing for the first time. You can dip into the waters of this stream, again and again, at any point finding refreshment and perspective on Ch'an and Zen as practice, as presentation of the Main Fact, and as a culture and tradition. A year from now you can dip again and find treasures that were not at all evident the first time.

Moreover, you can get acquainted with the old teachers as individuals. The advisor to the emperor and the poet in a cave are very different fellows. Their words differ, their manner differs, their social views differ. Yet read side by side in this volume, their intimate kinship in the Buddha-Dharma becomes evident, their intimate kinship with us in our own living rooms today becomes clear, and our understanding of the Buddha-Dharma itself is vastly enriched.

—Robert Aitken

Introduction

Zen has a peculiar hold on the public imagination, it seems, and certainly on public discourse. In the hundred-odd years since the first Zen master traveled to the United States, Zen has steadily, mysteriously migrated from the peripheral realms of interreligious dialogue and academic study toward the pumping, thumping heart of popular culture. A movie critic describes Sean Connery's costuming as "Zenned-out black Armanis." Patagonia flogs hats in a pattern it calls "Zen Turtles." In the funnies, Calvin questions Hobbes about being a tiger: "Kind of a Zen thing, huh?" Skaters and gymnasts executing flawless routines, golfers sinking long putts, and other athletes displaying impressive powers of concentration all demonstrate, color commentators declare, the Zen of their respective sports. Beneath the surface of Stephen Bochco's *Hill Street Blues, L.A. Law,* and *N.Y.P.D. Blue,* a reviewer for the *New Yorker* discerns "an almost Zen nonattachment," while *Newsweek* stretched the limits of credulity by reporting, in the wake of the 1992 presidential campaign, that Bill Clinton had been "a model of Zen-like equanimity." And of course any moderate-sized bookstore offers a panoply of Zen titles these days; the several hundred currently in print include *The Zen of Bowel Movements: A Spiritual Approach to Constipation.*

Behind the proliferating uses and meanings of Zen—well behind—lies the fifteen-hundred-year Buddhist tradition represented in this book. Whatever we make of it in postmodern America, it comes to us as a religious culture of profound wisdom and extraordinary vigor, of earthiness and elegance, that has transformed the great societies that have been its prior hosts. Arising in China by a now-obscure pathway, it came to dominate the religious life of its sprawling native land, where it has always been called *Ch'an*, after the Sanskrit word meaning *meditation.* In medieval times, as pilgrims carried it home to other nations, its teachings and practices took new forms, and its name adapted to other tongues, becoming *Sŏn* in Korea, *Thien* in Vietnam, *Zen* in Japan. By any name, it has very rarely assumed a missionizing stance, yet in the past century, it has reached every continent except perhaps Antarctica. It wouldn't be surprising if, there too, a few scientists today cross their legs daily in Ch'an-style practice. Maybe they're even getting instruction via Cybermonk, an on-line service operated by an enterprising New York Zen group.

This ever-evolving tradition has sometimes been referred to as "the stream of Ts'ao-ch'i," the stream that splashes, purls, glides, or roars, maybe, from the mountain where Hui-neng, the semi-legendary Sixth Ancestor, lived. If "Ch'an" and "Zen" soon feel dry and doctrinaire, this fluid name reminds us that the whole phenomenon is alive and that we would be wise to stay alert and to look back, upstream, from time to time. It suggests the mystery of its coming down to us—something so yielding, so diffuse, in many respects so vulnerable that has proven, nonetheless, so robust and powerful and long-lasting. Much of its vitality must spring from the fact that, as the epigraph reminds us, it is always near at hand. The rippling stream of Ts'ao-ch'i runs right through *here.*

All of that makes it impossible to contain—between the covers of this book or anywhere else. We began this collection aware that it could not encompass the whole tradition, even the whole textual dimension of the tradition, and we finish it yet more aware of how incomplete it is, and how inevitably. Right away we found it necessary to limit the anthology's scope geographically and culturally— to restrict its contents to Ch'an and Zen writings. We did so, reasoning that the original Chinese way and its Japanese development constitute the common heritage of most practitioners today in English-speaking countries. The other old forks of the Ch'an stream, son and Thien, have meandered relatively recently into Anglophone nations, and not much of their literature is yet in translation. The same is true even of the later Ch'an lineages, and we have not tried to represent them here. All these branches of the ancient stream deserve volumes of their own.

Our decision to gather writings wholly from the literature of early Ch'an and Zen also reflects the direction that scholarship and publishing have taken. Thanks to a recent profusion of translations and studies, the lives and work of eminent Chinese and Japanese masters today lie open to readers of English as they never have before, and to an extent far greater than those of their Korean and Vietnamese counterparts. As compilers of this anthology and as students of the Way, we are deeply indebted to the dozens of translators whose efforts, over generations, have brought in this rich harvest.

The number of good translations published in the past fifteen years not only presents the opportunity to assemble a collection such as this but also makes it almost necessary: rare is the reader, much less the book buyer, who has kept up with the outpouring from the presses. Thus in selecting materials for *The Roaring Stream,* our first goal has been to provide a compact, broadly representative library of Ch'an and Zen literature. We hope it will be useful, among other ways, as a sampler, a means of identifying people and texts that you want to explore further. With few exceptions, our selections come from readily available books, and the listing "Sources and Resources" furnishes the particulars needed to track them down.

Several factors have guided our selections. We have looked for readability, for clarity and creativity in original texts as well as grace and care in their translations. We've sought a pleasing mix of contents, ranging from two-line poems to extended disquisitions, from formal lectures delivered before august audiences to brief letters dashed off to encourage flagging students far away, from impromptu dialogues to finely crafted masterpieces of prose and poetry. Variety has been a goal, too, in terms of subject matter and level of difficulty; within the space of a few pages, utterly practical instruction about the rudiments of meditation bumps up against wise counsel on the perplexities of daily life and expressions of fundamental reality that have confounded the best Zen students for centuries.

Though *The Roaring Stream* also presents as wide a spectrum of Ch'an and Zen writers as currently possible, it is a spectrum terribly narrowed by historic forces. Of its gaps, most striking is the absence of women, the result of East Asian gender biases at least as sharp and deep as those of Euro-American civilization. Not one of the forty-six chapters that follow is devoted to a woman because the voluminous canon of Ch'an and Zen allows them only the most marginal presence. They appear very rarely and, when they do, nearly always stand in the shadow of male teachers or even of monks who are clearly their inferior in religious accomplishment. Most go nameless, which suggests that the few whose names survive were truly exceptional in their talent and impact. Relative to the place that the traditional record accords them, women occupy a disproportionately large part of this book.

Gender discrimination is not the only thing that has kept individuals from taking their rightful place in *The Roaring Stream.* Inclusion in the Chinese canon required a social, or at least religious, standing that rank-and-file monastics lacked. Whatever they may have written has vanished, while the records of many mediocre masters have been preserved. Even teaching credentials did not guarantee one a spot in the canon, however. Among the myriad people of the Way who are effectively lost to history may be superb masters who chose to maintain a low public profile or who went unnoticed by the opinion-makers and chroniclers of their time. One such case is that of Kanzan Egen, a major figure in Rinzai Zen, who shunned attention, neither wrote nor lectured, and thus left precious little to fatten a book.

Sectarian disputes and practical considerations have kept others from these pages. Recent scholarship has convincingly demonstrated that orthodox histories of Ch'an have understated the importance of teachers and teachings outside the lineage of Hui-neng (Chapter 3); as is so often the case, the survivors of a complex historical process wrote the record as they saw fit, downplaying others' contributions or even claiming them for their own. Other worthy people are absent owing to their preferred means of expression. The early nineteenth-century Japanese master Sengai Gibon, for example, left a large, brilliant Dharma legacy that consists primarily of paintings and calligraphy and thus falls beyond the scope of a literary anthology.

Laypeople, too, would be thinly represented in this collection if we confined it to Ch'an and Zen literature as customarily defined—that is, to writings of recognized masters and to records of their sayings and doings. To heighten the lay presence in these pages, we both have favored lay subjects in our selections from the traditional literature and have opened the book to a group of lay writers who made their names primarily in the literary, rather than religious, sphere. These are five great poets—Wang Wei, Po Chü-i, Su T'ung-po, Ishikawa Jōzan, and Bashō—who were associated closely with Ch'an or Zen and whose work reflects the tradition's influence. Their lives and work help illustrate the part that Ch'an and Zen played in society, especially among members of the artistic community but also in forming the aesthetics of China and Japan. Reading their poems alongside the tradition's standard literature suggests a two-way flow of influence, from literary circles to the monastery, as well as the reverse. Great Chinese writers, in particular, seem to have anticipated and pointed the way to the pithy and graceful expression of mature Ch'an and Zen.

Besides striving to bring into *The Roaring Stream* a diverse group of authors, we have sought to make it representative of the major branches of Ch'an and Zen—the so-called "Five Houses and Seven Schools" of Ch'an, plus the three enduring lineages of Zen (Sōtō, Rinzai, and Ōbaku). Though we have borrowed the classical terminology to distinguish the various branches from one another, this is not to suggest that the distinction has a strong basis in fact. On the contrary, the houses and schools were largely constructed in retrospect, as a means of telling an otherwise unmanageable history, of imposing a rough order on the organic disarray that is life. While employing the conventional terms, we have interjected periodic reminders that the actuality was not so tidy, that people and ideas often moved freely across sectarian lines because the lines rarely stood out as crisply and clearly in everyday affairs of centuries past as they do today, on paper. We hope they will be understood much like the grid lines superimposed on a street map, dividing it into numbered and lettered squares as a convenient, provisional device to name and locate points in the landscape. Readers may ignore these and all the book's other historical points of reference without reducing the pleasure or principal value of perusing the selections themselves, just as one can enjoy a great painting without knowing whether its creator subscribed to an Expressionist or Fauvist philosophy.

At the same time, since *The Roaring Stream* is broadly representative of the tradition, it presents an ad hoc, composite image of Ch'an and Zen. It may be sampled in any sequence, but if read from front to back, chronologically, it offers a sense of the tradition's evolution and of the forces, including powerful social phenomena, that have shaped it. This is important to us, as editors of the anthology, because we observe a tendency in recent publishing to decontextualize Ch'an and Zen—to snip anecdotes, dialogues, and luminous phrases out of the source works as if they had no social or cultural underpinnings, as if the tradition were a spiritual scrap heap from which we can pick what pleases us, leaving the rest behind.

Of course, we are quite free to do that, with this or any other body of cultural material. The error lies in supposing that, once removed from its context, a word or object remains what it was. Transport a urinal from a scrapyard to an exhibition hall, as Marcel Duchamp did in 1917, and it becomes something else—a sculptural form, a revolutionary aesthetic statement. Similarly, a T'ang-dynasty Ch'an master's remark on the self, translated into English, plucked from its context, and inserted into a late-twentieth-century American essay, is highly unlikely to convey what was originally intended. In ancient China, the very word we translate as "self" denoted something quite different from the self we know in post-Freudian, post-industrial America.

Placing things in new contexts, as Duchamp illustrated, may be illuminating, may even help us see them more clearly in their original settings. To get this benefit, however, we need a sense of the old context as well as the new, and most of us have a considerably hazier grasp of ancient Chinese and Japanese religious ways than we do of restroom porcelain. Thus it is relatively easy for us to overlook the profound shifts of meaning that occur when an old Ch'an or Zen passage is quoted out of context. It is easy to suppose that something "Zen" is still Zen when it appears in an advertisement or a self-help book or a pop spirituality lecture. We hope the structure and content of this collection will hold the context clear. Though we have often selected excerpts from much longer works, we have avoided the temptation to choose little snippets, preferring substantial enough pieces to give a reasonably faithful impression of the texts, and the contexts, from which they come. Likewise, we have decided to order the selections chronologically (rather than thematically or according to literary genre) and to provide background information about both the authors and their writings in order to keep the relevant temporal and cultural frames apparent and strong.

One of the cultural frames that we have reproduced and that might be invisible to the unwarned reader is the custom of presenting the heritage of Ch'an and Zen as a pageant of lives, as a succession of stories about its leaders. This approach became standard more than a thousand years ago, replicating a widely established pattern in Chinese historiography. The tradition could have been memorialized with accounts of monastic communities or ordinary monk's lives, of ideas or economic realities, but in East Asian civilizations, as in many others worldwide, the Great Man theory of history prevailed. Although we don't buy that theory—for any history narrowly focused on individual achievements (and in the Ch'an case, mainly those of ordained men) leaves out far too much to be credible—the sequential presentation of the writers and their works seems the most advantageous method of organizing an anthology of this nature. We hope that flagging the issue here and resisting Great Man notions in the biographical sketches that introduce each chapter will offset the shortcomings of this scheme.

Chief among these shortcomings is the risk of perpetuating perhaps the most deep-seated and damaging image in Ch'an and Zen, the heavily idealized image of the teacher-sage. While the tradition has long stressed that a deeply enlightened person is completely ordinary, it has also advanced a countervailing discourse proclaiming the extraordinary capacities of the awakened ones, or buddhas, and of forerunners in the tradition, commonly referred to as "patriarchs" or "ancestors." This exaltation of enlightened teachers has, no doubt, served a motivational purpose, but over the ages, it has been so repeated, formalized, and in the end accepted literally that a leading Zen scholar has characterized the result as "the cult of the Zen master."

In introducing the forty-six chapters of *The Roaring Stream,* we have described the people they feature as evenhandedly as we know how. If we haven't altogether escaped the tendency to make heroes of them, we have certainly sought to separate historical fact from the later accretions of legend and to indicate the issues and processes that shaped their reputations. The task of portraying them as flesh-and-blood individuals is vastly complicated by the prevalence of legendary, even propagandistic, material in the classical sources and the dearth of what we moderns consider basic personal information. A typical Ch'an or Zen biography is concerned almost exclusively with just four elements of its subject's experience: his course of maturation as a student of the Dharma, his authorization as a master, his teaching, and the successor he named to carry on his work. Family history and life prior to monkhood are usually dispensed with in a few perfunctory sentences indicating such simple facts as birthplace and surname. Physical description is essentially nil, with exceptions made for characteristics that stuck out as really peculiar in Chinese or Japanese society. Living conditions receive similarly short shrift, and psychological or emotional factors are registered vaguely, if at all.

Our efforts to probe behind the canonical accounts and blow life back into the old worthies is motivated not just by the desire for a colorful book but also by interest in exploring Ch'an and Zen as an embodied tradition. It may sound wonderful on the page, but like other religions and other pursuits of all kinds, it has to prove itself on the road and in the field, in the living and the dying. We have accented features of both the careers and the texts that might hold particular meaning for students of the Way in our own time and place: the tradition's stance on women and laypeople, as already noted; its adaptations to changing social and cultural circumstances; its engagement in, or aloofness from, public problems; its understanding of the good life; its counsel on moral issues; and its relationship to the various power structures that conditioned its existence. In pursuit of this last point and as a gauge of the prominence teachers attained during their lifetimes, in our biographical sketches we have made it a point to mention the governmental honors, if any, a master received. Some will be surprised to discover the degree of attention that rulers paid these gentlemen.

In many other respects, our efforts to orient readers to our subjects's lives and writings are spotty at best. We have made very limited attempts to place them in terms of national history or geography or to explain the technical details of Ch'an and Zen training, although we have made reference to some of the historic divisions within the tradition and to underlying differences of experience, understanding, or opinion that may have given rise to them. Doctrinal and sectarian distinctions are not of central importance either to us personally or, we dare suggest, to a true grasp of the Way; accordingly, we have given them relatively little ink here.

As these omissions indicate, *The Roaring Stream* is not a complete source on any individual, much less on the entire tradition. Nor is it a scholarly work. Neither of us possesses credentials in the field of Buddhist studies, and the information offered here is all secondary in nature, derived from others' original, often highly creative, work. While Ch'an and Zen masters have long ridiculed scholars as hopeless know-nothings, we feel profound gratitude to the many researchers who, along with the translators (indeed, sometimes doubling *as* translators), have helped inform our understanding of the tradition and supplied ingredients for this book. In preparing it, we have sought out the best of the current scholarship, and we hope, fervently, that we've interpreted it responsibly. The reader inclined to delve more deeply into Ch'an and Zen history, biography, texts, and topics will find abundant leads in the citations and recommendations of the Sources and Resources section of the book.

Throughout *The Roaring Stream,* we have rendered Chinese names and terms according to the Wade-Giles system. Where translators have used the pinyin system now favored by the Chinese government or other orthographies, for consistency's sake and to avoid cluttering the text with brackets, we've substituted the Wade-Giles equivalent without so indicating. In the same way, we have harmonized the names used and have substituted "ancestor" for "patriarch" wherever the latter appeared in the selections; while either is a valid translation and "patriarch" was preferred by prior generations of translators, the present generation tends to favor "ancestor," as we do. We apologize to scholars and translators who may feel, in this or other decisions, that we have emended their work inappropriately.

This book results from close and happy collaboration between two friends and fellow students of the Way. Jack Shoemaker conceived the project and has guided its development ever since, while Nelson Foster has handled the assembling, ordering, and interpretation of selections, including initial preparation of editorial comments. From the outset, we envisioned ourselves simply as anthologers, gathering the work of others, and feel some chagrin that the finished book contains so many of our own words. We certainly did not anticipate making new translations for its pages, but as our work progressed, we felt a mounting dissatisfaction with existing translations of some of the great texts, especially early texts, and finally desperation got the better of prudence, propelling Nelson to undertake improved versions. He could not, and would not, have done so without generous assistance on the Chinese and Japanese from Joan Iten Sutherland and Masa Uehara. We are deeply grateful to them both.

Many others have contributed to the preparation of this book as well. Besides furnishing the foreword, Robert Aitken called a number of sources to our attention and lent hard-to-find materials. Gary Snyder supported the project enthusiastically from the first, giving us good counsel and the run of his library. Peigwang Dowiat assisted very generously in providing translations for Chapter 27. Scholars at the University of Hawai'i—David Chappell of the Department of Religion and Roger T. Ames and Daniel Cole of the Center for Chinese Studies—graciously volunteered to answer questions on fine points of Chinese language and history. The editorial work of Alan Turkus, Tom Christensen, and Carol Christensen brought the book to a level of clarity and consistency it would not have reached otherwise. We also received advice, source materials, or much-needed logistical help from Judyth Collin, Chuck Dockham, Harry Ednie, Pat Ferris, Trish Hoard, Kenneth Kraft, Eric Larsen, Anne Lazerove, Jennifer Long, Marsha Stone, Jim Sylva, Jack Turner, and no doubt others who have escaped our files and short-term memories. Nine bows to all.

May this book repay the resources expended in its production, benefitting not only its readers but, through them, the many beings of the Triple World.

—Nelson Foster and Jack Shoemaker

CHINA

1

Bodhidharma

(D. CA. 533)

For more than a thousand years, students of Ch'an and Zen have looked to Bodhidharma as the founder of their strand of Buddhist tradition, the person who singlehandedly carried the ineffable essence of Buddhism from India to China. This understanding, we now know, belongs to the sphere of mythology rather than to the realm of historical fact. That Bodhidharma (J., Bodaidaruma or simply Daruma) lived seems reasonably certain, but if scholarly standards of evidence are maintained, everything else about him is subject to question, including his role, if any, in the establishment of Ch'an.

Shreds of documentary evidence indicate that a South Indian meditation teacher going by the name of Dharma or Bodhidharma arrived in China by the year 479. Over the next half century, he (or another monk of like name) pops up here and there in the carefully kept, voluminous annals of Chinese history, but his biography lacks even a single firm detail. Though numerous writings attached themselves to this phantom, the only text that now can be credibly attributed to him is a brief treatise titled "The Two Entrances and Four Practices." Ascribed to Bodhidharma in manuscripts dated as early as the mid-seventh century, it describes two approaches to gaining the Way, the first of which bears a tantalizing resemblance to Ch'an.

The most distinctive feature of this first approach, known as "entering through the Principle," is its recommendation of *pi-kuan*, which translates literally as "wall gaze" or "wall contemplation." This unusual phrase has long been identified with Bodhidharma and with the practice of *tso-ch'an*, seated meditation (J., zazen). It has been interpreted in two ways, either or both of which may have intended: to face a wall physically or to meditate *like* a wall—to cultivate a mind that is firm, ungraspable, free of all concepts and concerns. Over the centuries, both interpretations have found their way into Ch'an and Zen meditation instruction, and in many temples today, it remains standard practice to do zazen facing a partition of some sort, if not actually a wall. ⊗

THE TWO ENTRANCES AND FOUR PRACTICES

There are many avenues for entering the Way, but essentially they all are of two kinds: entering through the Principle[1] and entering through practice.

1 Principle (*li*) is a central concept in classical Chinese thought, where it refers to the cosmic order.

"Entering through the Principle" is awakening to the essential by means of the teachings. It requires a profound trust that all living beings, both enlightened and ordinary, share the same true nature, which is obscured and unseen due only to mistaken perception. If you turn from the false to the true, dwelling steadily in wall contemplation, there is no self or other, and ordinary people and sages are one and the same. You abide unmoving and unwavering, never again confused by written teachings. Complete, ineffable accord with the Principle is without discrimination, still, effortless. This is called entering through the Principle.

"Entering through practice" refers to four all-encompassing practices: the practice of requiting animosity, the practice of accepting one's circumstances, the practice of craving nothing, and the practice of accord with the Dharma.

What is the practice of requiting animosity? When experiencing suffering, a practitioner of the Way should reflect: "For innumerable eons, I have preferred the superficial to the fundamental, drifting through various states of existence, creating much animosity and hatred, bringing endless harm and discord. Though I have done nothing wrong in this life, I am reaping the natural consequences of past offenses, my evil karma. It is not meted out by some heavenly agency. I accept it patiently and with contentment, utterly without animosity or complaint." A sutra says, "When you encounter suffering, do not be distressed. Why? Because your consciousness opens up to the fundamental." Cultivating this attitude, you are in accord with the Principle, advancing on the path through the experience of animosity. Thus it is called the practice of requiting animosity.

Second is the practice of accepting circumstances. Living beings, having no [fixed] self, are entirely shaped by the impact of circumstances. Both suffering and pleasure are produced by circumstances. If you experience such positive rewards as wealth and fame, this results from past causes. You receive the benefits now, but as soon as these circumstances are played out, it will be over. Why should you celebrate? Success and failure depend upon circumstances, while the Mind does not gain or lose. Not being moved even by the winds of good fortune is ineffable accord with the Way. Thus it is called the practice of accepting one's circumstances.

Third is the practice of craving nothing. The various sorts of longing and attachment that people experience in their unending ignorance are regarded as craving. The wise awaken to the truth, going with the Principle rather than with conventional ideas. Peaceful at heart, with nothing to do,[2] they change in accord with the seasons. All existence lacking substance, they desire nothing. [They

Early Buddhist thinkers borrowed and reinterpreted the term as a means of expressing the absolute, the unconditioned.

2. *Wu-wei*, translated here as "nothing to do," is an expression Ch'an borrowed from Taoism. It connotes not manipulating things, taking them as they are instead of seeking to control them.

know that] the goddesses of good and bad fortune always travel as a pair and that the Triple World,[3] where you have lived so long, is like a burning house. Suffering inevitably comes with having a body—who can find peace? If you understand this fully, you quit all thoughts of other states of being, no longer crave them. A sutra says, "To crave is to suffer; to crave nothing is bliss." Thus we understand clearly that craving nothing is the true practice of the Way.

Fourth is the practice of accord with the Dharma. The principle of essential purity is the Dharma. Under this principle, all form is without substance, undefilable and without attachment, neither "this" nor "that."[4] The *Vimalakīrti Sūtra* says, "In this Dharma, there are no living beings because it transcends the defiling [concept] of 'living beings.' In this Dharma, there is no self because it transcends the defiling [concept] of 'self.'" When the wise embrace and understand this principle, they are practicing accord with the Dharma. Since in the Dharma there is fundamentally nothing to withhold, [the wise] practice generosity, giving their bodies, lives, and possessions without any regret in their minds. Fully understanding the emptiness of giver, gift, and recipient, they do not fall into bias or attachment. Ridding themselves of all defilements, they aid in the liberation of living beings without grasping at appearances. In this way they benefit themselves and others both, gracing the Way of Enlightenment. In the same fashion, they practice the other five perfections.[5] To eliminate false thinking in practicing the six perfections means having no thought of practicing them. This is practicing accord with the Dharma.

Whatever Bodhidharma may have contributed to the teaching, style, or practice of Ch'an, certainly its origination was not one man's doing. Indeed, it would be incorrect even to say that Ch'an arose out of one culture, let alone a single person, for in fact it developed out of a mingling of Indian and Chinese traditions. The Indian sources, which Bodhidharma represents in the mythic account, were diverse schools of Mahāyāna (Great Vehicle) Buddhism, which emerged in northern India during the first century of the Christian era. The Mahāyāna schools held the inherent and actual liberation of all beings as a cardinal principle, whereas the earlier forms of Buddhism, dismissed by the Mahāyānists as "Small Vehicle," emphasized enlightenment as an option for monastics, achieved only by rare individuals. As the Mahāyāna sutras were carried north and translated, Chinese readers recognized an affinity between the Dharma set forth in these Indian scriptures and the Tao, the Way, as it had long been taught in their indigenous traditions of Confucianism and Taoism. The

3. The Triple World (Skt., *Triloka*) is an Indian Buddhist term for the universe of birth-and-death, conceived of as three worlds of desire, of form, and of formlessness.
4. That is, inseparable one from another, not to be divided into subject and object, self and other.
5. An allusion to the six *pāramitās*, or perfections, of classical Buddhism. Generosity headed the list customarily, followed by morality, patience, zeal, meditation, and wisdom.

subsequent renaissance of religious culture produced distinctly Chinese forms of Buddhism, including Ch'an, whose teachings and language still show the marked influence of Taoism.

In the late seventh and early eighth centuries, as the newly developed schools of Chinese Buddhism sought to assert their legitimacy and distinguish themselves from one another, several hit upon the strategy of tracing their roots back to India and of thus establishing direct descent from Shākyamuni Buddha. So it happened that the mysterious Bodhidharma became a key figure in the institutional development and mythos of Ch'an: as early as 689, he was nominated as the young sect's Indian connection. His obscurity may actually have made him the best candidate for this position. His near-perfect absence from the historical record allowed Ch'an chroniclers to portray Bodhidharma however they saw fit, and not too surprisingly, as a body of legend grew up around him in the next few centuries, he came to embody many of the sect's central tenets. Among these was the proposition that Ch'an, unlike other sects, need not justify itself in terms of the Indian doctrines because it constituted "A separate transmission outside the sutras, not dependent on words and letters." This unique formulation, customarily credited to Bodhidharma, amounts to a claim that Ch'an had been secretly transmitted from teacher to student for a thousand years before it reached China.

In 1004, the Chinese monk Tao-yüan included much of the dubious lore about Bodhidharma in *The Transmission of the Lamp*, an enormous text laying out the Ch'an line of succession from time immemorial. Here he appears in his full mythic proportions and in vivid detail. Uncompromising in his practice, in his rejection of fame and profit, and in his treatment of would-be disciples, he exemplifies the virtues traditionally esteemed in a Ch'an master. Problems of historicity aside, this is the Bodhidharma revered by generations of Ch'an and Zen students. Affectionately known as "the red-bearded barbarian," he is always depicted big-nosed and hirsute, wearing an earring—highly exotic, by medieval Chinese standards. In most of the innumerable ink paintings made of him, he sits glowering sternly, even reproachfully, but in others, he shows a very different aspect, peering out in bug-eyed amazement, as if to say, "I've caused an awful lot of trouble, haven't I?" 🕸

FROM THE TRANSMISSION OF THE LAMP

Residing at Shao-lin Temple of Sung Mountain, Master Bodhidharma sat [in meditation] facing the wall all day long in silence. People wondered who he was and called him the Wall-Gazing Brahmin.

At that time there was a Buddhist monk named Shen-kuang who was widely informed and who had been living in Lo-yang for a long time. He read [great] quantities of all kinds of books which told of the profound Principle. He sighed and said, "The teachings of Confucius and Lao-tzu are but customs and etiquette, and the books of Chuang-tzu and the *I Ching* still do not plumb the depths of the wonderful Principle. Lately I hear that Master Dharma is living in Shao-lin Temple. With this supreme man so near, I should reach the deeper realms [of understanding]." Then he went to him, wanting to be instructed from morning till night. The Master, however, would give him no instruction, but sat in meditation all the time facing the wall.

Kuang thought to himself: "Men of old sought the Way by smashing their bones to take out the marrow, slashing their veins to feed hungry [animals], spreading their hair to cover the muddy road in order to let a spiritual man pass through safely, or leaping off a cliff to feed a hungry tigress. All through the ages people have behaved like this. Who am I [not to do so]?"

On December 9th of that year it snowed heavily in the night. Shen-kuang stood firmly without moving [in the yard of Shao-lin Temple]. By dawn of the next day, the falling snow had piled so deep that it reached his knees.

Master Bodhidharma then took pity on him and asked him, "What are you seeking, standing in the snow for this long time?"

Shen-kuang sobbed, and in tears begged him, "Please, Master, have mercy. Open the gate of nectar. Deliver the message that liberates sentient beings!"

The master said, "The supreme, unequalled, spiritual Way of the buddhas is accessible only after vast eons of striving to overcome the impossible and to bear the unbearable. How could a man of small virtue, little wisdom, slight interest, and slow mind attain the True Vehicle? Striving for it would be vain effort."

After listening to this exhortation from the master, Shen-kuang secretly took a sharp knife and cut off his own left arm, placing it in front of the master.

Realizing that he was a good vessel for the dharma, the master said, "All buddhas in search of the Way have begun by ignoring their bodies for the sake of the Dharma. Now you have cut off your arm in front of me. You may have the right disposition."

The master then renamed him Hui-k'o. Hui-k'o asked, "May I hear about the Dharma-seal of the Buddha?"

The master said, "The Dharma-seal is not something that can be heard about from others."

Hui-k'o said, "My mind is not yet at peace. Pray set it at peace for me, Master!"

The master said, "Bring me your mind, and I will set it at peace for you."

Hui-k'o answered, "I have searched for it, but in the end it is unobtainable."

The master said, "Your mind has been set at peace."

Later on, Emperor Hsiao-ming heard about the marvellous deeds of the master. He dispatched a messenger with an imperial invitation to the palace. Three times in all the imperial messenger came to urge him [to accept the invitation], but the master would not come down from the mountain. The emperor's warm respect for the master increased more and more, and he sent gifts of two linen robes, a golden bowl, a silver pitcher, silken cloth, and other articles. Three times the master firmly refused them, which only confirmed still more the wish of the emperor. At last the master accepted them. From this time the devotion of his congregation, robed and lay, increased more and more.

After nine years had passed, the master wished to return to the western land of India. He said to his disciples, "The time has come [for me to go back home]. I want each of you to show your understanding."

One disciple, Tao-fu, answered, "According to what I understand, the function of the Tao cannot be grasped through literal knowledge, nor is it apart from literal knowledge."

The master remarked, "You have gained my skin!"

A nun, Tsung-ch'ih, said, "What I understand now is like Ānanda's glimpse of the realm of Akshobhya Buddha. It may be seen in oneness, but never in duality."

The master said, "You have gained my flesh!"

Tao-yu said, "The four great [elements] are originally empty, the five aggregates (physical form, sensation, perception, impulse, and thought) do not exist, and in my comprehension there is not a single thing to be found."

The master declared, "You have gained my bone!"

Finally Hui-k'o bowed and remained standing at his seat.

The master said, "You have gained my marrow!"

Looking at Hui-k'o, the master told him, "In days gone by, the Tathāgata handed on to Mahākāshyapa the true Dharma-eye. Through the Ancestors, from one to another, it then came into my hands. Now I am giving it to you, and you must take good care of it. Besides this, I will give you my yellow robe, which shall be the testimony of faith in the Dharma. Each has a significance which you should know."

Hui-k'o said, "Will you please reveal to me the significance?"

The master said, "By carrying the Dharma-seal you will be inwardly in accord with the approved mind, and the keeping of the robe will fix the outward spiritual message. In later generations, when mutual trust is slight and doubts arise, people may say, 'He was a man of India and you are a son of this land—how could the Dharma be transmitted? What proof is there?' Now that you are receiving the robe and the dharma, they can be produced as proof, and the activity of the message will be freed from obstacles.

"After two hundred years it will be time to stop transmitting the robe. Then the Dharma will be spread all over the world. But although many people will know of the Tao, few will practice it; and although there will be many who preach the Principle, few will penetrate it. More than a thousand, or ten thousand, people will concur with the innermost [teaching] and bear private witness. When you expound the truth, do not slight the man who is not yet enlightened. Should his essential nature suddenly turn, he would be equal in original enlightenment. Listen to my poem:

> Originally I came to this land
> To rescue deluded people by transmitting the Dharma.
> One flower will open with five petals
> And the fruit will ripen by itself."

2

Seng-ts'an

(D. 606)

Though he lived later than Bodhidharma, Seng-ts'an is an even more obscure and problematic figure. According to traditional transmission records, which were constructed well after the fact, he inherited the Dharma from Hui-k'o, Bodhidharma's successor, thus becoming the Third Ancestor in the Ch'an bloodline. History offers every reason to consign this account to the category of legend, however. Seng-ts'an (J., Sōzan) may owe his place in the lineage to a single mention in an early document naming him as a student of Hui-k'o. The author of a 712 treatise, describing the early masters of Ch'an in an attempt to bolster the credibility of the mythic lineage, candidly acknowledges conspicuous holes in Seng-ts'an's biography, going so far as to remark, "No one ever knew where he ended up."

This underground teacher owes his fame to the Dharma poem *Relying on Mind*, whose authorship has long been credited to him. Among the earliest and best-known of all Ch'an texts, it consists of seventy-three couplets, each of the paired lines containing just four characters. Over the centuries, countless Ch'an and Zen students have committed this pithy verse to memory, and it turns up with remarkable frequency in the lectures and dialogues of both Chinese and Japanese teachers. Even within this brief collection, quotations from it appear in several chapters.

Like the four-line poem Bodhidharma offers in *The Transmission of the Lamp* after entrusting the Dharma to Hui-k'o, *Relying on Mind* belongs to an Indian-derived genre, the *gāthā*, rather than to the mainstream of Chinese poetry. The early sutras of southern Buddhism are larded with *gāthās*, usually short and probably archaic verses—vestiges of the oral tradition that preserved the sutras in the centuries before they were written down. Authors of the later, Mahāyāna sutras punctuated them with *gāthās* as well. Chinese Buddhists put the old form to new use as a means of opening the Way for their compatriots and perhaps to lend latter-day writings a resemblance to ancient texts.

Relying on Mind seems to have been composed—or at least edited and popularized—long after Seng-ts'an's time. It contains thoughts and language highly unlikely for a text dating to his day and, even more tellingly, does not make its appearance in Ch'an literature until two centuries after 606, the date conventionally given for his death. All the same, it is a challenging and very important work representing the tradition in its formative stages. In its lines, understandings of Mind, and nonduality that trace to the Perfection of Wisdom school of Mahāyāna Buddhism blend harmoniously with the Taoist emphasis on letting things be that is expressed in the term *wu-wei* (lit., no doing or nothing to do). In reading the poem, it may be useful to recall a key passage on *wu-wei* from the *Tao Te Ching*:

> Those who pursue learning gain something every day.
> We who pursue the Tao lose something every day,
> loss after loss until we reach nothing to do—
> no doing, yet nothing is not done. ⌘

RELYING ON MIND

The Supreme Way is not difficult;
    it just precludes picking and choosing.
Without yearning or loathing,
    the Way is perfectly apparent,
while even a hairbreadth difference
    separates heaven and earth.
To see the Way with your own eyes,
    quit agreeing and disagreeing.
The battling of likes and dislikes—
    that's the disease of the mind.
Misunderstanding the great mystery,
    people labor in vain for peace.
Mind has the totality of space:
    nothing lacking, nothing extra.
It's just selecting and rejecting
    that make it seem otherwise.
Don't pursue worldly concerns,
    don't dwell passively in emptiness;
in the peace of absolute identity,[1]
    confusion vanishes by itself.
Suppressing activity to reach stillness
    just creates agitation.
Dwelling in such dualities,
    how can you know identity?

---

1. The character rendered here as "identity" is often translated "oneness," and literally means "one kind" or "one kindedness." It denotes the fundamental sameness of all things. Likewise, "peace" might be translated "equanimity" or "serenity," and refers to the even-mindedness that comes of realizing the identity of all things.

People who don't know identity
    bog down on both sides—
rejecting form, they get stuck in it,
    seeking emptiness, turn away from it.[2]
The more people talk and ponder,
    the further they spin out of accord.[3]
Bring gabbing and speculation to a stop,
    and the whole world opens up to you.
If you want the essence, get right to the root;
    chasing reflections, you lose sight of the source.
Turning the light around for an instant[4]
    routs becoming, abiding, and decay.
The changing phases, the ups and downs,
    all result from misperception.
There's no need to seek the truth—
    just put a stop to your opinions!
Dualistic constructs don't endure,
    so take care not to pursue them.
As soon as positive and negative arise,
    the mind is lost in confusion.
The two exist because of the one,
    but don't cling to oneness either.
If you don't conceive even oneness of mind,
    the ten thousand things are all flawless.
In this flawlessness there's nothing at all,
    no conception, no mind.
The subject disappears with its objects,
    objects vanish without a subject.
Objects are objects because of subjects,
    subjects subjects because of objects.
If you want to know both these aspects,
    originally they're one and empty.
A single emptiness unites opposites,
    pervading all things equally.

2. In other words, by rejecting the world of form, one implicitly acknowledges its reality, and to seek emptiness is to mistake it for some kind of object.

3. *Accord* is a key term in Chinese thought as a whole and in Zen in particular. It connotes seeing things as they truly are and acting in harmony with the forces at play.

4. The phrase *turning back the light* crops up repeatedly in Ch'an and Zen texts and is a metaphor for turning awareness away from objects and focusing it on the mind. Instead of preoccupying ourselves with reflections created as our mental "light" plays off of objects, we are instructed to see the source of the light itself.

If we didn't see things as fine and coarse,
   how could prejudice exist?
The Supreme Way by nature is all-embracing,
   not easy, not difficult,
but quibbling and hesitating,
   the more you hurry, the slower you go.
Holding onto things wrecks your balance,
   inevitably throwing you off-course,
but let everything go, be genuine,
   and the essence won't leave or stay.
Accept your nature, accord with the Way
   and stroll at ease, trouble-free.
Tying up thoughts denies reality,
   and you sink into a stupor of resistance.
Resisting thoughts perturbs the spirit!
   Why treat what's yours as foreign?
If you want to enter the One Vehicle,
   don't disdain the six senses.[5]
Not disdaining the six senses—
   that's enlightenment itself.
The wise have nothing to do,[6]
   while the unwise tie themselves in knots.
Since things aren't different in essence,
   it's stupid to hanker and cling.
To get hold of the mind by using the mind,
   isn't that a gross error, too?
Delusion creates calm and chaos,
   enlightenment entails no good or evil.
Every opposition under the sun
   derives merely from false thinking.
Like dreams, illusions, spots before your eyes—
   why bother grasping at them?
Gain and loss, right and wrong—
   let them go, once and for all.
If you don't fall asleep,
   dreams cease on their own.

---

5. The various paths and schools of Indian Buddhism were regarded as different vehicles. The One Vehicle (Skt., *Ekayāna*) is that of the buddhas and bodhisattvas or, metaphorically, the mind of identity itself. As for the senses, Buddhism has traditionally counted consciousness as a sixth sense, along with sight, hearing, smell, taste, and touch.

6. This "nothing to do" is *wu-wei,* the virtue of nondoing. See the introduction to this chapter.

If you don't conjure up differences,
    all things are of one kind.
In the essential mystery of identity,
    eternal and ephemeral are forgotten.[7]
Seeing the things of the world evenly
    restores their genuine character;
without grounds and criteria,
    they can't be judged or compared.
Still or active, nothing moves,
    and active or still, nothing ceases.
If you don't perpetuate duality,
    how can even identity remain?
In the very end, at the ultimate,
    there's no room for rules or measures.
The harmonious, equanimous mind—
    here, all effort subsides.
Doubt is wiped utterly away,
    what's truly reliable established.[8]
Nothing hangs in the mind,
    there's nothing to remember;
empty, luminous, genuine,
    the mind needs no exertion.
This isn't the sphere of thought,
    can't be gauged by reason or feeling.
The Dharma-realm of true actuality[9]
    harbors neither self nor other.
To reach accord with it at once,
    just say, "Not two!"[10]
Without duality, all beings are the same,
    not a single one excluded.
Sages throughout the world

7. Translated literally, "the unmoving and conditioned are both forgotten." *The conditioned* is a Buddhist term for things produced or destroyed by conditions—things that come and go, that are born and die.

8. The ideogram translated here as "reliable" represents a person standing by his or her word and has a rich set of possible meanings—sincerity, honesty, faith, belief, credibility, fidelity, confidence, trust (as well as verbal and adjectival forms of all these nouns). Here it indicates a quality of the mind that the poem describes—the mind that is never lacking, always present and complete, and in that sense absolutely trustworthy, or faithful. It occurs also in the poem's title and final lines.

9. *Dharmadhātu*, or Dharma-realm, is another expression for the mind of identity. It is the fundamental reality of all things.

10. "Say" here implies making a practice of nonduality, perhaps even taking "not two" as a theme of meditation.

all find entry to this source.
Here hurry and delay have no bearing;
    an instant is ten thousand years.
"Here" and "not here" don't apply either.
    Everywhere it's right before your eyes.
The tiny is the same as the large
    once boundaries are forgotten;
the huge is the same as the small
    if they're not seen in terms of limits.
Likewise, being is actually nonbeing,
    nonbeing the very same as being.
Any understanding short of this
    you should definitely abandon.
One is no other than all,
    all no other than one.
If your insight matched this,
    what anxieties could remain?
The reliable mind lacks dualities;
    nonduality is relying on mind.
Here the way of words is cut—
    no past, no future, no present.

3

Hui-neng

(638–713)

With Hui-neng (J., Eno), the fabled Sixth Ancestor, we arrive at a figure who can be said with certainty to have played a part in the development of Ch'an. His exact role and his relationship to the text attributed to him, usually known as the *Platform Sutra,* are fraught with unresolved questions, and a large amount of legendary material has accrued to his account as well, but he left more discernible traces in the historical record than did Bodhidharma and Seng-ts'an. One document reliably places him among the students of Hung-jen, the Fifth Ancestor. Another, a memorial inscription written not long after his death by the famous poet and Ch'an practitioner Wang Wei (see Chapter 5), outlines his life and teachings.

None of this, however, offers much support for traditional images of Hui-neng or of Ch'an in his time. While the later transmission chronicles would have us believe that the young sect was in full flower by this point, historical sources make it evident that Ch'an was still finding its identity. Neither its teachings nor its institution were well defined—far from it. To the extent that it had a leader in Hui-neng's generation, that was plainly Shen-hsiu, another student of Hung-jen, who rose to prominence in northern China, winning support from the imperial family and developing a large following in the twin capitals of Lo-yang and Chang-nan. Not until he and Shen-hsiu both were dead did Hui-neng's name become the focus of public discussion, when one of his heirs, an ambitious and apparently persuasive man named Shen-hui, launched an attack on Shen-hsiu and his successors. Charging that this "Northern School" was preaching an inferior doctrine of gradual enlightenment, Shen-hui argued that the true teaching of sudden awakening had passed from Hung-jen to Hui-neng—a claim now recognized as baseless but that caused sufficient stir then to get Shen-hui exiled.

Despite its title, *The Platform Sutra of the Sixth Ancestor* cannot be Hui-neng's work. It is now thought to have been composed by a member of the Ox-head School, a third constellation of monks in the unstable galaxy of eighth-century Ch'an, maybe in an effort to reconcile the differences between Shen-hui's camp and the Northern School. Whoever wrote it and for whatever reason, *The Platform Sutra* presented Hui-neng in such a flattering light that it effectively sealed his place as sixth man in the mythic bloodline. After a few more generations, Shen-hsiu's line died out, and so did all the others. From that point on, Ch'an teachers universally traced their pedigrees through Hui-neng.

Like Bodhidharma, Hui-neng lives on principally in a set of stories—stories whose truth lies safely beyond history. Along with the red-bearded barbarian, the one-armed Hui-k'o, and Seng-ts'an, who is said to have had leprosy, the Hui-neng of legend stands outside the norms of Chinese culture. He is depicted as a native of a barbarian village, an illiterate, a manual laborer—and a man who happened to have an extraordinary knack for Ch'an. *The Platform Sutra* portrays him, as an unseasoned layman, defeating Shen-hsiu and all the other monks at Hung-jen's monastery in a competition to express the Dharma—and thus receiving Bodhidharma's robe and alms bowl from Hung-jen, as proof of succession. In this appealing tale, Hui-neng triumphs by dictating a *gāthā* brilliantly expressing *shūnyatā*, the fundamental emptiness of all things. This event is celebrated in the Ch'an proverb, "The seven hundred eminent monks understood the Dharma; only Hui-neng didn't. That's why he obtained the Ancestor's robe and bowl." The irrelevance of status, intellect, and learning in Ch'an is a central theme of *The Platform Sutra*, as is the importance of not understanding, of no-thought or non-thinking. ⊗

FROM THE PLATFORM SUTRA

"Good friends, how then are meditation and wisdom alike? They are like the lamp and the light it gives forth. If there is a lamp there is light; if there is no lamp there is no light. The lamp is the substance of light; the light is the function of the lamp. Thus, although they have two names, in substance they are not two. Meditation and wisdom are also like this.

Good friends, in the Dharma there is no sudden or gradual, but among people some are keen and others dull. The deluded recommend the gradual method, the enlightened practice the sudden teaching. To understand the original mind . . . is to see into your own original nature. Once enlightened, there is from the outset no distinction between these two methods; those who are not enlightened will for long *kalpas* [eons] be caught in the cycle of transmigration.

"Good friends, in this teaching of mine, from ancient times up to the present, all have set up no-thought[1] as the main doctrine, nonform as the substance, and nonabiding as the basis. Nonform is to be separated from form even when associated with form. No-thought is not to think even when involved in thought. Nonabiding is the original nature of man.

"Successive thoughts do not stop; prior thoughts, present thoughts, and future thoughts follow one after the other without cessation. If one instant of thought is cut off, the Dharma-body separates from the physical body, and in the midst of successive thoughts there will be no place for attachment to any-

1. *Wu-nien.* Often rendered as the equivalent of *wu-hsin* [no mind]. A term widely used in Ch'an, it is considered one of the most important and characteristic elements in the teaching of the Sixth Ancestor.

thing. If one instant of thought clings, then successive thoughts cling; this is known as being fettered. If in all things successive thoughts do not cling, then you are unfettered. Therefore, nonabiding is made the basis.

"Good friends, being outwardly separated from all forms, this is nonform. When you are separated from form, the substance of your nature is pure. Therefore, nonform is made the substance.

"To be unstained in all environments is called no-thought. If on the basis of your own thoughts you separate from environment, then, in regard to things, thoughts are not produced. If you stop thinking of the myriad things, and cast aside all thoughts, as soon as one instant of thought is cut off, you will be reborn in another realm. Students, take care! Don't rest in objective things and the subjective mind. [If you do so] it will be bad enough that you yourself are in error, yet how much worse that you encourage others in their mistakes. The deluded man, however, does not himself see and slanders the teachings of the sutras. Therefore, no-thought is established as a doctrine. Because man in his delusion has thoughts in relation to his environment, heterodox ideas stemming from these thoughts arise, and passions and false views are produced from them. Therefore this teaching has established no-thought as a doctrine.

"Men of the world, separate yourselves from views; do not activate thoughts. If there were no thinking, then no-thought would have no place to exist. 'No' is the 'no' of what? 'Thought' means 'thinking' of what? 'No' is the separation from the dualism that produces the passions. 'Thought' means thinking of the original nature of the True Reality. True Reality is the substance of thoughts; thoughts are the function of True Reality. If you give rise to thoughts from your self-nature, then, although you see, hear, perceive, and know, you are not stained by the manifold environments, and are always free. The *Vimalakīrti Sūtra* says: 'Externally, while distinguishing well all the forms of the various dharmas, internally he stands firm within the First Principle.'

"Now that we know that this is so, what is it in this teaching that we call 'sitting in meditation' [*tso-ch'an*]? In this teaching 'sitting' means without any obstruction anywhere, outwardly and under all circumstances, not to activate thoughts. 'Meditation' is internally to see the original nature and not become confused.

"And what do we call Ch'an meditation [*ch'an-ting*]?[2] Outwardly to exclude form is 'ch'an'; inwardly to be unconfused is meditation [*ting*]. Even though there is form on the outside, when internally the nature is not confused, then, from the outset, you are of yourself pure and of yourself in meditation. The very contact with circumstances itself causes confusion. Separation from form on the

---

2. *Ch'an* is *dhyāna*; *ting* is its Chinese translation. The meaning is equivalent to *tso-ch'an,* above.

outside is 'ch'an'; being untouched on the inside is meditation [*ting*]. Being 'ch'an' externally and meditation [*ting*] internally, it is known as ch'an meditation [*ch'an-ting*]. The *Vimalakīrti Sūtra* says: 'At once, suddenly, you regain the original mind.' The *P'u-sa-chieh* says: 'From the outset your own nature is pure.'

"Good friends, see for yourselves the purity of your own natures, practice and accomplish for yourselves. Your own nature is the Dharmakāya and self-practice is the practice of Buddha; by self-accomplishment you may achieve the Buddha Way for yourselves.

The Master said: "Good friends, if you wish to practice, it is all right to do so as laymen; you don't have to be in a temple. If you are in a temple but do not practice, you are like the evil-minded people of the West. If you are a layman but do practice, you are practicing the good of the people of the East. Only I beg of you, practice purity yourselves; this then is the Western Land."

The prefect asked: "Master, how should we practice as laymen? I wish you would instruct us."

The Master said: "Good friends, I shall make a formless verse for you monks and laymen. When all of you recite it and practice according to it, then you will always be in the same place as I am. The verse says:

> Proficiency in preaching and proficiency in the mind,
> Are like the sun and empty space.
> Handing down this sudden teaching alone,
> Enter into the world and destroy erroneous doctrines.
> Although in the teaching there is no sudden and gradual,
> In delusion and awakening there is slowness and speed.
> In studying the teaching of the sudden doctrine,
> Ignorant persons cannot understand completely.
> Although explanations are made in ten thousand ways,
> If you combine them with the Principle, they become one.
> Within the dark home of the passions,
> The sun of wisdom must at all times shine.
> Erroneous [thoughts] come because of the passions;
> When correct [thoughts] come the passions are cast aside.
> Use neither the erroneous nor the correct,
> And with purity you will attain to complete nirvana.[3]
> Although enlightenment [*bodhi*] is originally pure,
> Creating the mind that seeks it is then delusion.

3. *Wu-ch'u*; ashesa. The extinction of both birth and death, where nothing more remains to be discarded.

The pure nature exists in the midst of delusions,
With correct [thoughts] alone remove the three obstacles.[4]
If people in this world practice the Way,
There is nothing whatsoever to hinder them.
If they always make clear the guilt within themselves,
Then they will accord with the Way.
All living things of themselves possess the Way;
If you part from the Way and seek it elsewhere,
Seek it you may but you will not find it,
And in the end, indeed, you will be disappointed.
If you aspire to attain the Way,
Practice correctly; this is the Way.
If in yourselves you do not have the correct mind,
You will be walking in darkness and will not see the Way.
If you are a person who truly practices the Way,
Do not look at the ignorance of the world,
For if you see the wrong of people in the world,
Being wrong yourself, *you* will be evil.
The wrong in others is not your own crime,
Your own wrong is of itself your crime.
Only remove the wrong in your own mind,
Crush the passions and destroy them.
If you wish to convert an ignorant person,
Then you must have expedients.
Do not allow him to have doubts,
Then enlightenment [*bodhi*] will appear.
From the outset the Dharma has been in the world;
Being in the world, it transcends the world.
Hence do not seek the transcendental world outside,
By discarding the present world itself.
Erroneous views are of this world,
Correct views transcend this world.
If you smash completely the erroneous and the correct,
[Then the nature of enlightenment (*bodhi*) will be revealed as it is].
Just this is the Sudden Teaching;
Another name for it is the Mahāyāna.
Having been deluded throughout a multitude of *kalpas*,
One gains awakening within an instant.

---

4. *San-chang*. The three *vighna*. There are several groups. The *Hōbō dankyō kōkan* . . . identifies
them as the passions, deeds done, and retributions.

The Master said: "Good friends, if all of you recite this verse and practice in accordance with it, even if you are a thousand *li*[5] away from me, you will always be in my presence. If you do not practice it, even if we are face to face, we will always be a thousand *li* apart. Each of you yourselves must practice. The Dharma doesn't wait for you.

"Let us disperse for a while. I am going back to Mt. Ts'ao-ch'i. If any of you have great doubt, come to that mountain and I shall resolve that doubt for you and show you the Buddha-world as well."

All the officials, monks, and laymen who were sitting together bowed low before the Master, and there was none who did not sigh: "Wonderful, great awakening! These are things we have never heard before. Who would have expected Ling-nan to be so fortunate as to have had a buddha born there!" The entire assembly dispersed.

5. [*Li*: a measure of distance equivalent to the English league.—Eds.]

4

Yung-chia

(D. 713)

Yung-chia Hsüan-chüeh is known in the annals of Ch'an as the Master Who Spent One Night with the Ancestor. The Ancestor in question is Hui-neng, whom Yung-chia (J., Yōka) visited at Mt. Ts'ao-ch'i after decades of study in other Buddhist traditions, notably the T'ien-t'ai sect. He had awakened upon reading a passage from the *Vimalakīrti Sūtra* and traveled to see Hui-neng, at the urging of another monk, in order to have his realization checked. On his arrival, he went before Hui-neng. Rather than touching his head to the ground in the *k'ou-t'ou* prescribed by custom, he flourished his staff and circled the celebrated teacher three times. "A monk must maintain the exacting rules and etiquette of his station," said Hui-neng. "Where have you come from, and why do you carry on in this arrogant way?"

"Birth-and-death is a matter of terrible urgency," answered the visitor. "Death follows birth with great speed."

"Why don't you grasp the Unborn and see that there's no early or late?" asked the Ancestor.

"What grasps is the Unborn, and what sees is neither early nor late," answered Yung-chia.

"That's right!" Hui-neng exclaimed. Others looking on were astonished. Having reached accord with the Ancestor, Yung-chia prostrated himself and announced his intention to depart. Asked why he was leaving so soon, Yung-chia declared that, even in the midst of motion, our fundamental nature does not move. How could it be considered, then, that he was leaving, much less leaving too soon? The dialogue continued, with Hui-neng confirming the responses of his reluctant guest and eventually prevailing upon him to spend at least one night in the monastery at Ts'ao-ch'i. Thus Yung-chia acquired his unwieldy nickname. At least so goes the customary account, which may well have been concocted simply to link him to the Sixth Ancestor.

The famous *Song of Realizing the Way* alludes to this legendary meeting of minds and to transmission of the Buddha's message to Ts'ao-ch'i through twenty-eight generations of teachers in India and six more in China. In so doing, the poem gives evidence that it was composed (or substantially modified, at least) well after Yung-chia's death, for at that time neither the twenty-eight step Indian sequence nor Hui-neng's place in the line of succession was securely established.

The poem is credited to Yung-chia all the same and is the only piece of writing ascribed to him that students of Ch'an and Zen commonly know, recite, and even memorize.

Though the author of the poem refers to himself as a mountain monk and sings the praises of hermit life, the Yung-chia of record was hardly a reclusive or obscure figure. He attracted enough notice during his lifetime to draw numerous disciples, and after his death, the imperial court honored him with the title Master of Formlessness, a memorial pagoda, and recognition in the official dynastic history. Moreover, the state governor preserved his teachings in a ten-part text that later entered the Chinese canon. This dry prose work is distant in both spirit and content from the lively poem for which Yung-chia is remembered.

The poem's title, *Cheng-tao ke,* is often translated *Song of Enlightenment,* but it is interesting to retain the meaning and flavor of the Chinese characters that form the compound for enlightenment. *Cheng* may mean "confirm," "verify," "prove," or "certify." In the present case, it refers to corroborating the Dharma through one's own experience. *Tao* (J., *dō*) appears frequently in Ch'an and Zen literature and is sometimes preserved in English for that reason, but fortunately, its double import is nicely conveyed by the word *way.* The *tao* is at once the way things are and the way to such experience, the path of practice and realization. Inevitably *tao* carries at least a whiff of the grand old Chinese tradition of Taoism, and in this instance, it's a rather strong whiff. The initial three lines of this Way-verification song are especially redolent of Lao-tzu and Chuang-tzu.

Along with traces of Taoism, the *Cheng-tao ke* contains numerous references to the teachings, metaphors, and mythology of Indian Buddhism, holding far more tightly to these foreign precedents than later Ch'an tradition would. All the same, it is unmistakably a Ch'an poem, laying out many of the school's central themes, including the futility of conceptual study as a means to true understanding, the necessity of realization, its suddenness and availability to all, and the nature and importance of emptiness and not-knowing. The manner in which the poem covers this ground—zigzagging from topic to topic, mixing personal matters with lofty insights in language ranging from the highly poetic to the purely expository—suggests an attractive flair and idiosyncrasy in its author, whether that was really Yung-chia or someone else. ⊗

SONG OF REALIZING THE WAY

Haven't you met someone seasoned in the Way of Ease,
    a person with nothing to do and nothing to master,
    who neither rejects thought nor seeks truth?
The real nature of ignorance is buddha-nature itself.
    The empty, illusory body is the very body of the Dharma.[1]

---

1. Sutras distinguish three bodies, or aspects, of the Buddha. Yung-chia is equating our physical bodies with the Dharma-body (Skt., Dharmakāya), the pure, clear body of fundamental reality.

When the Dharma-body is realized, there's nothing at all.
    The original nature of all things is innately Buddha.[2]
Elements of the self come and go like clouds, without purpose.[3]
    Greed, hate, and delusion appear and disappear like ocean foam.
When you reach the heart of reality, you find neither self nor other,
    and even the worst kind of karma dissolves at once.
If these words were lies, uttered to deceive others,
    my tongue would be torn out forever!
The instant you awaken to the *ch'an* of the Tathāgatā,[4]
    all practices and means of liberation are perfected at once.
In life's dream, passing from heaven to hell, each realm seems real,[5]
    but with awakening, the whole cosmos is completely empty.
No bad fortune, no good fortune, no loss, no gain—
    in nirvana, there's nothing to ask or to seek
Dust builds up on a mind-mirror not cleaned.
    With one decisive stroke now, lay the glass bare!
Who is it that has no thought? Who is it that's unborn?
    It's as if really not born, yet not unborn either.
Put this question to a wooden puppet:
    can buddhahood be gained by seeking it?[6]
Just let everything go—earth, water, fire, wind—
    then drink and eat as you please, in nirvana.
Everything in the universe is fleeting and vacant;
    this is the perfect enlightenment of the Tathāgatā.
A true follower of the Way speaks with certainty.
    You who lack will and self-discipline, be inquiring!
Going straight to the root is the hallmark of the Buddha;

2. The Chinese characters rendered "innately Buddha" translate the Sanskrit word *bhūtatathāta,* a name for the unnameable. It signifies the changeless reality of things as they simply are and is taken as a synonym for Dharmakāya (note 1).
3. The literal reference is to the five *skandhas* (bundles, aggregates), that constitute each person—form, sensation, perception, impulse, and consciousness.
4. Tathāgatā (lit., thus-come, thus-gone) is a common designation for the Buddha and, at the same time, indicates the nature of the buddha-mind, which all beings share. This is the mind of perfect freedom, of coming and going without obstruction. In Yung-chia's time, *Ch'an* probably meant meditation more often than it meant a particular tradition. In each case, whether it should be capitalized or not is a judgment call.
5. Classical Buddhism taught a cycle of birth and death that takes us through six realms or modes of existence, ranging from hell to heaven. Which realm one is born into next time depends on the karma built up in this round. Ch'an masters early on began to interpret this teaching metaphorically, as an expression of continual passage through states of suffering, happiness, hunger, greed, and so forth.
6. Here the poet borrows an image from the Perfection of Wisdom sutras, which liken the nature of a bodhisattva to that of a marionette. The point is that both act freely, without the confusion brought on by dualistic thinking. The answer to this rhetorical question is plainly meant to be "no."

picking up leaves and collecting branches is no use at all.
Most people don't know the pearl that answers all wishes,
    the great pearl found in the treasurehouse of the Tathāgatā.[7]
Its miraculous workings are neither empty nor not empty,
    a single sphere of light without form yet not formless.
Opening the eyes of wisdom, gaining powers to save others—[8]
    these come only when you realize the inconceivable.
It's not difficult to see the reflections in a mirror,
    but can you take hold of the moon in the water?
Though they always travel alone, always walk alone,
    the enlightened all tread the same path of nirvana.
Their air is ancient, their spirit pure and bearing noble.
    Lean-faced and bony, they pass unnoticed in the world.
Disciples of the Buddha renounce all their possessions,
    but they're poor in body only, not in the Way.
Poverty shows forever in their patch-cloth garb,
    but they hold in mind the precious jewel of the Way.
This jewel is beyond price and can never be exhausted,
    though used ceaselessly to help others, as conditions permit.
A buddha's three bodies and fourfold wisdom are complete within it.[9]
    The six powers and eight freedoms of a sage all bear its stamp.[10]
With just one look, a superior student understands everything;
    those of less talent learn a lot but can be certain of little.
Strip the filthy clothes from your own breast!
    Why make a show of outward effort?
Let others criticize you, let them condemn you—
    trying to set the sky on fire, they'll just end up exhausted.
I hear abusive words as though I were drinking ambrosia:
    everything melts, and suddenly I enter the inconceivable.
When you understand the real value of abuse,

7. *Chintāmani,* sometimes rendered *mani*-jewel, refers to a brilliant pearl or gem that grants every wish made upon it. Though it is usually depicted in the hands of a buddha or bodhisattva, Yung-chia construes it as the pearl of our own nature and locates it in the *Tathāgatā-garbha* (lit., Tathāgatā womb or treasury).

8. This line refers to five kinds of insight and five powers that, according to the classical teachings, accompany enlightenment.

9. Regarding the three bodies, see note 1, above. Sutras list the four aspects of a buddha's wisdom as the wisdom of identity, subtle understanding of relationships, great mirror wisdom, and insight into effective action.

10. According to classical teachings, a buddha proceeds through an eight-step sequence of progressively greater liberations and comes to obtain six supernatural powers. Yung-chia makes clear that these attributes of liberation are not acquired one by one but occur all at once in the simple act of seeing the treasure with one's own eyes.

your worst critic becomes a wise friend.[11]
If harsh words raise no waves of bitterness or pride—
    how better to show the persistence and compassion of the Unborn?[12]
Seeing into the fundamental fact, you see into its expression as well.
    Your *samādhi* and *prajñā* are full, not stagnantly empty.[13]
Nor is this something that you accomplish alone;
    it's the essence of buddhas as countless as sands of the Ganges.
The lion-roar teaching of fearlessness
    strikes terror in the hearts of all other animals.
Even the great elephant gallops off, its dignity shattered.
    Only the heavenly dragon listens calmly, in pure delight.
Once I traveled rivers and seas, crossed mountains and streams,
    visiting teachers to seek the Way and delve into Ch'an,
but ever since I recognized the Dharma path at Ts'ao-ch'i,
    I've known for myself what's beyond birth and death.
Walking is *ch'an* and sitting is *ch'an*;
    speaking or silent, moving or still, the essence is at peace.
Even under threat of sword and spear, it's undisturbed;
    even a cup of poison won't destroy this serenity.
Before Shākyamuni could meet Dīpankara Buddha,
    he had to train endless eons in perseverance.[14]
Round after round after round of birth and death,
    the cycle of *samsāra* continues without cease.
Only those who abruptly realize the Unborn
    no longer feel the grip of shame and honor.
Deep in the mountains, on an isolated peak,
    I live on my own in a stand of pines.
In a simple hut, I sit meditating without concerns,
    silent and alone, dwelling peacefully, lighthearted.
Once you've awakened, it's done: no effort needed.
    The world of affairs knows nothing like this.
Generous behavior might get you to heaven,[15]

---

11. The Chinese phrase given here as "wise friend" is a translation of the Sanskrit word *kalyānamitra*, denoting a religious guide or teacher.
12. Along with the wish-fulfilling pearl and the treasure beyond price, the Unborn is an expression for essential nature, emphasizing that this nature is not born and does not die.
13. *Samādhi* is meditative absorption, *prajñā* the wisdom of enlightenment.
14. In Buddhist mythology, Shākyamuni was preceded in the world by numerous other buddhas. It was meeting the first of these ancient buddhas, Dīpankara, that confirmed the future Shākyamuni's incalculably long path to buddhahood.
15. Practicing generosity for karmic reasons might work in the short term by getting you a heavenly birth in the next round of being.

but it's like shooting an arrow into vast space:
when its force is exhausted, it falls back to earth,
   bad fortune inevitably following after good.
How can this compare to the true gate of nondoing,
   a leap directly to the ground of the Tathāgatā?
Just get to the root—never mind the branches!
   It's like the fire in the heart of a crystal.
Once you've seen the bliss-bestowing jewel,
   you and all beings benefit endlessly.
The moon shines on the river, a breeze stirs the pines—
   what's there to do this clear, boundless evening?
The morality-jewel of Buddha-nature adorns my mind;
   I'm clothed in the dew, the fog, the cloud, and the mist.
A monk's dragon-subduing bowl and tiger-parting staff,
   its linked rings jingling musically—[16]
these aren't just symbolic, superficial things;
   the Tathāgatā's treasure staff marked out the trail!
Don't seek the true and don't reject the false;
   realize the emptiness and formlessness of both.
Formless, neither empty nor not empty—
   these are the true signs of the Tathāgatā.
The mind-mirror shines brilliantly, without obstruction,
   its light reaching worlds as countless as sands of the Ganges.
The ten thousand things are all reflected here,
   illumined perfectly, neither inside nor outside.
If you cling to emptiness, denying cause and effect,
   your confusion and carelessness bring disaster all around.
Clinging to being and denying emptiness is just as bad—
   you've escaped drowning but leapt into the fire.
Rejecting illusion and holding onto truth,
   the discriminating mind becomes falsely clever.
To engage in practice without understanding this
   is to mistake a thief for your own child.
Losing the Dharma treasure, destroying natural virtue—
   that's what comes from the churning of consciousness.
The gateway to Ch'an is cutting mind off completely,
   suddenly entering the power and wisdom of the Unborn.

16. Hui-neng is said to have tricked an evil-doing dragon into shrinking itself and coming close enough that he could catch it in his alms bowl. Similarly, a Ch'an master was reputed to have used his traveling staff to break up a tiger fight, saving the tigers' lives. Such staffs are topped with two sets of rings, whose jingling is intended to warn off nearby animals.

People of heroic will wield the sword of wisdom,
    its *prajñā* blade blazing with a diamond fire.
It shreds the logic of other paths,
    drives off the demons of heaven, too.
Roll the Dharma thunder, pound the Dharma drum!
    Raise clouds of compassion, shower life-giving dew!
Wherever they go, giants of the Way nourish one and all;
    people of every kind and capacity all find freedom.
From virgin meadows of the snow-crested peaks
    comes the pure food I continually enjoy.[17]
This single, perfect nature pervades all natures;
    the sole, universal Dharma encompasses all dharmas.
One moon shines in the water everywhere;
    all the reflected moons are just that one moon.
The Dharma-body of all buddhas suffuses your nature,
    your nature inseparable from the Tathāgatā's.
A single stage of awakening includes all stages,
    transcending mind, matter, and activity.
All the teachings are fulfilled in a snap of the fingers;
    in the blink of an eye, the regime of time ends.
Numbers, names, the whole list of negations—
    what have they got to do with real awakening?[18]
Beyond praise, beyond reproach,
    like space itself, it has no bounds.
Never coming or going, it's always full and clear,
    but if you go looking for it, it won't be found.
It can't be acquired and can't be lost,
    only attained without attaining anything.
It speaks in silence and is silent in speech.
    The great gift-gate stands open, unobstructed.
If someone asks me my guiding principle,
    I call it the power of great *prajñā*!
People who say right or wrong—they don't know.
    Agreeing and disagreeing, even *devas* don't get it.[19]

17. This food (actually ghee, clarified butter) is yet another metaphor for the pure, clear Dharmakāya. "Snow-crested peaks" is a figure of speech for the Himalaya.

18. "Negations" here probably refers to Mahāyāna philosophical systems that attempted to identify the Dharmakāya through an exhaustive sequence of negations—not being, not non-being, neither being nor non-being, etc.

19. In the cosmology of classical Buddhism, *devas* (lit., shining ones) enjoy long, blissful lives in the heavenly realm. Though this is the most pleasant of the six realms, *devas* still suffer the delusions of duality and are bound for rebirth.

I've already practiced this for ages and ages;
    it's not an idler's wild notion put out to mislead you.
I hoist the Dharma banner and present the very teaching
    set forth by Shākyamuni, carried down to Ts'ao-ch'i.
Mahākāshyapa received the lamp first and handed it on
    through twenty-eight generations of teachers in India.
Then, crossing rivers and seas to reach this land,
    Bodhidharma came to be our first ancestor here.
His robe, we all know, has been passed down through six teachers,
    and how many people since have realized the Way?
Truth can't be established, the false is empty from the outset.
    Set aside being and non-being, and even non-emptiness is empty.
From the start, the twenty types of emptiness were nothing to cling to;
    the nature of the Tathāgata is always one, its essence the same.
The mind, as a sense organ, takes all things as objects—
    a double blotch that darkens the mind-mirror[20]—
but the moment it's wiped it clean, the light shines again;
    mind and things both forgotten, true nature comes clear.
Sad, sad, this age of corruption and decline!
    Hard times make discipline difficult.[21]
As the era of the great sages recedes, delusions run deep.
    Demons strong and Dharma weak, hatred and mayhem abound.
When people hear the Buddha's word of immediate perfection,
    they're mad they can't smash it as they would a roof tile.
The workings of your mind bring suffering on your body,
    so don't blame your troubles on anyone else,
and unless you want a ticket to unending hell,
    don't malign the true Dharma of the Tathāgatā,
In a sandalwood forest, where no other trees grow,
    lions live alone in the dense, luxuriant groves,
prowling undisturbed and utterly at peace,
    while other animals, even birds, stay far away.
Only their cubs follow closely behind,
    already roaring loudly by the age of three.
Even if a jackal took after the King of the Dharma,

20. The natural clarity of mind is obscured, in other words, by dividing the world into subject and object, perceiver and perceived.
21. Yung-chia here alludes to a prediction that the Buddha's teaching would deteriorate over time. After being rightly remembered and practiced for its first thousand years, its second millennium was to be the age of "semblance," when people wouldn't understand the Dharma but would still go through the motions. Yung-chia lived in this latter period. A third and final age, lasting ten thousand years and expected to culminate in complete ignorance of the Way, is now in progress.

it would forever open its ogreish mouth in vain.[22]
The Dharma of sudden awakening isn't a matter of our feelings;
    doubts and hesitations must be confronted and cleared away.
This old mountain monk doesn't hold himself above others!
    I just worry some will stick in eternalism or extinction.[23]
Wrong is not wrong, and right is not right—
    miss this by a hair, and you're off a thousand miles.
Right, a dragon-girl instantly achieved buddhahood.
    Wrong, a great scholar plummeted into hell.[24]
In my early years, I sought to amass great learning,
    studying commentaries, reading sutras and *shastras*,
tirelessly drawing distinctions among names and forms—
    just as futile as diving into the sea to count its sands.
This the Tathāgatā condemned sharply in saying,
    "What's the use of reckoning someone else's fortune?"
All my efforts, I realized, had been misguided and useless;
    I'd wasted many years, blowing like dust in the wind.
If your disposition is wrong, misunderstandings occur,
    and the Tathāgatā's sudden awakening is out of reach.
Southern Buddhists may try diligently but miss the Way.[25]
    Non-Buddhists may be very astute but lack *prajñā*.
People who are ignorant, people who are childish—
    they suppose an empty fist or raised finger holds the truth.
Mistaking the pointing finger for the moon, they practice fruitlessly,
    devising weird ideas in the realm of form and sensation.
Not perceiving a single thing—that's the Tathāgatā!
    Only then can one be called "Supreme Seer."[26]
With awakening, we find karmic burdens empty;
    without it, all our debts continue to come due.
A royal feast is spread for the hungry, but they don't eat.

22. Try as they might, in other words, imitators can never give the roar of the Dharma.
23. That is, get stuck in concepts about Buddha-nature, considering it a permanent entity or absolute nothingness.
24. Yung-chia here offers episodes from the sutras as evidence that one's birth, gender, and social status have no bearing upon buddhahood. All that counts is realization.
25. Mahāyāna Buddhists looked down upon the older forms of Buddhism maintained in South Asia, terming them Hīnayāna, "small vehicle," in contrast to Mahāyāna, "big vehicle." Hīnayāna is the term actually employed here.
26. Supreme Seer is an epithet for Avalokiteshvara, the bodhisattva of compassion, who sees the suffering of the world. The implication is that realizing emptiness, breaking through the dualism of perceiver and perceived, makes it possible to see without obstruction—no *you* separate from *me*, no *self* and *other*.

The sick meet a peerless doctor—why don't they recover?[27]
To practice Ch'an in the world of desire takes powerful discernment,
    but the lotus that blooms in the midst of fire can never be destroyed.
Pradhānashūra broke the gravest precepts yet awoke to the Unborn,
    and the buddhahood he achieved long ago endures to this day.[28]
The dharma of fearlessness comes forth like a lion's roar!
    What a pity confused minds just grow denser, tough as leather.
Persisting in the belief that moral failures block enlightenment,
    people can't see the secret the Tathāgatā revealed.
Long ago, two monks broke the precepts on sex and killing.
    Upāli, his light like a glowworm's, only worsened their plight,
but the great Vimalakīrti cleared their doubts at once,
    as the fiery sun melts frost and snow.[29]
The power of liberation is beyond comprehension,
    working wonders as countless as sands of the Ganges.
Who wouldn't offer food, clothing, shelter, and medicine
    to one who deserves ten thousand pieces of gold?[30]
Breaking your body, grinding your bones—even that's not enough!
    A single phrase of awakening beats eons and eons of practice.
The king of all dharmas ranks second to none;
    tathāgatās countless as sands of the Ganges all gain it alike.
I reveal the bliss-bestowing pearl to you now,
    and all who take this to heart will come to accord:
When you see clearly, there's nothing at all;
    there are no people, there are no buddhas.
The myriad worlds are like so much foam on the sea,
    old worthies and great sages merely flashes of lightning.
Even if a red-hot iron wheel were spinning around your skull,
    it wouldn't dispel the perfect clarity of *samādhi* and *prajñā*.
Though the sun might turn cold and the moon hot,
    demon forces could never destroy the true teaching.

27. The metaphors of a great Dharma feast and of Shākyamuni as incomparable physician are drawn from the *Lotus Sutra*.

28. Yung-chia errs on this name. Pradhānashūra is said to have awakened *another* monk to the fact that his transgressions, like all else, had no fundamental basis.

29. Here Yung-chia draws on a sutra to counter a misunderstanding of karma, namely that misdeeds of the past make liberation in this lifetime impossible. Upāli, whom Yung-chia dismisses as a dimwit, was an elder of Shākyamuni's time, while Vimalakīrti appears in the Mahāyāna sutras as exemplar par excellence of enlightened lay life.

30. In early Chinese Buddhism, as in Southern Buddhism to this day, monks depended on offerings of the "four necessities." One should not begrudge these, Yung-chia suggests, to those like Vimalakīrti who have reached enlightenment and thus are able to free others.

An elephant cart moves along majestically.
   How could a mantis block its progress?
Just as elephants don't travel on rabbit paths,
   great enlightenment isn't a matter of details.
Why diminish the sky by looking at it through a reed?
   If you haven't yet found clarity, take this song as your key.

5

Wang Wei

(c. 699–761)

Wang Wei had a distinguished career in the vast civil service apparatus of the Chinese empire, but his reputation is for art, not statescraft. He excelled in music, painting, and calligraphy as well as poetry, earning himself an undisputed place among the giants of Chinese high culture. Though he left a modest body of work—some four hundred poems—he is recognized as a major contributor to the literary flowering that occurred during the T'ang dynasty (618–907). This golden age of Chinese letters coincided with the rise of Ch'an, and Ch'an is often credited for stimulating the creativity of the era.

In Wang Wei's case, certainly, Ch'an and poetry went hand in hand. His writings are laced with allusions to sutras, teachings, personages, and places—not all of them strictly associated with Ch'an, though clearly his interest centered on the stream from Ts'ao-ch'i. His memorial for Hui-neng, already mentioned, is one of three such funerary inscriptions that Wang Wei composed, all of which link him with prominent Ch'an figures. The other two celebrate the monk Ching-chüeh, author of an early Ch'an history, and the teacher Tao-kuang, not much known now but eminent enough in his time to warrant a memorial pagoda and the title Ch'an Master of Great Virtue.

The inscription for Tao-kuang, written after his death in 739, contains our best evidence that Wang Wei studied Ch'an not just through reading and periodic temple visits but in a serious and protracted fashion. "For ten years," he reports, "I sat at his feet and obediently received the teachings." Wang Wei lost his wife in about 730, and biographers suggest that her death prompted a deepening involvement in Ch'an and in Buddhism generally. That he did not remarry—indeed, maintained celibacy—was highly unusual for a layman and is taken, along with his declared vegetarianism, as testimony to his earnestness as a practitioner. For many of his fellow literati, Ch'an was principally an intellectual interest, but the same cannot be said of Wang Wei.

Wang Wei's poems often depict him turning reluctantly away from the monk's life to return to his life as a government official and man of the world. In "On Leaving Monk Wen-ku in the Mountains," he places himself midway between his brother Chin, who held a very high place at court, and an unnamed elder relative who had taken the monk's tonsure. True to the dictates of Chinese tradition, Wang Wei proposes that seclusion is justified in times of disorder but that, "when the Way pre-vails," one must serve the nation. Serving the nation, in this view, is accord with the Way here. So is sadness when leaving a place one loves.

Emblematic of Wang Wei's stance is the epithet he adopted, Mo-chieh. Added to his given name, it forms Wei-mo-chieh, the Chinese transliteration of Vimalakīrti—the name of an Indian householder revered by Mahāyāna Bud-dhists as a model of wisdom. Styling himself a latter-day Vimalakīrti framed Wang Wei's dual life in the most positive terms: not as a split or a straddle—one foot in affairs of state, the other in monkhood—but as a unity, the best of both worlds. It states his understanding that fundamentally there are *not* two worlds, pure and impure, and that a true person of the Way may go anywhere, unhampered. 🕸

VISITING HSIANG-CHI TEMPLE

Unknown, Hsiang-chi Temple—
miles and miles into cloud-draped peaks.
Among the old trees, a path no one travels,
a bell deep in the mountains but where from?
A brook gulps among protruding boulders,
and though the sun glows, it's cool beneath the pines.
At dusk, by a bend in an empty pool,
meditating quietly I rout the deadly dragon.

OFFERING A MEAL FOR THE MONKS OF MOUNT FU-FU

Having come late to the pure truth,
every day I withdraw farther from the crowd.
Expecting monks from a distant mountain,
I prepare, sweeping out my simple thatch hut.
It's true: from their place in the clouds,
they come to my poor house in the weeds.
On grass mats, we have a meal of pine nuts.
Burning incense, we read books about the Way.
I light the oil lamp as daylight thins,
ring the stone chimes as night comes on.
Once you've realized the joys of stillness,
your days hold ample peace and leisure.
Why give serious thought to returning?
Life now looks completely vacant.

ON LEAVING MONK WEN-KU IN THE MOUNTAINS, SHARED ALSO WITH YOUNGER BROTHER CHIN

I remove my hemp robe to head back to the court,
leaving my master, rejoining the sages of our time.
It's not just this man of the mountains I leave—
I'm turning my back even on the moon in the pines.
These past days we've wandered, taking life easy,
going right to the edge of the pinkening clouds.
Opening a window over the river's north bank,
from bed we watched birds fly till they vanished.
We enjoyed meals sprawled on the flat rocks,
lounged often by a plunging stream.
In orderly times, people rarely enter seclusion.
When the Way prevails, why leave the world?
My younger brother holds a high position;
an elder relation has become a monk.
Keep the path to your reed gate clear—
whenever time allows, I'll come knock.

FALL NIGHT, SITTING ALONE

Sitting alone, I mourn my thinning hair.
The hall is empty at not yet nine o'clock,
wild fruit thuds down in a rainstorm,
insects from outdoors chirp beneath the lamp.
White hair's very, very hard to change,
and real gold can't be manufactured.
To get rid of the ailments of age,
there's just one thing: study the Unborn!

SENT TO A MONK AT CH'UNG-FAN MONASTERY

Ch'ung-fan monk! This Ch'ung-fan monk!
Went home to the mountains last fall, didn't return this spring.
Falling flowers, warbling birds—so many, all mixed up.
A door on the creek, a window on the peaks—so quiet, closeted.
Up there on the cliffs, who knows the affairs of people below?
Seen from the city's distance: just an empty, cloud-covered range.

Poems like the foregoing, touching more or less overtly on Buddhism, are hardly exceptional in Wang Wei's oeuvre. Many others report visits to temples and monasteries, exalt particular Ch'an teachers, or address explicitly Buddhist topics, sometimes in quite specialized language. More numerous, however, and generally of greater literary value are the poems making no direct reference to the Dharma, poems that seem to carry its resonance as all things do, simply by nature. Here, the clouds are clouds, and what lies concealed behind them is Mount Chung-nan. If you say the clouds represent delusion and Chung-nan the unmoving reality of buddha-nature, you ruin the poem and defile the world. ☙

AN ANSWER FOR VICE-PREFECT CHANG

Late in life, all I want is peace.
The million pursuits aren't my concern.
Looking myself over—no future plans.
I just know: go back to the ancient forest.
A breeze in the pines, loosening my belt,
I pick my lute under the mountain moon.
What's the logic, you ask, of success and failure?
A fisherman's song carries far past the shore.

WRITTEN AFTER STEADY RAIN AT MY WANG RIVER ESTATE

Steady rain in the vacant woods, smoke rising lazily—
greens steaming, millet cooking for those in the fields.
Across the foggy paddies flaps a white egret,
orioles sing in the summer trees' dense foliage.
In the mountain quiet, I learn to see a morning hibiscus.
Beneath the pines, I pick damp mallows for a meatless meal.
An old man of the wild, done battling for position—
why would the gulls still be fearful of me?

Lines 6–8 After noting his harmlessness—his vegetarian ways and disinclination to struggle for status—Wang Wei closes with an allusion to a Taoist story about a man who kept company with seagulls until one day his father directed him to catch one; from then on, the gulls gave him a wide berth.

ANSWER TO P'EI TI'S QUESTION ABOUT MY LIFE

Vast, wide, the expanse of the cold river.
Gray, blue, the curtain of autumn rain.
You ask if Mt. Chung-nan's still there—
my heart knows what's beyond the white clouds!

MY RETREAT AT MT. CHUNG-NAN

In midlife, I've come to cherish the Way;
for late life, I've built a home near Chung-nan.
I head out there alone anytime the urge strikes.
It's glorious the things an empty self sees!
I walk the stream to its very source,
sit and watch the clouds rise. . . .
If by chance I meet an old woodsman,
we talk and laugh—no rush to get home!

IN THE MOUNTAINS

Up Bramble Creek, white stones jut out.
Cold weather—hardly any red leaves left.
Along the mountain trail, there's no rain;
the vacant blue itself soaks one's clothes.

6

Shih-t'ou

(700–790)

Shih-t'ou Hsi-ch'ien received relatively little public notice in his own lifetime but looms large in Ch'an histories. *The Transmission of the Lamp* places him among Hui-neng's students when the great master died, which would mean that Shih-t'ou had launched his religious career auspiciously by the age of thirteen—not impossible but almost surely an embellishment upon the historical facts. He went on to study with one of Hui-neng's successors, the obscure master Ch'ing-yüan Hsing-szu (J., Seigen Gyōshi). This too may be legendary, however, for he appears wise beyond his years in the traditional account of their first meeting:

After determining that the young monk had come from the monastery at Ts'ao-ch'i, Ch'ing-yüan asked what Shih-t'ou had brought from Hui-neng. "Even before I went to Ts'ao-ch'i, I lacked nothing," Shih-t'ou replied.

"If that's so," said the master, "what do you expect to pursue after leaving Ts'ao-ch'i?"

"If I hadn't gone to Ts'ao-ch'i, how could I have understood that I lacked nothing?" said Shih-t'ou, and he asked, "Did you know the master of Ts'ao-ch'i or not?"

"Do you know me now or not?" countered Ch'ing-yüan.

"Though I might know you," answered the boy, "how can I realize it?"

Impressed, Ch'ing-yüan said, "There are many horned animals in this assembly, but a single unicorn is enough!" Shih-t'ou thus joined the monks of Ch'ing-yüan's assembly and, in due course, received Dharma-transmission from him. His great awakening is said to have occurred as he read a passage from Seng-chao, an early Chinese scholar-monk whose writings presaged Ch'an: "The ultimate self is empty and void. Though it lacks form, the myriad things are all of its making. One who understands the myriad things as the self—isn't that a sage?"

In 742, two years after Ch'ing-yüan's death, Shih-t'ou built himself a hut on a broad stone bench near an old temple on the mountain of Nan-yüeh, in southern China. Already the site of three Ch'an monasteries, this mountain attracted Ch'an students in droves, and word soon began circulating among them about the fellow they dubbed Shih-t'ou Ho-shang, the Stone-top Monk (J., Sekitō Oshō), presumably in honor of his dwelling place. Inquirers came flocking to his door throughout a teaching career believed to have lasted fifty years. ⚏

FROM THE TRANSMISSION OF THE LAMP

Shih-t'ou: "My teaching which has come down from the ancient buddhas is not dependent on meditation [*dhyāna*] or on diligent application of any kind. When you attain the insight as attained by the Buddha, you realize that Mind is Buddha and Buddha is Mind, that Mind, Buddha, sentient beings, *bodhi* [enlightenment], and *klesha* [passions] are of one and the same substance while they vary in names. You should know that your own mind-essence is neither subject to annihilation nor eternally subsisting, is neither pure nor defiled, that it remains perfectly undisturbed and self-sufficient and the same with the wise and the ignorant, that it is not limited in its working, and that it is not included in the category of mind [*chitta*], consciousness [*manas*], or thought [*vijñāna*]. The three worlds of desire, form, and no-form, and the six paths of existence are no more than manifestations of your mind itself. They are all like the moon reflected in water or images in the mirror. How can we speak of them as being born or as passing away? When you come to this understanding, you will be furnished with all the things you are in need of."

Tao-wu, one of Shih-t'ou's disciples, then asked: "Who has attained to the understanding of Hui-neng's teaching?"

T'ou: "The one who understands Buddhism."

Wu: "Have you then attained it?"

T'ou: "No, I do not understand Buddhism."

A monk asked: "How does one get emancipated?"

The Master said: "Who has ever put you in bondage?"

Monk: "What is the Pure Land?"

Master: "Who has ever defiled you?"

Monk: "What is nirvana?"

Master: "Who has ever subjected you to birth-and-death?"

Shih-t'ou asked a monk newly arrived: "Where do you come from?"

"From Kiangsi."

"Did you see Ma the great teacher?"[1]

"Yes, Master."

Shih-t'ou then pointed at a bundle of kindling and said: "How does Ma the teacher resemble this?"

The monk made no answer. Returning to Ma the teacher, he reported the interview with Shih-t'ou. Ma asked: "Did you notice how large the bundle was?"

"An immensely large one it was."

"You are a very strong man indeed."

1. [A reference to Ma-tsu, often called Ma Ta-shih (Great Master Ma). See Chapter 7.—Eds.]

"How so?" asked the monk.

"Because you have carried that huge bundle from Nan-yüeh even up to this monastery. Only a strong man can accomplish such a feat."

A monk asked: "What is the meaning of the First Ancestor's coming from the West?"

Master: "Ask the post over there."

Monk: "I do not understand . . ."

Master: "I do not either, any more than you."

Ta-tien asked: "According to an ancient sage it is a dualism to take the tao either as existing or as not-existing. Please tell me how to remove this obstruction."

"Not a thing here, and what do you wish to remove?"

Shih-t'ou turned about and demanded: "Do away with your throat and lips, and let me see what you can say."

Said Ta-tien: "No such things have I."

"If so, you may enter the gate."

"What is Ch'an?" asked a monk.

"Brick and stone."

"What is the tao?"

"A block of wood."

If these exchanges faithfully represent Shih-t'ou's teaching style, it is not hard to understand why he became a major figure in early Ch'an, carrying it rapidly toward its mature form. Lineage histories credit his Dharma descendants with establishing three of the so-called Five Houses of Ch'an—the Ts'ao-t'ung (J., Sōtō), Yun-men (J., Unmon) and Fa-yen (J., Hōgen) lines of the teaching. Though his literary record is not voluminous, Shih-t'ou is noted for two exceptional poems. The first, "Song of the Grass-Roof Hermitage," begins as if it were a simple celebration of his cliff-top hut, but by its final lines, the hermitage under consideration has become ours—that most intimate place of habitation, the body. The artistry of the poem sets it apart from *Relying on Mind* and *Song of Realizing the Way* suggesting that Wang Wei and others in the Chinese literary tradition may have had good effect on Ch'an expression. ❧

SONG OF THE GRASS-ROOF HERMITAGE

I've build a grass hut where there's nothing of value.

After eating, I relax and enjoy a nap.

When it was completed, fresh weeds appeared.

Now it's been lived in—covered by weeds.

The person in the hut lives here calmly,
not stuck to inside, outside, or in between.
Places worldly people live, he doesn't live.
Realms worldly people love, he doesn't love.
Though the hut is small, it includes the entire world.
In ten square feet, an old man illumines forms and their nature.
A Great Vehicle bodhisattva trusts without doubt.
The middling or lowly can't help wondering;
Will this hut perish or not?
Perishable or not, the original master is present,
not dwelling south or north, east or west.
Firmly based on steadiness, it can't be surpassed.
A shining window below the green pines—
jade palaces or vermilion towers can't compare with it.
Just sitting with head covered all things are at rest.
Thus, this mountain monk doesn't understand at all.
Living here he no longer works to get free.
Who would proudly arrange seats, trying to entice guests?
Turn around the light to shine within, then just return.
The vast inconceivable source can't be faced or turned away from.
Meet the ancestral teachers, be familiar with their instruction,
bind grasses to build a hut, and don't give up.
Let go of hundreds of years and relax completely.
Open your hands and walk, innocent.
Thousands of words, myriad interpretations,
are only to free you from obstructions.
If you want to know the undying person in the hut,
don't separate from this skin bag here and now.

The Coincidence of Opposites has proved to be an even more influential verse than "Song of the Grass-Roof Hermitage." Though it falls short in terms of grace and coherence, it opened up for Ch'an a rich territory of experience and metaphor that Taoist writers and the Hua-yen school of Buddhism had previously staked out: the mutuality of all beings and the inextricable unity of opposites. It seems natural that Shih-t'ou would explore this terrain, for it is the realm of his own reported realization and offered Ch'an new ways of expressing the enlightened mind.

The poem borrows its title from a Taoist text on the *I Ching* and, in doing so, presents itself explicitly in juxtaposition to the older tradition. It also borrows the imagery of light and darkness that Taoists had developed in expressing the harmonies of yin and yang. The poem plays off these metaphors, taking light and dark in turn as organic expressions of Buddha-nature, of what is brightly manifested all around us and the dark mind of nonduality. Its originality in treating these two aspects of the great matter—by turns distinguishing them, identifying them, and showing their complementarity—made *The Coincidence of Opposites* famous and inspired such later, finely articulated formulations of these interrelationships as the Five Modes of Tung-shan (see Chapter 18). ஐ

THE COINCIDENCE OF OPPOSITES

The mind of the great sage of India
    was intimately conveyed from west to east.
Though people may be sharp-witted or dull,
    there's no north and south in the Way.[2]
The deep spring sparkles in the pure light,[3]
    its branches streaming through the darkness.
Grasping at phenomena is the source of delusion;
    uniting with the absolute falls short of awakening.[4]
All of the senses, all the things sensed—
    they interact without interaction.
Interacting, they permeate one another,
    yet each remains in its own place.
By nature, forms differ in shape and appearance.
    By nature, sounds bring pleasure or pain.
In darkness, the fine and mediocre accord;
    brightness makes clear and murky distinct.
Each element comes back to its own nature[5]
    just as a child finds it own mother.
Fire is hot, the wind blows,
    water is wet and earth solid,
eyes see forms, ears hear sounds,
    noses smell, tongues tell salty from sour—
so it is with everything everywhere.
    The root puts forth each separate shoot.[6]

2. Lit., "In the Way, no northern or southern ancestor." This probably alludes to the famous comeback Hui-neng is said to have made in answer to the Fifth Ancestor's challenge, "If you're from Ling-nan [in the far south of China], you're a barbarian! How could you ever become a buddha?" Hui-neng: "Though people of the north and south differ, there's no north or south in Buddha-nature."

3. The word translated "deep" here also means "subtle," "mysterious," "profound," even "obscure" or "spiritual." It characterizes the "spring" (lit., source) that is the original nature of all things.

4. Uniting with the absolute, in other words, is still a kind of grasping.

5. The elements referred to are earth, water, fire, and wind, which the Chinese classically recognized as the four basic elements.

6. "Root" and "shoot" are conventional metaphors for cause and effect.

Both root and shoot go back to the fundamental fact.
  Exalted and lowly is just a matter of words.[7]
In the very midst of light, there's darkness;
  don't meet another in the darkness.
In the very midst of darkness, there's light;
  don't observe another in the light.
Light and darkness complement each other,
  like stepping forward and stepping back.
Each of the myriad things has its particular virtue
  inevitably expressed in its use and station.[8]
Phenomena accord with the fundamental as a lid fits its box;
  the fundamental meets phenomena like arrows in mid-air.
Hearing these words, understand the fundamental;
  don't cook up principles from your own ideas.[9]
If you overlook the Way right before your eyes,
  how will you know the path beneath your feet?
Advancing has nothing to do with near and far,[10]
  yet delusion creates obstacles high and wide.
Students of the mystery, I humbly urge you,
  don't waste a moment, night or day!

7. "Exalted and lowly" represents differences in general. Shih-t'ou doesn't deny the reality of differences but points out that such terms as high and low are concepts, labels of human invention that hold no valid claim on the truth. Just as there is no north and south in Buddha-nature, there is no exalted and lowly.

8. That is, a cup is no better or worse than a torque wrench, a cab driver no higher or lower than a physician. Each has its own value, and as the next couplet suggests, this jibes precisely with Buddha-nature. In his famous "Song of Zazen," Hakuin Zenji expresses the same point: "All beings by nature are Buddha / as ice by nature is water. / Apart from water, there is no ice, / apart from beings, no Buddha."

9. As Yung-chia says in *Song of Realizing the Way*, all those who awaken share the same realization and tread the same path. In that sense, it's a mistake to judge a matter of the Way by one's personal standards.

10. Advancing on the Way, that is. To paraphrase Seng-ts'an's line in *Relying on Mind*, the terms "here" and "not here" don't apply to the fundamental. Call it what you will, it isn't absent anywhere, so it can't be near or far.

7

Ma-tsu

(709–788)

Ma-tsu Tao-i and Shih-t'ou are often paired as heroes of Ch'an. Though the records of their lives are patchy and subject to question on historical grounds, these eighth-century colleagues stand out unambiguously as teachers who creatively articulated and established the way of Ch'an. As three of its Five Houses arose from Shih-t'ou's line, so the remaining two—the Lin-chi (J., Rinzai) and Yang-ch'i (J., Yōgi)—trace their origins to Ma-tsu (J., Baso).

Their contemporaries could not know of these downstream developments, but they had no difficulty recognizing the two masters' importance. It was said that a monk remained ignorant unless he made pilgrimage west of the river and south of the lake—journeyed, that is, to see Ma-tsu in Kiangsi Province (lit., West of the River) and Shih-t'ou in Hunan (South of the Lake). Their monasteries were about two hundred miles apart, and though apparently they never met, they knew each other's teaching through word of mouth and seem to have referred students to one another with some frequency.

Ma-tsu excelled at training monks, and no one before or since has equalled his record at producing successors. Available accounts furnish numbers from 84 to 139, but even the low figure, adjusted for biographical inflation, represents an extraordinary accomplishment. *The Transmission of the Lamp* notes that Ma-tsu's heirs fanned out widely, spreading the Dharma throughout China, which helps to explain the Ch'an boom that occurred in the following centuries. The tremendous impact of his teaching is reflected in the way he came to be known: the *tsu* attached to his family name means "ancestor" and is the term applied to Hui-neng and the earlier Chinese and Indian masters of the school's mythic lineage. After Hui-neng, no Ch'an teacher but Ma-tsu was honored with this designation.

Chronicles of his life and work demonstrate Ma-tsu's talent for expressing the Dharma and opening his students' minds. To present the great matter vividly and appropriately, he freely employed whatever tools were at hand, holding up his fly whisk, shouting, grabbing people, hitting them—methods widely emulated by other teachers. In contrast to Shih-t'ou, he left a substantial personal record, and the brilliance of his dialogues gave them a prominent place in the body of Ch'an literature and, later, in the form of practice known as *kung-an* (J., *kōan*) study. ❈

FROM THE RECORD OF MA-TSU

The Ancestor said to the assembly, "The Way needs no cultivation, just do not defile. What is defilement? When with a mind of birth and death one acts in a contrived way, then everything is defilement. If one wants to know the Way directly: Ordinary Mind is the Way![1] What is meant by Ordinary Mind? No activity, no right or wrong, no grasping or rejecting, neither terminable nor permanent, without worldly or holy. The sutra says, 'Neither the practice of ordinary people, nor the practice of sages, that is the bodhisattva's practice.'[2] Just like now, whether walking, standing, sitting, or reclining, responding to situations and dealing with people as they come: everything is the Way. The Way is identical with the *dharmadhātu*. Out of sublime functions as numerous as the sands of the Ganges, none of them is outside the *dharmadhātu*. If that was not so, how could it have been said that the mind-ground is a Dharma gate, that it is an inexhaustible lamp.

"All dharmas are mind dharmas; all names are mind names. The myriad dharmas are all born from the mind; the mind is the root of the myriad dharmas. The sutra says, 'It is because of knowing the mind and penetrating the original source that one is called a *shramaṇa* [monk].' The names are equal, the meanings are equal: all dharmas are equal. They are all pure without mixing. If one attains to this teaching, then one is always free. If the *dharmadhātu* is established, then everything is the *dharmadhātu*. If suchness is established, then everything is suchness. If the principle is established, then all dharmas are the principle. If phenomena are established, then all dharmas are phenomena. When one is raised, thousands follow. The principle and phenomena are not different; everything is wonderful function, and there is no other principle. They all come from the mind.

"For instance, though the reflections of the moon are many, the real moon is only one. Though there are many springs of water, water has only one nature. There are myriad phenomena in the universe, but empty space is only one. There are many principles that are spoken of, but 'unobstructed wisdom is only one.'[3] Whatever is established, it all comes from One Mind. Whether constructing or sweeping away, all is sublime function; all is oneself. There is no place to stand where one leaves the Truth. The very place one stands on is the Truth; it is all one's being. If that was not so, then who is that? All dharmas are Buddhadharmas and all dharmas are liberation. Liberation is identical with suchness: all

---

1. Together with "mind is Buddha," "Ordinary Mind is the Way" became known as the hallmark of Ma-tsu's teaching.
2. Quotation from the *Vimalakīrti Sūtra*.
3. The sentence "Unobstructed wisdom is only one" (lit., "is not many") appears in the *Vimalakīrti Sūtra*.

dharmas never leave suchness. Whether walking, standing, sitting, or reclining, everything is always inconceivable function. The sutras say that the Buddha is everywhere.

"The Buddha is merciful and has wisdom. Knowing well the nature and characters of all beings,[4] he is able to break through the net of beings' doubts. He has left the bondages of existence and nothingness; with all feelings of worldliness and holiness extinguished, [he perceives that] both self and dharmas are empty. He turns the incomparable [Dharma] wheel. Going beyond numbers and measures, his activity is unobstructed and he penetrates both the principle and phenomena.

"Like a cloud in the sky that suddenly appears and then is gone without leaving any traces; also like writing on water, neither born nor perishable: that is the Great Nirvana."

When Ta-chu came to see the Ancestor for the first time, the Ancestor asked him, "Where are you coming from?"

"I am coming from Ta-yün Monastery in Yüeh-chou." replied Ta-chu.

The Ancestor asked him, "What is your intention in coming here?"

Ta-chu said, "I have come here to seek the Buddha-dharma."

The Ancestor said, "Without looking at your own treasure, for what purpose are you leaving your home and walking around? Here I do not have a single thing. What Buddha-dharma are you looking for?"

Ta-chu bowed, and asked, "What is Hui-hai's own treasure?"[5]

The Ancestor said, "That which is asking me right now is your own treasure—perfectly complete, it lacks nothing. You are free to use it; why are you seeking outside?" Upon hearing this, Ta-chu realized the original mind without relying on knowledge and understanding. Overjoyed, he paid his respects to the Ancestor and thanked him. After this he stayed with him for six years and served him as his disciple.

Later he returned [to Yüeh-chou][6] and composed a treatise entitled *Essentials of Entering the Way Through Sudden Awakening* in one *chüan*. When the Ancestor saw the text, he said to the assembly, "In Yüeh-chou there is a great pearl [*ta-chu*]; its perfect brilliance shines freely without obstruction."

4. The meaning of the Chinese phrase *shan chi hsing,* which here has been translated as "well knowing the nature and characters of all beings," is that the Buddha has the ability to know the particular character of each individual and is able to give a teaching which is best suited to the needs of the person it is given to.

5. Hui-hai is Ta-chu's name.

6. The text simply says "he returned," without specifying the place. Other sources provide the information that Ta-chu returned to his old teacher in Yüeh-chou to attend to his needs as he was getting old and sick.

Ch'an Master Hui-tsang of Shih-kung used to be a hunter [before becoming a monk]. He disliked monks. One day, as he was chasing a herd of deer, he happened to pass in front of the Ancestor's hermitage. The Ancestor greeted him. Hui-tsang asked, "Has the Venerable seen a herd of deer passing nearby?"

The Ancestor asked him, "Who are you?"

Hui-tsang replied, "I am a hunter."

The Ancestor asked, "Do you know how to shoot?"

Hui-tsang said, "Yes, I know."

The Ancestor asked, "How many deer can you shoot with a single arrow?"

Hui-tsang said, "With a single arrow I can shoot only one [deer]."

The Ancestor said, "You don't know how to shoot."

Then Hui-tsang asked, "Does the Venerable know how to shoot?"

The Ancestor said, "Yes, I know."

Hui-tsang asked, "How many can the Venerable shoot with a single arrow?"

The Ancestor said, "With a single arrow I can shoot the whole herd."

Hui-tsang said, "They also have life; why shoot the whole herd?"

The Ancestor said, "If you know that, then why don't you shoot yourself?"

Hui-tsang replied, "If you ask me to shoot myself, I cannot do that."

The Ancestor said, "Ah, this man. All his ignorance and defilements accumulated over vast *kalpas* have today suddenly come to an end." At that point Hui-tsang destroyed his bow and arrows. He cut off his hair with a knife, and became a monk with the Ancestor.

One day, as Hui-tsang was working in the kitchen, the Ancestor asked him, "What are you doing?"

Hui-tsang replied, "I am tending an ox."

The Ancestor asked, "How do you tend an ox?"

Hui-tsang replied, "When he wants to enter the grass, I grab his nostrils and pull him away."

"You are really tending an ox," commented the Ancestor.[7]

When Ch'an Master Wu-yeh of Fen-chou went to see the Ancestor, the Ancestor noticed that his appearance was extraordinary and that his voice was like [the sound of] a bell. He said, "Such an imposing Buddha hall, but no Buddha in it."

Wu-yeh respectfully kneeled down, and said, "I have studied the texts that contain the teachings of the Three Vehicles and have been able to roughly understand their meaning. I have also often heard about the teaching of the Ch'an school that mind is Buddha: this is something I have not yet been able to understand."

The Ancestor said, "This very mind that does not understand is it. There is no other thing."

7. The use of the image of tending an ox as an allegory for spiritual training is very common in the Ch'an school.

Wu-yeh further asked, "What is the mind-seal that the Ancestor has secretly transmitted from the West?"

The Ancestor said, "The Venerable looks rather disturbed right now. Go and come some other time."

As Wu-yeh was just about to step out, the Ancestor called him, "Venerable!" Wu-yeh turned his head and the Ancestor asked him, "What is it?" [On hearing this] Wu-yeh experienced awakening. He bowed to the Ancestor, who said, "This stupid fellow! What is this bowing all about?"

When Teng Ying-feng was about to leave the Ancestor, the Ancestor asked him, "Where are you going?"

"To Shih-t'ou." replied Yin-feng.

The Ancestor said, "Shih-t'ou's path is slippery."

Yin-feng said, "I will use my own skills to deal with the situation as it presents itself."[8] Then he left.

As soon as he arrived in front of Shih-t'ou, he walked around the Ch'an seat once, struck his staff on the ground, and asked, "What is the meaning?"

Shih-t'ou said, "Heavens! Heavens!" Yin-feng was left speechless.

He returned to the Ancestor and reported what has happened. The Ancestor said, "Go back to see him again. When he says, 'Heavens! Heavens!' you make a deep sigh twice."

Yin-feng went back to Shih-t'ou and asked the same question as before. Shih-t'ou made a deep sigh twice. Yin-feng was left speechless again. He returned to the Ancestor and related what had happened.

The Ancestor said, "I told you that Shih-t'ou's path is slippery."

When Venerable Shui-lao of Hung-chou came to see the Ancestor for the first time, he asked. "What is the meaning of [Bodhidharma's] coming from the West?"

The Ancestor said, "Bow down!"

As soon as Shui-lao went down to bow, the Ancestor kicked him. Shui-lao had great awakening. He rose up clapping his hands and laughing heartily, and said, "Wonderful! Wonderful! The source of myriad samādhis and limitless subtle meanings can all be realized on the tip of a single hair." He then paid his respects to the Ancestor and withdrew.

Later he told the assembly, "Since the day I was kicked by Master Ma, I have not stopped laughing."

8. The translation is tentative. The literal meaning of the Chinese is something like: "I will have a bamboo pole with me and will perform a play when I get there." I have understood it to be a statement of self-confidence on the part of Yin-feng, claiming that he has his own tricks (a bamboo pole), which he can use to deal with Shih-t'ou (to perform a play) when he gets there.

Once a lecturing monk came and asked, "What Dharma does the Ch'an school teach?"

The Ancestor asked him, "What Dharma does the Lecture Master teach?"

The lecturer replied, "I have lectured on over twenty sutras and *shastras.*"

The Ancestor said, "Aren't you a lion?"

The lecturer said, "Thank you." Thereupon, the Ancestor hissed.

The lecturer said, "That is Dharma."

The Ancestor asked, "What Dharma is it?"

The lecturer said, "It is the lion coming out of a cave." The Ancestor kept silent. The lecturer said, "That is also Dharma."

The Ancestor asked, "What Dharma is it?"

The lecturer said, "It is the lion in a cave."

Then the Ancestor asked, "When there is neither coming out nor going in, what Dharma is that?" The lecturer had no reply. He then started to leave. When he reached the door, the Ancestor called him, "Lecture Master!" The lecturer turned his head and the Ancestor asked him, "What is it?" The lecturer had no reply again. "This stupid lecturer," said the Ancestor.

8

Han-shan

For obscurity, Han-shan rivals Bodhidharma and Seng-ts'an. Trying to ascertain the facts of his life is like crossing a bog: things may look solid, but they all give way. A number of fine scholars have waded into the evidentiary mire and have managed to bring forth a great deal of information and insight but nothing conclusive about his biography. His dates of birth and death, his family, his career, the site of his hermitage, his relationships with known Ch'an figures, even the authorship of "his" three hundred or so poems—all this remains unclear. The eminent translator Arthur Waley long ago suggested that he be regarded as a state of mind rather than flesh and blood. By this point, he might also warrant nomination as a field of study.

Plausible dates for Han-shan (J., Kanzan) begin shortly before the rise of the T'ang dynasty and extend for its duration, which is to say from the early seventh to early tenth centuries. Painstaking linguistic analysis has convinced one scholar that he lived during the first part of this span and that later, toward its end, one or more other writers added to his work. Our selections are drawn entirely from the poems attributed to "Han-shan I," but for purposes of the book's authorial sequence, he is placed midway between the first and last dates proposed for him.

Two things seem sure: that Han-shan gained notoriety only after his death and that Ch'an people, feeling kinship with him through his poems, then swiftly adopted him into the family. By 1004, when *The Transmission of the Lamp* was completed, he was honored with a place among the masters and a few decades later, when Hsüeh-tou composed the poems subsequently made famous by *The Blue Cliff Record* (see Chapter 23), he saw fit to cite Han-shan by name and to quote his poems. Apparently Ch'an chroniclers pegged Han-shan as a ninth-century figure, grafting into the school's annals unlikely tales of meetings with two eminent teachers of that time, Kuei-shan (Chapter 12) and Chao-chou (Chapter 15).

The poems, if we take them at face value, indicate that Han-shan was born into a prosperous family and educated for the elite ranks of scholar-officials but that he repeatedly failed to qualify, perhaps because he had a bad leg and thus was considered unpresentable in high society. He married, became a farmer, and had a son before withdrawing, for unstated reasons, to spend the rest of his life on a crag called Han-shan, Cold Mountain, in the T'ien-t'ai range of eastern China. He remained a layman and occasionally descended to see the world he left behind—probably to pick up a few supplies, too. Legend associates him with Kuo-ching Monastery, but he is never said to have resided there or studied formally with any Ch'an master.

Han-shan wears the mantle of the untutored sage but wrote sturdy classical verse spiced with vigorous colloquialisms and clearly knew not only Buddhism but also the great Taoist texts and other mainstays of the Chinese canon. Unlike Wang Wei, whose position ensured his poems the circulation they deserved, Han-shan occupied a marginal spot literarily as well as socially, and it took some time for his work to come down from Cold Mountain. Whatever their initial circulation in Ch'an circles, not until 1189 did they get published and receive much wider currency.

Thereafter, both in China and Japan, Han-shan and his sidekick Shih-te became icons of the enlightened life, depicted in spirited ink paintings—and in other art forms, including kabuki theater—as ragged, wild-haired characters, free from all convention, cackling over the cosmic joke. Han-shan is identified with the Bodhisattva of Great Wisdom, Mañjushrī, and is typically portrayed either holding an empty scroll, as Mañjushrī is, or pointing gleefully to the full moon. Since the 1950s, especially through outstanding translations by Gary Snyder and Burton Watson, Han-shan's fame has spread throughout the English-speaking world, where today he is surely China's best-known poet. ∞

1
I climb the road to Cold Mountain,
the road to Cold Mountain that never ends.
The valleys are long and strewn with stones,
the streams broad and banked with thick grass.
Moss is slippery, though no rain has fallen;
pines sigh, but it isn't the wind.
Who can break from the snares of the world
and sit with me among the white clouds?

2
Yes, there are stingy people,
but I'm not one of the stingy kind.
The robe I wear is flimsy? The better to dance in.
Wine gone? It went with a toast and a song.
Just so you keep your belly full—
never let those two legs go weary.
When the weeds are poking through your skull,
that's the day you'll have regrets!

3
As for me, I delight in the everyday Way
among mist-wrapped vines and rocky caves.
Here in the wilderness I'm completely free,
with my friends, the white clouds, idling forever.
There are roads but they do not reach the world.
Since I'm mindless, who can rouse my thoughts?
On a bed of stone I sit, alone in the night,
while the round moon climbs up Cold Mountain.

LINE 1   "The everyday Way" is a reference perhaps to the words attributed to
the Zen Master Ma-tsu Tao-i (709–788): "The everyday mind—that is the Way."

LINE 6   "Mindless" (*wu-hsin*) is a Buddhist term indicating the state in which
all ordinary processes of discriminatory thinking have been stilled. [An alternative translation would be, "Since I have no-mind. . . . " In this reading, Han-
shan refers not to a quiet condition of mind but to the original emptiness of our
common nature.—Eds.]

4
Now I have a single robe,
not made of gauze or of figured silk.
Do you ask what color it is?
Not crimson, nor purple either.
Summer days I wear it as a cloak,
in winter it serves for a quilt.
Summer and winter in turn I use it;
year after year, only this.

5
Want to know a simile for life and death?
Compare them then to water and ice.
Water binds together to become ice;
ice melts and turns back into water.
What has died must live again,
what has been born will return to death.
Water and ice do no harm to each other;
life and death are both of them good.

6
Have I a body or have I none?
Am I who I am or am I not?

Pondering these questions,
I sit leaning against the cliff while the years go by,
till the green grass grows between my feet
and the red dust settles on my head,
and the men of the world, thinking me dead,
come with offerings of wine and fruit to lay by my corpse.

7

My mind is like the autumn moon
shining clean and clear in the green pool.
No, that's not a good comparison.
Tell me, how shall I explain?

8

Chattering about food won't fill your belly,
Blabbing about clothes won't stop the cold.
To fill you up, only food will do.
Putting on clothes—that keeps out winter.
But misunderstanding, you mull things over,
always saying, "Seeking the Buddha's too hard!"
Turn your mind back—that's the Buddha!
Don't swivel your eyes around outside.

9

I wanted to go off to the eastern cliff—
how many years now I've planned the trip?
Yesterday I pulled myself up by the vines,
but wind and fog forced me to stop halfway.
The path was narrow and my clothes kept catching,
the moss so spongy I couldn't move my feet.
So I stopped under this red cinnamon tree.
I guess I'll lay my head on a cloud and sleep.

10

By chance I happened to visit an eminent priest
among mist-wrapped mountains piled peak on peak.
As he pointed out for me the road home,
the moon hung out its single round lamp.

11
I divined and chose a distant place to dwell—
T'ien-t'ai: what more is there to say?
Monkeys cry where valley mists are cold;
my grass gate blends with the color of the crags.
I pick leaves to thatch a hut among the pines,
scoop out a pond and lead a runnel from the spring.
By now I'm used to doing without the world.
Picking ferns, I pass the years that are left.

12
High, high from the summit of the peak,
whatever way I look, no limit in sight!
No one knows I am sitting here alone.
A solitary moon shines in the cold spring.
Here in the spring—this is not the moon.
The moon is where it always is—in the sky above.
And though I sing this one little song,
in the song there is no Ch'an.

The psychologist James Hillman has observed that religious traditions, in-cluding Buddhism, tend toward escapism. They favor the summits of spirit and neglect the valleys of soul—the down-and-dirty terrain of everyday experi-ence. Han-shan in many ways epitomizes the peak-dweller, and such poems as the preceding, shimmering with mountain light, have made his name. Only in a geographic sense, however, can he be said to have shunned the lowlands. Other of his poems swell with earthy feelings, not just compassion or delight but also anger, longing, sourness, pride, loneliness, sorrow, worry. How could these not also be the feelings, and the poems, of an awakened mind? ❀

13
I think of all the places I've been,
chasing from one famous spot to another.
Delighting in mountains, I scaled the mile-high peaks;
loving the water, I sailed a thousand rivers.
I held farewell parties with my friends in Lute Valley;
I brought my zither and played on Parrot Shoals.
Who would guess I'd end up under a pine tree,
clasping my knees in the whispering cold?

14

Last night in a dream I returned to my old home
and saw my wife weaving at her loom.
She held her shuttle poised, as though lost in thought,
as though she had no strength to lift it further.
I called. She turned her head to look
but her eyes were blank—she didn't know me.
So many years we've been parted
the hair at my temples has lost its old color.

15

A swarm of beauties play in the glowing dusk,
each gust of wind filling the road with their perfume.
Gold butterflies are stitched into their skirts,
and jade ducks nestle, paired, in their hair.
Their ladies-in-waiting are swathed in sheer red silk,
their eunuchs attend in pants of plum brocade.
Taking this in: someone who's lost his way,
with whitened hair and troubled, troubled heart.

LINE 7   Ambiguous. The elegant young women (imperial concubines, it seems)
and their entourage may be "taking in" the old man, he may be watching them,
or both.

16

Wise men, you have cast me aside.
Fools, I do the same to you.
I would be neither wise man nor fool;
from now on let's hear no more from each other.
When night comes I sing to the bright moon;
at dawn I dance with white clouds.
How could I still my voice and my hands
and sit stiff as a stick with my gray hair rumpled?

17

A man sitting in a mountain pass—
robed in clouds, tricked out in sunset's rose.
In his fingers a fragrant flower, to pass along,
but the road's so long and hard to climb!
In his mind: disappointment and doubt;

old as he is, he's accomplished nothing.
People laugh at him, call him a cripple,
yet he stands alone—constant, untouched.

18
Poems of five-character lines, five hundred,
of seven-character lines, seventy-nine,
of three-character lines, twenty-one—
six hundred poems in all.
Usually I write them up on a rock face
and praise myself: "Very good calligraphy!"
Anyone who can understand my poems—
you must be the Buddha's mother!

LINE 4   If there really were six hundred poems, half of them have not survived.

LINE 8   Translates more literally, "truly you're the Tathāgatha mother," with
the possible interpretation, "you're the true mother of all things."

9

Pai-chang

(720–814)

Of all great master Ma-tsu's many Dharma heirs, Pai-chang Huai-hai played the most important role in forming and perpetuating the still-young tradition. In terms of Ch'an genealogy, he belongs to the ninth generation in China, just the third after Hui-neng. At this time, lines among Buddhist schools remained quite blurry; in many respects, they were still different teachings more than different sects. Movement among the country's five thousand Buddhist monasteries and temples was quite free, and as students and lecturers circulated, they carried texts, ideas, metaphors, teaching methods, and the like, creating an active exchange among the diverse traditions.

When Pai-chang was nine, the emperor ordered a registration of monks and nuns, beginning a gradual extension of government control over the Buddhist community. This pressure from central authority, along with criticism from Confucian intellectuals and growing competition for adherents and material support, accelerated a process of self-definition already under way, both among the Buddhist groups and within them. In some quarters, differentiation led to rivalry and rancor. A few years after Pai-chang's death, the prominent Buddhist layman P'ei Hsiu would bemoan the strife among what by then had truly become sects:

> "[Students] take written teachings as spears and shields and attack each other. . . . Teachings are considered high or low depending on whether they are one's own or someone else's. Right and wrong are confused and made complicated, and no one can tell them apart. Thus, the various teachings of the Buddhas and bodhisattvas of the past are now used to create controversy."

Ch'an chronicles praise Pai-chang (J., Hyakujō) for strengthening the sect's institutional identity, not through intra-Buddhist bickering but by formulating its monastic regimen and literally getting Ch'an monks out from under others' roofs. *The Transmission of the Lamp* records Pai-chang's rationale as follows: taking shelter in other schools' facilities, especially those of the Lü-tsung, required Ch'an monks to devote "too much attention . . . to details all the time." Whereas Lü-tsung taught and practiced the minutely specific Vinaya (rules of discipline) developed to govern the Buddhist community in India, Ch'an monks needed a simpler monastic code. They should, Pai-chang declared, "enlarge, with restraint," on the received Indian models and should "separate [them-selves] to establish the regulations and practices appropriate to their own needs."

Several of Pai-chang's innovations deserve particular notice. He stipulated that a Ch'an monastery should center on a Dharma Hall rather than the usual Buddha Hall, to emphasize that a Ch'an master conveys the teaching freshly rather than merely parroting or celebrating the founder's message. He also broke with custom in insisting that the Ch'an community allow no spiritual hier-archy among its members, no distinction in title or accommodations between those who had awakened and those who had not. This rule gave expression to the realization that there is no "high" or "low" in Buddha-nature, that all beings share it alike. To this day, Ch'an and Zen monasteries disregard the hierarchies of age, class, and education that structure life elsewhere, cutting across them all with a simple order of priority based on one's date of admission.

Pai-chang's leveling principle held for all members, including himself, and it was strictly applied in the area of work, where again he departed dramatically from precedent by initiating the practice of *pu-ch'ing,* general labor. Previously, Ch'an monks had adhered to the Vinaya's proscriptions against farming, which were designed to prevent them from doing unintended harm to creatures of wa-ter, soil, and vegetation. This made Buddhist monasteries dependent on govern-ment grants, private charity, and field labor by slaves, prisoners, or tenant farmers. In setting the old rule aside, as Kenneth Ch'en notes in *The Chinese Transformation of Buddhism,* Pai-chang "made some accommodation to the pre-vailing Chinese work ethic . . . and was able to counteract the criticism that monks were parasites on society."

Pai-chang is famous for the dictum, "A day without work is a day without eating," and is said to have stopped eating when, as he reached advanced age, his monks hid his tools to discourage him from expending his limited energy in the fields. (They quickly returned them, and he worked until the end of his days.) For his role in forging the monastic order, later generations of teachers and stu-dents have revered him as the Ancestor Who Planted the Forest—monks here being likened to trees.

Pai-chang's willingness to overturn ancient precedents and trust his own in-stincts says much about the man's temperament, and so does his name, which derives from the mountain where he taught. Properly known as Ta-hsiung, it was an exceptionally sheer peak and thus gained the common name Pai-chang, Ten-Thousand-Feet-High. People thought the name apt for the master's char-acter and teaching style—lofty, unrelenting. Pai-chang faithfully carried for-ward Ma-tsu's Dharma but seems to have given instruction quite differently. Whereas Ma-tsu's record is composed mainly of pithy exchanges with his stu-dents, Pai-chang's tilts strongly toward lectures. He also appears less inclined than Ma-tsu to make bold and sudden interventions, which is interesting since, according to the record, both his reported awakenings were triggered by such moves. ❁

FROM THE SAYINGS OF PAI-CHANG

One day as the master was walking along with Ma-tsu, they saw a flock of wild ducks fly by. The Ancestor said, "What is that?" The master said, "Wild ducks." Ma-tsu said, "Where have they gone?" The master said, "Flown away." Ma-tsu then turned around and grabbed the master's nose; feeling pain, the master let out a cry. The Ancestor said, "Still you say, 'Flown away'?" At these words the master had insight.

Then the master returned to the attendants' quarters, wailing pitifully. Another monk who worked as an attendant for Ma-tsu asked him, "Are you thinking of your parents?" The master said no. The fellow attendant said, "Has someone reviled you?" The master said no. The attendant said, "Then why are you crying?" The master said, "My nose was grabbed by the great teacher, and the pain hasn't stopped." The attendant said, "What happened? What didn't you realize?"[1] The master said, "Go ask the teacher."

The attendant went and asked the great teacher Ma-tsu, "What incident happened that attendant Huai-hai failed to accord with? He is in the attendants' quarters crying. Please explain this to me."

The great teacher, Ancestor Ma, explained simply that Huai-hai did indeed understand, and told the other attendant to go ask him. So the attendant went back and said to the master, "The teacher says you understand; he told me to ask you myself." The master then laughed. The attendant said, "Just a minute ago you were crying; now why are you laughing?"

The master said, "Just then I was crying; right now I am laughing."

The attendant was at a loss.

The next day Ma-tsu went into the teaching hall; as soon as the community had assembled, the master came forward and rolled up the prostration mat,[2] whereupon Ma-tsu got down from his seat and went back to his room with the master following behind.

Ma-tsu said, "Just then I had not yet said anything; why did you roll up the mat?" The master said, "Yesterday you grabbed my nose, and it hurt." Ma-tsu said, "Yesterday where did you set your mind?" The master said, "My nose doesn't hurt anymore today." Ma-tsu said, "You have deeply understood yesterday's event." The master bowed and withdrew.

The master called on Ma-tsu a second time; as he stood by, Ma-tsu looked at

1. "In what incident did you not accord [with reality, or the enlightened teacher]?" The Chinese word *yin-yuan*, "cause and condition," is used to mean "circumstances, event, incident," hence "story." Any *kung-an*, "public record" of Ch'an teachings in sayings and doings, is referred to as *yin-yuan*. The word for "accord" means "merging," "meshing," as of meeting minds, in this case; it is commonly used in Ch'an texts for understanding, realization.

2. A mat was placed in front of the teacher's seat in the teaching hall when he was teaching, where anyone who came forth from the crowd to ask a question would prostrate himself before and after.

the whisk on the corner of the rope seat. The master said, "Do you identify with
the function, or detach from the function?" Ma-tsu said, "Later on, when you
open your lips, what will you use to help people?" The master took the whisk
and held it up; Ma-tsu said, "Do you identify with this function, or detach from
this function?" The master hung the whisk back where it had been before; Ma-
tsu drew himself up and shouted so loud that the master's ears were deafened for
three days.[3]

Henceforth the sound of thunder would roll. Generous believers invited
him to the region of Hsin-wu in Hung-chou, where he dwelt on Ta-hsiung
Mountain. Because of the precipitous steepness of the cliffs and crags where he
dwelt, the mountain was called Pai-chang. Once he was there, before even a
month had passed, guests studying the mystery came like deer from all four directions; Kuei-shan[4] and Huang-po[5] were foremost among them.

When Huang-po came to the master's place, [after] one day[6] he took leave
and said, "I want to go pay respects to Ancestor Ma." The master said, "Ancestor
Ma has already passed on." Huang-po said, "What were Ancestor Ma's sayings?"
The master then cited the circumstances of his second calling on Ancestor Ma
and the raising of the whisk; he said, "The way of enlightenment is not a small
matter; at that time, I was actually deafened for three days by Ma-tsu's shout."

When Huang-po heard this, he unconsciously stuck out his tongue [in awe].
The master said, "Will you not succeed to Ma-tsu hereafter?" Huang-po said,
"No. Today, thanks to your recital, I have been able to see Ancestor Ma's great
capacity in action; but I do not know Ancestor Ma. If I were to succeed to Ancestor Ma, later on I would be bereft of descendants." The master said, "Right,
right! When one's view is equal to the teacher's he diminishes his teacher's virtue
by half; only when his view surpasses the teacher's is he qualified to pass on the
transmission. You sure have a view that goes beyond a teacher's.[7]

3. This famous incident is known as Pai-chang's second call on Ma-tsu; the previous *kung-an* about
Pai-chang and the ducks is included as one of the main cases of *The Blue Cliff Record,* and the second
calling is told in the commentary on that story.
4. Kuei-shan Ling-yu (771–854) came to Pai-chang around 794 and spent many years there as chief
cook for the community. [See Chapter 12—Eds.]
5. Huang-po Hsi-yun (d. 855). [See Chapter 14—Eds.]
6. This could be read simply, "One day he took leave . . . " It is not clear how long Huang-po did eventually stay with Pai-chang, and there is no special record of his enlightenment there or anywhere else.
7. A Ch'an master's "duty" is to pass on the transmission, or witness of enlightenment, to a worthy
successor, who must in turn pass it on to students of yet a later generation. Hence the successor must
"equal" the teacher by way of his own realization of the source, yet he must eventually "surpass" his
teacher in order to renew the teaching for the benefit of others. With continuous variation of time,
circumstance, and potential, a succession of true teachers cannot adhere to a mold, but must contin-
ually be surpassing their ancestors in order to meet the special needs of their own times and communities to successfully communicate the living reality of the Way. One evidence of this is the renewal of
Ch'an teaching as manifest in the production of new literature and new techniques over the centuries. To "diminish the teacher's virtue by half" means that if the successor cannot pass on the trans-

In the teaching hall the master said, "The spiritual light shines alone, far transcending the senses and their fields; the essential substance is exposed, real and eternal. It is not contained in written words. The nature of mind has no defilement; it is basically perfect and complete in itself. Just get rid of delusive attachments, and merge with realization of thusness."

This principle from the extensive record of Pai-chang is originally present in everyone.[8] All the buddhas and bodhisattvas may be called people pointing out a jewel. Fundamentally it is not a thing—you don't need to know or understand it, you don't need to affirm or deny it. Just cut off dualism; cut off the supposition "it exists" and the supposition "it does not exist." Cut off the supposition "it is nonexistent" and the supposition "it is not nonexistent." When traces do not appear on either side, then neither lack nor sufficiency, neither profane nor holy, not light or dark. This is not having knowledge, yet not lacking knowledge, not bondage, not liberation. It is not any name or category at all. Why is this not true speech? How can you carve and polish emptiness to make an image of Buddha? How can you say that emptiness is blue, yellow, red, or white?

As it is said, "Reality has no comparison, because there is nothing to which it may be likened; the body or reality is not constructed and does not fall within the scope of any classification." That is why it is said, "The substance of the sage is nameless and cannot be spoken of; the empty door of truth as it really is cannot be tarried in." It is like the case of insects being able to alight anywhere, only they can't alight on the flames of a fire—sentient beings' minds are also like this in that they can form relations anywhere, only they cannot relate to transcendent wisdom.

As you are inherently equal, your words are equal, and I am also the same—a Buddha field of sound, a Buddha field of smell, a Buddha field of taste, a Buddha field of feeling, a Buddha field of phenomena—all are thus. From here all the way to the world of the lotus treasury,[9] up and across, all is thus. If you hold onto the elementary knowledge as your understanding, this is called bondage at the pinnacle, and it is also called falling into bondage at the pinnacle.[10] This

mission himself, his own teacher has in a sense failed to produce a complete heir, and half his virtue (helping others) is lacking (even though he has realized his own deliverance from confusion). This could be read, " . . . has less than half the teacher's virtue," focusing on the student, who cannot produce an heir equal to himself as his own teacher had at least done, according to this old saying.

8. [Pai-chang is using "principle" in the same special sense that Bodhidharma uses it in "The Two Entrances and Four Practices" (Chapter 1), signifying original nature.—Eds.]

9. The ocean of worlds described in the *Avatamsaka Sūtra* [*Flower Garland Scripture*], said to be lotus born and adorned by the deeds and practices vowed by Vairochana, the universal sun Buddha, the cosmic illuminator. Esoterically, Vairochana is the mind and his world is the field of mind

10. This has a different meaning in Mahāyāna Buddhism than in elementary Buddhism; here it means staying in personal nirvana, never coming out of absorption, forever detached and quiescent, without realization of emptiness and selflessness of things, forced to choose between stillness and confusion.

is the basis of all mundane troubles—giving rise to knowledge and opinion on your own, you "bind yourself without rope."

In reading scriptures and studying the doctrines, you should turn all words right around and apply them to yourself. But all verbal teachings only point to the inherent nature of the present mirror awareness—as long as this is not affected by any existent or nonexistent objects at all, it is your guide; it can shine through all various existent and nonexistent realms. This is adamantine wisdom, where you have your share of freedom and independence. If you cannot understand in this way, then even if you could recite the whole canon and all its branches of knowledge, it would only make you conceited, and conversely shows contempt for Buddha—it is not true practice.

Just detach from all sound and form, and do not dwell in detachment, and do not dwell in intellectual understanding—this is practice. As for reading scriptures and studying the doctrines, according to worldly convention it is a good thing, but if assessed from the standpoint of one who is aware of the inner truth, this [reading and study] chokes people up. Even people of the tenth stage cannot escape completely, and flow into the river of birth and death.

But the teachings of the Three Vehicles all cure diseases such as greed and hatred. Right now, thought after thought, if you have such sicknesses as greed or hatred, you should first cure them—don't seek intellectual understanding of meanings and expressions. Understanding is in the province of desire, and desire turns into disease. Right now just detach from all things, existent or nonexistent, and even detach from detachment. Having passed beyond these three phases, you will naturally be no different from a buddha. Since you yourself are Buddha, why worry that the Buddha will not know how to talk? Just beware of not being Buddha.

As long as you are bound by various existent or nonexistent things, you can't be free. This is because before the inner truth is firmly established, you first have virtue and knowledge; you are ridden by virtue and knowledge, like the menial employing the noble. It is not as good as first settling the inner truth and then afterwards having virtue and knowledge—then if you need virtue and knowledge, as the occasion appears you will be able to take gold and make it into earth, take earth and make it into gold, change sea water into buttermilk, smash [Mt. Sumeru][11] into fine dust, and pick up the waters of the four great oceans and put them into a single hair pore. Within one meaning you create unlimited meanings, and within unlimited meanings you make one meaning.

The discipline of doing is to cut off the things of the world. Just do not do anything yourself, and there is no fault—this is called the discipline of nondoing. It

11. [In Buddhist cosmology, Mt. Sumeru is the peak at the center of the universe.—Eds.]

is also called unmanifested discipline, and it is also called the discipline of non-indulgence. As long as there is arousal of mind and movement of thoughts, this is all called breaking discipline.

For now just do not be confused and disturbed by any existent or nonexistent objects; and do not stop and abide in disillusion, and yet have no understanding of nonabiding. This is called all-embracing study; this is called effort, praise, and remembrance, and it is called widespread circulation of truth.

When not yet enlightened, not yet liberated, it is called mother; after enlightenment, it is called child. When there is not even any knowledge or understanding of the absence of enlightenment or liberation, that is called "mother and child both perish." There is no confinement by good, no confinement by evil; no confinement by Buddha, no confinement by sentient beings. The same goes for all assessments or measurements, to the extent that there is no confinement by any calculating measurements at all. Therefore it is said that a Buddha is someone who has left confinement and goes beyond measure.

[To say that] "the Buddha appears in the world and saves sentient beings" are words of the nine-part teachings; they are words of the incomplete teaching. Anger and joy, sickness and medicine, are all oneself; there is no one else. Where is there a Buddha appearing in the world? Where are there sentient beings to be saved? As the *Diamond-Cutter Scripture* says, "In reality, there are no sentient beings who attain extinction and deliverance."

Not to love Buddhas or bodhisattvas, not to be affected by greed for anything existent or nonexistent, is called "saving others." Also not to keep dwelling in the self is called "saving oneself." Because the sicknesses are not the same, the medicines are not the same, and the prescriptions are also not the same—you should not one-sidedly hold fast [to any of them]. If you depend on such things as buddhas or bodhisattvas, all this is dependence upon the prescription. Therefore it is said, "One who has arrived at wisdom cannot be one-sided." That which is discussed in the teachings is likened to yellow leaves;[12] it is also like an empty fist deceiving a small child [pretending there is something in it]. If someone does not realize this principle, this is called the same as ignorance. As it is said, "Bodhisattvas who practice transcendent wisdom should not grasp my words or depend on the commands of the teachings."

Anger is like a rock, love is like river water. Right now, just have no anger, no love; this is passing through mountains, rivers, and stone walls.

12. The simile of yellow leaves presented as gold to a child to stop its crying appears in the *Mahāpā-rinirvāna Sūtra.*

10

The P'ang Family

Though Hui-neng promotes Ch'an practice for laypeople in the *Platform Sutra* and though many later masters followed suit, Ch'an and Zen literature may create the impression that the Way was pursued almost exclusively by monks. The renowned Layman P'ang (J., Ho Koji), his wife, and their two children provide a sparkling counterexample. Soon after the Layman's death in 808, a friendly and highly placed government official saw to it that his life story, poems, and sayings were preserved—in the same manner as those of the great Ch'an teachers. Fortunately, the resulting record also affords glimpses of his wife and daughter, Ling-chao, though not of his son. On the strength of her showing in its pages, Ling-chao became one of the few acclaimed women in the history of Ch'an, while the P'angs together became the model of enlightened family life.

A preface to the record indicates that the P'angs lived in southern China and practiced Buddhism at a hermitage they maintained near their home. Once "his entire household attained the Way," the Layman gave away their house for conversion into a temple, loaded his family's possessions—all but the bare necessities—on a boat, and sank it in deep water. Thereafter, the family subsisted by making bamboo utensils, and the Layman and Ling-chao used their leisure to trek about the country, visiting its finest Ch'an masters. The Layman's initial awakening with Shih-t'ou evidently was shallow, as is often the case but, thorough-going awakening followed with Ma-tsu. Layman P'ang is regarded as a successor of both these masters.

Layman P'ang acquired a reputation as a poet as well as a sage. Masters of later generations often quoted his poems in their teachings, and his lines on the miraculous activities of drawing water and hauling wood have become especially famous, even achieving notoriety in modern-day America. Though the Layman obviously took pleasure in words, he seems to have viewed his poems primarily as vehicles of Dharma inspiration and instruction. They stand closer to the tradition of the *gāthā* than to the mainstream Chinese literary tradition and closer to the work of Han-shan than to that of Wang Wei.

FROM THE RECORD OF LAYMAN P'ANG

At the beginning of the Chen-yüan era [785–804] of T'ang, the Layman visited Ch'an Master Shih-t'ou. He asked the Master: "Who is the man who doesn't accompany the ten thousand dharmas?"[1]

Shih-t'ou covered the Layman's mouth with his hand. In a flash he realized!

One day Shih-t'ou said to the Layman: "Since seeing me, what have your daily activities been?"

"When you ask me about my daily activities, I can't open my mouth," the Layman replied.

"Just because I know you are thus I now ask you," said Shih-t'ou.

Whereupon the Layman offered this verse:

> My daily activities are not unusual,
> I'm just naturally in harmony with them.
> Grasping nothing, discarding nothing,
> In every place there's no hindrance, no conflict.
> Who assigns the ranks of vermilion and purple?[2]
> The hills' and mountains' last speck of dust is extinguished.
> [My] supernatural power and marvelous activity—
> Drawing water and carrying firewood.

Shih-t'ou gave his assent. Then he asked: "Will you put on black robes or will you continue wearing white?"[3]

"I want to do what I like," replied the Layman. So he did not shave his head or dye his clothing.

Later the Layman went to Kiangsi to visit Ch'an Master Ma-tsu. He asked Ma-tsu: "Who is the man who doesn't accompany the ten thousand dharmas?"

"Wait till you've swallowed in one swig all the water of the West River, then I'll tell you," replied Ma-tsu.

At these words the Layman suddenly understood the Mysterious Principle. He offered the verse containing the phrase, "empty-minded having passed the exam."[4]

1. [This question, which seems to have been the Layman's self-discovered koan, asks who or what is free of all phenomena, all "others."]

2. The color of clothing worn by high government officials.

3. "White-clothed" is a conventional term indicating a commoner. White is here used in contrast to the black robes of a Ch'an Buddhist monk.

4. [The full poem is "The whole world is the same, single community; / each and every one learns there's nothing to do. / This is the very place to select a buddha! / I return empty-minded, having passed the exam."—Eds.]

He remained with Ma-tsu two years, practicing and receiving instruction.
He wrote a verse which says:

> I've a boy who has no bride,
> I've a girl who has no groom;
> Forming a happy family circle,
> We speak about the [Unborn].

One day the Layman addressed Ma-tsu, saying: "A man of unobscured original
nature asks you please to look upward."

Ma-tsu looked straight down.

The Layman said: "You alone play marvelously on the stringless *ch'in*."[5]

Ma-tsu looked straight up.

The Layman bowed low. Ma-tsu returned to his quarters.

"Just now bungled it trying to be smart," then said the Layman.

One day Ch'an Master Tan-hsia T'ien-jan[6] came to visit the Layman. As soon as
he reached the gate he saw [the Layman's] daughter Ling-chao carrying a basket
of greens.

"Is the Layman here?" asked Tan-hsia.

Ling-chao put down the basket of greens, politely folded her arms [one on
top of the other] and stood still.

"Is the Layman here?" asked Tan-hsia again.

Ling-chao picked up the basket and walked away. Tan-hsia then departed.

When the Layman returned a little later, Ling-chao told him of the conversation.

"Is Tan-hsia here?" asked the Layman.

"He's gone," replied Ling-chao.

"Red earth painted with milk,"[7] remarked the Layman.

Later, when Tan-hsia came to see the Layman, though the Layman saw him coming, he neither rose nor spoke to him. Tan-hsia raised his whisk; the Layman
raised his mallet.[8]

"Just this, or is there something else?" asked Tan-hsia.

"Seeing you this time is not the same as seeing you before," observed the
Layman.

5. The Chinese lute.
6. Tan-hsia T'ien-jan (738–823), one of Layman P'ang's best friends, was a Dharma heir of Shih-t'ou.
7. This expression denotes an action that is needless, useless, or defiling.
8. The *fu-tzu* or whisk consisted of long white yak- or horse-hairs bound atop a wooden handle, and
was used originally by Indian Buddhist monks to brush away insects without injuring them. Later the
whisk was carried as a symbol of authority by Ch'an teachers. The *ch'ui-tzu* was an eight-sided wooden
mallet. One of its uses was as a gavel in Ch'an ceremonies to call the assembly of monks to order.

"Go on and belittle my reputation as you please," said Tan-hsia.

"A while ago you took a hit [from my daughter]," returned the Layman.

"If that's so," said Tan-hsia, "then you've made [my] T'ien-jan's mouth dumb."

"You're dumb because of your intrinsic nature," said the Layman, "and now you afflict me with dumbness."

Tan-hsia threw down his whisk and departed.

"Jan Āchārya, Jan Āchārya!"⁹ called the Layman.

But Tan-hsia did not look back.

"He's come down not only with dumbness but with deafness as well," remarked the Layman.

The Layman was once lying on his couch reading a sutra. A monk saw him and said: "Layman! You must maintain dignity when reading a sutra."

The Layman raised up one leg.

The monk had nothing to say.

The Layman was visiting a lecture-mart,¹⁰ listening to a discourse on the *Diamond Sutra*. When the "no self, no person" line was reached,¹¹ he asked: "Lecture-master, since there is no self and no person, who is he who's lecturing, who is he who's listening?"

The lecture-master had no reply.

"Though I'm just a commoner," said the Layman, "I know a little about faith."

"What is your idea?" inquired the lecture-master.

The Layman replied with a verse:

> There's no self and no person,
> How then kinfolk and stranger!
> I beg you, cease going from lecture to lecture;
> It's better to seek truth directly.
> The nature of Diamond Wisdom
> Excludes even a speck of dust.
> From "Thus have I heard" to "This I believe,"¹²
> All's but an array of unreal names.

9. Skt., *āchārya* spiritual teacher, master, or preceptor. "Jan" is an abbreviation of Tan-hsia's other name, T'ien-jan.

10. *Chiang-ssu,* a place where Buddhist monks other than those of the Ch'an and Vinaya sects discoursed on the meaning of the sutras to the general public. Such professional lecturers supported themselves by contributions received from the audience.

11. The line in question is probably "Furthermore, Subhūti, this Dharma, being universally the same, has no high or low—this is called Supreme Perfect Enlightenment. Because of [having] no self, no person, no sentient being, and no life when cultivating all good practices, Supreme Perfect Enlightenment is attained."

12. Set phrases that mark respectively the beginning and end of Buddhist sutras.

When the lecture-master heard this verse, he sighed with admiration.

Wherever the Layman dwelt there was much coming and going of venerable priests, and many exchanges of questions. According to the capacity of each the Layman responded as an echo to a sound. He was not a man to be categorized by any rule or measure.

One day Mrs. P'ang went into the Deer Gate Temple to make an offering of food. The temple priest asked her the purpose [of the offering] in order to transfer the merit.[13] Mrs. P'ang took her comb and stuck it in the back of her hair. "Transference of merit is completed," she said, and walked out.

The Layman was sitting in his thatched cottage one day. "Difficult, difficult, difficult," he suddenly exclaimed, "[like trying] to scatter ten measures of sesame seed all over a tree!"

"Easy, easy, easy," returned Mrs. P'ang, "just like touching your feet to the ground when you get out of bed."

"Neither difficult nor easy," said Ling-chao. "On the hundred grass-tips, the Patriarchs' meaning."

During the Yüan-ho era [806–820] the Layman traveled northward to Hsiang-han, stopping here and there. His daughter Ling-chao sold bamboo baskets for their morning and evening meals. The Layman had these verses, which say:

> When the mind's as is, circumstances also are as is;
> There's no real and also no unreal.
> Giving no heed to existence,
> And holding not to nonexistence—
> You're neither saint nor sage, just
> An ordinary man who has settled his affairs.
>
> To preserve your life you must destroy it;
> Having completely destroyed it you dwell at ease.
> When you attain the inmost meaning of this,
> An iron boat floats upon water.

The Layman was once selling bamboo baskets. Coming down off a bridge he stumbled and fell. When Ling-chao saw this she ran to her father's side and threw herself down.

"What are you doing!" cried the Layman.

13. It was customary for a temple priest to write on a slip of paper the donor's name, the gift and its purpose, and the date. This would then be displayed in public so that the donor's merit would become known to others, i.e., "transferred."

"I saw Papa fall to the ground, so I'm helping," replied Ling-chao.

"Luckily no one was looking," remarked the Layman.

The Layman was about to die. He spoke to Ling-chao, saying: "See how high the sun is and report to me when it's noon."

Ling-chao quickly reported: "The sun has already reached the zenith, and there's an eclipse." While the Layman went to the door to look out, Ling-chao seated herself in her father's chair and, putting her palms together reverently, passed away.

The Layman smiled and said: "My daughter has anticipated me."

He postponed [his going] for seven days.

The Prefect Yü-ti came to inquire about his illness. The Layman said to him: "I beg you just to regard as empty all that is existent and to beware of taking as real all that is nonexistent. Fare you well in the world. All is like shadows and echoes." His words ended. He pillowed his head on Mr. Yü's knee and died.

His final request was that he be cremated and [the ashes] scattered over rivers and lakes. Monks and laity mourned him and said that the Ch'an adherent Layman P'ang was indeed a Vimalakīrti. He left three hundred poems to the world.

11

Nan-ch'üan

(747–834)

Like Pai-chang and Layman P'ang, Nan-ch'üan P'u-yüan reseized the Way under Ma-tsu. He became, next to Pai-chang, the great teacher's most illustrious successor. (J., Nansen) According to traditional accounts, he came to awakening sometime before Ma-tsu's death in 788, spent a while on pilgrimage, and then, at forty-eight, retired to the top of Mount Nan-ch'üan to live in seclusion for the next three decades. His example helped such periods of "cultivating the sacred seedling" the rule for upcoming Ch'an masters. Though not always so protracted, these intervals alone or in the company of a few like-minded fellows afforded an opportunity not only to deepen in realization but also to study texts, to get some practice at teaching, and to season a bit, especially to eliminate the traces of enlightenment, the "stink of Ch'an."

Nan-ch'üan finally emerged at the request of the provincial governor Lu Hsüan (also known as Lu Keng), who became first his patron and later his devoted student. By this date, despite harsh criticism and periodic reversals in its fortunes, Ch'an had assumed a prominent place in Chinese cultural life. Adventurous scholar-officials had followed in Wang Wei's footsteps, forming a new constituency of committed lay practitioners. Since people of high station like Lu Hsüan wielded tremendous power, close association with them produced problems as well as patronage. While monks and nuns officially stood outside the Confucian hierarchy and thus were not required to bow even before the emperor, their freedom had its limits; to insult the dignity of the mighty was to risk serious reprisal.

Nan-ch'üan typically taught without regard to decorum, surprising monks with the same sort of direct, even painful presentations of the great matter that Ma-tsu had made, but with Governor Lu he had to behave differently. In one famous meeting recorded in *The Transmission of the Lamp,* Lu appreciatively quoted the statement of the pre-Ch'an monk Seng-chao that all things have the same root and that right and wrong have the same essence. Nan-ch'üan replied by pointing out a peony in the courtyard and saying, "People of the present day"—a polite, indirect reference to Lu himself—"see these blossoms as if in a dream!" A later master likened this to leading Lu to the brink of a cliff and pushing him off, but the governor evidently neither took offense nor tumbled to the truth. Both men persevered, however, and in time Lu awoke from his dream so completely as to become one of Nan-ch'üan's seventeen successors.

Nan-ch'üan taught with great acuity and passion, in one notorious instance going so far as to cut a cat in two in order to make a Dharma point. More often, he used his blade bloodlessly. One day as he was gardening, for example, a monk passing by asked him the way to Nan-ch'üan. The master held up his sickle, exclaiming, "This sickle cost three dollars!" The monk rejoined that he had not asked about the sickle and repeated his question about the way to Nan-ch'üan. "I always enjoy using it!" replied the teacher.

Nan-ch'üan's public career was brief—less than a decade—but his inspired instruction earned him a brilliant reputation even before he came down from the mountain. Avid and discerning students sought him out there, including his great successor Chao-chou (Chapter 15). His capacity, noted in *The Blue Cliff Record,* "to capture rhinos and tigers, to judge dragons and snakes" made visiting him an important experience for Huang-po (Chapter 14), principal heir of Pai-chang, and for Tung-shan (Chapter 18), the progenitor of the Ts'ao-tung lineage. ⊗

FROM THE TRANSMISSION OF THE LAMP

Ch'an Master Nan-ch'üan P'u-yüan of Ch'ih-chou was a native of Hsin-cheng in Cheng-chou. His original surname was Wang. . . . When he was thirty he went to the Sung Mountain for his ordination. He began his studies with the ancient text of the *Four-Division Vinaya* and devoted himself to the refinements of disciplinary rules. Later he visited various centers and listened to the lectures on the *Lankāvatāra* and *Avatamsaka Sūtras.* He also delved into the doctrine of the Middle Way given in the *Mādhyamika Shāstra,* the *Shata Shāstra,* and the *Dvādasanikāya Shāstra.* Thus he acquired a thorough discipline in Buddhist philosophy. Finally he came to Ma-tsu and studied Ch'an Buddhism with him, and achieved sudden enlightenment. He immediately freed himself from what he had previously learned and obtained the joy of *samādhi.*

One day while Nan-ch'üan was serving rice gruel to his fellow monks, his master, Ma-tsu, asked him, "What is in the wooden bucket?"

"This old fellow should keep his mouth shut and not say such words," remarked Nan-ch'üan. The rest of the monks who were studying with him did not dare to raise any questions about the exchange.

In the eleventh year [795] of the period of Chen-yüan, Master Nan-ch'üan moved to Ch'ih-yang and built a small temple on the top of Mt. Nan-ch'üan. He remained there for thirty years, never once coming down. At the beginning of the period of Ta-ho (827–835), Lu Hsüan, a provincial governor in Hsüanch'eng, admired the spirit of the Master's Ch'an teachings. He and his supervisor from the Royal Court invited the Master to come down to the city to promote the learning of Ch'an, and both of these high officials assumed the position of disciple to the Master. Thereafter several hundred disciples gathered around him, and his teachings were widely disseminated. Master Nan-ch'üan came to be highly esteemed as a teacher of Ch'an.

Once the Master planned to visit a village on the following day. During the night the God of Earth[1] informed the head of the village of the Master's coming, and consequently everything was prepared for his visit. When the Master arrived, he was surprised and asked, "You have prepared everything well. How did you know I was coming?" The village head replied that the God of Earth had informed him. Thereupon Master Nan-ch'üan proclaimed, "[My] achievement was not high enough; [my] mind was observed by the spirits and gods." A monk immediately asked him, "Master, as you are a man of great virtue, why should you be watched by spirits and gods?" Nan-ch'üan replied, "Offer a portion of food before the Earth God's shrine."

On one occasion the Master stated, "Ma-tsu of Kiangsi maintained that the Mind is the Buddha. However, Teacher Wang[2] would not say it this way. He would advocate 'Not Mind, not Buddha, not things.' Is there any mistake when I say it this way?" After listening to this, Chao-chou made a bow and went away. Thereupon a monk followed him, saying, "What did you mean just now, when you bowed and left the Master?" Chao-chou replied, "Sir, you will have to ask the Master." The monk went to the Master and said, "Why did Ts'ung-shen [Chao-chou] behave that way a moment ago?" "He understood my meaning!" Nan-ch'üan exclaimed.

Another day Master Nan-ch'üan spoke to Huang-po thus: "There is a kingdom of yellow gold and houses of white silver. Who do you suppose lives there?"

"It is the dwelling place of the saints," replied Huang-po.

"There is another man.[3] Do you know in what country he lives?" asked the Master.

Huang-po folded his hands and stood still.

"You cannot give an answer. Why don't you ask Teacher Wang?" asked the Master.

Huang-po, in turn, repeated his master's question: "There is another man. Do you know in what country he lives?"

"Oh, what a pity this is!" said Nan-ch'üan.

---

1. In Chinese literature and tradition, spirits or gods often appear in dreams to deliver messages, such as happened in the case of the village leader. The highest achievement of Ch'an should be free from this. Because his visit was predicted by the Earth God, Nan-ch'üan said that his achievement of Ch'an was not high enough.

2. [Himself. Nan-chüan was often called Teacher Wang and sometimes refers to himself that way, in the third-person.—Eds.]

3. I.e., the real self.

Once the monks in the two wings of the monastery were disputing over the possession of a cat when the Master appeared on the scene. He took hold of the animal and said to the quarreling monks:

"If any one of you can say something to the point, he will save the life of this creature; if nobody can, it will be killed." Unfortunately, no one could, so the cat was killed. Later on, when Chao-chou came back, Master Nan-ch'üan told him about the incident that had taken place during his absence. At once Chao-chou took off a sandal and put it on top of his head, and then went away.

The Master said, "Had you been here a moment ago, you would have saved the animal's life."

One day Master Nan-ch'üan was sitting with Shan-shan by the fire in his chamber. Said the Master, "Do not point to the east or to the west, but go straight to what is fundamental."

Putting down the fire tongs, Shan-shan folded his hands and stood silently. The Master said, "Although you have reached such an answer, there is still a difference from the tao maintained by Teacher Wang."

Once when Master Nan-ch'üan went to the vegetable garden, he saw a monk there and threw a brick at him. When the monk turned his head to look, the Master lifted one of his feet. The monk said nothing, but when the Master returned to his room the monk followed him there and asked, "A moment ago you threw a brick at me. Did you not mean to give me some warning?" The Master said, "Then why did I lift my foot?" The monk made no reply.

Once Master Nan-ch'üan addressed the assembly: "Teacher Wang wants to sell his body. Who would like to buy it?" A monk stepped forward and said, "I want to buy it."

"He does not ask for a high price, nor does he ask for a low one. What can you do?" asked the Master. The monk made no answer.

One day Master Nan-ch'üan spread ashes outside his doorway and closed the doors. Then he announced that if anyone could comment correctly, the door would be opened. A number of answers were given, but none of them satisfied the Master. Thereupon, Chao-chou cried out, "Good heavens!" and immediately the door was thrown open by the Master.

One evening when Master Nan-ch'üan was enjoying the moonlight, a monk asked him when one could be equal to the moonlight. The Master said, "Twenty years ago I attained that state." The monk continued, "What about right now?" The Master went immediately to his room.

One day when the Master came to the assembly hall, Governor Lu said, "Master, please teach dharma to all of us!"

"What do you want to talk about?" asked the Master.

"Don't you have any expedients for attaining enlightenment?" Lu continued.

"What is it that you want me to say?" asked the Master.

"Why should we have four modes of birth and six levels of reincarnation?"[4] asked the governor.

"This is not what I teach," replied the Master.

Once Governor Lu together with Master Nan-ch'üan saw someone playing dice. Lu picked up the dice and asked, "How is it that one can let his luck decide whether things turn out to be this or that?"

"These are indeed dirty pieces of bone!" said the Master.

The governor then said, "There is a piece of stone in my house. Sometimes it stands up and sometimes it lies down. Now, can it be carved into the image of a buddha?"

"Yes, it is possible," answered the Master.

"But is it impossible to do so?" countered the governor.

"It is impossible! It is impossible!" exclaimed the Master.

Chao-chou asked, "Tao is not external to things; the externality of things is not Tao. Then what is the Tao that is beyond things?" The Master struck him. Thereupon Chao-chou took hold of the stick and said, "From now on, do not strike a man by mistake!" The Master said, "We can easily differentiate between a dragon and a snake, but nobody can fool a Ch'an monk."

The Master asked the supervisor,[5] "What is the purpose of our working together today?" The answer was, "To turn the millstone." The Master stated, "As for the millstone, I'll let you turn it. But as for the axle, be sure not to move it." The supervisor uttered no word.

One day an elder monk asked the Master, "When we say, 'The Mind is the Buddha,' we are wrong. But when we say, 'Not Mind, not Buddha,' we are not correct either. What is your idea about this?" Master Nan-ch'üan answered, "You should believe 'The Mind is the Buddha' and let it go at that. Why should you talk about right or wrong? It is just the same as when you come to eat your meal. Do you choose to come to it through the west corridor, or by another way? You cannot ask others which is wrong."

When the Master was living in a small temple a monk came to visit him. Master Nan-ch'üan told the monk that he was going to the top of the hill, and asked

4. The four modes of birth are: from the womb, from the egg, from moisture, and through the transformation of forms. The six levels of reincarnation are: that of a spirit in hell, that of a bodiless ghost, that of an animal body, that of a malevolent spirit, that of a human form, and that of a *deva* on a high level of existence.

5. *Wei-na* is the Chinese transliteration of *karmadana*, the duty-distributor, the second in command in a monastery.

the monk to have his own meal at lunchtime and then bring another portion up the hill for the Master. The monk, however, when he had had his lunch, broke his regular routine and went to bed. The Master waited for him on the hill, but the monk did not come. Eventually he returned to the temple and found the monk lying asleep. The Master lay down on the other side of the bed and went to sleep himself. Thereupon the monk got up and left. Some years later the Master recalled this, saying, "In the temple where I lived in my early years, there was a talented monk who came to visit me. I have not seen him since."

The Master once picked up a ball and asked a monk, "How do you compare that one to this one?" The answer was, "It is incomparable." The Master continued, "What difference did you see that made you say that one is incomparable to this one?" "If you want me to tell you the difference that I see, you must put down the ball," answered the monk. The Master remarked, "I must admit you have one eye open to wisdom."

When Governor Lu was about to return to his office in Hsüan-cheng, he came to bid the Master good-bye. The latter asked him, "Governor! You are going back to the capital. How will you govern the people?" The governor replied, "I will govern them through wisdom." The Master remarked, "If this is true, the people will suffer for it."

Once Master Nan-ch'üan went to Hsüan-cheng. Governor Lu came out of the city gate to welcome him, and pointing to the gate, said, "Everybody here calls it Yung-men, or the Gate of the Jar. What would you call it?" The Master said to him, "If I should say what I would like to call it, it would blemish your rule." Lu Hsüan further asked, "If the bandits should come into the town suddenly, what should we do?" The Master answered, "It is the fault of Teacher Wang." Lu Hsüan again asked, "What is the purpose of the many hands and eyes of the Bodhisattva of Great Compassion, Kuan-yin?" The Master answered, "Just as our nation employs you."

When the Master was washing his clothes, a monk said, "Master! You still are not free from 'this'?" Master Nan-ch'üan replied, lifting the clothes, "What can you do to 'this'?"

The Master asked Liang-hsin, a monk, whether there is a Buddha in the *kalpa* of the void.[6] The monk answered, "There is." The Master asked, "Who?" "It is Liang-hsin!" the monk replied. "In what country do you live?" pressed the Master. The monk made no answer.

---

6. *Kalpa* means eon. More specifically, it refers to the period of time between the creation and the re-creation of the universe. This Great Kalpa is divided into four lesser *kalpas:* formation, existence, destruction, and void. The *kalpa* of the void is the last stage in the cycle.

A monk inquired, "From Ancestor to Ancestor there is a transmission. What is it that they transmit to one another?" The Master said, "One, two, three, four, five!"

Master Nan-ch'üan asked a Vinaya monk, "Please explain the sutra to me, will you?" The monk answered, "If I explain the sutra to you, you tell me about Ch'an. Thus you have my explanation." The Master said, "How could a golden ball be exchanged for a silver one?" The Vinaya monk said, "I do not understand." The Master said, "Suppose there is a cloud in the sky. Is it to be held there by driving nails or tied up with vines?" The monk asked, "Should there be a pearl in the sky, how would you fetch it?" The Master said, "Chop the bamboo and make it into a ladle, and we will use it to fetch the pearl from the sky." The monk challenged him: "How would it be possible to use the ladle in the sky?" The Master answered, "What do you suggest we do to fetch the pearl from the sky?" The monk then bid the Master good-bye, saying to him, "I am going to travel far. If anyone asks me what you are doing these days, I will not know how to answer." The Master replied, "You tell them that recently I have come to understand how to rush upon another." The monk said, "How is that?" The Master answered, "With one rush, both sides are destroyed."

A monk asked, "Where are one's nostrils before one is born?" The Master replied, "Where are one's nostrils after one has been born?"

Before the Master passed away, the head monk asked him, "Where are you going after your death?" The Master answered, "I am going down the hill to be a water buffalo." The monk continued, "Would it be possible to follow you there?" The Master said, "If you want to follow me, you must come with a piece of straw in your mouth."

Thereafter the illness of Master Nan-ch'üan was announced. On the twenty-fifth day of the twelfth month in the eighth year of the Ta-ho period, early in the morning, he told his disciples, "For a long time the stars have been blurring and the lamplight dimming; don't say that I alone have to come and go." After saying this, he passed away. He was then eighty-seven years of age and in the fifty-eighth year of his ordination. The year after his death his body was enshrined in a pagoda.

12

Kuei-shan

(771–853)

Kuei-shan Ling-yu and his principal successor, Yang-shan Hui-chi (807–883), are regarded as founders of the first of the Five Houses of Ch'an, and its name has linked theirs for posterity: Kuei-yang (J., Igyō). Recognition of these houses, it should be noted, occurred after the fact, as chroniclers interpreted Ch'an history. In life, Kuei-shan and Yang-shan were intimately associated and developed what came to be referred to as a "family style," but they did not set themselves apart from the rest of Ch'an. On the contrary, records show that they mixed with all comers in the fluid, exciting scene of the time, trading insights with other masters, either in face-to-face encounters or via the bamboo telegraph that carried stories and repartee from mountain to mountain throughout the Ch'an universe.

Kuei-shan (J., Isan) studied for many years with Pai-chang, arriving as a promising inquirer at age twenty-three and staying to become a senior member of the assembly. He worked—for twenty years, some say—in the position of head cook, which Ch'an texts without exception identify as an office of immense trust and responsibility. This should not seem odd to anyone who has experienced the effect that institutional cooking may have on personal and collective well-being, although in this case what came out of the kitchen was judged to reflect the cook's wisdom and character more than culinary talent. Over the centuries, an informal pantheon of Ch'an chefs has developed, in which Kuei-shan holds a place of high honor.

Kuei-shan's biography from *The Transmission of the Lamp* reports that he was still serving as head cook at the time Pai-chang picked him to establish a monastery on Mt. Kuei. Elsewhere, Kuei-shan is said to have spent eight years on this wild peak before the world realized his presence and assembled to build the monastery foreseen for him there. He eventually attracted considerable notice, we are told, obtaining a general's intercession on behalf of his project and winning support from P'ei Hsiu, a future prime minister (or grand councillor) and author of the complaint about Buddhist infighting quoted in Chapter 9. By the time he died, Kuei-shan was perhaps the nation's most highly touted master. Counted among his forty-one successors is the nun Liu T'ieh-mo, known as Iron Grinder Liu, one of the rare women whose accomplishments won her name a place in Ch'an literature. (A famous dialogue between her and Kuei-shan is recounted in Chapter 25.) The Ch'an library contains numerous and wonderful tales of Kuei-shan, many of them involving Yang-shan (J., Kyōzan) as well.

The Kuei-yang house only lasted a few generations, and some ascribe its early demise to insufficient strictness in the training of students—a readiness to assent and praise, thus a failure to push students beyond small insights to great awakenings. Gentleness and harmony does indeed prevail in many interactions between the house's founders, but its records certainly show evidence of rigor, too. Kuei-shan and Yang-shan take each other to task on occasion, and their most widely read work, Kuei-shan's "Admonitions," blasts monks for indolence, urging them on with great heat and passion. The harmony between the founders may best be explained as a near-perfect meeting of minds at peace. As Yang-shan put it, they were "two mouths without a single tongue." ⊗

FROM THE TRANSMISSION OF THE LAMP

Mt. Kuei had formerly been an inaccessible region. The rocks were steep and high, and no one lived there. Only monkeys could be found for companions and only chestnuts were available as food. When people at the foot of the mountain heard that Master Ling-yu was living there they assembled to build a monastery for him. Through General Li Ching-jang's recommendation the Royal Court granted the title Tung-ching to the monastery. Often the Prime Minister, P'ei Hsiu, came to the Master to ask questions about the meaning of Ch'an, and from this period onward devotees from all over the country journeyed to Mt. Kuei.

One day Master Kuei-shan Ling-yu came into the assembly and said:

"The mind of one who understands Ch'an is plain and straightforward without pretense. It has neither front nor back and is without deceit or delusion. Every hour of the day, what one hears and sees are ordinary things and ordinary actions. Nothing is distorted. One does not need to shut one's eyes and ears to be non-attached to things. In the early days many sages stressed the follies and dangers of impurity. When delusion, perverted views, and bad thinking habits are eliminated, the mind is as clear and tranquil as the autumn stream. It is pure and quiescent, placid and free from attachment. . . ."

During an assembly period [Kuei-shan said,] "When one hears the truth one penetrates immediately to the ultimate reality, the realization of which is profound and wondrous. The mind is illuminated naturally and perfectly, free from confusion. On the other hand, in the present-day world there are numerous theories being expounded about Buddhism. These theories are advocated by those who wish to earn a seat in the temple and wear an abbot's robe to justify their work. But reality itself cannot be stained by even a speck of dust, and no action can distort the truth. When the approach to enlightenment is like the swift thrust of a sword to the center of things, then both worldliness and holiness are completely eliminated and Absolute Reality is revealed. Thus the One and the Many are identified. This is the Suchness of Buddha."

Yang-shan asked, "What was the meaning of Bodhidharma coming from the West?"

The Master answered, "A fine large lantern."

"Is it not 'this'?"

"What is 'this'?"

"A fine large lantern," Yang-shan said.

"You do not really *know*."

One day the Master said to the assembly, "There are many people who experience the great moment, but few who can perform the great function." Yang-shan went with this statement to the abbot of the temple at the foot of the mountain and asked him its meaning. The abbot said, "Try to repeat your question to me." As Yang-shan began to do so, the abbot kicked him and knocked him down. When Yang-shan returned and repeated this to the Master, Kuei-shan laughed heartily.

Once when all the monks were out picking tea leaves the Master said to Yang-shan, "All day as we were picking tea leaves I have heard your voice, but I have not seen you yourself. Show me your original self." Yang-shan thereupon shook the tea bush.

The Master said, "You have attained only the function, not the substance." Yang-shan remarked, "I do not know how you yourself would answer the question." The Master was silent for a time. Yang-shan commented, "You, Master, have attained only the substance, not the function." Master Kuei-shan responded, "I absolve you from twenty blows!"

When the Master came to the assembly, a monk stepped forward and said to him, "Please, Master, give us the Dharma." "Have I not taught you thoroughly already?" asked the Master, and the monk bowed.

The Master told Yang-shan, "You should speak immediately. Do not enter the realm of illusion."

Yang-shan replied, "My faith in reality is not even established."

The Master said, "Have you had faith and been unable to establish it, or is it because you never had faith that you could not establish it?"

Yang-shan said, "What I believe in is Hui-chi [himself]. Why should I have faith in anyone else?"

The Master replied, "If this is the case, you have attained *arhatship*."[1]

Yang-shan answered, "I have not even seen the Buddha."

1. [This is as much a challenge as a compliment. Though Southern Buddhists regarded an *arhat* as second only to a buddha, Mahāyāna Buddhists considered them inferior to *bodhisattvas*.—Eds.]

The Master asked Yang-shan, "In the forty volumes of the *Nirvāna Sūtra,* how many words were spoken by Buddha and how many by devils?"

Yang-shan answered, "They are all devils' words."

Master Kuei-shan said, "From now on, no one can [overcome] you."

Yang-shan said, "I, Hui-chi, have simply seen the truth in this one instant. How should I apply it to my daily conduct?" The Master replied, "It is important that you see things correctly. I do not talk about your daily conduct."

Once when Yang-shan was washing his clothes, he lifted them up and asked the Master, "At this very moment, what are you doing?" The Master answered, "At this moment I am doing nothing." Yang-shan said, "Master! You have substance, but no function." The Master was silent for a while, then picked up the clothes and asked Yang-shan, "At this very moment, what are you doing?" Yang-shan replied, "At this moment, Master, do you still see 'this'?" The Master said, "You have function, but no substance."

One day the Master suddenly spoke to Yang-shan, "Last spring you made an incomplete statement. Can you complete it now?" Yang-shan answered, "At this very moment? One should not make a clay image in a moment." The Master said, "A retained prisoner improves in judgment."

The Master asked a newly arrived monk what his name was. The monk said, "Yüeh-lun [Full Moon]." The Master then drew a circle in the air with his hand. "How do you compare with this?" he asked. The monk replied, "Master, if you ask me in such a way, a great many people will not agree with you." Then the Master said, "As for me, this is my way. What is yours?" The monk said, "Do you still see Yüeh-lun?" The Master answered, "You can say it your way, but there are a great many people here who do not agree with you."

The Master was about to pass a pitcher to Yang-shan, who had put out his hands to receive it. But he suddenly withdrew the pitcher, saying, "What is this pitcher?" Yang-shan replied, "What have you discovered from it, Master?" The Master said, "If you challenge me in this way, why do you study with me?" Yang-shan explained, "Even though I challenge, it is still my duty to carry water for you in the pitcher." The Master then passed the pitcher to him.

During a stroll with Yang-shan, the Master pointed to a cypress tree and asked, "What is this in front of you?" Yang-shan answered, "As for this, it is just a cypress tree." The Master then pointed back to an old farmer and said, "This old man will one day have five hundred disciples."

The Master said to Yang-shan, "Where have you been?" Yang-shan answered, "At the farm." The Master said, "Are the rice plants ready for the harvest?" Yang-shan replied, "They are ready." The Master asked, "Do they appear to you to be green, or yellow, or neither green nor yellow?" Yang-shan answered,

"Master, what is behind you?" The Master said, "Do you see it?" Then Yang-shan picked up an ear of grain and said, "Are you not asking about *this?*" The Master [praised him highly].

One winter the Master asked Yang-shan whether it was the weather that was cold or whether it was man who felt cold. Yang-shan replied, "We are all here!" "Why don't you answer directly?" asked the Master. Then Yang-shan said, "My answer just now cannot be considered indirect. How about you?" The Master said, "If it is direct, it flows with the current."

A monk came to bow in front of the Master, who made a gesture of getting up. The monk said, "Please, Master, do not get up!" The Master said, "I have not yet sat down." "I have not yet bowed," retorted the monk. The Master replied, "Why should you be ill-mannered?" The monk made no answer.

Two Ch'an followers came from the assembly of Master Shih-shuang to the monastery of Master Kuei-shan, where they complained that no one there understood Ch'an. Later on everyone in the temple was ordered to bring firewood. Yang-shan encountered the two visitors as they were resting. He picked up a piece of firewood and asked, "Can you make a correct statement about this?" Neither made an answer. Yang-shan said, "Then you had better not say that no one here understands Ch'an." After going back inside the monastery, Yang-shan reported to Master Kuei-shan, "I [saw through] the two Ch'an followers here for Shih-shuang." The Master asked, "Where did you come upon them?" Yang-shan reported the encounter, and thereupon the Master said, "Hui-chi is now being [seen through] by me."

When the Master was in bed Yang-shan came to speak to him, but the Master turned his face to the wall. Yang-shan said, "How can you do this?" The Master rose and said, "A moment ago I had a dream. Won't you try to interpret it for me?" Thereupon Yang-shan brought in a basin of water for the Master to wash his face. A little later Hsiang-yen also appeared to speak to the Master. The Master repeated, "I just had a dream. Yang-shan interpreted it. Now it is your turn." Hsiang-yen then brought in a cup of tea. The Master said, "The insight of both of you excels that of Sāriputra."[2]

Once a monk said, "If one cannot be the straw hat on top of Mt. Kuei, how can one reach the village that is free from forced labor? What is this straw hat of Mt. Kuei?" The Master thereupon stamped his foot.

The Master came to the assembly and said, "After I have passed away I shall become a water buffalo at the foot of the mountain. On the left side of the buffalo's chest five characters, *Kuei-shan-Monk-Ling-yu,* will be inscribed. At that time you may call me the monk of Kuei-shan, but at the same time I shall also be the water buffalo. When you call me water buffalo, I am also the monk of Kuei-shan. What is my correct name?"

2. One of the ten finest disciples of Buddha, whose widsom is considered the greatest of all.

The Master propagated the teachings of Ch'an for more than forty years. Numerous followers achieved self-realization, and forty-one disciples penetrated to the final profundity of his teaching. On the ninth day of the first month of the seventh year [853] of T'ai-chung of the T'ang Dynasty, the Master washed his face and rinsed his mouth and then seated himself and, smiling, passed away. This was sixty-four years after he was ordained. He was eighty-three years old. He was buried on Mt. Kuei where he had taught. His posthumous name, received from the Royal Court, was Great Perfection, and his pagoda was called Purity and Quiescence.

13

Po Chü-i

(772–846)

Po Chü-i covered a lot of ground—and inked a lot of rice paper—in his seventy-four years. Like fellow poet-officials Wang Wei before him and Su T'ung-po (Chapter 24) after him, he saw much of China in the course of his long government service and took the opportunity to call on numerous teachers and temples, eagerly sampling the diverse schools of Buddhism. Everywhere Po Chü-i went, he wrote poems, and as more than three thousand of them have survived, he takes the prize for most prolific poet of the T'ang Dynasty. He also ranged widely in terms of subjects and genres, yet he always kept his language simple, reading his poems to a washerwoman, it is said, to ensure their comprehensibility even to the uneducated. For that reason, in part, he enjoyed extraordinary popularity in his own day, his work known, recited, copied, and posted all over China and in Japan, too.

Throughout his life, Po Chü-i held to the Confucian rule that poetry should edify, not merely entertain. In his late work, he tended to touch—lightly—on philosophical, psychological, and religious matters, while his earlier poems more often addressed concerns of a social or moral nature, evoking injustices and chiding those responsible. Though Po couched his youthful condemnations in allegory, cloaked them in history, or tempered them with humor, they rankled higher-ups all the same, and twice he was shunted into provincial positions as a consequence. His ascent of the bureaucratic ladder continued, however, ultimately bringing far loftier titles and far greater wealth than Wang Wei or Su T'ung-po ever achieved.

Throughout his life, Po Chü-i expressed a taste for mountain scenery and seclusion, but how much of this was genuine and how much was poetic convention no one can say. During one of his provincial assignments, he built—that is, he had others build—a "thatch hut" on Mount Lu, the site of many Buddhist temples and hermitages. This was the rustic retreat of a wealthy man, not Hanshan's spartan hideaway; Po had no great appetite for discomfort. In a poem written when he held a comfortable job in the cultural capital of Lo-yang, he depicted himself as a "semi-recluse," claiming that he had all the pleasures of a hermit's life and none of the hardships. On retiring, he remained in Lo-yang and continued to enjoy ample social interaction while continuing in his poems to sound notes of simplicity and seclusion.

Like many other Chinese intellectuals of his time, Po saw no contradiction between the teachings of Ch'an and those of Lao-tzu and Chuang-tzu. Indeed, he may have belonged to a then-popular school of thought that advocated "the unity of the three doctrines"—Buddhism, Taoism, and Confucianism—and he often explicitly coupled Ch'an with Taoism in his writings. One of his poems flatly equates Chuang-tzu's favored method of "sitting and forgetting" (*tso-wang*) with zazen (*tso-ch'an*): "Practicing Ch'an and 'sitting and forgetting': / the end is identical, they're not two different roads."

Po Chü-i's principal interests, besides poetry and the Way, were friendship and family, music, and wine. To judge by his literary record, he struggled all his life to meet the standards of relinquishment laid out in Taoist and Buddhist doctrine, seeing the pursuits and people that he loved as his greatest obstacles on the path. In "Madly Singing in the Mountains," he called poetry his "special failing" and lamented, "I've broken free from the thousand bonds of life, / but this weakness still remains."

In retirement, Po appears to have resolved his conflict about writing, perhaps through his acquaintance with the noted teacher and scholar Kuei-feng Tsung-mi (J., Keihō Shūmitsu), a master of the Hua-yen school as well as a fifth-generation heir of Hui-neng's apostle Shen-hui. Tsung-mi criticized the ascendant southern Ch'an of Ma-tsu and his heirs for departing from scriptural tradition in favor of direct, mind-to-mind transmission of the Dharma. In a tribute to Tsung-mi composed in this late period, Po Chü-i seconded the point:

> The word-treasury carries afar every division of the Dharma,
> and the mind-beacon lights a thousand lamps.
> Abandoning the written word completely is not the Middle Way;
> dwelling forever in the empty void is the Lesser Path.

Among his final poems was a witty riposte to the Taoists on this point, too:

> "Those who speak don't know;
> those who know don't speak"—
> I'm told those are Lao-tzu's words,
> but if we believe that Lao-tzu knew,
> how is it he wrote five thousand words?

Po's enthusiasm for the Dharma increased with age. "Half my friends are monks," he declared in a poem written at sixty-one and dedicated to four Ch'an monks. Five years later, in his prose *Biography of a Master of Wine and Song*, he confessed that, in addition to enjoying the pleasures advertised in his title, he was "addicted to Buddhism." This addiction went well beyond words. Po contributed vast sums to Ch'an institutions, most notably Hsiang-shan Temple near Lo-yang, where he spent so much time that he began to consider it his "home in old age" and to style himself the Lay Buddhist of Hsiang-shan.

As for Ch'an, it welcomed Po Chü-i as one of its own—at heart, if not in every last detail. Within a century and a half of his death, *The Transmission of the Lamp* placed his biography among those of the masters, recording his study with several teachers, including the colorful Niao K'o, known to posterity as the

Bird's Nest Master for his peculiar place of residence, the branches of a spreading pine. Po had once governed that neck of the woods and had gone to interview him, calling up, "Your Reverence, isn't your dwelling place dangerous?"

"Isn't Your Excellency's position more dangerous?" responded the master.

"I defend the borders," said Po. "What's the danger in that?"

"When fire comes in contact with fuel," replied the master, alluding to the contacts that inflame our passions, "and when consciousness is never still, how can you avoid danger?"

"What is the essence of the Dharma?" asked Po, changing tack.

The master answered, "Always do good, never do evil."

"Even a child of three knows enough to say that!" exclaimed Po.

"A three-year-old can say it," agreed the master, "but an eighty-year-old has difficulty practicing it." Hearing this, the governor prostrated himself.

In his later years, Po's guide to Ch'an was Ju-man Fu-kuang, a successor of Ma-tsu whom Po claims in his bibulous biography as his "religious friend." In sketching Po's Ch'an creditials, *The Transmission of the Lamp* reports that he practiced for an extended period with Ju-man but also makes the unusual comment "He had no constant teacher." All the same, it praises his Dharma-eye unreservedly and leaves open the possibility he gave instruction, perhaps secretly: "He was not observed to behave as a Dharma teacher; still, there were few men who could give answers regarding the matter as well as Po Chü-i. . . . " ⊗

SICK LEAVE
(While Chief Clerk to the subprefecture of Chou-chih, near Ch'ang-an, in 806)

Propped on pillows, not attending to business;
For two days I've lain behind locked doors.
I begin to think that those who hold office
Get no rest, except by falling ill!
For restful thoughts one does not need space;
The room where I lie is ten foot square.
By the western eaves, above the bamboo-twigs,
From my couch I see the White Mountain rise.
But the clouds that hover on its far-distant peak
Bring shame to a face that is buried in the world's dust.

THE CHANCELLOR'S GRAVEL-DRIVE
(A satire on the maltreatment of subordinates)

A government bull yoked to a government cart!
Moored by the bank of Ch'an River, a barge loaded with gravel.
A single load of gravel,
How many pounds it weighs!

Carrying at dawn, carrying at dusk, what is it all for?
They are carrying it towards the Five Gates,
To the west of the main road.
Under the shadow of green laurels they are making a gravel-drive.
For yesterday arrived, newly appointed,
The Assistant Chancellor of the Realm,
And was terribly afraid that the wet and mud
Would dirty his horse's hoofs.
The Chancellor's horse's hoofs
Stepped on the gravel and remained perfectly clean;
But the bull employed in dragging the cart
Was almost sweating blood.
The Assistant Chancellor's business
Is to "save men, govern the country
And harmonize yin and yang."
Whether the bull's neck is sore
Need not trouble him at all.

ON BOARD SHIP: READING YÜAN CHEN'S POEMS

I take your poems in my hand and read them beside the candle;
The poems are finished, the candle is low, dawn not yet come.
My eyes smart; I put out the lamp and go on sitting in the dark,
Listening to waves that, driven by the wind, strike the prow of the ship.

AFTER LUNCH

After lunch—one short nap;
On waking up—two cups of tea.
Raising my head, I see the sun's light
Once again slanting to the southwest.
Those who are happy regret the shortness of the day;
Those who are sad tire of the year's sloth.
But those whose hearts are devoid of joy or sadness
Just go on living, regardless of "short" or "long."

SLEEPING ON HORSEBACK

We had ridden long and were still far from the inn;
My eyes grew dim; for a moment I fell asleep.
Under my right arm the whip still dangled;

In my left hand the reins for an instant slackened.
Suddenly I woke and turned to question my groom.
"We have gone a hundred paces since you fell asleep."
Body and spirit for a while had changed place;
Swift and slow had turned to their contraries.
For these few steps that my horse had carried me
Had taken in my dream countless eons of time!
True indeed is that saying of wise men
"A hundred years are but a moment of sleep."

PARTING FROM THE WINTER STOVE

On the fifth day after the rise of Spring,
Everywhere the season's gracious attitudes!
The white sun gradually lengthening its course,
The blue-gray clouds hanging as though they would fall;
The last icicle breaking into splinters of jade:
The new stems marshalling red sprouts.
The things I meet are all full of gladness;
It is not only *I* who love the Spring.
To welcome the flowers I stand in the back garden;
To enjoy the sunlight I sit under the front eaves.
Yet still in my heart there lingers one regret;
Soon I shall part with the flame of my red stove!

GETTING UP EARLY ON A SPRING MORNING
(*Part of a poem written when Governor of Soochow in 825*)

The early light of the rising sun shines on the beams of my house;
The first banging of opened doors echoes like the roll of a drum.
The dog lies curled on the stone step, for the earth is wet with dew;
The birds come near to the window and chatter, telling that the day is fine.
With the lingering fumes of yesterday's wine my head is still heavy;
With new doffing of winter clothes my body has grown light.
I woke up with heart empty and mind utterly extinct;
Lately, for many nights on end, I have not dreamt of home.

HALF IN THE FAMILY, HALF OUT
(*Written in 840, when the poet was around seventy. To be "in the family"
means to be a lay Buddhist believer; to be "out of the family" means to be a*

monk. The cranes in line five are pet birds that Po kept in his garden. The daughter mentioned in the last line was Po's eldest daughter, who had recently been widowed and had returned with her infant son to live with her parents.)

Comfortably fixed for clothing and food, children married off,
from now on family affairs are no concern of mine.
In nightly rest, I'm a bird who's found his way to the forest;
at morning meals, I'm one in heart with the monk who begs his food.
Clear cries, several voices—cranes under the pines;
one spot of cold light—the lamp among the bamboo.
Late at night I practice meditation, sitting in lotus position.
My daughter calls, my wife hoots—I don't answer either of them.

SITTING ALONE IN THE PLACE OF PRACTICE

I straighten and adjust robe and headcloth, wipe clean the platform:
one pitcher of autumn water, one burner of incense.
Needless to say, cares and delusions must first be gotten rid of;
then when it comes to enlightenment, you try to forget that too.
Morning visits to court long suspended, I've put away sword and pendants;
feasts and outings gradually abandoned, jars and wine cups are neglected.
In these last years, when I'm no more use to the world,
best just to be free and easy, sitting here in the place of practice.

THE CRANES

The western wind has blown but a few days;
Yet the first leaf already flies from the bough.
On the drying paths I walk in my thin shoes;
In the first cold I have donned my quilted coat.
Through shallow ditches the floods are clearing away;
Through sparse bamboos trickles a slanting light.
In the early dusk, down an alley of green moss,
The garden-boy is leading the cranes home.

RISING LATE, AND PLAYING WITH A-TS'UI, AGED TWO

All the morning I have lain snugly in bed;
Now at dusk I rise with many yawns.
My warm stove is quick to get ablaze;

At the cold mirror I am slow in doing my hair.
With melted snow I boil fragrant tea;
I cook a milk-pudding seasoned with curds
At my sloth and greed there is no one but me to laugh;
My cheerful vigor none but myself knows.
The taste of my wine is mild and works no poison;
The notes of my lute are soft and bring no sadness.
To the three joys in the book of Mencius
I have added the fourth of playing with my baby boy.

EASE
(*Congratulating himself on the comforts of his life during a temporary retirement from office.*)

Lined coat, warm cap and easy felt slippers,
In the little tower, at the low window, sitting over the sunken brazier.
Body at rest, heart at peace; no need to rise early.
I wonder if the courtiers at the Western Capital know of these things, or not?

A DREAM OF MOUNTAINEERING
(*Written when he was seventy.*)

At night, in my dream, I stoutly climbed a mountain
Going out alone with my staff of holly-wood.
A thousand crags, a hundred hundred valleys—
In my dream-journey none were unexplored
And all the while my feet never grew tired
And my step was as strong as in my young days.
Can it be that when the mind travels backward
The body also returns to its old state?
And can it be, as between body and soul,
That the body may languish, while the soul is still strong?
Soul and body—both are vanities;
Dreaming and waking—both alike unreal.
In the day my feet are palsied and tottering;
In the night my steps go striding over the hills.
As day and night are divided in equal parts—
Between the two, I get as much as I *lose*.

14

Huang-po

(D. 850)

P'ei Hsiu, the same high official who visited Kuei-shan for instruction, figured prominently in the career of Huang-po Hsi-yün, serving as both his sponsor and his amanuensis. In 843, P'ei wrote, he asked Huang-po (J.,Ōbaku) to join him in residence at a monastery in Chün-chou and there, "day and night, I questioned him about the Way." Six years later, P'ei invited Huang-po to the district he was then governing, of Wan-ling, and installed him in a monastery built expressly for him. The master, obviously pleased, named the new place for the mountain where he had lived as a novice monk, and the name stuck, first to the monastery and then to him: Huang-po.

Here, the two men resumed their discussions, and as he had on the earlier occasion, P'ei took the trouble to write down what he had heard. Thus we possess for Huang-po, unlike other masters of the age, an authoritative and contemporaneous document of his words. He would probably not be pleased by this, judging from his reaction one day when P'ei presented him with a poem:

He took it in his hands, but soon sat down and pushed it away. "Do you understand?" he asked.

"No, Master."

"But why don't you understand? Think a little! If things could be expressed like this with ink and paper, what would be the purpose of a sect like ours?"

Huang-po seems to have exercised a measure of deference in teaching P'ei, as Nan-ch'üan did with his well-placed lay disciple, but as a rule he practiced the no-holds-barred teaching method pioneered by his Dharma grandfather, Ma-tsu, frequently swatting or bellowing at students in an attempt to open their eyes. The most outstanding instance of such behavior came when Huang-po encountered a novice monk at a Dharma assembly conducted in a government complex. As P'ei reports this event:

The [novice] noticed our Master enter the hall of worship and make a triple prostration to the Buddha, whereupon he asked: "If we are to seek nothing from the Buddha, Dharma, or Sangha, what does Your Reverence seek by such prostrations?"

"Though I seek nothing from the Buddha," replied our Master, "or from the Dharma, or from the Sangha, it is my custom to show respect this way."

"But what purpose does it serve?" insisted the [novice], whereupon he suddenly received a slap.

"Oh," he exclaimed, "How uncouth you are!"

"What is this?" cried the Master. "Imagine making a distinction between refined and uncouth!" So saying, he administered another slap. . . .

What makes this incident remarkable, *The Blue Cliff Record* explains, is that the inquisitive novice was a future emperor, hiding himself in the Ch'an *sangha* until his political troubles receded. When he emerged and took power, "he bestowed on Huang-po the title of Uncouth Ascetic. Later, when Prime Minister P'ei Hsiu was at court, P'ei advanced the proposal that Huang-po be granted the [posthumous] title, "Ch'an Master Without Limits"—a positive twist that was duly accepted.

This freewheeling teacher, by all accounts, cut a very impressive figure. P'ei describes him as extraordinarily tall, with "a small lump shaped like a pearl" in the middle of his forehead. (Huang-po seems to have made prostrations before the Buddha a regular part of his practice, and other writers suggested that this protuberance resulted from so frequently touching his head to the floor.) *The Blue Cliff Record* notes that "When Huang-po first met Pai-chang, Pai-chang said, 'Magnificent! Imposing! Where have you come from?' Huang-po said, 'Magnificent and imposing, I've come from the mountains.' " P'ei observed that Huang-po's "words were simple, his reasoning direct, his way of life exalted, and his habits unlike the habits of other men."

At some point, Huang-po trained under his Dharma uncle Nan-ch'üan, but the bulk of his preparation was with Pai-chang, and it was the latter he succeeded in the Dharma. Upon acknowledging him as an heir, Pai-chang made a statement that has reverberated ever since through the halls of Ch'an and Zen: "If a student's insight is equal to the teacher's, the student will have merely half the teacher's capacity. Only a student whose insight exceeds the teacher's is worthy of receiving transmission." Huang-po apparently took this injunction to heart, in due course producing thirteen successors of his own, among them one of the greatest Ch'an masters of all time, Lin-chi (Chapter 17).

FROM THE CHÜN-CHOU RECORD

The Master said to me: All the Buddhas and all sentient beings are nothing but the One Mind, beside which nothing exists. This Mind, which is without beginning, is unborn and indestructible. It is not green nor yellow, and has neither form nor appearance. It does not belong to the categories of things which exist or do not exist, nor can it be thought of in terms of new or old. It is neither long nor short, big nor small, for it transcends all limits, measures, names, traces and comparisons. It is that which you see before you—begin to reason about it and you at once fall into error. It is like the boundless void that cannot be fathomed

or measured. The One Mind alone is the Buddha, and there is no distinction between the Buddha and sentient things, but that sentient beings are attached to
forms and so seek externally for Buddhahood. By their very seeking they lose it,
for that is using the Buddha to seek for the Buddha and using mind to grasp
Mind. Even though they do their utmost for a full eon, they will not be able to attain to it. They do not know that, if they put a stop to conceptual thought and
forget their anxiety, the Buddha will appear before them, for this Mind is the
Buddha and the Buddha is all living beings. It is not the less for being manifested
in ordinary beings, nor is it greater for being manifested in the Buddhas.

The building up of good and evil both involve attachment to form. Those who,
being attached to form, do evil have to undergo various incarnations unneces-
sarily; while those who, being attached to form, do good, subject themselves to
toil and privation equally to no purpose. In either case it is better to achieve sudden self-realization and to grasp the fundamental Dharma. This Dharma is
Mind, beyond which there *is* no Dharma; and this Mind is the Dharma, beyond
which there *is* no mind. Mind in itself is not mind, yet neither is it no-mind. To
say that Mind is no-mind implies something existent. Let there be a silent understanding and no more. Away with all thinking and explaining. Then we may say
that the Way of Words has been cut off and movements of the mind eliminated.
This Mind is the pure Buddha-Source inherent in all men. All wriggling beings
possessed of sentient life and all the Buddhas and bodhisattvas are of this one
substance and do not differ. Differences arise from wrong-thinking only and
lead to the creation of all kinds of karma.

Our original Buddha-nature is, in highest truth, devoid of any atom of objectiv-
ity. It is void, omnipresent, silent, pure; it is glorious and mysterious peaceful
joy—and that is all. Enter deeply into it by awaking to it yourself. That which is
before you is it, in all its fullness, utterly complete. There is naught beside. Even
if you go through all the stages of a bodhisattva's progress towards Buddhahood,
one by one; when at last, in a single flash you attain to full realization, you will
only be realizing the Buddha-nature, which has been with you all the time; and
by all the foregoing stages you will have added to it nothing at all. You will come
to look upon those eons of work and achievement as no better than unreal actions performed in a dream. That is why the Tathāgata said: "I truly attained
nothing from complete, unexcelled Enlightenment. Had there been anything attained, Dīpankara Buddha would not have made the prophecy concerning me."[1]
He also said: "This Dharma is absolutely without distinctions, neither high nor

1. This quotation refers to the *Diamond Sutra,* as do many of the others either directly or indirectly.
Dīpankara Buddha, during a former life of Gautama Buddha, prophesied that he would one day attain to Buddhahood.

low, and its name is Bodhi." It is pure Mind, which is the source of everything and which, whether appearing as sentient beings or as Buddhas, as the rivers and mountains of the world which has form, as that which is formless, or as penetrating the whole universe, is absolutely without distinctions, there being no such entities as selfness and otherness.

Q: From all you have just said, Mind is the Buddha; but it is not clear as to what sort of mind is meant by this "Mind which is the Buddha."

A: How many minds have you got?

Q: But is the Buddha the ordinary mind or the enlightened mind?

A: Where on earth do you keep your "ordinary mind" and your "enlightened mind?"

Q: In the teaching of the Three Vehicles it is stated that there are both. Why does Your Reverence deny it?

A: In the teaching of the Three Vehicles it is clearly explained that the ordinary and enlightened minds are illusions. You don't understand. All this clinging to the idea of things existing is to mistake vacuity for the truth. How can such conceptions not be illusory? Being illusory, they hide Mind from you. If you would only rid yourselves of the concepts of ordinary and enlightened, you would find that there is no other Buddha than the Buddha in your own Mind. When Bodhidharma came from the West, he just pointed out that the substance of which all men are composed is the Buddha. You people go on misunderstanding; you hold to concepts such as "ordinary" and "enlightened," directing your thoughts outwards where they gallop about like horses! All this amounts to beclouding your own minds! So I tell you Mind is the Buddha. As soon as thought or sensation arises, you fall into dualism. Beginningless time and the present moment are the same. There is no this and no that. To understand this truth is called compete and unexcelled enlightenment.

Q: Upon what doctrine does Your Reverence base these words?

A: Why seek a doctrine? As soon as you have a doctrine, you fall into dualistic thought.

Q: Just now you said that the beginningless past and the present are the same. What do you mean by that?

A: It is just because of your *seeking* that you make a difference between them. If you were to stop seeking, how could there be any difference between them?

Q: If they are not different, why did you employ separate terms for them?

A: If you hadn't mentioned ordinary and enlightened, who would have bothered to say such things? Just as those categories have no real existence, so Mind is not really "mind." And, as both Mind and those categories are really illusions, wherever can you hope to find anything?

If you would spend all your time—walking, standing, sitting or lying down—learning to halt the concept-forming activities of your own mind, you could be sure of ultimately attaining the goal. Since your strength is insufficient, you might not be able to transcend *samsāra* by a single leap; but, after five or ten years, you would surely have made a good beginning and be able to make further progress spontaneously. It is because you are not that sort of man that you feel obliged to employ your mind "studying dhyāna" and "studying the Way." What has all that got to do with Buddhism? So it is said that all the Tathāgata taught was just to convert people; it was like pretending yellow leaves are real gold just to stop the flow of a child's tears; it must by no means be regarded as though it were ultimate truth. If you take it for truth, you are no member of our sect; and what bearing can it have on your original substance? So the sutra says: "What is called supreme perfect wisdom implies that there is really nothing whatever to be attained." If you are also able to understand this, you will realize that the Way of the Buddhas and the Way of devils are equally wide of the mark. The original pure, glistening universe is neither square nor round, big nor small; it is without any such distinctions as long and short, it is beyond attachment and activity, ignorance and enlightenment. You must see clearly that there is really nothing at all—no humans and no Buddhas. The great chiliocosms, numberless as grains of sand, are mere bubbles. All wisdom and all holiness are but streaks of lightning. None of them have the reality of Mind. The Dharmakāya, from ancient times until today, together with the Buddhas and Ancestors, is One. How can it lack a single hair of anything? Even if you understand this, you must make the most strenuous efforts. Throughout this life, you can never be certain of living long enough to take another breath.

FROM THE WAN-LING RECORD

Q: But what if in previous lives I have behaved like Kalirāja, slicing the limbs from living men?

A: The holy sages tortured by him represent your own Mind, while Kalirāja symbolizes that part of you which goes out *seeking.* Such unkingly behaviour is called lust for personal advantage. If you students of the Way, without making any attempt to live virtuously, just want to make a study of everything you perceive, then how are you different from him? By allowing your gaze to linger on a form, you wrench out the eyes of a sage [yourself]. And when you linger upon a sound, you slice off the ears of a sage—thus it is with all your senses and with cognition, for their varied perceptions are called slicers.

Q: When we meet all suffering with sagelike patience and avoid all mind-slicing perceptions, that which suffers with resignation surely cannot be the One Mind, for that cannot be subject to the endurance of pain.

A: You are one of those people who force the Unbecoming into conceptual molds, such as the *concept* of patient suffering or the *concept* of seeking nothing outside yourself. Thereby you do yourself violence!

Q: When the holy sages were dismembered, were they conscious of pain; and, if among them there were no entities capable of suffering, who or what did suffer?

A: If you are not suffering pain now, what is the point of chiming in like that?

During his travels, our Master paid a visit to Nan-ch'üan. One day at dinner-time, he took his bowl and seated himself opposite Nan-ch'üan's high chair. Noticing him there, Nan-ch'üan stepped down to receive him and asked: "How long has Your Reverence been following the Way?"

"Since before the era of Bhisma Rāja," came the reply.[2]

"Indeed?" exclaimed Nan-ch'üan. "It seems that Master Ma has a worthy grandson here." Our Master then walked quietly away.

A few days later, when our Master was going out, Nan-ch'üan remarked: "You are a huge man, so why wear a hat of such ridiculous size?"

"Ah, well," replied our Master. "It contains vast numbers of chiliocosms."

"Well, what of me?" inquired Nan-ch'üan, but the Master put on his hat and walked off.

Once, when our Master had just dismissed the first of the daily assemblies at the K'ai-yuan Monastery near Hung-chou, I [P'ei Hsiu] happened to enter its precincts. Presently I noticed a wall-painting and, by questioning the monk in charge of the monastery's administration, learnt that it portrayed a certain famous monk.

"Indeed?" I said. "Yes, I can see his likeness before me, but where is the man himself?" My question was received in silence.

So I remarked: "But surely there *are* Zen monks here in this temple, aren't there?"

"Yes," replied the monastery administrator, "*there is one.*"

After that, I requested an audience with the Master and repeated to him my recent conversation.

"P'ei Hsiu!" cried the Master.

"Sir!" I answered respectfully.

"Where are *you?*"

Realizing that no reply was possible to such a question, I hastened to ask our Master to re-enter the hall and continue his sermon.

2. This implies that he had been upon the Way many eons before the present world cycle began.

15

Chao-chou

(778–897)

In a time when human life expectancy was considerably shorter than it is today, many Ch'an masters enjoyed remarkable longevity—but none to compare with the 120-year span of Chao-chou Ts'ung-shen. The Methuselah of Ch'an began his practice early, seeking out Nan-ch'üan in his mountain-top retreat while still an unordained novice of seventeen. Chao-chou accompanied Nan-ch'üan when he accepted Lu Hsüan's invitation to head a monastery and continued his training there until the master's death in 834, when Chao-chou was fifty-seven. After the three-year period of mourning prescribed by Chinese culture, he wandered on pilgrimage for two decades before taking up residence at Kuan-yin Temple in the northern city and district that gave him the name Chao-chou. It must have been nice to rest his feet, but at eighty, he still had a forty-year teaching career ahead of him.

From this point on, people came to *him* rather than the other way around—and they came in large numbers, many of them from great distances. Two things drew them besides the teacher himself. The city boasted a stone bridge erected in the first or second century (and still standing today) that his compatriots regarded as one of the world's engineering wonders. In addition, the city's location made it a way station for travelers destined for Mt. Wu-t'ai, revered by Buddhists as the abode of Mañjushrī, the Bodhisattva of Great Wisdom. Two hundred monasteries were built there, of which fifty-eight remain even now. References both to the bridge and to Wu-t'ai occur repeatedly in Chao-chou's record.

Sightseers often feel disappointed by much-ballyhooed attractions—by the discrepancy, that is, between expectation and reality—and it was no different in ninth-century China. One monk came to the master and said that he had heard of the stone bridge of Chao-chou for a long time, but now had come and found just a simple wooden bridge. "You've only seen the simple wooden bridge," responded Chao-chou. "You haven't seen the stone bridge." When the monk then asked what the stone bridge was, Chao-chou answered, "Donkeys cross, horses cross."

This exchange exemplifies the "Ch'an of lips and tongue" for which the venerable master became known. What began as a complaint about the bridge—and, by implication, about Chao-chou himself—he deftly transformed into a direct presentation of the subtle bridge of Mind, over which not just donkeys and horses but all things pass. Speaking to his assembly one day, Chao-chou declared, "When I teach, I go directly to the core of the matter. If you say I should use the various techniques to fulfill your various needs, [you should] go to those who employ all the methods and teach all the doctrines." Plain speech was his way, and teachers ever since have expressed awe at his ability to illumine the great matter with a few ordinary words suited perfectly to the situation.

Chao-chou did not try to impress the crowd or even the high and mighty. At least two governors and various other officials called on him, offering support, but unlike Kuei-shan and Huang-po, he declined improvement or expansion of his small, rundown temple. In matters of social rank, Chao-chou consciously stood the norms on their heads: when people of high status came, he received them sitting where he was, but when people of low status came, he got up and went to meet them outside the temple gate.

Noteworthy in this connection is the unusually large number of women who appear in his record, most of them in settings outside the temple compound. Men still predominate numerically, but Chao-chou seems either to have appealed more to female students or to have made himself more accessible to them than did other T'ang-dynasty masters. The women he met seem well equipped for the encounter:

> When Chao-chou was outside of the monastery one day, he came across an old woman carrying a basket. He immediately asked, "Where are you going?"
> The old woman said, "I'm on my way to steal Chao-chou's bamboo shoots."
> Chao-chou said, "What will you do if you run into Chao-chou?"
> The old woman came up to Chao-chou and gave him a slap.

Eloquent and accessible though he was, Chao-chou left no successors who could meet Pai-chang's standard of bettering their master, and his line—indeed, the entire line of Nan-ch'üan—petered out after just a few more generations. Some commentators suggest that Chao-chou's "flavorless words" were too subtle for disciples to apprehend or to equal. Perhaps the stream of inquirers through the temple, together with his efforts outside the gate, made it impossible to give deserving students the sort of close and sustained training that Chao-chou had received from Nan-ch'üan. In any case, the old wizard's words spread far and wide, influencing all five houses of Ch'an in their formative stages, and they continue to befuddle and delight practitioners today. ⊗

FROM THE TRANSMISSION OF THE LAMP

Master Ts'ung-shen of the Kuan-yin Temple of Chao-chou was a native of Hao County of Ts'ao State. His family name was Ho. While still a young boy his head was shaved as a novice under a teacher of Hu-t'ung Temple of that state. Before he accepted the precepts he went to Ch'ih-yang to study Ch'an under Master Nan-ch'üan.

When he arrived, Nan-ch'üan was lying down and asked him, "Where have you come from lately?"

Ts'ung-shen replied, "I have just come from Shui-hsiang Temple."

Nan-ch'üan asked, "Have you seen the famous statue [of the Buddha there]?"

He said, "I have seen no celebrated image; I see only a reclining [Buddha]."

Nan-ch'üan asked, "Are you a novice under a master, or without a master?"

He replied, "I am a novice with a master."

Nan-ch'üan demanded, "Where is your master?"

Ts'ung-shen said, "The midwinter cold is now very severe. I am so happy to see you enjoying such good health, Master."

Nan-ch'üan recognized him as a promising vessel [of the dharma] and admitted him into his room for training in Ch'an.

On another occasion Ts'ung-shen asked, "What is the Tao?"

Nan-ch'üan replied, "Your everyday mind is the Tao."

He asked, "Can one reach towards it?"

Nan-ch'üan answered, "If you try to reach towards it, you will miss it."

Ts'ung-shen argued; "If I do not try to reach it, how can I know the Tao?"

Nan-ch'üan said, "The Tao has nothing to do with knowing it or not knowing it. Knowing it is merely deluded consciousness, and not knowing it is but nondifferentiation. When you enter the real Tao without doubt, it will be like the great sky, the vastness itself. How could it be right to argue within oneself whether it is right or wrong?"

One day Ts'ung-shen asked, "Where should he take rest who knows that he has it?"

Nan-ch'üan replied, "He should become a buffalo at the foot of the mountain."

Ts'ung-shen thanked him for this instruction, and Nan-ch'üan remarked, "In the middle of last night the moon appeared at the window."

Ts'ung-shen was made responsible for the fire at the monastery. One day he set fire to some wood and fastened the door; the smoke billowed up inside the roof. Then he yelled, "Help! Fire! Help! Fire!"

When all the monks came rushing up, he shouted out, "If anyone can say a word of Ch'an I will open the door."

Not one of the monks made an answer, but Nan-ch'üan passed the lock to him through the window and Ts'ung-shen opened the door.

The Master was planning a visit to Wu-t'ai [sometimes called Ching-liang: a sacred mountain dedicated to Mañjushrī and his golden lion]. Another monk wrote a poem to discourage him from going. It read:

What green mountain anywhere is not a place of training?
Why bother to trudge with a staff to Mt. Ching-liang?
Even if the Golden Lion reveals itself in the clouds,
This is not auspicious when looked at with the true eye.

The Master asked him, "What is the true eye?" The monk could find no answer.

After the Master had poured the influence of his Tao over the northern land, he was invited to live in Kuan-yin Temple of Chao-chou.

Mounting the dais in the dharma hall, the Master delivered this sermon to the congregation: "I feel as though a clear crystal is held in my hand. When a Mongolian comes before me, a Mongolian appears; when a Chinese man comes before me, a Chinese appears. I hold up a blade of grass to make use of the golden-bodied Buddha, sixteen feet high, and I hold up a golden-bodied Buddha, sixteen feet high, to make use of the blade of grass. The Buddha is distress and distress is the Buddha."

There was a monk present who said, "I wonder whose distress is the Buddha."

The Master replied, "The Buddha distresses himself for the sake of all other people."

The monk asked, "How can he get rid of it?"

The Master said, "Why should he get rid of it?"

When Master Chao-chou was sweeping the floor, a man observed, "You are a good Ch'an master. How is it that dust accumulates?"

The Master said, "It comes from outside."

The man said, "This is a pure clean monastery; how could there be specks of dust?"

The Master exclaimed, "Here comes another one!"

A monk on his way to visit Wu-t'ai Monastery asked an old woman, "Which way should I go for Mt. Wu-t'ai?"

The old woman answered, "Walk straight on."

The monk went on, whereupon the woman remarked, "He, too, has gone that way."

The monk mentioned this incident to the Master, who said, "Wait a little, I will inquire from the lady."

Next day the Master went out and asked the woman, "Which way must I follow for Mt. Wu-t'ai?"

She replied, "Walk straight on." As the Master was going, she remarked, "He, too, has gone that way."

The Master returned to the monastery and said to the monks, "I have tested the woman for you."

When the Master had gone out from the monastery, he met a woman who asked, "Where do you live, Venerable Sir?" He replied, "In the *hsi* of the Eastern Monastery of Chao-chou." The woman said nothing.

When he returned to the monastery, the Master asked the monks, "Which meaning of *hsi* should be applied?"

Some suggested *hsi* meaning "west" and others insisted on *hsi* meaning "dwelling."

The Master remarked, "You should all be judges in the administrative office."

The monks inquired, "O Master, why do you say that?"

The Master replied, "You are all literate."

A monk asked, "What is the treasure in the bag?"

The Master replied, "Keep your mouth closed."

A newly arrived monk had an interview with the Master and was asked, "Where do you come from?" He replied, "From the South, Sir."

The Master said, "Every form of Buddha-dharma is preserved in the South. What do you expect to gain by coming here?"

The monk said, "How could the dharma differ in the north or south?"

The Master remarked, "Even if you have come from Master Hsüeh-feng or Master Yün-chü, you still carry a board on one shoulder [have a one-sided view]."

A monk asked, "What is the Buddha?"

The Master replied, "The one in the shrine."

The monk protested, "But isn't the one in the shrine a clay figure made from mud?"

"Yes, that's right," said the Master.

"Then what is the Buddha?" asked the monk.

The Master said again, "The one in the shrine."

The monk asked, "What is my self-being?"

The Master said, "Have you had your breakfast?"

The monk replied, "Yes, I have."

The Master said, "Then wash your bowl."

All of a sudden the monk was enlightened.

When a monk was leaving the monastery, the Master asked him, "Where do you intend to go?"

The monk replied, "I am going to Hsüeh-feng Monastery."

The Master said, "If [I-ts'un of] Hsüeh-feng suddenly asks you, 'What message has your teacher?' how will you answer?"

The monk confessed, "I could not say. Please, Master, tell me."

The Master told him, "If it is winter, say 'How cold it is!' If it is summer, say 'How hot it is!'" Then he continued, "Hsüeh-feng may also ask you what the ultimate matter is."

The monk said, "I could not answer that."

The Master advised him, "Simply confess that you are not a messenger although you have really come from Chao-chou."

When the monk visited Hsüeh-feng, everything happened according to plan.

Hsüeh-feng remarked, "This can only have been devised by Chao-chou."

A monk asked, "What is the message of Bodhidharma?"

The Master knocked the leg of the Ch'an seat.

The monk queried, "Is it not the one thing only?"

The Master said, "If that is so, take it away."

Someone asked, "Master, will you enter into Hell?"

The Master answered, "[I'll be] the first to enter it."

The man said, "Why should a great and good Ch'an master enter Hell?"

The Master said, "Who would transform you through the teaching if I had not entered it?"

One day the Prince Governor of [the] Prefecture came with the royal princes and scholars to visit the temple. Remaining seated, the Master inquired, "Great Prince, have you understanding of this?"

The Prince replied, "No, I cannot grasp it."

The Master said, "Since my youth I have kept a vegetarian diet and my body is already aged. Even if I see people, I have no strength to descend from the Ch'an seat."

The Prince felt great admiration for the Master. The next day he sent a general to the Master with a message, and the Master came down from the seat in order to receive him.

Afterwards the Master's attendant said, "Master, you did not come down from the Ch'an seat even when you saw the great Prince coming to visit you. Why did you descend from it for the general who came to see you today?"

The Master replied, "My etiquette is not your etiquette. When a superior class of man comes, I deal with him from the Ch'an seat; when a middle grade of man comes, I get down to deal with him; and for dealings with men of the low grade, I step outside the temple gate. . . ."

The profound teaching of the Master spread widely across the country, and whenever people heard the name of Chao-chou they were all inspired to surrender themselves.

On November 2nd in the fourth year of Ch'ien-ning of T'ang [897], the Master laid himself down on his right side and passed away. He was 120 years old.

Once a man had asked the Master, "How old are you?" and he had replied, "There are numberless beads on the string of the rosary."

Later he received the posthumous title of Chen-chi Ta-shih [Great Master of Extreme Truth].

16

Te-shan

(780–865)

Te-shan Hsüan-ch'ien went down in annals of Ch'an as the unlikely savior of the line of Shih-t'ou, the person who kept the line alive at a time when it had begun to weaken, thus making possible the houses of Yün-men and Fa-yen. No one would have guessed this outcome when he set out for southern China in the first decades of the ninth century. Scholarly by nature, he had made his living until then as a Dharma lecturer, specializing in the brief text whose title, *The Diamond-Cutter Perfection of Wisdom Sutra,* is usually abbreviated to the *Diamond Sutra.* Surnamed Chou, he knew this ancient Indian scripture so well and spoke about it so frequently that people had nicknamed him Diamond Chou.

Like Tsung-mi, Po Chü-i, and many others hearing from afar about the Ch'an explosion that had occurred West of the River and South of the Lake, Te-shan (J., Tokusan) evidently felt concerned that the Dharma he dearly prized was being misrepresented. For a century or so, Hui-neng's descendants had advertised the *Diamond Sutra* as the Sixth Ancestor's favorite text, so Diamond Chou may have perceived these developments in the south as a professional affront or challenge. *The Blue Cliff Record* depicts him charging off in a considerable huff—and quickly getting his comeuppance at the hands of a little-known pair of "southern devils," an unnamed wise woman and the master Lung-t'an Ch'ung-hsin.

The latter was a Dharma grandson of Shih-t'ou, the former perhaps a student beyond the monastery walls. The question that she posed to Diamond Chou about his beloved sutra manifested the southern Ch'an approach of "direct pointing to the mind" and opened him up for the later ministrations of Lung-t'an (J., Ryūtan). Like Yung-chia, Te-shan is purported to have spent a single night under his teacher's roof, but in his case, the result was a complete religious turnaround, not just the confirmation of a prior realization.

The larger-than-life quality of this account marks it as a matter of mythos rather than of sober history, especially if one contrasts it with Chao-chou's forty years of training under Nan-ch'üan—or with the difficulty that we moderns have in changing our ways. Yet mythos and history rise, inevitably, from the same sources and hold much in common. Regard it as a mole or a pearl or a callous from bowing, but there probably was something unusual in the center of Huang-po's forehead. Likewise, the abrupt and thoroughgoing character of Te-shan's conversion experience, if we may use that term, probably has a basis in mundane fact.

Certainly it has doctrinal underpinnings going back to eighth-century debates about sudden and gradual enlightenment, but Ch'an writers have long remarked a psychological consistency in reports of Te-shan's life, a pattern that lends them a measure of historical credibility. In virtually every image the records give us, he demonstrates a peculiarly unyielding, even absolutist temperament. In his performance as a teacher, this characteristic expressed itself in an inclination either to keep silent or to apply his staff to students' backs, declaring "If you say a word, you get thirty blows. If you don't say a word, you get thirty blows." Whatever we make of this, the man who came to be called the Master of the Thirty Blows had an odd and successful career, capped with the development of two superb Dharma heirs, Yen-t'ou and Hsüeh-feng (Chapter 19). ⊗

FROM THE BLUE CLIFF RECORD

Originally Te-shan was a lecturing monk, expounding the *Diamond-Cutter Scripture* in western Shu [Szechwan]. According to what it says in that teaching, in the process of the knowledge attained after diamond-like concentration, one studies the majestic conduct of Buddhas for a thousand eons and studies the refined practices of Buddhas for ten thousand eons before finally fulfilling Buddhahood. On the other hand, the "southern devils" at this time were saying "Mind itself is Buddha." Consequently Te-shan became very incensed and went traveling on foot, carrying some commentaries; he went straight to the South to destroy this crew of devils. You see from how aroused he got what a fierce keen fellow he was.

When he first got to Li-chou [in Hunan], he met an old woman selling fried cakes by the roadside; he put down his commentaries to buy some refreshment to lighten his mind. The old woman said, "What is that you're carrying?" Te-shan said, "Commentaries on the *Diamond-Cutter [Sutra].*" The old woman said, "I have a question for you: if you can answer it I'll give you some fried cakes to refresh your mind; if you can't answer, you'll have to go somewhere else to buy." Te-shan said, "Just ask." The old woman said, "The *Diamond-Cutter [Sutra]* says, 'Past mind can't be grasped, present mind can't be grasped, future mind can't be grasped': which mind does the learned monk desire to refresh?" Te-shan was speechless. The old woman directed him to go call on Lung-t'an.

As soon as Te-shan crossed the threshold he said, "Long have I heard of Lung-t'an [Dragon Pond], but now that I've arrived here, there's no pond to see and no dragon appears." Master Lung-t'an came out from behind a screen and said, "You have really arrived at Lung-t'an." Te-shan bowed and withdrew. During the night Te-shan entered Lung-t'an's room and stood in attendance till late at night. Lung-t'an said, "Why don't you go?" Te-shan bade farewell, lifted up the curtain, and went out; he saw that it was dark outside, so he turned around and said, "It's dark outside." Lung-t'an lit a paper lantern and handed it to Te-shan; as soon as Te-shan took it, Lung-t'an blew it out. Te-shan was vastly and greatly enlightened.

Immediately he bowed to Lung-t'an, who said, "What have you seen that you bow?" Te-shan answered, "From now on I will never again doubt what's on the tongues of the venerable teaching masters of the world."

The next day Lung-t'an went up into the teaching hall and said, "There is one among you with teeth like a forest of swords and a mouth like a bowl of blood; even if you hit him with a staff, he wouldn't turn back. Another day he will ascend to the summit of a solitary peak and establish my path there." Then Te-shan took all his commentaries in front of the teaching hall and raised a torch over them, declaring, "Even to plumb all abstruse locutions is like a single hair in the great void; to exhaust the essential workings of the world is like a single drop of water cast into a vast valley." Then he burned the commentaries.

Later he heard the Kuei-shan's teaching was flourishing, so he traveled to Kuei-shan to meet him as an adept. Without even untying his bundle, he went straight to the teaching hall, where he walked back and forth from east to west and west to east, looked around, and said, "Nothing, no one." Then he went out. Tell me, what was his meaning? Wasn't he crazy?

This old fellow Kuei-shan still was not taken in by that [Te-shan]; anyone but Kuei-shan would have been crushed by him.

On his way out Te-shan got as far as the monastery gate, but then he said to himself, "Still, I shouldn't be so coarse." He wanted to bring out his guts, his innermost heart, in a Dharma battle with Kuei-shan; so he went back in with full ceremony to meet him. As Kuei-shan sat there, Te-shan lifted up his sitting mat and said, "Teacher!" Kuei-shan reached for his whisk; Te-shan then shouted, shook his sleeves, and left. How extraordinary!

Te-shan turned his back on the teaching hall, put on his straw sandals, and departed. Tell me, what was his meaning?

Afterwards, this old fellow [Kuei-shan] was unhurried; when evening came he finally asked the head monk, "Where is that newcomer who just came?" The head monk replied, "At that time, he turned his back on the teaching hall, put on his straw sandals, and left." Kuei-shan said, "Hereafter that lad will go up to the summit of a solitary peak, build himself a grass hut, and go on scolding the Buddhas and reviling the Ancestors."

FROM THE TRANSMISSION OF THE LAMP

In the beginning of the T'ai-chung era [847–860], Hsueh Yen-wang, the governor of Wu-ling [in Hunan], restored the monastery on Mt. Te and called it the Meditation Abode of Ancient Worthies. He was going to look for a man of knowledge to dwell there, when he heard of the master's practice of the Way. Though he repeatedly invited him, the master did not come down from the mountain. Yen-wang then fabricated a ruse, sending a runner to falsely accuse the master of having violated the laws regarding tea and salt. Having taken the master into his domain, he looked up to him with reverence and insisted that he dwell there, and reveal the way of the sect.

In the hall, the master said, "There is nothing in the self, so do not seek falsely; what is attained by false seeking is not real attainment. You just have nothing in your mind, and no mind in things; then you will be empty and spiritual, tranquil and sublime. Any talk of beginning or end would all be self-deception. The slightest entanglement of thought is the foundation of the three mires [hell, animality, hungry ghosthood]; a momentarily aroused feeling is a hindrance for ten thousand eons. The name 'sage' and the label 'ordinary man' are merely empty sounds; exceptional form and mean appearance are both illusions. If you want to seek them, how can you avoid trouble? Even if you despise them, they still become a great source of anxiety. In the end there is no benefit."

Hsüeh-feng asked, "In the immemorial custom of the sect, what doctrine is used to teach people?" The master said, "Our sect has no words; in reality there is no doctrine to be given to mankind."

Yen-t'ou heard of this and said, "The old man of Mt. Te has a spine as strong as iron; it cannot be broken. Even so, when it comes to the way of expounding the teaching, he still lacks something."

Before his death he said to his disciples, "Grasping emptiness and pursuing echoes wearies your mind and spirit. When awakened from a dream, you realize it was false; after all, what matter is there?" When he finished speaking, he died sitting at rest.

17

Lin-chi

(D. 867?)

Just as Te-shan is known for his blows and Chao-chou for his simple eloquence, Lin-chi I-hsüan is known for his shout—a roar sounding something like KHAT! that he issued as a presentation of Buddha-nature. While each of these reputations is deserved to a degree, they are grossly reductionistic. Lin-chi's bellow was no more than a small part of his rich, inventive, and highly effective teaching. His lively and extensive discourse record undercuts the popular image of him as a sort of Dharma thug, displaying his mastery of Mahāyāna sutras and his creativity in utilizing and interpreting them. He did shout at, beat, and berate his students, but he also originated some of the most sophisticated, even lovely, expressions of the fundamental matter ever to appear in Ch'an. And it was all to the same end: to introduce us to, as he put it, "the true person of no rank who is constantly going in and out the gateways of your face."

Born and raised in the north, Lin-chi (J., Rinzai) traveled far south to study with Huang-po and eventually received transmission from him. According to Lin-chi's record, three years passed before he even dared to approach Huang-po with a question, and when he did, he got no more than a taste of the old master's stick. Frustrated, supposing his way was blocked by bad karma, he decided to leave. Huang-po referred him to another teacher, Kao-an Ta-yü, who is reported to have brought him to awakening with a few well-chosen phrases. Lin-chi continued his training with Huang-po for an unspecified period thereafter, making at least one excursion to Mt. Kuei, where he had exchanges with both Kuei-shan and Yang-shan. He also studied with Te-shan at least for a while:

> The Master [Lin-chi] was standing in attendance at Te-shan's side. Te-shan said, "I'm tired today!"
> The Master said, "What's this old fellow doing talking in his sleep?"
> Te-shan struck the Master a blow.
> The Master grabbed the chair Te-shan was sitting on and turned it over.
> Te-shan let the matter end there.

Later, Lin-chi sent one of his best students to check on Te-shan, and Ch'an annals link the two masters closely for reasons of style and disposition as well as for their record of contact.

Lin-chi returned north to teach at a small temple called Lin-chi-yüan, the Monastery Overlooking the Ford, which was not far from the city of Chao-chou and likewise on the route to Mt. Wu-t'ai. Though older than Lin-chi, Chao-chou had not yet hung up his traveling staff at Kuan-yin Temple and paid a call before he did. Lin-chi's record says he was washing his feet when his visitor arrived, but Chao-chou put his question anyway, inquiring, "What's the meaning of Bodhi-dharma's coming from India?"

"I happen to be washing my feet just now," Lin-chi replied. Chao-chou came closer and made as if listening intently. "In that case, I'll ladle out another dipper of dirty water!" exclaimed Lin-chi. Chao-chou promptly took leave.

Scholars cannot pin down dates for Lin-chi, but he probably moved to the temple by the ford in about 850, at the age of about forty. By that time, political changes had created new circumstances in the north, helping open the way there for southern Ch'an. Northern Buddhist institutions had been hurt by the An Lu-shan Rebellion (755–763), and they suffered outright repression in the early 840s, climaxing with the all-out Hui ch'ang persecution of 845. During this lat-ter period, monks and nuns were defrocked en masse, some even executed, and thousands of monasteries and temples were destroyed. Southern Ch'an was largely protected from these developments by its distance from the capital, its relatively high degree of economic independence, its good standing with local officials, and a weakening of imperial authority that had occurred after 755. This last factor gave provincial rulers increased latitude to exercise their own prerog-ative, and the officials who welcomed both Lin-chi and Chao-chou to their new positions undoubtedly were doing exactly that.

Lin-chi's teaching was cut short by his death in 866 or early 867, when he was in his middle fifties. Despite his relatively brief tenure and isolated location, he had twenty-one successors and received the posthumous imperial honors that were becoming customary for noted Ch'an masters. Among his heirs, Hsing-hua Ts'ung-chiang established the lasting line that came to be thought of as the house of Lin-chi and that remains alive today, best known in the Rinzai Zen of Japan. Another successor, San-sheng Hui-jan, compiled the master's lectures and dia-logue into a sparkling record that spread Lin-chi's influence far and wide. ⊗

FROM THE RECORD OF LIN-CHI

The Master instructed the group, saying: "Followers of the Way, the Dharma of the buddhas calls for no special undertakings. Just act ordinary, without trying to do anything particular. Move your bowels, piss, get dressed, eat your rice, and if you get tired, then lie down. Fools may laugh at me, but wise men will know what I mean.

"A man of old said, 'People who try to do something about what is outside themselves are nothing but blockheads.'¹ If, wherever you are, you take the role of host, then whatever spot you stand in will be a true one. Then whatever circumstances surround you, they can never pull you awry. Even if you're faced with bad karma left over from the past, or the five crimes that bring on the hell of incessant suffering, these will of themselves become the great sea of emancipation.²

"Students these days haven't the slightest comprehension of the Dharma. They're like sheep poking with their noses—whatever they happen on they immediately put in their mouths. They can't tell a gentleman from a lackey, can't tell a host from a guest. People like that come to the Way with twisted minds, rushing in wherever they see a crowd. They don't deserve to be called true men who have left the household.³ All they are in fact is true householders, men of secular life.

"Someone who has left household life must know how to act ordinary and have a true and proper understanding, must know how to tell buddhas from devils, to tell true from sham, to tell common mortals from sages. If they can tell these apart, you can call them true men who have left the household. But if they can't tell a buddha from a devil, then all they've done is leave one household to enter another. You might describe them as living beings who are creating karma. But you could never call them true men who have left the household."

Someone asked, "What do you mean by the true Buddha, the true Dharma, and the true Way? Would you be good enough to explain to us?"

The Master said, "Buddha—this is the cleanness and purity of the mind. The Dharma—this is the shining brightness of the mind. The Way—this is the pure light that is never obstructed anywhere. The three are in fact one. All are empty names and have no true reality."

"Suppose you yearn to be a sage. Sage is just a word, *sage.* There are some types of students who go off to Mt. Wu-t'ai looking for Mañjushrī. They're wrong from the very start! Mañjushrī isn't on Mt. Wu-t'ai. Would you like to get to know Mañjushrī? You here in front of my eyes, carrying out your activities, from first to last never changing, wherever you go never doubting—this is the living Mañjushrī!

"Your mind that each moment shines with the light of nondiscrimination— wherever it may be, this is the true Samantabhadra. Your mind that each moment is capable of freeing itself from its shackles, everywhere emancipated—this is the

1. From a poem attributed to the eighth-century Ch'an master Ming-tsan, or Lan-tsan, of Mt. Nan-yüeh.
2. The five crimes are usually given as (1) killing one's father, (2) killing one's mother, (3) killing an *arhat*, (4) doing injury to a buddha, and (5) causing dissension in the Monastic Order. Any one of these condemns the doer to suffer in the *Avichi* hell, the hell of incessant suffering.
3. *Ch'u-chia,* to leave the family or the household life, is the common term in Chinese for becoming a monk or nun.

method of meditating on Kuan-yin.[4] These three act as host and companion to one another, all three appearing at the same time when they appear, one in three, three in one.[5] Only when you have understood all this will you be ready to read the scriptural teachings."

Someone asked, "What was Bodhidharma's purpose in coming from the west?"[6]

The Master said, "If he had had a purpose, he wouldn't have been able to save even himself!"

The questioner said, "If he had no purpose, then how did the Second Ancestor manage to get the Dharma?"

The Master said, "Getting means not getting."

"If it means not getting," said the questioner, "then what do you mean by 'not getting'?"

The Master said, "You can't seem to stop your mind from racing around everywhere seeking something. That's why the Ancestor said, 'Hopeless fellows— using their heads to look for their heads!'[7] You must right now turn your light around and shine it on yourselves, not go seeking somewhere else. Then you will understand that in body and mind you are no different from the Ancestors and buddhas, and that there is nothing to do. Do that and you may speak of 'getting the Dharma.'

"Fellow believers, at this time, having found it impossible to refuse, I have been addressing you, putting forth a lot of trashy talk. But make no mistake! In my view, there are in fact no great number of principles to be grasped. If you want to use the thing, then use it. If you don't want to use it, then let it be.

"People here and there talk about the six rules and the ten thousand practices, supposing that these constitute the Dharma of the buddhas.[8] But I say that these are just adornments of the sect, the trappings of Buddhism. They are not the Dharma of the buddhas. You may observe the fasts and observe the precepts, or carry a dish of oil without spilling it, but if your Dharma-eye is not wide open, then all you're doing is running up a big debt.[9] One day you'll have to pay for all the food wasted on you! . . .

4. The method of calling on the saving power of the Bodhisattva Avalokiteshvara, or Kuan-yin, described in chapter 25 of the *Lotus Sutra*.

5. The three bodhisattvas represent wisdom (Mañjushrī), religious practice (Samantabhadra), and compassion (Kuan-yin). At different times one or the other takes the leading role, with the other two acting as attendants.

6. A standard inquiry in Ch'an practice, similar to the question "What is the basic meaning of Buddhism?"

7. The identity of the Ancestor and source of the quotation are unknown.

8. The ten thousand practices are various kinds of devotional acts.

9. Monks were expected to fast from noon until morning of the following day. The practice of filling a dish with oil and carrying it on the head for a given distance without spilling any is . . . an exercise for cultivating concentration of mind.

"As for those who go off to live all alone on a solitary peak, eating only one meal a day at the hour of dawn, sitting in meditation for long periods without lying down, performing circumambulations six times a day—such persons are all just creating karma.[10] Then there are those who cast away their head and eyes, marrow and brains, their domains and cities, wives and children, elephants, horses, the seven precious things, throwing them all away.[11] People who think in that way are all inflicting pain on their body and mind, and in consequence will invite some kind of painful retribution. Better to do nothing, to be simple, direct, with nothing mixed in.

"Followers of the Way, don't take the Buddha to be some sort of ultimate goal. In my view he's more like the hole in a privy. Bodhisattvas and *arhats* are all so many *cangues* and chains, things for fettering people. . . .

"Followers of the Way, there is no Buddha to be gained, and the Three Vehicles, the five natures, the teaching of the perfect and immediate enlightenment are all simply medicines to cure diseases of the moment.[12] None have any true reality. Even if they had, they would still all be mere shams, placards proclaiming superficial matters, so many words lined up, pronouncements of such kind.

"Followers of the Way, even if you can understand a hundred sutras and treatises, you're not as good as one plain monk who does nothing. As soon as you acquire a little of such understanding, you start treating others with scorn and contempt, vying and struggling with them like so many *asuras*,[13] blinded by the ignorance of self and others, forever creating karma that will send you to hell. You're like the monk Good Star who understood all the twelve divisions of the teachings but fell into hell alive, the earth unwilling to tolerate him.[14] Better to do nothing, to leave off all that.

> When you get hungry, eat your rice;
> when you get sleepy, close your eyes.

10. Circumambulating a statue of the Buddha and paying obedience to it at six fixed times, three in the daytime and three in the night.

11. As the ruler did who is described in chapter 12 of the *Lotus Sutra*. The seven precious things in the *Lotus Sutra* are gold, silver, lapis lazuli, seashell, agate, pearl, and carnelian.

12. The Three Vehicles [are the three main streams of Buddhism]. The five natures, a doctrine of the Fa-hsiang school, divides human beings into five groups according to their inborn capacity for enlightenment. The teaching of the perfect and immediate enlightenment is the One Vehicle doctrine of Mahāyāna Buddhism, especially as expounded in the T'ien-t'ai and Hua-yen schools.

13. [The *asuras* are fighting titans, one of the six forms of being in classical Buddhism, here (as customary in Ch'an) interpreted as representing human experience.—Eds.]

14. Good Star, or Sunakshatra, was a disciple of the Buddha who was proficient at reciting the scriptures but could not understand their true meaning. As a result of his mistaken views he fell into hell while still alive. (See Chapter 33 of the *Nirvāna Sūtra*.)

Fools may laugh at me,
but wise men will know what I mean.[15]

"Followers of the Way, don't search for anything in written words. The exertions of your mind will tire it out, you'll gulp cold air and gain nothing.[16] Better to realize that at every moment all is conditioned and without true birth, to go beyond the bodhisattvas of the Three Vehicle provisional doctrines.

"Fellow believers, don't dawdle your days away! In the past, before I had come to see things right, there was nothing but blackness all around me. But I knew that I shouldn't let the time slip by in vain, and so, belly all afire, mind in a rush, I raced all over in search of the Way. Later I was able to get help from others, so that finally I could do as I'm doing today, talking with you followers of the Way. As followers of the Way, let me urge you not to do what you are doing just for the sake of clothing and food. See how quickly the world goes by! A good friend and teacher is hard to find, as rarely met with as the *udumbara* flower.[17]

"You've heard here and there that there's this old fellow Lin-chi, and so you come here intending to confront him in debate and push him to the point where he can't answer. But when I come at students like that with my whole body, their eyes are wide open enough but their mouths can't utter a word. Dumbfounded, they have no idea how to answer me. Then I say to them, 'The trampling of a bull elephant is more than a donkey can stand!'[18]

"You go all around pointing to your chest, puffing out your sides, saying, '*I* understand Ch'an! *I* understand the Way!' But when two or three of you turn up here, you're completely helpless. For shame! With that body and mind of yours you go around everywhere flapping your two lips, hoodwinking the village people, but the day will come when you'll taste the iron cudgels of hell! You're not men who have left the household—you belong, all of you, in the realm of the *asuras!*

"Followers of the Way, if you wish to be always in accord with the Dharma, never give way to doubt. 'Spread it out and it fills the whole Dharma-realm, gather it up and it's tinier than a thread of hair.'[19] Its lone brightness gleaming forth, it has never lacked anything. 'The eye doesn't see it, the ear doesn't hear it.'[20] What shall we call this thing? A man of old said, 'Say something about a

15. From the poem by Ming-tsan, or Lan-tsan, of Mt. Nan-yüeh.
16. It has been suggested that the person "gulps cold air" because he is reading aloud, though the meaning is uncertain.
17. The *udumbara,* an imaginary plant often mentioned in Buddhist writings, blooms only once in three thousand years.
18. Lin-chi is quoting from the end of chapter 6 of the *Vimalakīrti Sūtra.*
19. From the *Chüeh-kuan lun* by Niu-t'ou Fa-jung (594–657).
20. From the *I-po-ko* or "Song of One Alms Bowl" by the Ch'an master Pei-tu.

thing and already you're off the mark.'²¹ You'll just have to see it for yourselves. What other way is there? But there's no end to this talk. Each of you, do your best! Thank you for your trouble."

The Master said to a nun, "Well come, or ill come?"²²
    The nun gave a shout.
    The Master picked up his stick and said, "Speak then, speak!"
    The nun shouted once more.
    The Master struck her.

The Master said to Hsing-shan, "How about that white ox on the bare ground?"²³
    Hsing-shan said, "Moo, moo!"
    The Master said, "Lost your voice?"
    Hsing-shan said, "How about you, Reverend?"
    The Master said, "This beast!"

One day Constant Attendant Wang called on the Master and together they went to look at the monks' hall.
    Constant Attendant Wang said, "This hallful of monks—do they read sutras perhaps?"
    The Master said, "No, they don't read sutras."
    "Do they perhaps learn how to meditate?" asked the Constant Attendant.
    "No, they don't learn how to meditate," said the Master.
    The Constant Attendant said, "If they don't read sutras and they don't learn how to meditate, what in fact *do* they do?"
    The Master said, "We're training all of them to become buddhas and Ancestors."
    The Constant Attendant said, "Gold dust may be precious, but if it gets in the eye it can blind.²⁴ What about it?"
    The Master said, "And I always thought you were just an ordinary fellow!"

21. The words of Nan-yüeh Huai-jang (677–744).
22. In early Buddhism, novices entering a monastery were greeted with the words, "Well come, monk!" Lin-chi is playing on the conventional phrase.
23. Hsing-shan is Chien-hung of Hsing-shan in Cho-chou, a Dharma heir of Yün-yen T'an-sheng (780–841). Lin-chi is referring to the parable in chapter 3 of the *Lotus Sutra,* in which a rich man, in order to lure his unwary children out of the burning house where they are playing, offers them a beautiful carriage drawn by a white ox, promising to give it to them after they get out of the house. The burning house represents the realm of delusion or ignorance, the carriage with the white ox is the One Vehicle of the Buddha's teaching as set forth in the *Lotus Sutra,* and the "bare ground" is the area outside the house, the realm of enlightenment.
24. A proverb of the time. In Ch'an, of course, any talk of becoming a buddha is taboo.

The Master went to see Feng-lin.[25] On the way he met an old woman. "Off some-where?" she asked.

"Off to Feng-lin," the Master said.

"I think you'll find that Feng-lin isn't in right now," the old woman said.

"Off somewhere?" said the Master.

The old woman walked away.

The Master called after her. She turned her head, whereupon the Master walked away.

LIN-CHI'S "FOUR PROCEDURES"

The Master gave an evening lecture, instructing the group as follows: "At times one takes away the person but does not take away the environment. At times one takes away the environment but does not take away the person. At times one takes away both the person and the environment. At times one takes away neither the person nor the environment."[26]

At that time a monk asked, "What does it mean to take away the person but not take away the environment?"

The Master said, "Warm sun shines forth, spreading the earth with brocade. The little child's hair hangs down, white as silk thread."

The monk asked, "What does it mean to take away the environment but not take away the person?"

The Master said, "The king's commands have spread throughout the realm. Generals beyond the border no longer taste the smoke and dust of battle."

The monk asked. "What does it mean to take away both the person and the environment?"

The Master said, "All word cut off from Ping and Fen—they stand alone, a region apart."[27]

The monk said, "What does it mean to take away neither the person nor the environment?"

The Master said, "The king ascends his jeweled hall; country oldsters sing their songs."

25. The identity of Feng-lin is not known.
26. *Ching,* the word translated here as "environment," could perhaps better be rendered as "circumstances" or "surroundings" in many contexts, but [Watson] translated it as "environment" throughout because it is such a key concept in Buddhist thought.
27. Ping and Fen are outlying regions in northern China. In Lin-chi's time, local military governors often defied the central government and established their areas as virtually independent states.

18

Tung-shan

(807–869)

L in-chi's life coincided almost exactly with that of Tung-shan Liang-chieh principal source of the Ch'an house known as Ts'ao-tung (J., Sōtō). Over the next several centuries, the Lin-chi and Ts'ao-tung houses solidified into sects clearly distinguishable by their diverging approaches to practice and, later, by their institutional structures. A rivalry developed between them, especially in Japan, but it seems to have no basis in the lives, words, or methods of their founders. Tung-shan and Lin-chi literally walked the same paths as they took part in the great Dharma free-for-all of the late T'ang period. Their backgrounds, natures, and teaching styles differed, yet they shared a genius for expressing the Way in direct, impromptu exchanges, and both felt a call to synthesize from the ever-growing store of Ch'an teachings and metaphors a few succinct and subtle formulations that future generations came to revere. These include Lin-chi's "Four Procedures" and Tung-shan's "Five Degrees of Honor and Virtue," the final text of this chapter.

Having grown up in far eastern China, Tung-shan journeyed not south but west to reach the flourishing nexus of Ch'an established by Shih-t'ou and Ma-tsu. He visited both Nan-ch'üan and Kuei-shan before settling down to study in earnest with Yün-yen T'an-sheng (780?–841). A Dharma grandson of Shih-t'ou, Yün-yen (J., Ungan) lived in a stone chamber on the mountain that gave him his name. The phrase in Tung-shan's record describing the master's domicile (translated in our selection as "linked caves") indicates a series of interconnected hermit cells hewn in a cliff face; such cells remain not merely in evidence but in active use in China today. The colony of hermits dwelling there constituted Yün-yen's assembly.

This was the right place for Tung-shan to pose the burning question that motivated his search: how can inanimate things teach the Dharma? In one form or another, such questions were in the air. "Does a dog have Buddha-nature?" one of his contemporaries asked Chao-chou, drawing the famous "No" (Ch., *wu*; J., *mu*) that would, within a couple of centuries, come into play as a koan. Tung-shan's record quotes both Kuei-shan and Yün-yen answering his question in the affirmative and citing Mahāyāna sutras in support of their position. But the idea that inanimate things teach the Dharma was a new one, and both masters bent the letter, and probably even the spirit, of the texts they quoted. Later Ch'an firmly resolved this matter in favor of inanimate things both having and expressing Buddha-nature, a position that remains controversial even today.

Its doctrinal weaknesses notwithstanding, Yün-yen's teaching on this question evidently sufficed to open young Tung-shan's eyes, for his record continues with a poem expressing what he realized. The word used here is the Chinese for *gāthā*, but Tung-shan's verse scarcely resembles the *gāthās* of old. Rather, it belongs to a new genre of enlightenment poems that arose about this time and soon became a fixture in Ch'an and Zen literature. Such poems were later termed *tou-chi-chieh* (J., *tokinoge*), which translates as "*gāthās* of mutual understanding"—poems that reflect a true meeting of minds. The minds involved are those of the student and the teacher but also, implicitly, of the student and all enlightened Dharma ancestors, of mind and Mind.

Tung-shan was just thirty-four when Yün-yen died, and he had already taken leave to continue on pilgrimage. He is said to have practiced after Yün-yen's death with Tao-wu Yüan-chih (J., Dōgo Enchi), who was Yün-yen's brother through ties of both blood and Dharma lineage. Tao-wu's biography puts his demise six years before Yün-yen's, however, so one chronicler or another has obviously erred. In any case, Tung-shan did study further, testing and sharpening his insight through many encounters on the road. A great second awakening occurred one day when he glimpsed his own reflection as he crossed a river, and again he marked the experience with a *gāthā*, this one manifesting his delight at seeing Yün-yen truly eye to eye, everywhere he looked.

Tung-shan's record contains a number of other poems as well, both long and short, doctrinal and occasional. His doctrinal poems hark back to those of his Dharma ancestor Shih-t'ou, while the occasional verses anticipate the flowering of Ch'an poetry yet to come. His legacy also included twenty-six successors, of whom Ts'ao-shan Pen-chi (Chapter 20) came to be considered co-founder of the Ts'ao-tung house. The only enduring Ts'ao-tung lineage, however, flowed from Yün-chü Tao-ying (J., Ungo Dōyō), who figures more conspicuously in Tung-shan's record than any other successor and developed the widest reputation as a teacher. Tung-shan himself, again like Lin-chi, seems to have risen in prominence after his death, but he was known well enough in his own day to attract correspondence from Po Chü-i and receive the usual imperial honors marking his career. 〰

FROM THE RECORD OF TUNG-SHAN

The Master, whose personal name was Liang-chieh, was a member of the Yü family of Kuei-chi. Once, as a child, when reading the *Heart Sutra* with his tutor, he came to the line, "There is no eye, no ear, no nose, no tongue, no body, no mind." He immediately felt his face with his hand, then said to his tutor, "I have eyes, ears, a nose, a tongue, and so on; why does the sutra say they don't exist?"[1]

---

1. The *Heart Sutra*, an abbreviated Perfection of Wisdom text, is a body of thought central to much of the Mahāyāna tradition. It teaches, in part, the ultimate emptiness of all things, including the Dharmas of the earlier Buddhist teachings.

This took the tutor by surprise, and, recognizing Tung-shan's uniqueness, he said, "I am not capable of being your teacher."

From there the Master went to Wu-hsieh Mountain, where, after making obeisance to Ch'an Master Mo, he took the robe and shaved his head.[2] When he was twenty-one he went to Sung Mountain[3] and took the Complete Precepts.

[After visiting Nan-ch'üan,] the Master made a visit to Kuei-shan and said to him, "I have recently heard that the National Teacher Chung of Nan-yang[4] maintains the doctrine that nonsentient beings expound the Dharma.[5] I have not yet comprehended the subtleties of this teaching."

Kuei-shan said, "Can you, Acarya, remember the details of what you heard?"

"Yes, I can," said the Master.

"Then why don't you try to repeat it for me?" said Kuei-shan.

The Master began, "A monk asked Hui-chung, 'What sort of thing is the mind of the ancient buddhas?'"[6]

"The National Teacher replied, 'It's wall and tile rubble.' "[7]

" 'Wall and tile rubble! Isn't that something nonsentient?' asked the monk.

" 'It is,' replied the National Teacher.

"The monk said, 'And yet it can expound the Dharma?'

" 'It is constantly expounding it, radiantly expounding it, expounding it without ceasing,' replied the National Teacher.

2. Wu-hsieh Mountain is located in Chu-chi hsien, Chekiang. Ch'an Master Mo (747–818), a member of the second generation of Ma-tsu's line, made this his center, becoming known as Ling-mo of Wu-hsieh.

3. Sung Mountain, which is in northern Teng-feng hsien, Honan, is the central peak of China's "Five Peaks" and the location of the Shaolin Temple with its ordination platform.

4. Chung of Nan-yang is Hui-chung (d. 775), a disciple of Hui-neng. According to his biography, until he was sixteen, he never spoke, nor did he leave the immediate vicinity of his house. However, when he saw a Ch'an monk passing his house one day, he began speaking and requested ordination. As a result, the monk directed him to Hui-neng. He is said to have lived forty years on Po-yai Mountain in Nan-yang, modern Honan, without leaving. However, by 761 his fame had spread, and he was summoned to the capital, where he received the title "National Teacher" (kuo-shih).

5. The question of whether nonsentient beings possess Buddha-nature and thus, by extension, are capable of expressing Dharma—a major controversy in early T'ang China—grew out of differing interpretations of the Nirvāna Sūtra, particularly the line, "All beings, without exception, possess Buddha-nature." Hui-chung was a prominent spokesman for the belief that nonsentient beings are included under "all beings." On one occasion he cited the Avatamsaka Sūtra, "The Buddha's body completely fills the Dharma-realm and is manifest to all beings." Often cited in opposition to this is the following passage from the Nirvāna Sūtra: "Such nonsentient things as walls, tile, and stones lack Buddha-nature. All else can be said to have Buddha-nature." Hui-chung could not have been unaware of this passage when he used wall and tile rubble as examples of the mind of the ancient Buddhas.

6. "Ancient buddha" is a term commonly used in Ch'an literature to refer to distinguished former masters.

7. Chuang-tzu, when asked whether the Tao was found among the lowly, replied that the Tao "exists in the crickets, . . . in the grasses, . . . in tiles and bricks, . . . and in shit and piss."

"The monk asked, 'Then why haven't I heard it?'

"The National Teacher said, 'You yourself haven't heard it, but this can't hinder those who are able to hear it.'

" 'What sort of person acquires such hearing?' asked the monk.

" 'All the sages have acquired such hearing,' replied the National Teacher.

"The monk asked, 'Can you hear it, Ho-shang?'

" 'No, I can't,' replied the National Teacher.

"The monk said, 'If you haven't heard it, how do you know that nonsentient beings expound the Dharma?'

"The National Teacher said, 'Fortunately, I haven't heard it. If I had, I would be the same as the sages, and you, therefore, would not hear the Dharma that I teach.'

" 'In that case, ordinary people would have no part in it,' said the monk.

" 'I teach for ordinary people, not sages,' replied the National Teacher.

" 'What happens after ordinary people hear you?' asked the monk.

" 'Then they are no longer ordinary people,' said the National Teacher.

"The monk asked, 'According to which sutra does it say that nonsentient beings expound the Dharma?'

" 'Clearly, you shouldn't suggest that it's not part of the sutras. Haven't you seen it in the *Avatamsaka Sūtra?* It says, "The earth expounds Dharma, living beings expound it, throughout the three times, everything expounds it." ' "[8] The Master thus completed his narration.

Kuei-shan said, "That teaching also exists here. However, one seldom encounters someone capable of understanding it."

Tung-shan said, "I still don't understand it clearly. Would the Master please comment?"

Kuei-shan raised his fly whisk,[9] saying, "Do you understand?"

"No, I don't. Please, Ho-shang, explain," replied Tung-shan.

Kuei-shan said, "It can never be explained to you by means of the mouth of one born of mother and father."

Tung-shan asked, "Does the Master have any contemporaries in the Way who might clarify this problem for me?"

"From here, go to Yu-hsien of Li-ling where you will find some linked caves.[10]

8. *Avatamsaka Sūtra.* The "three times" are past, present, and future, i.e., always.

9. The fly whisk usually consisted of the tail hair of some animal attached to a handle. According to tradition, the Buddha had approved of its use by the monks as a means of brushing off bothersome insects without killing them. However, because there was a tendency to use rare and expensive materials to construct the whisk, the Buddha stipulated that only certain ordinary materials be used: felt, hemp, finely torn cloth, tattered items, or tree twigs. Paintings of Buddhist monks indicate that in China this stipulation was ignored. In Ch'an it was a symbol of authority, generally held, when teaching, as an indication that the teaching was the correct Dharma.

10. Yu-hsien of Li-ling is in the northwest part of Ch'ang-sha in modern Hunan.

Living in those caves is a man of the Way, Yün-yen.[11] If you are able to 'push aside the grass and gaze into the wind,'[12] then you will find him worthy of your respect," said Kuei-shan.

"Just what sort of man is he?" asked Tung-shan.

Kuei-shan replied, "Once he said to this old monk,[13] 'What should I do if I wish to follow the Master?'

"This old monk replied, 'You must immediately cut off your defilements.'

"He said, 'Then will I come up to the Master's expectation?'

"This old monk replied, 'You will get absolutely no answer as long as I am here.' "

Tung-shan accordingly took leave of Kuei-shan and proceeded directly to Yün-yen's. Making reference to his previous encounter with Kuei-shan, he immediately asked what sort of person was able to hear the Dharma expounded by nonsentient beings.

Yün-yen said, "Nonsentient beings are able to hear it."

"Can you hear it, Ho-shang?" asked Tung-shan.

Yün-yen replied, "If I could hear it, then you would not be able to hear the Dharma that I teach."

"Why can't I hear it?" asked Tung-shan.

Yün-yen raised his fly whisk and said, "Can you hear it yet?"

Tung-shan replied, "No, I can't."

Yün-yen said, "You can't even hear it when I expound the Dharma; how do you expect to hear when a nonsentient being expounds the Dharma?"

Tung-shan asked, "In which sutra is it taught that nonsentient beings expound the Dharma?"

Yün-yen replied, "Haven't you seen it? In the *Amitābha Sūtra* it says, 'Water birds, tree groves, all without exception recite the Buddha's name, recite the Dharma.' "[14]

Reflecting on this, Tung-shan composed the following *gāthā*:

How amazing, how amazing!
Hard to comprehend that nonsentient beings expound the Dharma.

11. T'an-sheng of Yün-yen (780–841), although in the third generation of the Shih-to'u line, began his career as a monk together with Kuei-shan under Pai-ch'ang in the Ma-tsu line. He remained with Pai-ch'ang for more than twenty years before going to Yao-shan, a disciple of Shih-t'ou. Yün-yen Mountain is in T'an-chou, modern Ch'ang-sha, Hunan.

12. "To push aside the grass and gaze into the wind" is a play on a line from the Confucian *Analects* suggesting the ability to distinguish the superior man from ordinary people. "The superior man's deportment is like the wind; ordinary people's is like grass. When the wind blows over it, the grass bends."

13. "This old monk" is a self-deprecating term often used by monks to refer to themselves.

14. The sentence quoted from the *Amitābha Sūtra* is part of Shâkyamuni's description of the Pure Land of Ultimate Bliss, the Western Paradise. Thus, since Yün-yen could not have been unaware of this fact, it must be assumed that he has tacitly equated this world with the Pure Land.

It simply cannot be heard with the ear,
But when sound is heard with the eye, then it is understood.

Tung-shan said to Yün-yen, "I have some habits that are not yet eradicated."

Yün-yen said, "What have you been doing?"

Tung-shan replied, "I have not concerned myself with the Four Noble Truths."

Yün-yen said, "Are you joyful yet?"[15]

Tung-shan said, "It would be untrue to say that I am not joyful. It is as though I have grasped a bright pearl in a pile of shit."

Tung-shan asked Yün-yen, "When I wish to meet you, what shall I do?"

"Make an inquiry with the chamberlain," replied Yün-yen.[16]

Tung-shan said, "I am inquiring right now."

"What does he say to you?" asked Yün-yen.

Just before leaving, Tung-shan asked, "If, after many years, someone should ask if I am able to portray the Master's likeness, how should I respond?"[17]

After remaining quiet for a while, Yün-yen said, "Just this person."[18]

Tung-shan was lost in thought. Yün-yen said, "Chieh Āchārya, having assumed the burden of this Great Matter,[19] you must be very cautious."

Tung-shan remained dubious about what Yün-yen had said. Later, as he was crossing a river, he saw his reflected image and experienced a great awakening to the meaning of the previous exchange. He composed the following *gāthā:*

Earnestly avoid seeking without,
Lest it recede far from you.
Today I am walking alone,
Yet everywhere I meet him.
He is now no other than myself,
But I am not now him.

15. The Chinese term for "joyful" translates the Sanskrit, *pramuditā,* the name of the first of ten levels (*bhumi*) attained by a bodhisattva in his ripening to perfect enlightenment. Though he attains sainthood at this level, certain defilements remain.

16. "Chamberlain" was a title used during various dynasties, including the T'ang, for the court official who waited on the emperor and served as an intermediary between him and the court nobility.

17. Traditionally, a disciple was allowed to draw his master's portrait only when the master acknowledged that the disciple had received the transmission of his Dharma.

18. "Just this person" is a variant of "just this man of Han." According to medieval Chinese legal custom this is the phrase by which a criminal formally confessed his guilt in court. Comparison with other occurrences of the phrase in Ch'an works suggests that it expresses a thoroughgoing assumption of responsibility for one's being.

19. "Having assumed the burden" was another expression used when a criminal acknowledged his crime and personally accepted responsibility for it.

It must be understood in this way
In order to merge with Suchness.

Yün-yen, addressing the assembly, said, "A son exists in a certain household who always answers whatever is asked."

The Master came forward and asked, "How big a library does he have in his room?"

Yün-yen said, "Not a single word."

The Master said, "Then how does he know so much?"

"Day or night, he never sleeps," replied Yün-yen.

"Is it all right to ask him a question?" asked the Master.

"He could answer, but he won't," said Yün-yen.

When the Master first set out on a pilgrimage, he met an old woman carrying water. The Master asked for some water to drink.

The old woman said, "I will not stop you from drinking, but I have a question I must ask first. Tell me, how dirty is the water?"

"The water is not dirty at all," said the Master.

"Go away and don't contaminate my water buckets," replied the old woman.

Once, while the Master was on pilgrimage with Shen-shan, they saw a white rabbit suddenly cross in front of them. Shen-shan remarked, "How elegant!"

"In what way?" asked the Master.

"It is just like a white-robed commoner paying respects to a high minister."

"At your venerable age, how can you say such a thing!" said the Master.

"What about you?" asked Shen-shan.

"After generations of serving as a high official, to temporarily fall into reduced circumstances," replied the Master.

When Shen-shan had picked up a needle to mend clothes, the Master asked, "What are you doing?"

"Mending," answered Shen-shan.

"In what way do you mend?" asked the Master.

"One stitch is like the next," said Shen-shan.

"We've been traveling together for twenty years, and you can still say such a thing! How can there be such craftiness?" said the Master.

"How then does the venerable monk mend?" asked Shen-shan.

"Just as though the entire earth were spewing flame," replied the Master.

The Master asked Yün-chü, "Where have you been?"

"I've been walking the mountains," replied Yün-chü.

"Which mountain was suitable for residing on?" asked the Master.

"None was suitable for residing on," said Yün-chü.

"In that case, have you been on all the country's mountains?" said the Master.

"No, that isn't so," said Yün-chü.

"Then you must have found an entry-path," said the Master.

"No, there is no path," replied Yün-chü.

"If there is no path, I wonder how you have come to lay eyes on this old monk," said the Master.

"If there were a path, then a mountain would stand between us, Ho-shang," said Yün-chü.

The Master said, "Henceforth, not by a thousand, not even by ten thousand people will Yün-chü be held fast."

A monk said, "The Master normally tells us to follow the bird path. I wonder what the bird path is?"[20]

"One does not encounter a single person," replied the Master.

"How does one follow such a path?" asked the monk.

"One should go without hemp sandals on one's feet," replied the Master.

"If one follows the bird path, isn't that seeing one's original face?"[21] said the monk.

"Why do you turn things upside down so?" asked the Master.

"But where have I turned things upside down?" asked the monk.

"If you haven't turned things upside down, then why do you regard the slave as master?" said the Master.

"What is one's original face?" asked the monk.

"Not to follow the bird path," responded the Master.

One time when the Master was washing his bowls, he saw two birds contending over a frog. A monk who also saw this asked, "Why does it come to that?"

The Master replied, "It's only for your benefit, Āchārya."

The Master asked a monk, "What is the most tormenting thing in this world?"

"Hell is the most tormenting thing," answered the monk.

"Not so. When that which is draped in these robe threads is unaware of the Great Matter, that I call the most tormenting thing," said the Master.

20. "The bird path," an image encountered throughout Buddhist literature, is used to describe the path of an enlightened being.

21. The image of one's original face appears in the *Hsing-yu* section of the *Platform Sutra of the Sixth Ancestor.*

The Master went up to the hall and said, "When looking upon, what is it? When serving, what is it? When accomplishing, what is it? When accomplishing mutually, what is it? When there is the accomplishment of accomplishment, what is it?"

A monk asked, "What is 'looking upon'?"

"When eating, what is it?" replied the Master.

"What is 'serving'?" asked the monk.

"When ignoring, what is it?" replied the Master.

"What is 'accomplishing'?" asked the monk.

"When throwing down a mattock, what is it?" replied the Master.

"What is 'accomplishing mutually'?" asked the monk.

"Not attaining things," replied the Master.

"What is the 'accomplishment of accomplishment'?" asked the monk.

"Nothing shared," replied the Master.

The Master offered the following *gāthā*:[22]

> The sage kings from the beginning made Yao the norm;
> He governed the people by means of rites and kept his dragon-waist bent.
> When once he passed from one end of the market to the other,
> He found that everywhere culture flourished and the august dynasty was
>   celebrated.

> For whom do you wash your face and apply makeup?
> The sound of the cuckoo's call urges one home;
> Countless multitudes of flowers have fallen, yet the cuckoo's call is not stilled;
> Going farther into the jumbled peaks, in deep places its call continues.

> The blooming of a flower on a sear old tree, a spring outside of kalpas;
> Riding backwards on a jade elephant, chasing the *ch'i lin*.[23]
> Now hidden far beyond the innumerable peaks,
> The moon is white, the breeze cool at the approach of sunrise.

> Ordinary beings and Buddha have no truck with each other;
> Mountains are naturally high, waters naturally deep.
> What the myriad distinctions and numerous differences show is that
> Where the chukar cries, many flowers are blooming.

22. [This passage has come to be known as Tung-shan's "Five Degrees of Honor and Virtue."—Eds.]

23. The *ch'i lin* is a mythological beast, with the characteristics of a dragon, a deer, and the Greek Pegasus. It is traditionally regarded as the mount of sylphs.

Can't stand head sprouting horns anymore;[24]
When the mind rouses to seek the Buddha, it's time for compunction.
In the unimpeded vista of the *Kalpa* of Emptiness, when no one is perceived,
Why go south in search of the fifty-three?[25]

---

24. Nan-ch'üan asks Tao-wu, "What can you say about that place that knowledge does not reach?" Tao-wu replied, "One should absolutely avoid talking about that." Nan-ch'üan said, "Truly, as soon as one explains, horns sprout on one's head, and one becomes a beast."
25. The "fifty-three" is a reference to Sudhana's fifty-three teachers in the *Gandavyūha* section of the *Avatamsaka Sūtra.*

19

Hsüeh-feng

(822–908)

Ch'an historians rank Hsüeh-feng I-ts'un along with Tung-shan's successor Yün-chü as the two most eminent teachers of their generation. What makes this remarkable in Hsüeh-feng's case is his epic struggle to gain the Way, two decades of traipsing about the Ch'an mountains in a determined quest for certainty. *The Transmission of the Lamp* preserves dozens of unflattering reports about these efforts, noting his nine fruitless trips to see Tung-shan and three sojourns with the master T'ou-tzu Ta-t'ung, during which he was four times branded a "black lacquer bucket"—shorthand for *dimwit*. Hsüeh-feng stands out in Ch'an history as a plodding student who became a teacher of great effectiveness and importance, and that undoubtedly explains the chronicles' close attention to his misfortunes. Failure is the Way, his life has reminded later students, or as one Ch'an proverb says, "A superior vessel takes a long time to complete."

Hsüeh-feng (J., Seppō) lived for some years at Te-shan's monastery and won himself a place among the stars of Ch'an chefdom by serving in the position of head cook there, as he also had at Tung-shan's. Though Ch'an genealogies list him as one of Te-shan's successors, the last word was still eluding him when the Master of Thirty Blows died in 865. His turning point, according to *The Blue Cliff Record,* came during a pilgrimage with a fellow monk, the brilliant Yen-t'ou Ch'uan-huo (828–887), when the two got snowed in on Tortoise Mountain. Yen-t'ou (J., Gantō), also regarded as an heir of Te-shan, used the opportunity to catch up on his rest, while Hsüeh-feng sat meditating hour after hour. When Yen-t'ou chastised him for imitating a clay statue and urged him to get some sleep, Hsüeh-feng gestured to his chest and confessed that his heart was not at peace.

This moment of candor led Yen-t'ou to propose that he review his elder colleague's prior Ch'an experience for him. Hsüeh-feng then laid out the glimmers of insight he had gotten as a novice studying with one of Ma-tsu's heirs, upon reading Tung-shan's poem about crossing the river, when Te-shan hit him with his stick. . . . Finally Yen-t'ou burst out, "Haven't you heard that what enters through the gate is not the family treasure? Let it flow forth from your breast, covering heaven and earth!" Suddenly Hsüeh-feng came to and rejoiced, saying over and over, "Today Tortoise Mountain has finally gained the Way! Today Tortoise Mountain finally has gained the Way!"

Even so, Hsüeh-feng persisted in steadfastness, retiring to a hermitage in his native eastern China, far from the centers of Ch'an ferment and national life:

> Human life so hectic and hurried is but a brief instant;
> How can one dwell for long in the fleeting world?
> As I reached thirty-two I emerged from the mountains;
> Already well pasty forty, now I return to Min.
> No use bringing up others' faults again and again;
> One's own mistakes must be continually cleared away.
> I humbly report to the purple-clad nobles at court:
> The King of Death feels no awe for golden badges of rank.

Min, on the coast opposite Taiwan, was not exactly the boondocks, however. Sea trade had made it prosperous, and Hsüeh-feng eventually forged close ties with its ruler, who took an interest in Buddhism and gave him a great deal of support. The master settled on Hsiang-ku-shan, in an area that was often snow-capped and thus called Hsüeh-feng, Snowy Peak; he was mainly known by that name but was also dubbed Old Elephant Bones, from the name of the mountain itself.

As the T'ang dynasty entered its death throes, China underwent a period of instability that led many to seek cover. Yen-t'ou hid out as a ferryman, it is said, and finally was murdered by a bandit gang as he sat calmly meditating in an otherwise deserted monastery. Order prevailed in Hsüeh-feng's part of the world, however, and monks drifted there from all over, forming a diverse community of, by many reports, fifteen hundred people. Under Hsüeh-feng's leadership life was spartan, practice arduous, and teaching strict. Knowing the virtues of a clear phrase and a stinging insult, he let the assembly have it right between the eyes: "When I pick it up, this great earth is the size of a grain of millet. I cast it down before you. You lacquer buckets don't understand! Sound the drum! Call everyone to look!"

Like his old boss, Te-shan, he wielded his stick vigorously, frequently dealing students a blow even when they made good responses, as if to say, "But don't stop *there!*" His record also shows him making Dharma points in gentler fashion, often using his horsehair whisk—an implement originally designed for chasing flies but adopted by Ch'an masters as an instructional tool. Probably as a result of his own hard experience, he guided struggling practitioners with great proficiency. He told the faltering Ch'ang-ch'ing Hui-leng, later among his Dharma heirs, "I'll give you medicine that would revive a dead horse. Can you swallow it?" Ch'ang-ch'ing (J., Chōkei) said he would do whatever Hsüeh-feng recommended. "Then don't bother coming to me many times a day," the teacher said. "Just make yourself like a burnt stump on the mountainside. If you put your body and mind at rest for ten years or maybe seven or even just three, you'll surely discover something."

Hsüeh-feng's abilities brought him a purple robe from the court and great renown among Ch'an people, who now said "Chao-chou in the North, Hsüeh-feng in the South," as before they had touted Shih-t'ou and Ma-tsu's precincts

West of the River and South of the Lake. Far more important, Old Elephant Bones raised a herd of fifty-six talented successors. Besides Ch'ang-ch'ing, they included Hsüan-sha Shih-pei, whose descendants originated the Fa-yen school (Chapter 22), and Yün-men Wen-yen (Chapter 21), who founded the house that bore his name. Not bad for a black lacquer bucket. ⌘

FROM THE RECORD OF TUNG-SHAN

Hsüeh-feng went to pay his respects to [Tung-shan].

The Master said, "When you enter the door, you must say something. It won't do to say that you have already entered."

"I have no mouth," said Hsüeh-feng.

"Although you may have no mouth, you should still give me back my eyes," said the Master.

Hsüeh-feng said nothing.

Once, when Hsüeh-feng was carrying a bundle of firewood, he arrived in front of the Master and threw the bundle down.

"How heavy is it?" asked the Master.

"There is no one on earth who could lift it," replied Hsüeh-feng.

"Then how did it get here?" asked the Master.

Hsüeh-feng said nothing.

Hsüeh-feng was serving as the rice cook.[1] Once, while he was culling pebbles from the rice, the Master asked, "Do you cull out the pebbles and set the rice aside, or do you cull out the rice and set the pebbles aside?"

"I set aside the rice and pebbles at one and the same time," replied Hsüeh-feng.

"What will the monks eat?" asked the Master.

Hsüeh-feng immediately turned over the rice bucket.

The Master said, "Given your basic affinities, you will be most compatible with Te-shan."

FROM THE IRON FLUTE

Hsüeh-feng asked Te-shan, "Can I also share the ultimate teaching the old Ancestors attained?"

Te-shan hit him with a stick, saying, "What are you talking about?"

---

1. According to the monastic regulations attributed to Pai-chang . . . , the Rice Cook is one of the ten kitchen positions under the Chief Cook. The preparation of vegetables is delegated to another cook, and so on.

Hsüeh-feng did not realize Te-shan's meaning, so the next day he repeated his question.

Te-shan answered, "Zen has no words, neither does it have anything to give."

Yen-t'ou heard about the dialogue and said, "Te-shan has an iron backbone, but he spoils Zen with his soft words."

Three monks, Hsüeh-feng, Ch'in-shan, and Yen-t'ou, met in the temple garden. Hsüeh-feng saw a water pail and pointed to it. Ch'in-shan said, "The water is clear, and the moon reflects its image."

"No, no," said Hsüeh-feng, "it is not water, it is not moon."

Yen-t'ou turned over the pail.

A monk said to Hsüeh-feng, "I understand that a person in the stage of Shrāvaka sees his Buddha-nature as he sees the moon at night, and a person in the stage of bodhisattva sees his Buddha-nature as he sees the sun at day. Tell me how you see your own Buddha-nature."

For answer Hsüeh-feng gave the monk three blows with his stick. The monk went to another teacher, Yen-t'ou, and asked the same thing. Yen-t'ou slapped the monk three times.

A monk asked Hsüeh-feng, "How can one touch sanctity?"

Hsüeh-feng answered, "A mere innocent cannot do it."

"If he forgets himself," the monk asked again, "can he touch sanctity?"

He may do so in so far as he is concerned," Hsüeh-feng replied.

"Then," continued the monk, "what happens to him?"

"A bee never returns to his abandoned hive," came the answer.

Hsüeh-feng went to the forest to cut trees with his disciple, Chang-sheng. "Do not stop until your axe cuts the very center of the tree," warned the teacher.

"I have cut it," the disciple replied.

"The old masters transmitted the teaching to their disciples from heart to heart," Hsüeh-feng continued, "how about your own case?"

Chang-sheng threw his axe to the ground, saying, "Transmitted." The teacher took up his walking stick and struck his beloved disciple.

One day Hsüeh-feng began a lecture to the monks gathered around the little platform by rolling down a wooden ball. Hsüan-sha went after the ball, picked it up and replaced it on the stand.

Hsüan-sha sent a monk to his old teacher, Hsüeh-feng, with a letter of greeting. Hsüeh-feng gathered his monks and opened the letter in their presence. The envelope contained nothing but three sheets of blank paper. Hsüeh-feng showed the paper to the monks, saying, "Do you understand?" There was no answer, and Hsüeh-feng continued, "My prodigal son writes just what I think."

When the messenger monk returned to Hsüan-sha, he told him what had happened at Hsüeh-feng's monastery. "My old man is in his dotage," said Hsüan-sha.

FROM THE TRANSMISSION OF THE LAMP

A monk began, "In ancient times there was a saying . . . " [Hsüeh-feng] immediately lay down. After a while he stood up and said, "What were you asking?" As the monk started to repeat the question the Master commented, "This fellow wastes his life and will die in vain!"

Another monk asked, "What does it mean when the arrow is about to leave the bow?"

Master: "When the archer is an expert he does not try to hit the target."

Monk: "If the eyes of all the people do not aim at the target, what will happen?"

Master: "Be expert according to your talent."

Question: "An early master said that when one meets a man who understands Tao, one should reply to him neither by words nor by silence. How should one reply?"

Master: "Go and have a cup of tea."

The Master asked a monk where he came from. The answer was, "From the Monastery of Spiritual Light." The Master commented, "In the daytime we have sunlight; in the evening we have lamplight. What is spiritual light?" The monk made no answer. The Master answered for him: "Sunlight, lamplight."

The Master asked a monk, "How old is this water buffalo?" He received no reply and answered himself, saying, "It is seventy-seven." A monk asked him, "Why should you, Master, become a water buffalo?"[2] The Master said, "What is wrong with that?"

The Master asked a monk, "Where did you come from?"

Answer: "From Kiangsi."

Master: "How far is Kiangsi from here?"

Answer: "Not far."

The Master held up his fly whisk and said, "Is there any space for this?"

Answer: "If there were space enough for that, then Kiangsi would be far away."

The Master struck the monk.

2. The Master was seventy-seven at the time, hence the monk's response.

There was a monk who left the Master to visit Ling-yün,[3] whom he asked, "Before Buddha was born, what was he?" Ling-yün lifted his fly whisk. The monk asked, "What was he after he was born?" Ling-yün again lifted his fly whisk. The monk, failing to understand this, returned to the Master. The Master asked him, "You just left and now you have come back. Is this not too soon?" The monk replied, "When I asked Ling-yün about Buddhism, his answers did not satisfy me, so I have returned here." The Master demanded, "What did you ask?" The monk then recounted his experience with Ling-yün. Whereupon the Master said, "Please put the same question to me and I will answer you." The monk then asked, "Before Buddha was born, what was he?" The Master lifted his fly whisk. The monk asked, "What was he after he was born?" The Master put down his fly whisk. The monk made a deep bow and the Master struck him.

The Master mentioned a saying of the Sixth Ancestor: "It is neither the wind nor the banner that moves. It is your mind that moves." He commented, "Such a great patriarch! He has 'a dragon's head but a snake's tail.'[4] I will give him twenty blows." The monk Fu of T'ai-yüan, who was standing beside the Master, gnashed his teeth when he heard this. The Master confessed, "After what I said a moment ago, I also should be given twenty blows."

A monk pleaded, "Master! Please express what I cannot express myself." The Master answered, "For the Dharma's sake I have to save you!" Thereupon he lifted his fly whisk and flourished it before the monk. The monk departed immediately.

The Master asked a monk, "Where did you come from?"
    Answer: "From across the mountain range."
    The Master: "Have you met Bodhidharma?"
    Answer: "Blue sky, bright sun."
    The Master: "How about yourself?"
    Answer: "What more do you want?"
    The Master struck him.
    Later Master Hsüeh-feng saw this monk off. When he had gone several steps, the Master called to him. As the monk turned his head to look back, the Master said, "Do your best while you are traveling."
    A monk asked, "What do you think of the idea that picking up a hammer or lifting up a fly whisk is not teaching Ch'an?" The Master lifted up his fly whisk. The monk who had raised the question lowered his head and departed while Hsüeh-feng ignored him.

3. Ling-yün Chih-ch'in.
4. A common expression, which means dwindling away to nothing after an initial display of greatness.

The General of Fukien donated a silver chair to the Master. A monk asked the Master, "You have received a fine gift from the General. What are you going to give him in return?" The Master laid both hands upon the ground and said, "Please strike me lightly."

The Master stayed in Fukien for more than forty years. Every winter and every summer no fewer than one thousand five hundred people came to learn from him. In the third month of the second year of K'ai-p'ing [908] in the Liang dynasty, the Master announced his illness. The General of Fukien sent a physician to examine him. The Master said, "My illness is not an illness." He declined to take the medicine prescribed for him, but devoted himself to composing a *gāthā* for the transmitting of the Dharma.

On the second day of the fifth month he visited Lan-t'ien in the morning. When he returned in the evening he bathed and, in the middle of the night, entered nirvana. He was then eighty-seven, and it had been fifty-nine years since he was ordained.

20

Ts'ao-shan

(840–901)

Mystery shrouds the figure of Ts'ao-shan Pen-chi. Long ago, Ch'an people linked his name with Tung-shan's and recognized him as junior partner in the founding of the Ts'ao-tung house. Scraps of evidence make plausible a close association between him and Tung-shan, although counter-evidence calls that into question. Only in late versions of Tung-shan's biography does Ts'ao-shan (J., Sōzan) appear at all—and then barely, more like a name attached as an afterthought than as a flesh-and-blood character. Even in his own record, we find just two exchanges with his supposed teacher, one at the time he enters the monastery and the other, an indefinite number of years later, as he leaves. Sometime during this period, it says, Tung-shan secretly approved him as his successor.

Maybe so. Hui-neng's transmission occurred secretly, at least in legendary accounts, and at least one Sung-dynasty master guarded the details of his succession until he was about to die. Ts'ao-shan's claim of secrecy contrasts comically, however, with another report of the event that occurs in the biography of Su-shan Kuang-jen, who is better represented in Tung-shan's record than Ts'ao-shan and figures alongside him among the successors. Su-shan's exceptionally small stature, besides getting him the nicknames of Bantam Master and Uncle Dwarf, made it possible for him (or so the story goes) to hide beneath Tung-shan's seat and listen in as the master conveyed certain secret teachings to Ts'ao-shan. "When the transmission was completed, Ts'ao-shan bowed twice and hurried out. Uncle Dwarf now stuck out his head and bawled, 'Tung-shan's Ch'an is in the palm of my hand!' Tung-shan was greatly astonished and said, 'Stealing the Dharma by the dirtiest of means will avail you nothing.' "

By some means, probably quite proper, Ts'ao-shan came into possession of doctrinal writings consistently attributed to Tung-shan, notably a long verse titled "The Jeweled Mirror Samadhi" and the Five Ranks (or Five Modes), an esoteric scheme presenting the relationship between the universal and the particular, the absolute and the relative. If these were secret when Ts'ao-shan received them, they did not remain secret under his care. On the contrary, his reputation rests largely on his development and promotion of them. The Five Ranks circulated widely in Ch'an circles. Although generally ignored by others in Tung-shan's line, in just one century they took hold in the Lin-chi house, where they have been taught ever since.

Only the slightest allusion to all this appears in Ts'ao-shan's record, which reads as a conventional document except that it makes scant mention of his Ch'an connections. The Ts'ao-shan it depicts handles inquirers as artfully and discreetly as Tung-shan himself, refraining from shouts, blows, and nose-pulling, not even brandishing the whisk. We may never know with certainty whether the master of these dialogues was an invention of later chroniclers or the actual public persona of the man better known for his verse and commentaries. The record offers good reasons for his shadowy presence: he declined to lecture publicly and never stayed more than ninety days (a three-month training period) at any monastery. Of course, this could be no more than a smokescreen. In terms of effectiveness, his voice certainly placed a pale second to his brush: his literary works were a lasting contribution to the school, while his line of succession swiftly came to nothing. ⊗

FROM THE TRANSMISSION OF THE LAMP

The Master Pen-chi of Mt. Ts'ao in Fu-chou was a native of P'u-t'ien in Ch'üan-chou. His family name was Huang. While young he was interested in Confucianism, but at nineteen he left his home to become a monk, entering the temple at Mt. Ling-shih in Fu-t'ang hsien in Fu-chou, where at twenty-five he took the precepts. In the early years of the Hsien-t'ung era (860–872) the Ch'an sect flourished greatly and just at this time the Master [Liang]-chieh (807–869) was in charge of the monastery at Tung-shan. Pen-chi went there to request instruction of him.

Tung-shan asked: "What's your name, monk?"

"Pen-chi."

Tung-shan said: "Say something more."

"I won't."

"Why not?"

"My name is not Pen-chi."

Tung-shan was much impressed with his potential, allowed him entry to his quarters and in secret gave sanction to his understanding. After staying there for several years he took his leave of Tung-shan.

Tung-shan asked: "Where are you going?"

Pen-chi answered: "I'm going to a changeless place."

Tung-shan said: "If there's a changeless place you won't be going there."

Pen-chi replied: "Going is also changeless."

Then he said good-bye and left, wandering about and doing as he pleased. At first he was asked to stay at Mt. Ts'ao in Fu-chou and later he lived at Mt. Ho-yü. At both places students flocked to him in great numbers.

Someone asked: "What sort of person is he who is not a companion to the ten thousand dharmas?"

The Master said: "You tell me! Where have all the people in Hung-chou gone?"

Someone asked: "In phenomena what is true?"
The Master said: "The very phenomena are themselves truth."
"Then how should it be revealed?" he asked.
The Master lifted the tea tray.

Someone asked: "In illusion what is true?"
The Master said: "Illusion is from the outset true."
"In illusion what is manifested?" he asked.
The Master said: "The very illusion is itself manifestation."
"If this is so then one can never be apart from illusion," he said.
The Master replied: "No matter how you seek illusion you won't find it."

Someone asked: "What about a person who is always present?"
The Master said: "He met me just now and has gone out."
"What about a person who is never present?" he asked.
The Master said: "It is difficult to find such a person."

A monk called Ch'ing-jui said: "I am alone and poor; I beg of you to help me."
The Master said: "Monk Jui, come close." When he approached the Master added: "You've had three cups of wine at Po's house in Ch'üan-chou and yet you say that your lips are still dry."

Ching-ch'ing asked: "What is the principle of pure emptiness when the time comes that the body no longer exists?"
The Master said: "The principle is just like this. What about things then?"
Ching-ch'ing said: "Like principle as it is; also like things as they are."
The Master said: "It's all right to trick me, but what are you going to do about the eyes of all the sages?"
Ching-ch'ing said: "If the eyes of the sages don't exist, how is it possible to tell that it's not like this?"
The Master said: "Officially a needle is not allowed through, but horses and carriages enter by the back door."

Yün-men asked: "If a person who doesn't change himself should come would you receive him?"
The Master said: "I haven't got time to waste with such business."

Someone asked: "A man of old has said: 'Men all have it,' but I'm covered with the dusts of the world and wonder whether I do or not."

The Master said: "Show me your hand." Then he pointed to the man's fingers: "One, two, three, four, five. Enough!"

Someone asked: "The Ancestor Lu sat facing the wall. What was he trying to show?"

The Master covered his ears with his hands.

Someone asked: "I've heard that the teachings (*Nirvāna Sūtra*) say: 'The great sea does not harbor a corpse.' What is the 'sea?' "

The Master said: "It includes the whole universe."

He asked: "Then why doesn't it harbor a corpse?"

The Master said: "It doesn't let one whose breath has been cut off stay."

The man asked: "Since it includes the whole universe, why doesn't it let one whose breath has been cut off stay?"

The Master said: "In the whole universe there is no virtue; if the breath is cut off there is virtue."

He asked: "Is there anything more?"

The Master said: "You can say there is or there isn't, but what are you going to do about the dragon king who holds the sword?"

Someone asked: "With what sort of understanding should one be equipped to satisfactorily cope with the cross-examinations of others?"

The Master said: "Don't use words and phrases."

"Then what are you going to cross-examine about?"

The Master said: "Even the sword and axe cannot pierce it through!"

He said: "What a fine cross-examination! But aren't there people who don't agree?"

The Master said: "There are."

"Who?" he asked.

The Master said: "Me."

Someone asked: "Without words how can things be expressed?"

The Master said: "Don't express them here."

"Where can they be expressed?" he asked.

The Master said: "Last night at midnight I lost three coins by my bed."

Someone asked: "How should I take charge [of It] all day long?"

The Master said: "When passing through a village where there's an epidemic, don't let even a single drop of water touch you."

Someone asked: "What is the master of the Body of Essence?"

The Master said: "They say: 'There are no people in Ch'in.' "[1]

The monk said: "You're talking about the Master of the Body of Essence, aren't you?"

The Master said: "Kill!"

Someone asked: "With what sort of person should one associate in order always to hear the unheard?"

The Master said: "Sleep under the same canopy."

He said: "But that way it's still you who can hear it. How can I always hear the unheard?"

The Master said: "By not being the same as trees and rocks."

"Which comes before and which afterwards?" he asked.

The Master said: "Haven't you ever heard the saying: 'Always to hear the unheard?' "

Someone asked: "Who is he in this nation who is putting his hand to the hilt of his sword?"

"Me!" said the Master.

"Whom are you trying to kill?" he asked.

The Master said: "Everyone in the world."

He asked: "What would you do if you met your original father and mother?"

The Master said: "What is there to choose?"

He said: "What are you going to do about yourself?"

The Master said: "Who can do anything about me?"

"Why don't you kill yourself?" he asked.

"No place to lay hold of," the Master said.

Someone asked: "What about: 'When the ox drinks water and the five horses do not neigh?' "[2]

The Master said: "I can abstain from harmful foods." On another occasion he answered the same question with: "I've just come out of mourning."

Someone asked: "What do you think about: 'As soon as positive and negative arises / the mind is lost in confusion?' "[3]

The Master said: "Kill, kill!"

A monk brought up the story: "Someone asked Hsiang-yen: 'What is the Way?' and Hsiang-yen answered: 'A dragon's song from a withered tree.' This person

---

1. Reference is to a passage in a story in the *Tso Chuan,* Wen 13.
2. The "ox" is the mind; the "horses" the five sense organs.
3. Quotation from the *Hsin-hsin ming.* [We have modified this translation to jibe with that in Chapter 2.—Eds.]

then said: 'I don't understand,' and Hsiang-yen replied: 'An eye in the skull.' The same person later asked Shih-shuang: 'What is a dragon's song from a withered tree?' and Shih-shuang replied: 'There's still some joy remaining.' Then he asked: 'What is an eye in the skull?' and Shih-shuang replied, 'There's still some consciousness remaining.' "

The Master then responded with a verse:

> A dragon's song from a withered tree—this is truly seeing the Way.
> No consciousness in the skull—now for the first time the eye is clear.
> Yet when joy and consciousness are exhausted, they still do not
>   completely disappear;
> How can that person distinguish purity amidst the turbid?

The monk then asked the Master: "What about 'a dragon's song from a withered tree?' "

The Master said: "The blood vessel is not cut off."

The monk asked: "What about 'an eye in the skull?' "

The Master said: "It can't be completely dried up."

The monk said: "I don't know whether there is somebody who can hear?"

The Master said: "In the great earth there is not a single person who has not heard."

The monk said: "Then what kind of a phrase is 'a dragon's song from a withered tree?' "

The Master said: "I don't know what phrase this is, but [I do know that] all who hear are doomed."

Although the Master furthered the development of those of superior capacity, he did not leave any pattern by which he could be traced. After he was examined by Tung-shan's Five Ranks [and passed it], he was esteemed as an authority throughout the Ch'an world. At one time Mr. Chung of Hung-chou repeatedly urged him [to preach in public], but he declined. In return he copied a verse on the secluded life in the mountains composed by the Master Ta-mei (752–839) and sent it to him. One night in late summer of the first year of Tien-fu (901) he asked a senior monk: "What's the date today?"

The monk answered: "The fifteenth day of the sixth month."

The Master said: "I've spent my whole life going on pilgrimages [from one Ch'an temple to another], but every place I came to I limited my meditation sessions to the ninety days." Next day at the hour of the dragon he passed away.

He was sixty-two years of age and had been a monk for thirty-seven years. His disciples erected a pagoda for him and installed his bones within it. The Imperial Court bestowed on him the posthumous title Yüan-cheng Ta-shih and on his pagoda the name Fu-yüan.

21

Yün-men

(864–949)

Many consider Yün-men Wen-yen the last great genius of Ch'an. Keen-witted and sharp-tongued, he taught with a passion that can still be felt in his words. When read, they scorch your eyeballs; heard, they just make your ears drop off. At a time when the Ch'an school was slipping into a retrospective mood, inclined to collect, codify, and preserve accomplishments of the past, Yün-men (J., Unmon) pressed enthusiastically ahead, discovering new means to teach the ancient Way. He, too, prized the stories of the old masters, but when he took them up, he always gave them a new twist.

Yün-men trained with eminent descendants of both Ma-tsu and Shih-t'ou. First, in Ancestor Ma's wing of the school, he studied with the unusual teacher Mu-chou Tao-tsung, a successor of Huang-po. Head monk in Huang-po's assembly at the time Lin-chi held down a cushion there, Mu-chou (J., Bokushū) had quit the monkhood as well as the monastery by the time Yün-men caught up with him. Aged and flinty, he made himself scarce, and only the extremely persistent could get in his door—briefly. Legend has it that the old layman ended his first meeting with Yün-men by literally slamming the door on him, at once crushing his leg and opening his mind.

Judging by the amount of ground Yün-men covered in the seventeen years after leaving Mu-chou, he cannot have sustained the crippling injury that this late tale alleges, but it does vividly convey the tenor of Mu-chou's instruction. At the old teacher's direction, Yün-men went next to Elephant Bone Mountain, where he came beneath the cudgel of the ever-demanding Hsüeh-feng, successor in the fifth generation of Shih-t'ou's line. By present-day humanistic standards, the ruthless training he received under these teachers may seem all wrong, but in medieval Chinese apprenticeships and in Ch'an study, in particular, it was considered a master's ultimate kindness.

In this view, the obduracy of bad habits made strict teaching and training a necessity and a good student willingly took whatever the master prescribed—"medicine that would revive a dead horse," as already noted in the instance of Yün-men's brother monk Ch'ang-ch'ing. The severity of his own teaching style made Yün-men a model for later teachers. "Though it was hard to approach him," one wrote, "he had the hammer and tongs to pull out nails and wrench out pegs"—the means, in other words, to cause the collapse of old mental structures. "Hammer and tongs" became the byword for effective Ch'an training, as opposed to the coddling of "grandmotherly kindness."

After seven years or so, Yün-men received transmission from Hsüeh-feng and began a meandering pilgrimage that enabled him to visit many monasteries, especially of the Ts'ao-tung line, and carried him all the way to the southern coast of China. The T'ang dynasty had entered its death throes by this date (ca. 900), so it makes sense that Yün-men, like Hsüeh-feng before him, would seek a teaching platform on the secure periphery. He found it near what today is Hong Kong and then was the capital of the Southern Han dynasty. Swiftly winning favor with its ruler, just twelve years after arriving he obtained approval for construction of a monastic complex at Mount Yün-men, Gate of the Clouds.

Six years later (but just one year after the monastery was finished), the emperor called Yün-men off the mountain for an audience that determined the rest of his life:

> "What is Ch'an all about?" the Son of Heaven wanted to know.
>
> Master [Yün-men] said, "Your Majesty has the question, and your servant the monk has the answer."
>
> The emperor inquired, "What answer?"
>
> Master [Yün-men] replied, "I request Your Majesty to reflect upon the words your servant has just uttered."

The emperor was pleased enough with this response to decree that Yün-men would henceforth hold the highest office in the monkhood, administering the capital's entire community of monks, Ch'an and otherwise. "The Master remained silent and did not respond." Luckily, an imperial advisor came to the rescue, suggesting that Yün-men might not "enjoy rising to a high post," and the emperor offered to withdraw the appointment, to which Yün-men "full of joy shouted thrice, 'Long live the emperor!' " Whether you judge this sycophancy, realpolitik, virtue, or simply accord with the Way, it freed him to spend his remaining eleven years doing what he loved.

A record kept by his juniors, one of the most quickly produced and best authenticated documents from Ch'an's heyday, affords a chance to watch Yün-men at work. Full of fire and creativity, he applies to his disciples every tool in the ancestral toolkit and a few others rarely, if ever, used before. His one-word phrases, answers on behalf of the audience, alternative responses to old sayings, and utilization of mime are especially original. His voluminous record was gathered and published within eighty-six years of his death (no mean feat, in an age of woodblock printing), and it had an extraordinary impact on the Ch'an world, thanks partly to an accident of timing. In the following two hundred years, all three of the great koan collections—*The Blue Cliff Record, The Book of Equanimity,* and *The Gateless Barrier*—would be prepared, and their authors must have had Yün-men's sayings at their elbows. Of all the Ch'an masters, none appears more often in these collections than he, though Chao-chou runs a close second. ∞

FROM THE RECORD OF YÜN-MEN

Having come to the Dharma Hall [to instruct the assembly],[1] the Master remained silent for a long time and then said:

"The knack of giving voice to the Tao is definitely difficult to figure out. Even if every word matches it, there still are a multitude of other ways; how much more so when I rattle on and on? So what's the point of talking to you right now?

"Though each of the three collections of Buddhist teaching[2] has its specific sphere—the *vinaya* pertains to the study of monastic discipline, the sutras to the study of meditative concentration, and the treatises to the study of wisdom—the [various parts of the Buddhist canon] really all boil down to just one thing, namely, the One Vehicle.[3] It is perfect and immediate—and extremely difficult to fathom. Even if you could understand it right now, you'd still be as different from this patch-robed monk as earth is from heaven. If in my assembly someone's ability is manifested in a phrase, you'll ponder in vain. Even if, in order to make progress, you sorted out all Ch'an teachings with their thousand differences and myriad distinctions, your mistake would still consist in searching for proclamations from other people's tongues.

"So how should one approach what has been transmitted? By talking in here about 'perfect' and 'immediate'? By [this] here or [that] there? Don't get me wrong: you must not hear me say this and then speculate that 'no perfect' and 'not sudden' are it!

"There *must* be a real *man* in here! Don't rely on some master's pretentious statements or hand-me-down phrases that you pass off everywhere as your own understanding! Don't get me wrong. Whatever your problem right now is: try settling it just here in front of the assembly!"

At the time Prefectural Governor Ho was present. He performed the customary bow and said, "Your disciple requests your instruction."

The Master replied, "This weed I see is no different!"[4]

Having entered the Dharma Hall, Master Yün-men said:

"If, in bringing up a case I cause you to accept it instantly, I am already spreading shit on top of your heads. Even if you could understand the whole world when I hold up a single hair, I'd still be operating on healthy flesh.

1. Formal lectures to the assembly by the master are usually introduced by this expression. Such discourses were formal in the sense that in principle all monks of a monastery (and often also visitors) were expected to be present when the master, seated on a wide chair on an elevated platform, addressed them.
2. Traditionally, the written teachings of Buddhism are classified in three "baskets" (Pali: *pitaka*): monastic rules (*vinaya*), sutras, and treatises (*shāstras*).
3. The singular or unique vehicle (*ekayāna*). In the Ch'an movement, one's own realization of the non-dual or mindless mind (Ch., *wu-hsin,* J., *mushin*) is regarded as the one vehicle.
4. In Ch'an texts, "weed" is used as a metaphor for illusions which the teacher steps into in order to save his disciples.

"At any rate, you must first truly attain this level of realization. If you're not yet there, you must not pretend that you are. Rather, you ought to take a step back, seek under your very feet, and see what there is to what I am saying!

"In reality, there is not the slightest thing that could be the source of understanding or doubt for you. Rather, you have the one thing that matters, each and every one of you! Its great function manifests without the slightest effort on your part; you are no different from the ancestor buddhas![5] [But since] the root of your faith has always been shallow and the influence of your evil actions massive, you find yourselves all of a sudden wearing many horns.[6] You're carrying your bowl bags[7] far and wide through thousands of villages and myriads of hamlets: what's the point of victimizing yourselves? Is there something you all are lacking? Which one of you full-fledged fellows hasn't got his share?

"Though you may accept what I am saying for yourself you're still in bad shape.[8] You must neither fall for the tricks of others nor simply accept their directives. The instant you see an old monk open his mouth, you tend to stuff those big rocks right into yours, and when you cluster in little groups to discuss [his words], you're exactly like those green flies on shit that struggle back to back to gobble it up! What a shame, brothers!

"The old masters could not help using up their whole lifetime for the sake of you all. So they dropped a word here and half a phrase there to give you a hint. You may have understood these things; put them aside and make some effort for yourselves, and you will certainly become a bit familiar with it. Hurry up! Hurry up! Times does not wait for any man, and breathing out is no guarantee for breathing in again! Or do you have a spare body and mind to fritter away? You absolutely must pay close attention! Take care!"

Having entered the Dharma Hall for a formal instruction, Master Yün-men said: "The Buddha attained the Way when the morning star appeared."

A monk asked: "What is it like when one attains the Way at the appearance of the morning star?"

Master Yün-men said: "Come here, come here!"

The monk went closer. Master Yün-men hit him with his staff and chased him out of the Dharma Hall.

Master Yün-men cited Master Hsüeh-feng's words: "The whole world is you.

5. This could also be translated as "ancestors and buddhas."
6. Horns are in Ch'an literature often associated with dualistic attachment or delusion in general, as are weeds. Cf. *The Blue Cliff Record*, case 95: "Where there is a buddha, you must not stay; if you do, horns sprout. Where there is no buddha, quickly run past; if you don't, the weeds will be ten feet high."
7. These bags were used by monks to carry their begging bowl and a few other possessions around on pilgrimage.
8. Or: out of luck.

Yet you keep thinking that there is something else . . ."⁹ Master Yün-men said:
"Haven't you read the *Shūrangama Sūtra* which says, 'Sentient beings are all up-
side-down; they delude themselves and chase after things'?"

He added, "If they could handle things, they would be identical to the Buddha."

"What is the Tao?"
The Master replied, "To break through this word."
"What is it like when one has broken through?"
"A thousand miles, the same mood."¹⁰

When Master Yün-men saw the characters that mean "dragon treasury," he
asked a monk, "What is it that can come out of the dragon's treasury?"¹¹
The monk had no answer.
The Master said, "Ask me, I'll tell you!"
So the monk asked, and the Master replied, "What comes out is a dead
frog."
On behalf of the [baffled] monk he said, "A fart!"
Again, he said, "Steam-breads and steam-cookies."

Someone asked Yün-men, "[It is said that] one should not leave home [to be-
come a monk] without one's parents' consent. How would one then be able to
leave home?"
The Master said, "Shallow!"
The questioner said, "I do not understand."
The Master remarked, "Deep!"

Someone asked Master Yün-men, "I request your instruction, Master!"
The Master said, "ABCDEF."
The questioner: "I don't understand."
The Master: "GHIJKL."¹²

Someone asked Yün-men, "I did all I could and came here. Will you accept?"
The Master said, "Nothing wrong with this question!"
The questioner went on, "Leaving aside this question: will you accept?"
The Master said, "Examine carefully what you first said!"

9. This saying is found in *The Record of Hsüeh-feng.*
10. This expresses the closeness good friends feel even when they are a thousand miles apart.
11. This treasury stands for the Buddhist canon, which is guarded by a dragon. The question thus
means something like: What can come out of the Buddhist teaching?
12. In the original, of course, the first Chinese characters a child had to learn to write are used.

Master Yün-men quoted: "All sounds are the Buddha's voice; all shapes are the Buddha's form." The Master picked up the fly whisk and said: "What is this? If you say it is a fly whisk, you won't even understand the Ch'an of a granny from a three-house hick town."

The Master once said: "Do you want to know the founding masters?" Pointing with his staff, he said: "They are jumping around on your heads! Do you want to know their eyeball?[13] It's right under your feet!"
   He added: "This [kind of guidance] is offering tea and food to ghosts and spirits. Nevertheless, these ghosts and spirits are not satisfied."

Once when the Master had finished drinking tea, he held up the cup and said: "All the buddhas of the three periods[14] have finished listening to the teaching; they have pierced the bottom of this cup and are going away. Do you see? Do you see? If you don't understand, look it up in an encyclopedia!"

Someone asked Master Yün-men, "What is the monk's practice?"
   The Master replied, "It cannot be understood."
   The questioner carried on, "Why can't it be understood?"
   "It just cannot be understood!"

"What is it like when all-embracing wisdom pervades and there is no hindrance?"
   The Master replied, "Clean up the ground and sprinkle it with water: His Excellency the Prime Minister is coming!"

Someone asked, "What is the place from which all buddhas come?"
   Master Yün-men said, "Next question, please!"

Master Yün-men quoted a saying by the Third Ancestor: "When mind does not arise, the myriad things have no fault.[15]"
   Master Yün-men said: "That's all he understood!"
   Then he raised his staff and added: "Is anything amiss in the whole universe?"

The Master told the following story:

   A monk said to Master Chao-chou, "I have just joined the monastery and am asking for your teaching."

13. The "eyeball of the founding masters" stands for their awakening—i.e., their realization of the core ("eye") of Buddhist teaching.
14. The awakened ones of the past, present, and future.
15. This is a quotation from the [*Relying on Mind,* Chapter 2].

Chao-chou asked back, "Have you already eaten your gruel?"
The monk replied, "Yes."
Chao-chou said: "Go wash your bowl!"[16]

Master Yün-men said: "Well, tell me: was what Chao-chou said a teaching or not? If you say that it was: what is it that Chao-chou told the monk? If you say that it wasn't: why did the monk in question attain awakening?"

Someone asked, "I heard a teaching that speaks of the purity of all-encompassing wisdom. What is that purity like?"
Master Yün-men spat at him.
The questioner continued, "How about some teaching method of the old masters?"
The Master said, "Come here! Cut off your feet, replace your skull, and take away the spoon and chopsticks from your bowl: now pick up your nose!"
The monk asked, "Where would one find such [teaching methods]?"
The Master said, "You windbag!" And he struck him.

Someone asked Master Yün-men "What is Ch'an?"
The Master replied, "That's it!"
The questioner went on, "What is the Tao?"
The Master said, "Okay!"

Someone asked Master Yün-men, "What is the eye of the genuine teaching?"
The Master said, "It's everywhere!"[17]

Someone asked Master Yün-men, "What is Ch'an?"
The Master said, "Is it all right to get rid of this word?"

One day the Master said, "I entangle myself in words with you every day; I can't go on till the night. Come on, ask me a question right here and now!"
In the place of his listeners, Master Yün-men said, "I'm just afraid that Reverend Yün-men won't answer."

16. In *The Record of Chao-chou* the initial question by the monk is different: "What is my self?"
17. This is one of Master Yün-men's famous one-word answers. In the original, the character in question has meanings such as: 1. vast, great; and 2. general, universal; all, everything, everywhere.

22

Fa-yen

(885–958)

F̶a-yen Wen-i is regarded as the founder of the fifth and last of the Ch'an houses, but at least one of his important descendants—and quite possibly he himself—saw his role as continuing and enlarging a house begun earlier by Hsüan-sha Shih-pei (835–908), a prominent successor of Hsüeh-feng. So well-attuned were Hsüan-sha (J., Gensha) and Hsüeh-feng that the two could communicate wordlessly, legend has it. Fa-yen (J., Hōgen) began his training under another of Hsüeh-feng's successors, Ch'ang-ch'ing (he of the horse medicine), but made little headway until he chanced to meet Hsüan-sha's principal heir, Lo-han Kuei-ch'en.

All this makes Fa-yen kin—Dharma nephew—to Yün-men, but since Fa-yen was still in his early twenties when Yün-men left for the far south, they probably never met. When his time came, Fa-yen carried the family tradition northward, establishing himself in another of the independent kingdoms that governed China during the Five Dynasties period (907–960). Following the pattern set by Hsüeh-feng and Yün-men, he formed close ties with the rulers of Nan-t'ang and received lavish honors and patronage from them in the course of his career.

Fa-yen read widely and wrote profusely, leaving "several hundred thousand words" when he died, according to *The Transmission of the Lamp.* Most of these have vanished, unfortunately, but what remains gives plain evidence of his learning, literary talent, and open mind. His writings manifest appreciation for the entire Ch'an heritage, irrespective of lineage, as well as a deep interest in the doctrines of other Buddhist schools, particularly the Hua-yen. He encouraged students to read the great Hua-yen teachers and apparently passed on, at least to some of them, his love of scholarship. One of his leading successors embraced the Tien-t'ai school, and the next generation of his line produced both Tao-yüan, the fair-handed compiler of *The Transmission of the Lamp,* and Yung-ming Yen-shou, who became a master in the Pure Land tradition as well as a Ch'an master and who wrote an even more gargantuan work harmonizing Ch'an teachings and those of other Chinese Buddhist schools.

Despite the extent of his other interests and the departures his successors would make, Fa-yen took a conservative attitude toward Ch'an. In his *Ten Guidelines for the Ch'an School,* he takes aim at weaknesses that he viewed as jeopardizing its future, including sectarian competitiveness among its lineages.

While masters before him had blasted Ch'an students for laziness and lack of insight, Fa-yen was the first to publish a treatise denouncing his fellow teachers for these failings. Too often, he charges, people preach the Dharma without having opened their eyes or found their own means of expressing it, merely parroting the words and imitating the actions of their predecessors.

Fa-yen reserved the ninth of his ten guidelines for Ch'an poetasters, titling it "On Indulging in Making Up Songs and Verses without Regard for the Rules of Sound and without Having Arrived at Reality." A fine poet himself, he extols the Ch'an tradition of verse, lauding its diversity, refinement, and unity of focus on "the one great matter." The trouble, he says, is "Ch'an teachers in various places and advanced students of meditation who consider songs and verse to be idle [pleasure], and take composition to be a trivial matter. . . . " Not only was bad poetry being produced he felt, but the Dharma itself was being damaged: "If you spout vulgar inanities, you disturb the influence of the Way; weaving miserable misconceptions, you cause trouble." ⊗

FROM TEN GUIDELINES FOR THE CH'AN SCHOOL

The purpose of Zen is to enable people to immediately transcend the ordinary and the holy, just getting people to awaken on their own, forever cutting off the root of doubt.

Many people in modern times disregard this. They may join Ch'an groups, but they are lazy about Ch'an study. Even if they achieve concentration, they do not choose real teachers. Through the errors of false teachers, they likewise lose the way.

Without having understood senses and objects, as soon as they possess themselves of some false interpretation they become obsessed by it and lose the correct basis completely.

They are only interested in becoming leaders and being known as teachers. While they value an empty reputation in the world, they bring ill on themselves. Not only do they make their successors blind and deaf, they also cause the influence of Ch'an to degenerate.

Ch'an is not founded or sustained on the premise that there is a doctrine to be transmitted. It is just a matter of direct guidance to the human mind, perception of its essence, and achievement of awakening. How could there be any sectarian styles to be valued?

There were differences in the modes of teaching set up by later Ch'an teachers, and there were both tradition and change. The methods employed by a number of famous Ch'an masters came to be continued as traditions, to the point where their descendants became sectarians and did not get to the original reality. Eventually they made many digressions, contradicting and attacking each other.

They do not distinguish the profound from the superficial, and do not know that the Great Way has no sides and the streams of truth have the same flavor.

If you memorize slogans, you are unable to make subtle adaptations according to the situation. It is not that there is no way to teach insight to learners, but once you have learned a way, it is essential that you get it to work completely. If you just stick to your teacher's school and memorize slogans, this is not enlightenment, it is a part of intellectual knowledge.

This is why it is said, "When your perception only equals that of your teacher, you lessen the teacher's virtue by half. When your perception goes beyond the teacher, only then can you express the teacher's teaching."

The Sixth Ancestor of Ch'an said to someone who had just been awakened, "What I tell you is not a secret. The secret is in you."

Another Ch'an master said to a companion, "Everything flows from your own heart."

See how those worthies of former times traversed mountains and seas, not shrinking from death or life, for the sake of one or two sayings. When there was the slightest tinge of doubt, the matter had to be submitted to certain discernment; what they wanted was distinct clarity.

First becoming standards of truth and falsehood, acting as eyes for intelligent beings, only after that did they raise the seal of the source on high and circulate the true teaching, bringing forth the rights and wrongs of former generations, bearing down on inconclusive cases.

If, without undergoing purification and clarification, you make your own personal judgment of past and present, how is that different from insisting on performing a sword dance without having learned how to handle a sword, or foolishly counting on getting across a pit without having found out its size? Can you avoid cutting yourself or falling?

THE COMPLETE PERFECTION OF TRUE NATURE

Reason exhausted, concerns forgotten—
how could this be adequately expressed?
Wherever I go, the icy moonlight's there,
falling just as it does on the valley ahead.
The fruit is ripe, trees heavy with monkeys,
mountains so endless I seem to have lost the way.
When I lift my head, some light still remains—
I see that I'm west of the place I call home.

Fa-yen's biography in *The Transmission of the Lamp* reads much like those of other T'ang and Five Dynasty teachers—surprisingly so, given that he stood so close to its author. Here the concerns of the *Guidelines* go unmentioned, but his taste for Buddhist literature and his belief in the value of study do arise, most conspicuously in a passage where, after observing that there are "many means to enlightenment," he immediately points out that Shih-t'ou awakened while he was *reading*. In exchanges with students, he makes two moves that seem distinctively his, sometimes repeating (or otherwise squarely affirming) what a student has offered, other times flatly contradicting it. His methods fall short of Yünmen's "hammer and tongs," and some would say that is why his house did not last long. Three of his immediate successors, including a Korean monk, became teachers of emperors, but the line soon lost steam and vanished after a few more generations. ⌘

FROM THE TRANSMISSION OF THE LAMP

Not long afterward Wen-i set out again with his friends across the lake.[1] Hardly had they started on their journey when a rainstorm began. The streams overflowed and flooded the land. Thereupon Wen-i and his companions took lodging temporarily at the Ti-ts'ang Monastery in the western part of the city of Fu-chou. While he was there, Wen-i took the opportunity to visit Lo-han Kueich'en,[2] who asked him:

"Where are you going, sir?"

"I shall continue my foot travels along the road."

"What is that which is called foot travel?"

"I do not know."

"Not-knowing [is most intimate]."

Wen-i was suddenly awakened. Hence he and his companions, Ch'ing-ch'i Hung-chin and others, four in all, determined to be disciples of Lo-han Kueich'en, and they consulted him freely in order to clear their doubts. They all gained a deep understanding of Ch'an, and one after another went through the ceremony of *shou-chi*.[3] Later, they were all to become the leading masters in their localities.

When they were ready to leave, Wen-i planned to stay and build a hut for himself in Kan-che Chou, but Ch'ing-ch'i and the other companions persuaded him to join them in visiting the monasteries south of the Yangtze River. When they arrived at Lin-ch'uan,[4] the governor invited Wen-i to be the abbot of the Ch'uing-shou Monastery. On the opening day, before the tea ceremony was completed, the audience were already gathered around his seat. The director of

1. The lake of Pan-yang, one of the five great lakes in China. The Yangtze River flows into it in northern Kiangsi Province. To the southwest of the Lake were many noted Ch'an Buddhist monasteries. [Wen-i is, of course, Fa-yen.—Eds.]
2. Lo-han Kuei-ch'en (867–928) was a disciple of Hsüan-sha Shih-pei.
3. In Sanskrit this ceremony is called *vyākarana,* which means being told that one will become a Buddha.
4. A town in northern Kiangsi Province.

the monks⁵ came up to him, saying, "All the audience are already gathered around your seat." Master Wen-i replied, "They really want to see the truly wise man." A moment later the Master walked up to his seat and all the audience made a deep bow. Then the Master said, "Since you all have come here, it is impossible for me not to make some remark. May I point out to you a way to truth that was given by our ancients? Be careful!" After saying this, he immediately left the seat.

At that moment a monk came forward and bowed to the Master. The Master said, "You may ask me a question!" But just as the monk was about to ask the question, the Master said, "The abbot has not yet begun his lecture, so no question will be answered."

From that time on, members of all the other congregations who had some understanding of Ch'an came to the Master. When they first arrived, they would be bold and self-confident, but as they were awakened by the Master's subtle words, they would begin to respect and believe in him. His visitors often exceeded one thousand in number.

Once when the Master came before the congregation, he let his disciples stand for a long time, and finally said:

"If your gathering should be dismissed [without a word], what is your opinion on whether or not Buddha's teaching is still implied? Try to tell me! If Buddha's teaching is not implied, why should you come here? Even if there is an implication of the Buddhist teaching, there are many gatherings in the city, so why should you come here?

"Every one of you may have read *Contemplations on Returning to the Source, Explanations of a Hundred Mental Qualities, Treatise on the Avatamsaka Sūtra, Nirvāna Sūtra,* and many another. Can you tell me in which of these teachings you find the absolute moment? If there is such a moment, please point it out to me. Are there no words in these sutras which indicate this absolute moment? . . . Do you understand? What is the use if you only read the sutra without understanding this?"

A monk asked, "How can you reveal yourself so as to identify with Tao?"

The Master answered, "When did you reveal yourself and not identify with Tao?"

A monk asked, "As for the finger, I will not ask you about it. But what is the moon?"⁶

The Master said, "Where is the finger that you do not ask about?" So the monk asked, "As for the moon, I will not ask you about it. But what is the finger?"

5. A monk was appointed as director by the government to administer monastic affairs and act as supervisor of all the monks in the area.

6. This refers to a famous statement: "The finger is what points at the moon, but it is not the moon."

The Master said, "The moon!"

The monk challenged him, "I asked about the finger; why should you answer me, 'the moon'?"

The Master replied, "Because you asked about the finger."

The Prince of Nan-t'ang esteemed the Master's teaching and invited him to stay in the Ch'an monastery of Pao-en, and bestowed upon him the title of Ch'an Master Ching-hui. The Master came to the assembly and said, "The ancients said, 'I will stand here until you see it.' Now I would like to sit here until you see it. Do you think that this is the Truth, too? Which of these statements is closest to the Truth? Try your judgment."

Question: "What is the direct way to obtain Buddha's wisdom?"

Master: "There is nothing more direct than this question."

Monk: "It is said that a chamber that has been dark for one hundred years can be made light by a single lamp. What is this single lamp?"

Master: "Why should you talk about one hundred years?"

Monk: "What is the ground of Absolute Truth?"

Master: "If there [were] a ground, it would not be Absolute Truth."

Monk: "What should one do during the twelve periods of the day?"

Master: "Tread firmly with each step."

Monk: "How can the ancient mirror reveal itself before it is uncovered?"

Master: "Why should you reveal it again?"

Monk: "What is the subtle idea of all Buddhas?"

Master: "It is what you also have."

The Master later stayed in the Ch'ing-liang Monastery. He came before the assembly and said:

"We Buddhists should be free to respond to whatever comes to us according to the moment and the cause. When it is cold, we respond to nothing else but cold; when it is hot, we respond to nothing else but heat. If we want to know the meaning of the Buddha-nature, we must watch the absolute moment and cause. In the past as well as at present there have been many means to enlightenment. Have you not read that when Shih-t'ou understood what was in the *Treatises of Seng-chao:* 'To unify ten thousand things into one's self is to be a sage indeed,' he immediately said that a sage has no self, yet nothing is not himself. In his work [*The Coincidence of Opposites*], he first points out that the mind of the Buddha in India cannot go beyond this. In this treatise he further expounds this idea. You, monks, need to be aware that all things are identified with yourself. Why? Because in this world not one isolated thing can be seen!"

The Master also said to the assembly, "You must not waste your time. A moment ago I told you that you must grasp the absolute moment and watch what is coming to you. If you lose the moment and miss the chance, you just waste your time and mistake what is formless for form.

"O monks, to take what is formless for form means losing the absolute moment and missing a chance. Just tell me whether it is correct to take the form for the formless. O monks, if you try to understand Ch'an in such a way, your efforts will be sadly wasted, because you are madly pursuing two extremes. What is the use of this? You should simply keep on doing your duty, follow what will come to you, take good care of yourself, and be careful."

23

Hsüeh-tou

(980–1052)

Ch'an master-poet Hsüeh-tou Ch'ung-hsien was born twenty-two years after Fa-yen's death and two decades after the rise of the Sung dynasty which restored stability in central China and reintegrated outlying states. Ch'an as a whole emerged undiminished from the Five Dynasties period and would flourish in the peace and prosperity of the Sung, but some parts of the sect did not survive to enjoy the new era. By the turn of the millennium, when his mother's sudden death propelled eighteen-year-old Hsüeh-tou into the monkhood, the Fa-yen line had already lost its vitality, and the Kuei-yang line, the first established, had slipped into decline as well.

Hsüeh-tou's search for the right Ch'an master carried him east from his native Szechwan into north-central China, where he entered the monastery of Chih-men Kuang-tsu, a teacher in the second generation of Yün-men's lineage. Chih-men (J., Chimon) did not leave a big footprint in the annals of Ch'an, but what we hear of him indicates a strong character and a teaching style that was poetic and elliptical. Another teacher later commented, "No one on earth can search out the stream of his words." Chih-men came to sufficient prominence late in life for the emperor to award him a purple robe, but he rejected it, and only imperial insistence brought him around.

As for Hsüeh-tou (J., Setchō), he was brought around with a well-timed whap of Chih-men's whisk, and no doubt the master's practice of writing verses in response to famous Ch'an sayings encouraged his student's development as a poet. Some fifteen years after entering the monastery, Hsüeh-tou received Dharma-transmission and resumed his eastward progress, ultimately settling not far from the ocean, at Mt. Hsüeh-tou. There he spent the final three decades of his life writing and teaching, becoming famous on both counts. When the time came to inscribe a tomb inscription for him, a prime minister who had studied under him would do the drafting!

In the opinion of noted zen scholar Yanagida Seizan, Hsüeh-tou's writings changed the course of Ch'an, precipitating "a shift toward the literary rather than the philosophical." Though the bulk of his carefully preserved work consists of Ch'an lectures and commentaries, it was a book of Ch'an sayings, offset by his poems, that became Hsüeh-tou's chief claim to fame. In making this text, he took as his model the important Lin-chi master Fen-yang Shan-chou (947–1024), who had assembled three collections of Ch'an sayings, one hundred sayings per collection, and had added a response or reflection to each saying. In one of these texts, Fen-yang (J., Fun'yō) made all his comments in verse form, and this example apparently inspired Hsüeh-tou to undertake a similar collection.

Hsüeh-tou drew ninety-eight of his cases from a pair of outstanding sources published since the turn of the century—*The Transmission of the Lamp*, with its biographies of almost a thousand Ch'an figures, and Yün-men's complete record, comprising nearly nine hundred talks and exchanges. He paid homage to his old teacher by rounding out the text with two of Chih-men's curious dialogues.

The result was a set of diverse and sparkling specimens from all of the Ch'an houses. In the manner of his great ancestor Yün-men, Hsüeh-tou interjected pungent comments or alternate responses in fifteen cases, in addition to appending his poems. Early in the next century, the master Yüan-wu K'o-ch'in (Chapter 25) attached extensive prose comments both to the cases and to Hsüeh-tou's poems, and the whole was published as *The Blue Cliff Record*. It remains one of the central texts of Ch'an and Zen. ⊗

FROM THE BLUE CLIFF RECORD

CASE 2: CHAO-CHOU'S THE SUPREME WAY

Case: Chao-chou addressed his assembly, saying, "The supreme way is not difficult; it just precludes picking and choosing. With even a few words, there will be delusion or enlightenment. This old monk does not dwell in enlightenment. Can you value this without reservation?"

A monk stepped forward and asked, "If you do not dwell in enlightenment, how can you value it without reservation?"

Chao-chou said, "I don't know that either."

The monk said, "If Your Reverence does not know, how can you say that you do not dwell in enlightenment?"

Chao-chou said, "Your questions are well asked. Make your bows and retire."

Verse: The supreme way is not difficult:
 The speech is to the point, the words are to the point.
 In one there are many kinds;
 In two there's no duality.
 On the horizon of the sky the sun rises and the moon sets;
 Beyond the balustrade, the mountains deepen, the waters grow chill.
 When the skull's consciousness is exhausted, how can joy remain?
 In a dead tree the dragon murmurs are not yet exhausted.
 Difficult, difficult!
 Picking and choosing? Clarity? You see for yourself!

CASE 3: MA-TSU UNWELL

Case: Great Master Ma-tsu was unwell. The monk in charge of monastery business asked him, "How is Your Reverence feeling these days?"

The Great Master said, "Sun-Face Buddha; Moon-Face Buddha."

Verse: Sun-Face Buddha, Moon-Face Buddha;
      What kind of people were the Ancient Emperors?
      For twenty years I have suffered bitterly;
      How many times I have gone down into the Blue Dragon's cave for
        you!
      This distress is worth recounting;
      Clear-eyed patch-robed monks should not take it lightly.

CASE 25: THE HERMIT OF LOTUS FLOWER PEAK

Case: The Hermit of Lotus Peak held up his staff before an assembly and said, "Why didn't the ancestors remain here after they reached it?"

The audience was silent. He himself answered, "It has no power for the way."

Again he said, "After all, what is it?" The assembly was again silent, and again he answered for them, "Carrying my staff across the back of my neck, paying others no heed, going to the thousand, the ten thousand peaks."

Verse: Dust and sand in his eyes, dirt in his ears,
      He doesn't consent to stay in the myriad peaks.
      Falling flowers, flowing streams, very vast.
      Suddenly raising my eyebrows [to look]—where has he gone?

CASE 34: YANG-SHAN'S NO VISIT TO THE MOUNTAIN

Case: Yang-shan asked a monk, "Where have you come from lately?"

"Mt. Lu," replied the monk.

"Did you go to the Five Elders Peak?" asked Yang-shan.

"I didn't visit there," answered the monk.

"Then you've never been to the mountain at all," said Yang-shan.

Yün-men commented, "These words were all spoken out of benevolence. The conversation fell into the weeds."

Verse: Leaving the weeds, entering the weeds;
      Who knows how to seek them out?
      White clouds, layer upon layer;
      Red sun, clear and bright.
      Looking to the left, there are no flaws;

Looking to the right, already old.
Have you not seen the man of Cold Mountain?
He traveled so swiftly;
Ten years he couldn't return,
And forgot the road by which he came.

CASE 36: CH'ANG-SHA WANDERS IN THE MOUNTAINS

Case: Ch'ang-sha one day went wandering in the mountains. When he returned to the gate, the head monk answered, "Your Reverence, where have you been wandering?"

"I've been strolling about in the hills," said Ch'ang-sha.

"Where did you go?" asked the head monk.

Ch'ang-sha said, "I went out following the scented grasses; I came back following the falling flowers."

"That's the spring mood itself," said the head monk.

Ch'ang-sha said, "It is better than autumn dew falling on the lotus flowers."

Hsüeh-tou commented: "I am grateful for that answer."

Verse: The earth is clear of any dust—
Whose eyes do not open?
First he went following the fragrant grasses,
Then he returned pursuing the falling flowers.
A weary crane alights on a withered tree,
A mad monkey cries on the ancient terrace.
Ch'ang-sha's boundless meaning—
Bah!

CASE 37: P'AN-SHAN'S NOTHING IN THE THREE WORLDS

Case: P'an-shan gave words of instruction, saying, "In the three worlds, there is nothing. Where shall we search for the mind?"

Verse: There is nothing in the triple world;
Where can mind be found?
The white clouds form a canopy;
The flowing spring makes a lute—
One tune, two tunes; no one understands.
When the rain has passed, the autumn water is deep in the evening pond.

CASE 58: CHAO-CHOU'S NON-EXPLANATION

Case: A monk asked Chao-chou, " 'The supreme way is not difficult; it just precludes picking and choosing.' Isn't that a rut into which people today have fallen?"

Chou said, "Once somebody asked me that. Since then, for five years, I haven't been able to explain."

Verse: The Elephant King trumpets,
         The Lion roars.
         Flavorless talk
         Blocks off people's mouths.
         South, north, east, west—
         The raven flies, the rabbit runs.

CASE 62: YÜN-MEN'S SINGLE TREASURE

Case: Yün-men said to the assembly, "Within heaven and earth, in the midst of the cosmos, there is one treasure, hidden in the body. Holding a lantern, it goes toward the Buddha Hall. It brings the great triple gate and puts it on the lantern."

Verse: Look! Look!
         On the ancient embankment, who holds the fishing pole?
         Clouds roll on.
         The water, vast and boundless—
         The white flowers in the moonlight, you must see for yourself.

CASE 82: TA-LUNG'S DHARMA-BODY

Case: A monk asked Ta-lung, "The body of form and color perishes. What is the indestructible Dharma-body?"
         Ta-lung said, "The mountain flowers bloom like brocade; / the river between the hills runs blue as indigo."

Verse: Asking without knowing.
         Answering, still not understanding.
         The moon is cold, the wind is high—
         On the ancient cliff, frigid juniper.
         How delightful: on the road he met a man who had attained the Path,
         And didn't use speech or silence to reply.
         His hand grasps the white jade whip.
         And smashes the black dragon's pearl.
         If he hadn't smashed it,
         He would have increased its flaws.
         The nation has a code of laws—
         Three thousand articles of offenses.

24

Su T'ung-po

(1037–1101)

If Hsüeh-tou was the Sung dynasty's consummate Ch'an poet, then Su T'ung-po was its consummate poet with an interest in Ch'an. Exactly how great an interest he had and how far he went in pursuing it, nobody knows. Like Po Chü-i, he left numerous signs of fondness for the Way, including his pen name, Layman of the Eastern Field, but in his case, we find no hard evidence of persistent practice or close study with a teacher. All the same, Ch'an and Zen people have long viewed him as an enlightened layperson par excellence. Hakuin (Chapter 44) placed him among a group of five Chinese laymen "possessed of insight far surpassing that of ordinary monks."

Su may not have had much time for focused pursuit of the Way, given his competing commitments as a public official and family man and his extraordinary career in the arts. He won national repute not only as a poet but also as a prose writer, a painter, and a calligrapher. His literary contributions ran the gamut from essays on aesthetics to a book of light humor titled *Master Mugwort's Miscellany.* Su once compared his writing to a "ten-thousand-gallon spring" that gushed forth unbidden and determined its own direction. "It can issue from the ground anywhere at all. On smooth ground it rushes swiftly and covers a thousand [leagues] in a single day without difficulty. When it twists and turns among mountains and rocks, it fits its form to the things it meets: unknowable. What can be known is, it always goes where it must go, always stops where it cannot help stopping—nothing else. More than that even I cannot know."

Though many of Su's poems refer to Buddhist sites or individuals, few of them bear a distinct Ch'an stamp; if anything, they carry a Ch'an watermark, only visible when held up to the moon. One of the few exceptions is a poem the masters have quoted for nine hundred years, said to record Su's awakening:

> The sound of the valley stream is the long, broad tongue;
> The form of the mountains—isn't that the pure, clear body?
> In the course of the night, eighty-four thousand *gāthās*—
> Tomorrow, how could I explain them to anyone else?

The sutras list a long, broad tongue among a buddha's distinguishing features, representing peerless capacity to express the Way, and "the pure, clear body" is the body of the Dharma, so the thrust of the poem cannot be mistaken. Its lucid,

elegant presentation of the preaching of inanimate things promptly won it a
place in *The Blue Cliff Record,* published just forty-four years later. Ch'an abbot
Ch'ang-tsung, to whom Su addressed the poem, succeeded the great Lin-chi
master Huang-lung Hui-nan and is usually taken, with little more evidence, as
Su's main teacher.

Su and his family moved frequently as his official posts changed and his political fortunes shifted. Criticism of imperial policy got him banished to the hinterlands for roughly half his forty-year career, even imprisoned at one point, but
the poems indicate that he took these reversals in stride and suggest that his
Ch'an study helped him do so. He likened his life in exile to a monk's casting off
family ties in order to find his true home, and he counted his blessings differently
than others:

> The weaker the wine,
> The easier it is to drink two cups.
> The thinner the robe,
> The easier it is to wear it double.

This represents, in part, a refusal to let his troubles get the better of him, but it
also reflects his ability to calculate the absolute bottom line:

> In all the world, good and evil,
> Joy and sorrow, are in fact
> Only aspects of the void.

However limited his actual practice of Ch'an, Su T'ung-po seems to have known
its heart and found novel, compelling means for its expression.⌘

THE STATUE OF VIMALAKĪRTI,
A CLAY FIGURE BY YANG HUI-CHIH OF THE T'ANG IN
THE TEMPLE OF THE PILLAR OF HEAVEN
(1061)

Long ago when Master Yü was sick and dying,
his friend Master Ssu went to visit him.
Stumbling to the well, Yü looked in and sighed,
"What will the Creator make out of me next?"
Now as I view this old clay image of Vimalakīrti,
ailing bones sharp and knobby, like a dried-up turtle,
I know that a great man is indifferent to life and death,
his body changing form, gone with the floating clouds.
Most people—yes, they're sturdy and handsome,
but though not sick in body, their minds are worn out.
This old fellow—his spirit's whole, something solid inside;
with quip and laughter he overpowers a thousand contenders.

When he was alive someone asked him about the Dharma;
he bowed his head, wordless, though at heart of course he knew.
To this day his likeness sits stolid, never speaking,
just as he was in life, nothing added, nothing lost.
Old farmers, village wives never deign to give a glance,
though field mice sometimes nibble at his whiskers.
Each time I look at him I'm lost in wonder—
Who can be like Vimalakīrti, a wordless teacher?

NOTE   Vimalakīrti was a wealthy lay follower of Shākyamuni Buddha in India,
famous for his masterful understanding of the Buddha's teachings and his skill in
propounding them. He is the central figure in the *Vimalakīrti Sūtra,* one of the
most important texts of Mahāyāna Buddhism. Yang Hui-chih was a painter and
sculptor active in the early eighth century. The T'ien-chu-ssu or Temple of the
Pillar of Heaven was in Feng-hsiang.

LINES 1–4   These lines are based on the passage in *Chuang-tzu* Sec. 6 that describes Master Yü's calm acceptance of death and tells how, dragging himself
haltingly to the well and looking in, he speculated on what form the Creator intended him to take next.

LINE 8   As a means of teaching the truths of Buddhism, Vimalakīrti took on the
form of an ailing man. In the *Vimalakīrti Sūtra* ch. 2 he says: "This body is like a
floating cloud, changing and fading away in an instant."

LINE 14   *Vimalakīrti Sūtra* ch. 9 describes how the bodhisattva Mañjushrī
asked Vimalakīrti to give his interpretation of nondualism, the core concept of
the Dharma or Buddhist doctrine. Vimalakīrti replied by remaining silent.

WINTER SOLSTICE
(1071)
(*I took an outing to Lone Hill and visited two Buddhist priests, Hui-ch'in
and Hui-ssu.*)

The sky threatens snow,
clouds cover the lake;
towers appear and disappear, hills loom and fade.
Clear water cut by rocks—you can count the fish;
deep woods deserted—birds call back and forth.
Winter solstice: I refuse to go home to my family;
I say I'm visiting priests, though really out for fun.
These priests I visit—where do they live?
The road by Jewel Cloud Mountain twists and turns.
Lone Hill's alone indeed—who'd live here?

These priests—the hill's not lonely after all.
Paper windows, bamboo roof—rooms sheltered and warm;
in coarse robes they doze on round rush mats.
Cold day, a long road—my servant grumbles,
brings the carriage, hurries me home before dark.
Down the hill, looking back, clouds and trees blend;
I can just make out a mountain eagle circling the pagoda.
Such trips—simple but with a joy that lasts;
back home, I'm lost in a dreamer's daze.
Write a poem quick before it gets away!
Once gone, a lovely sight is hard to catch again.

VISITING THE MONASTERY OF
THE ANCESTOR'S PAGODA WHILE ILL
(1073)

Purple plums, yellow melons—the village roads smell sweet;
black gauze cap, white hemp robe—traveling clothes are cool.
In a country temple, gate closed, pine shadows turning,
I prop pillows by a breezy window and dream long dreams.
A vacation due to illness—things could be worse;
stilling the mind—no medicine is better than this.
The priests aren't stingy with their well by the stairs;
they gave me pail and dipper and said help yourself!

LODGING AT HAI-HUI TEMPLE
(1073)

Three days by palanquin traveling through mountains;
beautiful mountains, but never a level stretch!
Dip toward the yellow springs, rise to the sky,
contest a threat-thin path with monkeys,
Till we reach a narrow hollow, pagoda tall and cramped in it;
thighs ache with bruises, empty stomach growls.
North across a high bridge, bearers' feet clomping;
walls like old battlements wind a hundred yards.
They sound the great bell—a crowd of monks appears,
leads me to the main hall, unbarred even at night.
Cedar tub and lacquer pail pour out rivers
to wash the body "spotless from the first."

I fall in bed and startle my neighbors with snoring;
the fifth-watch drum booms, the sky still dark.
Sharp and clear the wooden fish calls us to gruel;
I hear no voices, but the scuff of shoes.

LINE 3 "Yellow springs." A term for the underworld; Su uses it here face-
tiously.

LINE 12 "Spotless from the first." A Ch'an term derived from the *Vimalakīrti
Sūtra*, referring to the purity of the original nature.

LINE 15 "Wooden fish." A board shaped like a fish which was struck to summon the monks to meals.

WRITTEN FOR MASTER CHAN'S ROOM
AT THE DOUBLE BAMBOO TEMPLE
(1073)

Strike your own evening drum, morning bell,
then shut the door. Lamp burning low by a solitary pillow;
gray ashes where just now you stirred the stove to red.
Lie and listen to raindrops splattering the window.

BAD WINE IS LIKE BAD MEN
(1074)
*(Drank with Liu Tzu-yü at Gold Mountain Temple. Got very drunk, slept on
Pao-chüeh's meditation platform. Came to in the middle of the night and inscribed this on his wall.)*

Bad wine is like bad men,
deadlier in attack than arrows or knives.
I collapse on the platform;
victory hopeless, truce will have to do.
The old poet carries on bravely,
the Zen master's words are gentle and profound.
Too drunk to follow what they're saying,
I'm conscious only of a red and green blur.
I wake to find the moon sinking into the river,
the wind rustling with a different sound.
A lone lamp burns by the altar,
but the two heroes—both have disappeared.

WRITTEN ON ABBOT LUN'S WALL AT MOUNT CHIAO
(1074)

The master stays on Mount Chiao,
(though in fact he's never "stayed" anywhere).
No sooner had I arrived than I asked about the Way,
but the Master never said a word.
Not that he was lost for words—
he saw no reason for replying.
Then I thought, Look at your head and feet—
comfortable enough in hat and shoes, aren't they?
It's like the man with a long beard
who never worried how long it was.
But one day someone asked him,
"What do you do with it when you sleep?"
That night, pulling up the covers,
he couldn't decide if it went on top or under.
All night he tossed and turned, wondering where to put it,
till he felt like yanking it out by the roots.
These words may seem trite and shallow
but in fact they have deep meaning.
When I asked the Master what he thought,
the Master smiled his approval.

LINE 2 The Master dwells in the realm of Buddhist nondualism, where relative
concepts such as "staying" or "going" have no validity.

LOTUS VIEWING
(1079)
(*With the Wang brothers and my son Mai, went around the city looking at
lotus flowers. We climbed to the pavilion on Mt. Hsien, and in the evening
went to the Temple of Flying Petals.*)

The clear wind—what is it?
Something to be loved, not to be named,
moving like a prince wherever it goes;
the grass and trees whisper its praise.
This outing of ours never had a purpose;
let the lone boat swing about as it will.
In the middle of the current, lying face up,
I greet the breeze that happens along
and lift a cup to offer to the vastness:

how pleasant—that we have no thought for each other!
Coming back through two river valleys,
clouds and water shine in the night.

Clerks and townsmen pity my laziness;
day by day I have fewer disputes to settle.
So I can go drinking and wandering around,
even spending a whole night out.
We come looking for the Temple of Flying Petals,
making the most of the light that's left.
A bell ringing; the sound of gathering feet:
monks tumble out in mountain robes.
I may be dropping by at odd hours—
with foot and cane I'll open the door myself.
Don't treat me like a high official!
Outside I look like one, but inside I'm not.

WRITTEN ON THE WALL AT WEST FOREST TEMPLE
(1084)

From the side, a whole range; from the end, a single peak;
far, near, high, low, no two parts alike.
Why can't I tell the true shape of Lu-shan?
Because I myself am in the mountain.

NOTE   In the third month of this year, the poet was ordered to move to Ju-chou
in Honan, an indication that his sentence had been lightened and he was free to
move beyond the confines of Huang-chou. Before proceeding to Ju-chou, he
crossed the Yangtze and traveled south to visit his brother in Yün-chou. West
Forest Temple was in Kiangsi at Lu-shan or Mt. Lu, famous for its scenery and as
a center of Buddhist activity from early times. The poet stayed at the mountain
for a few days on his way to Yün-chou.

NEW YEAR'S EVE
(1084)
(*New Year's Eve at Ssu-chou; snow. Huang Shih-shih sent us a present of
cream and wine.*)

Twilight snow whirls down handfuls of powdered rice;
spring river whispers over yellow sand.
Past visits—dreams to be recounted only.

An exile is like a monk: where is home?
Before I can write, ink on the cold slab freezes;
lone lamp—I wonder why?—forms a flower.
In the middle of the night you send us cream and wine.
I jump up in surprise, my wife and children laugh and shout.

LINE 6 "Flower." The formation of a so-called snuff flower—a peculiar twisting of the wick—was believed to be a lucky omen.

BY THE RIVER AT T'ENG-CHOU,
GETTING UP AT NIGHT AND LOOKING AT THE MOON,
TO SEND TO THE MONK SHAO
(1100)

River moon to light my mind,
river water to wash my liver clean,
moon like an inch-round pearl
fallen into this white jade cup.
My mind too is like this:
a moon that's full, a river with no waves.
Who is it gets up to dance?
Let's hope there are more than three of you!
In this pestilent land south of the mountains,
still we have the cool river moonlight,
and I know that in all heaven and earth
there's no one not calm and at peace.
By the bedside I have milky wine;
the jar brims over as though full of white dew.
I get drunk alone, sober up alone,
the night air boundlessly fresh.
I'll send word to the monk Shao,
have him bring his zither and play under the moon,
and then we'll board a little boat
and in the night go down the Ts'ang-wu rapids.

NOTE   The poet, on his way home to the north, was about to leave T'eng-chou in Kwangsi and travel down the Ts'ang-wu River.

LINES 7–8 An allusion to Li Po's famous poem, "Drinking Alone Under the Moon," in which he speaks of three companions, the moon, his shadow, and himself, drinking and dancing together.

BELL AND DRUM ON THE SOUTH RIVER BANK
(1101)
(*Following the rhymes of Chiang Hui-shu: two poems.*)

Bell and drum on the south river bank:
home! I wake startled from a dream.
Drifting clouds—so the world shifts;
lone moon—such is the light of my mind.
Rain drenches down as from a tilted basin;
poems flow out like water spilled.
The two rivers vie to send me off;
beyond treetops I see the slant of a bridge.

NOTE   Written in the summer. The poet had traveled north, then east down the Yangtze to Chinkiang, and was now about to enter the Grand Canal to go south to Ch'ang-chou, where he planned to live the remainder of his life. He died on the eighteenth day of the seventh month of this year, shortly after reaching Ch'ang-chou. This is the second of the two poems.

25

Yüan-wu

(1063–1135)

After studying with teachers in several houses of Ch'an, Yüan-wu K'o-ch'in met his match in the great Lin-chi master Wu-tsu Fa-yen. In the early decades of the Sung dynasty, the Lin-chi line had forked into two "schools" named for teachers who began them, Huang-lung (J., Ōryō) and Yang-ch'i (J., Yōgi). Both schools flourished initially, absorbing other lineages, and Ch'an histories recognize their importance in a stock phrase used to describe the Chinese institution as a whole—"the Five Houses and the Seven Schools." Wu-tsu (J., Goso) and Yüan-wu (J., Engo), both natives of Szechwan, brought tremendous vitality to the Yang-ch'i school, and in the following generations, it eclipsed all other streams of Ch'an. The surviving tradition of Japanese Rinzai Zen descends entirely from Wu-tsu and Yüan-wu.

Yüan-wu's encounters with other teachers had gone so well that he came to Wu-tsu with an inflated sense of his understanding of Ch'an. Thus a rebuff that he received from Wu-tsu stung sharply, and he left in anger—but not before Wu-tsu sowed the seed of his return: "Remember me some day when you're seriously ill." When that day arrived, Yüan-wu decided to go back and see what the much-lauded master had to teach. From childhood, Yüan-wu had displayed exceptional intelligence, and the promise of this now humbled student must have been clear, for he soon received the honor of serving as Wu-tsu's attendant, a responsibility providing frequent and unusual access to instruction.

Indeed, in his capacity as attendant Yüan-wu heard the conversation that precipitated his awakening. As a certain high official took leave one day, Wu-tsu told him to reflect on a love song with two lines "very close to Ch'an"—"She often calls her servant Little Jade, though she doesn't really need her; / She calls just so her lover will recognize her voice." Yüan-wu inquired afterward if the visitor had understood. "He only recognized the voice," Wu-tsu replied. When Yüan-wu asked what more there *was* to understand, suddenly the great teacher quoted a famous dialogue from the record of Chao-chou: " 'What is the meaning of Bodhidharma's coming from the West?' 'The oak tree in the garden.' *See?*" Abruptly Yüan-wu saw, and he went on to become the foremost of Wu-tsu's several outstanding heirs.

Yüan-wu began to teach at the turn of the century, swiftly rising to national prominence. His deep realization, inborn talent for literature, and familiarity with other Ch'an lineages made him a superb representative not only of the Yang-

ch'i house or the Lin-chi school but of the entire stream from Ts'ao-chi. His reputation grew especially in the wake of lectures he delivered on a collection of one
hundred public cases assembled some sixty years before by the Yün-men master
Hsüeh-tou (Chapter 23). Yüan-wu added a pointer to each case, introducing its
subject, and interjected pithy, often caustic remarks into the body of both the case
and Hsüeh-tou's verse. His talks, however, consisted mainly of extended commentary on this material, exemplified in the selections which follow.

Yüan-wu's students gathered, edited, and published their notes on these lectures, producing the masterpiece commonly known in English as *The Blue Cliff
Record*. Despite the scale of this publishing endeavor—an English translation of
the text runs to 560 pages—and the labor-intensive nature of the wood-block
printing, publication was completed in 1128, no more than eighteen years after
the talks were given and seven years before Yüan-wu's death. The text is dense
with allusions to Ch'an traditions and literature and also draws heavily on Taoist
and secular sources, particularly on the Chinese classics, poetry, and folklore. Its
erudition dazzled readers and set a new standard for Ch'an writing. This was not
erudition for its own sake but rather, as Yüan-wu explains elsewhere, a princi-
pled practice of deciding current matters by reference to ancient precedents: "It
is not a matter of special liking for antiquity—it is simply that people today are
not sufficient as examples." As his precedent for such conservatism, he quotes
Wu-tsu's teacher: "Changing the old and constant is the big trouble of people today, and I will never do it."

Yüan-wu's life spanned a time when Chinese trade and culture boomed but
political discord enabled invaders from the north to drive the Sung dynasty
south of the Yangtze. This setback at the hands of a people that the Chinese considered barbarian did surprisingly little to diminish the vigor of Sung culture
and seems to have affected Yüan-wu's career only in its details. Before the south-
erly exodus of 1126, he was appointed abbot of several major monasteries in
north China and awarded a purple robe and an imperial title. Afterward, he was
selected to head equally prominent temples in the south and received, from the
new emperor, a second purple robe and a second imperial title, this being Yüan-
wu Ch'an-shih, Ch'an Master of Perfect Enlightenment.

Yüan-wu's career thus bore out his own dictum "Life, death, calamity, or
trouble—let them all be and you enter the realm of buddhahood without leaving
the realm of demons." Within a century of his death, his influence had spread as
far as Japan, carried overseas by descendants of his sixteen Dharma heirs and by
his brilliant writings. 88

FROM THE BLUE CLIFF RECORD

CASE 24: KUEI-SHAN AND IRON GRINDSTONE LIU

Case: Iron Grindstone Liu arrived at Kuei-shan. Kuei-shan said, "Old cow, so
you've come!"

The Grindstone said, "Tomorrow there's a great communal feast on Mt. T'ai, are you going to go, Teacher?"

Kuei-shan relaxed his body and lay down, the Grindstone immediately left.

Commentary: The nun "Iron Grindstone" Liu was like a stone-struck spark, like a lightning flash; hesitate and you lose your body and your life. In the path of meditation, if you get to the most essential place, where are there so many things? This meeting of adepts is like seeing horns on the other side of a wall and immediately knowing there's an ox, like seeing smoke on the other side of a mountain and immediately knowing there's a fire. When pushed they move, when pressed they turn about.

Kuei-shan said, "After I die, I'll go down the mountain to an alms-giver's house and be a water buffalo. On my left flank five words will be written, saying, 'A Kuei-shan monk, me.' At that time, would it be right to call it a Kuei-shan monk, or would it be right to call it a water buffalo?" When people these days are questioned about this, they are stymied and can't explain.

Iron Grindstone Liu had studied for a long time; her active edge was sharp and dangerous. People called her "Iron Grindstone Liu." She built a hut a few miles from Kuei Mountain. One day she went to call on Kuei-shan. When he saw her coming, he said, "Old cow, so you've come." The Grindstone said, "Tomorrow there's a great communal feast on Mt. T'ai; are you going to go, Teacher?" Kuei-shan relaxed his body and lay down, whereupon the Grindstone left. All of you look—throughout they seemed to be conversing, but this is not Ch'an, neither is it Tao. Can it be understood by calling it unconcern?

Kuei-shan is over six hundred miles from Mt. T'ai; how then did Iron Grindstone Liu want to have Kuei-shan go to the feast? Tell me, what was her meaning? This old lady understands Kuei-shan's conversation: fiber coming, thread going, one letting go, one gathering in; they answer back to each other like two mirrors reflecting each other, without any reflection image to be seen. Action to action, they complement each other; phrase to phrase, they accord.

People these days can be poked three times and not turn their heads, but this old lady couldn't be fooled one little bit. By no means is this an emotional view based on mundane truth; like a bright mirror on its stand, like a bright jewel in the palm of the hand, when a foreigner comes, a foreigner is reflected, and when a native comes a native is reflected. It's that she knows there is something transcendent; that's why she acts like this.

Right now you are content to understand this as unconcern. Master Yen of Wu-tsu said, "Don't take having concerns as not having concerns; time and time again concern is born of unconcern." If you can immerse yourself in this and penetrate through, you will see that Kuei-shan and Iron Grindstone Liu acting in this way is the same sort as ordinary people's conversation. People are often hindered by the words, that's why they don't understand. Only an intimate acquaintance can understand them thoroughly.

CASE 49: SAN-SHENG'S GOLDEN FISH
WHO HAS PASSED THROUGH THE NET

Case: San-sheng asked Hsüeh-feng, "I wonder, what does the golden fish who has passed through the net use for food?"

Feng said, "When you come out of the net I'll tell you."

Sheng said, "The teacher of fifteen-hundred people and you don't even know what to say!"

Feng said, "My affairs as abbot are many and complicated."

Commentary: With Hsüeh-feng and San-sheng, though there's one exit and one entry, one thrust and one parry, there is no division into victory and defeat. But say, what is the eye that these two venerable adepts possess?

San-sheng received the secret from Lin-chi. He traveled all over and everyone treated him as an eminent guest. Look at him posing a question. How many people look but cannot find him! He doesn't touch on inherent nature or the Buddha-Dharma: instead he asks, "What does the golden fish who has passed through the net use for food?" But say, what was his meaning? Since the golden fish who has passed through the net ordinarily does not eat the tasty food of others, what does he use for food?

Hsüeh-feng is an adept: in a casual fashion he replies to San-sheng with only ten or twenty percent. He just said to him, "When you come out of the net, I'll tell you." Fen-yang would call this "a question that displays one's understanding." In the Ts'ao-tung tradition it would be called "a question that uses things." You must be beyond categories and classifications, you must have obtained the use of the great function, you must have an eye on your forehead—only then can you be called a golden fish who has passed through the net. Nevertheless, Hsüeh-feng is an adept and can't help but diminish the other man's reputation by saying "When you come out of the net, I'll tell you."

Observe how the two of them held fast to their territories, towering up like ten thousand fathom walls. With this one sentence of Hsüeh-feng's anyone other than San-sheng would have been unable to go on. Yet San-sheng too was an adept: thus he knew how to say to him, "The teacher of fifteen hundred people and you don't even know what to say!" But Hsüeh-feng said, "My affairs as abbot are many and complicated." How obstinate this statement is!

When these adepts met, there was one capture and one release—(each) acted weak when encountering strength and acted noble when encountering meanness. If you form your understanding in terms of victory and defeat, you haven't seen Hsüeh-feng even in dreams. Look at these two men: initially both were solitary and dangerous, lofty and steep; in the end both were dead and decrepit. But say, was there still gain and loss, victory and defeat? When these adepts harmonized with each other, it was necessarily not this way.

San-sheng was the Temple Keeper at Lin-chi. When Lin-chi was about to pass on he directed, "After I'm gone you mustn't destroy the treasure of the eye of my correct teaching." San-Sheng came forward and said, "How could we dare destroy the treasure of the eye of your correct teaching, Master?" Chi said, "In the future, how will you act when people ask questions?" San-sheng then shouted. Chi said, "Who would have known that the treasure of the eye of my correct teaching would perish in this blind donkey?" San-sheng then bowed in homage. Since he was a true son of Lin-chi's, he dared to respond like this.

CASE 89: THE HANDS AND EYES OF
THE BODHISATTVA OF GREAT COMPASSION

Case: Yün-yen asked Tao-wu, "What does the Bodhisattva of Great Compassion use so many hands and eyes for?"

Wu said, "It's like someone reaching back groping for a pillow in the middle of the night."

Yen said, "I understand."

Wu said, "How do you understand it?"

Yen said: "All over the body are hands and eyes."

Wu said, "You have said quite a bit there, but you've only said eighty percent of it."

Yen said, "What do you say, Elder Brother?"

Wu said, "Throughout the body are hands and eyes."

Commentary: The Bodhisattva of Great Compassion [Avalokiteshvara] has eighty-four thousand symbolic arms. Great Compassion has this many hands and eyes—do all of you? Pai-chang said, "All sayings and writings return to one's self."

Yün-yen often followed Tao-wu, to study and ask questions to settle his discernment with certainty. One day he asked him, "What does the Bodhisattva of Great Compassion use so many hands and eyes for?" Right at the start Tao-wu should have given him a blow of the staff across his back, to avoid so many complications appearing later. But Tao-wu was compassionate—he couldn't be like this. Instead, he gave Yün-yen an explanation of the reason, meaning to make him understand immediately. Instead [of hitting him] Tao-wu said, "It's like someone reaching back groping for a pillow in the middle of the night." Groping for a pillow in the depths of the night without any lamplight—tell me, where are the eyes?

Yün-yen immediately said, "I understand." Wu said, "How do you understand it?" Yen said, "All over the body are hands and eyes." Wu said, "You have said quite a bit there, but you've only said eighty percent of it." Yen said, "What do you say, Elder Brother?" Wu said, "Throughout the body are hands and eyes."

But say, is "all over the body" right, or is "throughout the body" right? Although they seem covered with mud, nevertheless they are bright and clean. People these days often make up emotional interpretations and say that "all over the body" is wrong, while "throughout the body" is right—they're merely chewing over the Ancients' words and phrases. They have died in the Ancients' words, far from realizing that the Ancients' meaning isn't in the words, and that all talk is used as something that can't be avoided. People these days add footnotes and set up patterns, saying that if one can penetrate this case, then this can be considered understanding enough to put an end to study. Groping with their hands over their bodies and over the lamp and the pillow, they all make a literal understanding of "throughout the body." If you understand this way, you degrade those Ancients quite a bit.

Thus it is said, "He studies the living phrase; he doesn't study the dead phrase." You must cut off emotional defilements and conceptual thinking, become clean and naked, free and unbound—only then will you be able to see this saying about Great Compassion.

Haven't you heard how Ts'ao-shan asked a monk, "How is it when [the Dharmakāya, the body of reality] is manifesting form in accordance with beings, like the moon [reflected] in the water?" The monk said, "Like an ass looking at a well." Shan said, "You have said quite a lot, but you've only said eighty percent of it." The monk said, "What do you say, Teacher?" Shan said, "It's like the well looking at the ass." This is the same meaning as the main case.

While posterity knows Yüan-wu best for *The Blue Cliff Record,* he left his mark in other ways as well. In an effort to popularize Ch'an—and not without precedent—his teacher Wu-tsu is reported to have relaxed some of the traditional restrictions on monks' behavior, namely bans on contact with women and consumption of meat and alcohol. Though it is unclear whether Yüan-wu fully subscribed to these changes, he certainly continued Wu-tsu's project to propagate the Dharma among laypeople. He once delegated Ta-hui, who would become his highly influential successor, specifically to receive and instruct lay visitors. Enlightened laywomen appear conspicuously in both his and Ta-hui's records (Chapter 27). ※

INTERACTIONS WITH WOMEN

Fan Hsien-chien used to sit constantly, never lying down. When she heard that Yüan-wu was at Chao-chüeh temple in Ch'eng-tu [the province where she lived], she went to pay her respects to him and asked for guidance in the Way.

Yüan-wu told her to contemplate the saying, "It's not mind, it's not Buddha, it's not a thing."

She contemplated it for a long time without success. Finally, in frustration, she asked Yüan-wu, "What expedient method do you have to make it easier for me to understand?"

Yüan-wu said, "There is a method," and he had her contemplate simply, "What is it?"

Later she had an awakening and said, "After all, it was always so close!"

Chiao-an was the niece of a high official of the Sung dynasty. When she was young, she set her heart on the way of Ch'an; she decided early on not to marry or bear children. She experienced clear awakening at the words of Yüan-wu as he spoke to the assembly.

Yüan-wu said to her, "You should go on to erase your views—then you will finally be free."

She answered in verse,

> The pillar pulls out the bone sideways;
> The void shows its claws and fangs;
> Even if one profoundly understands,
> There is still sand in the eye.

Just as Yüan-wu approached the teaching seat on the day he began to teach at Chia-shan, Yü bounded forth from the assembly. She gave him a nudge with her body and went back into the crowd. Yüan-wu said, "When you see the strangeness as not strange, the strangeness disappears of itself."

The next day Yüan-wu went to her house. She shouted, "Such a yellow-mouthed little boy—and you say you're a teacher?"

Yüan-wu said, "Don't brag so much, lady. I've recognized you." Then she laughed and came out to meet him.

Besides offering face-to-face instruction, Yüan-wu conducted an extensive correspondence, laying out the path of Ch'an in plain language for people whose responsibilities did not permit much time at the monastery. In his letters, too, he makes frequent reference to the sages of old, but here his emphasis is much more practical than in the lofty *The Blue Cliff Record*. Such correspondence—or at least its inclusion as part of a master's formal record—was a relatively new phenomenon, dating back only half a century to Huang-lung (d. 1069). Yüan-wu's letters reflect both the widening audience Ch'an found in the Sung period and the increasingly engaged, egalitarian posture that he and other Ch'an leaders had started to take. Published under the title *Essentials of Mind,* the letters have had great impact on Ch'an and Zen students of later generations. 🞕

FROM ESSENTIALS OF MIND

ABANDONING ENTANGLEMENTS

Yen-t'ou said, "Abandoning things is superior, pursuing things is inferior." If your own state is empty and tranquil, perfectly illuminated and silently shining, then you will be able to confront whatever circumstances impinge on you with the indestructible sword of wisdom and cut everything off—everything from the myriad entangling objects to the verbal teachings of the past and present. Then your awesome, chilling spirit cuts off everything, and everything retreats of itself without having to be pushed away. Isn't this what it means to be well endowed and have plenty to spare?

If the basis you establish is not clear, if you are the least bit bogged down in hesitation and doubt, then you will be dragged off by entangling conditions, and obviously you will not be able to separate yourself from them. How can you avoid being turned around by other things. When you are following other things, you will never have any freedom.

SERENE AND FREE

People who study the Way begin by having the faith to turn toward it. They are fed up with the vexations and filth of the world and are always afraid they will not be able to find a road of entry into the Way.

Once you have been directed by a teacher or else discovered on your own the originally inherently complete real mind, then no matter what situations or circumstances you encounter, you know for yourself where it's really at.

But then if you hold fast to that real mind, the problem is you cannot get out, and it becomes a nest. You set up "illumination" and "function" in acts and states, snort and clap and glare and raise your eyebrows, deliberately putting on a scene.

When you meet a genuine expert of the school again, he removes all this knowledge and understanding for you, so you can merge directly with realization of the original uncontrived, unpreoccupied, unminding state. After this you will feel shame and repentance and know to cease and desist. You will proceed to vanish utterly, so that not even the sages can find you arising anywhere, much less anyone else.

That is why Yen-t'ou said, "Those people who actually realize it just keep serene and free at all times, without cravings, without dependence." Isn't this the door to peace and happiness?

In olden times Kuan-hsi went to Mo-shan.[1] Mo-shan asked him, "Where have you just come from?" Kuan-hsi said, "From the mouth of the road." Mo-shan said, "Why didn't you cover it?" Kuan-hsi had no reply.

---

1. [Mo-shan, a ninth-century nun, was a Ch'an master descended from Ma-tsu.—Eds.]

The next day Kuan-hsi asked, "What is the realm of Mt. Mo-shan like?" Mo-shan said, "The peak doesn't show." Kuan-hsi asked: "What is the man on the mountain like?" Mo-shan said, "Not any characteristics like male or female." Kuan-hsi said, "Why don't you transform?" Mo-shan said, "I'm not a spirit or a ghost—what would I transform?"

Weren't the Zen adepts in these stories treading on the ground of reality and reaching the level where one stands like a wall miles high?

Thus it is said: "At the Last Word, you finally reach the impenetrable barrier. Holding the essential crossing, you let neither holy nor ordinary pass."

Since the ancients were like this, how can it be that we modern people are lacking?

Luckily, there is the indestructible diamond sword of wisdom. You must meet someone who knows it intimately, and then you can bring it out.

HOW TO BE A HOUSEHOLDER-BODHISATTVA

This affair is a matter of people of sharp faculties and superior wisdom who do not consider it difficult to understand a thousand when hearing one. It requires a stand that is solid and true and faith that is thoroughgoing.

Then you can hold fast and act the master and take all sorts of adverse and favorable situations and differing circumstances and fuse them into one whole—a whole that is like empty space, without the least obstruction, profoundly clear and empty and illuminated, never changing even in a hundred eons or a thousand lifetimes, unitary from beginning to end. Only then do you find peace and tranquillity.

I have seen many people who are intellectually brilliant but whose faculties are unstable and whose practice is shallow. They think they witness transformation in verbal statements, and they assume that there is no way to go beyond the worldly. Thus they increase the thorns of arbitrary opinion as they show off their ability and understanding. They take advantage of their verbal agility and think that the Buddha-Dharma is like this. When situations are born from causal conditions, they cannot pass through to freedom, so they wind up vacillating back and forth. This is really a great pity!

This is why the ancients went through all sorts of experiences and faced all sorts of demons and difficulties. They might be cut to pieces, but they never gave it a thought; they took charge of their minds all the way along and made them as strong as iron or stone. Thus when it came to passing through birth-and-death, they didn't waste any effort. Isn't this where the special strength and generosity beyond emotionalism that truly great people possess lies?

When bodhisattvas who live a householder's life cultivate the practices of home-leavers, it is like a lotus blooming in fire. It will always be hard to tame the will for fame and rank and power and position, not to mention all the myriad starting points of vexation and turmoil associated with the burning house of worldly existence. The only way is for you yourself to realize your fundamental, real, wondrous wholeness and reach the stage of great calm and stability and rest.

It would be best if you managed to cast off everything and be empty and ordinary. Thoroughly experience the absence of conditioned mind, and observe that all phenomena are like dreams and magical illusions. Be empty all the way through, and continue on clearing out your mind according to the time and the situation. Then you will have the same correct foundation as all the great enlightened laymen in Buddhist tradition.

According to your own measure of power, you will transform those not yet enlightened so you can enter together into the uncontrived, uncluttered ocean of true nature. Then your life here on this earth will not be a loss.

26

Hung-chih

(1091–1157)

Hung-chih Cheng-chüeh is a poorly known but important master who played a pivotal role in development of the Ts'ao-tung house of Ch'an. Under the influence of his father, a zealous Ch'an layman, Hung-chih (J., Wanshi) began his career in the monkhood at the age of eleven. After serving a novitiate in the Huang-lung school of the Lin-chi line, at eighteen he entered the monastery of the highly respected Ts'ao-tung teacher K'u-mu Fa-cheng (n.d.), and he spent the remainder of his life solidly in the Ts'ao-tung fold. Like many monks of his generation, Hung-chih also studied for a while at Yüan-wu's feet, but for him, visiting the celebrated Lin-chi master constituted no more than a brief detour from the Ts'ao-tung path.

Training with K'u-mu (J., Komoku) set the direction of both Hung-chih's life and teaching. K'u-mu took his name, which means *dead tree*, from a long-established theme in Ts'ao-tung literature. The phrase gained prominence from an exchange in *The Transmission of the Lamp* biography of the house's supposed co-founder, Ts'ao-shan (Chapter 20). Asked about the Way, an earlier master had answered, "In a dead tree, the dragon sings." When questioned on the meaning of this expression, Ts'ao-shan presented a verse that began, "The person who says the dragon sings in a dead tree / is really one who knows the Way." Teachers in other lineages also took up the phrase, including Hsüeh-tou (see his poem on case 2, Chapter 23), but it echoed most resonantly in Ts'ao-tung halls. Another of the house's early masters, Shih-shuang Ch'ing-chu (J., Sekisō Keisho), won a reputation for teaching *k'u-mu* Ch'an, and his community of monks was dubbed the Dead Tree Assembly because its members sat upright in meditation at all hours, never lying down to sleep.

As his name implies, K'u-mu followed this example, practicing and advocating an exceptionally arduous program of seated meditation, zazen. Hung-chih moved on after a few years under K'u-mu's tutelage but later taught a similar form of practice, which he called *mo-chao* Ch'an, silent-illumination Ch'an. Beyond emphasizing strict and extensive zazen, this approach entailed objectless meditation, casting everything away to peer into the Void. Hung-chih's writings on the subject deeply influenced the thirteenth-century Japanese master Dōgen (Chapter 29) and, through him, shaped the future of the Sōtō sect. His method, as interpreted by Dōgen, is now widely known by the Japanese name *shikantaza* (lit., just exactly sitting) and is the principal practice in Sōtō training.

When he left K'u-mu, Hung-chih set off on a long pilgrimage of the sort that, by that era, had become a customary feature of serious Ch'an training. His rigorous preparation with K'u-mu, this period of walking meditation, and encounters with two teachers en route opened his mind, and great awakening came when he reached his destination, the monastery of Tan-hsia Tzu-ch'un (1054–1119). Like K'u-mu, Tan-hsia (J., Tanka) was a Dharma successor of Fu-yung Tao-kai, a prominent reviver of Ts'ao-tung Ch'an. Of a more literary bent than K'u-mu, Tan-hsia had compiled a collection of sayings and added his own verse comments, an undertaking somewhat unusual for a Ts'ao-tung teacher and one that evidently encouraged his new disciple to develop his own literary talents. Tan-hsia died within five years of Hung-chih's arrival but not before acknowledging the young monk, still only twenty-eight, as his Dharma heir.

For the next eleven years, Hung-chih peregrinated the Ch'an forest, looking in on Yüan-wu and other masters, teaching from time to time at various temples. At thirty-nine, he was tapped to head the small, ill-kept monastery at Mt. T'ien-t'ung in far eastern China, and there he remained the rest of his life, receiving no great notice nationally but attracting a group of disciples that grew gradually to sixteen hundred. Safely out of the way of the warfare that pushed the Sung empire south, yet still within its borders, he quietly rebuilt and expanded the monastery with the support of local merchants, officials, and military leaders. Legend has it that he descended the mountain only once in his nearly thirty years there, going down the day before he died to thank his circle of patrons.

Hung-chih did not hold himself aloof from worldly affairs, however. More than once when nearby villages faced hunger, he provided food from monastery stocks, and like other masters of the era, he opened the temple gates to earnest inquirers of diverse backgrounds. "Ever since the time of the Buddha and the founders of [Ch'an]," he wrote, "there has never been any distinction between ordained and laypeople, in the sense that everyone who has accurate personal experience of true realization is said to have entered the school of the enlightened mind and penetrated the source of religion."

Like Tan-hsia—and even more like Hsüeh-tou and Yüan-wu—Hung-chih immersed himself in the Ch'an literature and produced a pair of hundred-case koan collections, adding prose comments to one and poems to the other. The latter became the heart of a text usually called *The Book of Equanimity* in English (J., *Shōyōroku*) and widely regarded as equal to *The Blue Cliff Record* in beauty and profundity. His two anthologies represent only a small fraction of Hung-chih's record, which is more voluminous than any other Ts'ao-tung teacher's. It also contains lectures, informal talks and sayings, poems, and accounts of instruction given to particular students.

Hung-chih's writing has always received very high praise but unfortunately loses much of its grace and subtlety in English translation. Even so, it is not hard to appreciate the lyrical, evocative quality that is manifest in his prose as well as in his poetry. Stylistically, his work recalls the verse of his forerunners Shih-t'ou and Tung-shan, and as many have noted, it clearly became an inspiration, maybe even a model, for Dōgen's writing. The first selections below, drawn from Hung-chih's instructions on practice, represent his prose at its most direct yet demand to be read with the metaphoric mind—the right brain, if you will, rather than the left. They at once evoke the experience of meditative absorption and elucidate the fundamental nature of things.

Hung-chih's body of work includes some of the most elegant of all Chinese contributions to Ch'an doctrinal verse, his "Lancet of Seated Meditation" being a prime example. It also contains an especially serene specimen of a genre of poetry peculiar to Ch'an and Zen, the four-line *i-chieh* (J., *yuige*) or deathbed *gāthā:*

> Illusory dreams, phantom flowers—
> Sixty-seven years.
> A white bird vanishes in the mist,
> Autumn waters merge with the sky.

That a master could wield his brush with such composure on the brink of death came to be taken as incontrovertible proof of great enlightenment. In Hung-chih's case, it might also signify satisfaction with what he had accomplished. In addition to his literary legacy, he left eight successors who would rise to prominence. The imperial honors absent during his lifetime accrued to him swiftly on his demise. ☿

FROM HUNG-CHIH'S PRACTICE INSTRUCTIONS

THE CLOUDS' FASCINATION AND THE MOON'S CHERISHING

A person of the Way fundamentally does not dwell anywhere. The white clouds are fascinated with the green mountain's foundation. The bright moon cherishes being carried along with the flowing water. The clouds part and the mountain appears. The moon sets and the water is cool. Each bit of autumn contains vast interpenetration without bounds. Every dust is whole without reaching me; the ten thousand changes are stilled without shaking me. If you can sit here with stability, then you can freely step across and engage the world with energy. There is an excellent saying that the six sense-doors are not veiled, the highways in all directions have no footprints. Always arriving everywhere without being confused, gentle without hesitation, the perfected person knows where to go.

THE CONDUCT OF THE MOON AND CLOUDS

The consistent conduct of people of the Way is like the flowing clouds with no [grasping] mind, like the full moon reflecting universally, not confined anywhere, glistening within each of the ten thousand forms. Dignified and upright, emerge and make contact with the variety of phenomena, unstained and unconfused. Function the same toward all others since all have the same substance as you. Language cannot transmit [this conduct], speculation cannot reach it. Leaping beyond the infinite and cutting off the dependent, be obliging without looking for merit. This marvel cannot be measured with consciousness or emotion. On the journey accept your function, in your house please sustain it. Comprehending birth-and-death, leaving causes and conditions, genuinely realize that from the outset your spirit is not halted. So we have been told that the mind that embraces all the ten directions does not stop anywhere.

THE RESTING OF THE STREAMS AND TIDES

Just resting is like the great ocean accepting hundreds of streams, all absorbed into one flavor. Freely going ahead is like the great surging tides riding on the wind, all coming onto this shore together. How could they not reach into the genuine source? How could they not realize the great function that appears before us? A patch-robed monk follows movement and responds to changes in total harmony. Moreover, haven't you yourself established the mind that thinks up all the illusory conditions? This insight must be perfectly incorporated.

GRACIOUSLY SHARE YOURSELF

In the great rest and great halting the lips become moldy and mountains of grass grow on your tongue. Moving straight ahead [beyond this state], totally let go, washed clean and ground to a fine polish. Respond with brilliant light to such unfathomable depths as the waters of autumn or the moon stamped in the sky. Then you must know there is a path on which to turn yourself around. When you do turn yourself around you have no different face that can be recognized. Even if you do not recognize [your face], still nothing can hide it. This is penetrating from the topmost all the way down to the bottom. When you have thoroughly investigated your roots back to their ultimate source, a thousand or ten thousand sages are no more than footprints on the trail. In wonder return to the journey, avail yourself of the path and walk ahead. In light there is darkness; where it operates no traces remain. With the hundred grass tips in the busy marketplace graciously share yourself. Wide open and accessible, walking along, casually mount the sounds and straddle the colors while you transcend listening and surpass watching. Perfectly unifying in this manner is simply a patch-robed monk's appropriate activity.

PERFORMING THE BUDDHA WORK

[The empty field] cannot be cultivated or proven. From the beginning it is altogether complete, undefiled and clear down to the bottom. Where everything is correct and totally sufficient, attain the pure eye that illuminates thoroughly, fulfilling liberation. Enlightenment involves embodying this; stability develops from practicing it. Birth-and-death originally have no root or stem, appearing and disappearing originally have no defining signs or traces. The primal light, empty and effective, illumines the headtop. The primal wisdom, silent but also glorious, responds to conditions. When you reach the truth without middle or edge, cutting off before and after, then you realize one wholeness. Everywhere sense faculties and objects both just happen. The one who sticks out his broad long tongue transmits the inexhaustible lamp, radiates the great light, and performs the great buddha work, from the first not borrowing from others one atom from outside the dharma.[1] Clearly this affair occurs within your own house.

RELIGIOUS VERSES

THE GATE EMERGING FROM WITHIN THE BODY

Let go of emptiness and come back to the brambly forest.
Riding backward on the ox, drunken and singing,
Who could dislike the misty rain pattering on your bamboo raincoat and hat?
In the empty space you cannot stick a needle.

MEMORIAL IN HOMAGE TO THE THIRD ANCESTOR, ZEN MASTER CHIEN-CHIH[2]

The Way is without picking or choosing;[3]
   The waters are deep and the mountains steep.
The Ancestor does not appear or disappear.
   The moon is cold in the blue sky.
The unsprouting branches are awakened with spring flowers.
The tree top without shadows is the spiritual bird's dwelling.
The heavenly pillar so high and lofty;
   The River of Stars flows pure.
The stone ox roars!
   From the cave the clouds arise freely.[4]

---

1. The "broad long tongue" is one of the thirty-two physical marks of a buddha, indicating eloquent expression of the truth. "Dharma" is used here to mean the realm of reality and also the teaching that effects its realization.
2. "Memorial" means literally pagoda or stupa, a memorial structure housing the relics of a buddha or saint. Chien-chih Seng-ts'an (d. 606) was still a layperson when he received the transmission from the Second Ancestor.
3. A quote from the popular long poem [*Relying on Mind*] attributed to the Third Ancestor. [See Chapter 2.]
4. Cave (*tung*) and cloud (*yün*) may well refer to the Sōtō founder, Tung-shan Liang-chieh (807–869), and his successor Yün-chü Tao-ying (d. 902), or perhaps Tung-shan's teacher Yün-chü Tao-ying (781–841). Read thus, the last lines of this verse can be, "The stone ox roars! Tung-shan and Yün-chü (or Yün-yen) arose from this clarity."

LANCET OF SEATED MEDITATION

Essential function of all the Buddhas,
Functioning essence of all the Ancestors—
It knows without touching things,
It illumines without facing objects.
Knowing without touching things,
Its knowledge is inherently subtle;
Illumining without facing objects,
Its illumination is inherently mysterious.
Its knowledge inherently subtle,
It is ever without discriminatory thought;
Its illumination inherently mysterious,
It is ever without a hair's breadth of sign.
Ever without discriminatory thought,
Its knowledge is rare without peer;
Ever without a hair's breadth of sign,
Its illumination comprehends without grasping.
The water is clear right through to the bottom,
A fish goes lazily along.
The sky is vast without horizon,
A bird flies far far away.

FROM THE BOOK OF EQUANIMITY

CASE 38: LIN-CHI'S "TRUE MAN"

Case: Lin-chi said to the assembly, "There is a true man with no rank always going out and in through the portals of your face. Beginners who have not yet witnessed it, look! Look!"

Then a monk came forward and said, "What is the true man of no rank?"

Lin-chi got down from the seat, grabbed and held him: the monk hesitated. Lin-chi pushed him away and said, "The true man of no rank—what a piece of dry crap he is!"

Verse: Delusion and enlightenment are opposite,
        Subtly communicated, with simplicity;
        Spring opens the hundred flowers, in one puff,
        Power pulls back nine bulls, in one yank.
        It's hopeless—the mud and sand can't be cleared away;
        Clearly blocking off the eye of the sweet spring,
        If suddenly it burst forth, it would freely flow.

CASE 59: CH'ING-LIN'S "DEAD SNAKE"

Case: A monk asked Ch'ing-lin, "When the student goes by a short cut, then what?"

Ch'ing-lin said, "A dead snake lies across the great road: I urge you not to step on its head."

The monk said, "When one steps on its head, then what?"

Ch'ing-lin said, "You lose your life."

The monk said, "How about when one doesn't confront it?"

Ch'ing-lin said, "There's still nowhere to escape."

The monk said, "At just such a time, then what?"

Ch'ing-lin said, "It's lost."

The monk said, "Where has it gone?"

Ch'ing-lin said, "The grass is deep, there's no place to look for it."

The monk said, "You too should be on guard, Teacher."

Ch'ing-lin clapped and said, "This one's equally poisonous."

Verse: The boatman turns the rudder in the dark,
          The lone boat turns its bow in the night.
          Reed flowers—'snow' on both banks;
          Hazy water—autumn on one river.
          The power of the wind helps the sailboat go without rowing.
          The voice of the flute calls the moon down to the land of spring.

CASE 75: JUI-YEN'S "CONSTANT PRINCIPLE"

Case: Jui-yen asked Yen-t'ou, "What is the fundamental constant principle?"

Yen-t'ou said, "Moving."

Jui-yen said, "When moving, what then?"

Yen-t'ou said, "You don't see the fundamental constant principle."

Jui-yen stood there thinking.

Yen-t'ou said, "If you agree, you are not yet free of sense and matter: if you don't agree, you'll be forever sunk in birth-and-death."

Verse: The round pearl has no hollows,
          The great raw gem isn't polished.
          What is esteemed by people of the Way is having no edges.
          Removing the road of agreement, senses and matter are empty:
          The free body, resting on nothing, stands out unique and alive.

CASE 84: CHÜ-TI'S "ONE FINGER"

Case: Whenever Master Chü-ti was asked a question, he would just raise one finger.

Verse: Old Chü-ti's fingertip Ch'an—
    Thirty years he used it without wearing it out.
    Truly he has the unconventional technique of a man of the Way—
    Ultimately there are no mundane things before his eyes to see.
    His realization most simple,
    The device the more broad.
    An ocean of billions of worlds is drunk in the tip of a hair:
    Fish and dragons, limitless—into whose hands do they fall?
    Take, care Mr. Jen, holding the fishing pole![5]

---

5. [Chuang-tzu tells the tale of Mr. Jen, who baited his hook with fifty cattle and caught a fish big enough to feed half of humanity.—Eds.]

27

Ta-hui

(1089–1163)

Before inking his last poem, Hung-chih wrote his younger contemporary Ta-hui Tsung-kao, asking him to see to the disposition of his affairs. This act speaks volumes about the state of Ch'an in their time and the relationship between these two teachers, whom sectarian histories have depicted as opponents in a war of words regarding the right approach to Ch'an practice. Ta-hui (J., Daie), Yüan-wu's famed successor in the Yang-ch'i school of the Lin-chi line, espoused what he called *k'an-hua* Ch'an, the Ch'an of "contemplating sayings," and vociferously attacked the "silent-illumination" Ch'an taught by Hung-chih and other Ts'ao-tung masters. Recent scholarship makes it possible to see through the pair's ostensible antagonism to appreciate the harmony that, in fact, existed between them.

In his early wanderings, Ta-hui got broad exposure to prevailing trends in Ch'an, studying with an heir of Fu-yung in the Ts'ao-tung line, with one of Hsüeh-tou's successors in the Yün-men line, and with a Dharma grandson of Huang-lung in that branch of the Lin-chi line. This last master, who died when Ta-hui was just twenty-six, directed him to continue his practice under the guidance of Yüan-wu, whose star by then had begun its spectacular ascent. Ta-hui did as recommended, spending most of the next dozen years with Yüan-wu and ultimately developing such a clear Dharma-eye that the master deputized him to share teaching duties. Marveling at his abilities, some reckoned the thirty-seven-year-old monk a second coming of Lin-chi himself.

Officialdom took note. Scholar-officials sought out the younger teacher, and in 1126, remarkably soon after Yüan-wu had received *his* first purple robe and imperial title, the prime minister arranged similar honors for Ta-hui. When the Northern Sung dynasty collapsed shortly thereafter, Yüan-wu and Ta-hui fled to the south and soon were reassigned to lead one of the major monasteries there. During this period, Hung-chih entered the assembly, and Ta-hui probably met him, though the Ts'ao-tung master did not make an extended sojourn there.

Yüan-wu's retirement to Szechwan in 1130 and his death five years later left Ta-hui to make his own way, which he did very successfully. By 1137, he had become abbot of the Southern Sung's premier monastery, at Mt. Ching, near the capital of Hangchow. This position made it possible for him to widen his contacts with the literati who staffed the national bureaucracy, and Ta-hui formed close ties to a number of them, some very powerful. In doing so, he followed a growing trend in Sung Ch'an toward teaching for laypeople, but he also seems to have been acting on a keenly felt concern that China's inglorious retreat before its northern rivals signaled a serious decline not just in its military power or in its standing but in the wisdom and virtue upon which the nation's fortunes rested.

Ta-hui laid blame on those who had entered government service out of self-interest—"only interested in wealth and fame"—and worried that leaders had lost sight of the purpose of training people in the classics: "moral principles are basic and book learning is peripheral. Students of today tend to pursue the periphery and abandon the basis; they examine phrases and sentences, proudly enumerate flashy words and neglect the words of the sages. How lamentable this is!" This critique is couched in Confucian rather than Buddhist terms, but to Ta-hui, who subscribed to the unity of the three teachings (Confucianism, Buddhism, and Taoism), this did not matter.

His sentiments made Ta-hui a natural ally of officials hoping to shake up the government and mount a military campaign to take back northern China, and when these reformers lost a power struggle in 1141, he was charged with collusion and punished as one of them. Removed from the abbacy at Mt. Ching, stripped of his robes and honors, he was exiled first to the west and then, nine years later, to a disease-ridden region of the far south. Banishment of critical officials such as Su T'ung-po was almost routine, but Ta-hui's activism and exile put him in a class by himself among Ch'an masters of his epoch, and the posting of the initial order for his removal caused quite a stir at the monastery:

> The monks were weeping . . . like people who had lost their parents, lamenting sadly, unable to rest easy. Assembly Chief Yin went to the community quarters and said to them, "The calamities and stresses of human life are something that cannot be arbitrarily avoided. If we had [Ta-hui] be like a sissy all his life, submerged in the rank and file, keeping his mouth closed, not saying anything, surely this exile would not have happened."

Reminding the monks of hardships that their Dharma forebears had survived, Yin urged them to do whatever it took to follow Ta-hui, and "the next day they left in a continuous stream." A hundred monks joined even in the second, more hazardous phase of Ta-hui's exile, and half are said to have died in an epidemic.

Ta-hui kept busy during this period of forced isolation. In its initial stage, he seems to have devoted himself mainly to writing, preparing a collection of cases and commentaries titled *The Treasury of the True Dharma-Eye*. He also sustained a heavy correspondence, giving both monastics and laypeople (including some of his fellow exiles) practical instruction in Ch'an. In these endeavors, he may have taken inspiration from Yüan-wu's example, but Ta-hui was not just emulating his old teacher. Of all the elements in his record, including informal talks, accounts of private interviews, and poetry, his letters are considered the most original, prized especially because they offer the fullest, most explicit exposition of his innovative saying-contemplation method.

While Yün-men, Wu-tsu, and others had cited public cases to challenge and instruct students and while case anthologies and commentaries like *The Blue Cliff Record* had become fashionable, Ta-hui put the cases to a new use in directing his correspondents to adopt particular sayings as the exclusive focus of their practice. He taught them to call the assigned sayings to mind day and night, whatever their circumstances, promising that this would eventually precipitate a breakthrough to enlightenment. Though Ta-hui especially urged *k'an-hua* practice upon laypeople, believing that it was the approach to Ch'an best suited to busy lives, in the Lin-chi and Rinzai tradition it became the standard method of koan study for one and all. The saying that Ta-hui most frequently recommended, Chao-chou's *"wu"* (J., *mu;* see Chapter 18), assumed unprecedented importance in ensuing decades, to such an extent that the Yang-ch'i master Wu-men Hui-kai, writing in 1228, would place it first in his collection of forty-eight cases and call it the "one gate" of Ch'an. Even today it remains the koan of choice for beginning koan study.

Ta-hui might have been appalled by this outcome, which goes far beyond anything he seems to have foreseen, but he did argue adamantly for the *k'an-hua* approach. In doing so, he repeatedly and stridently contrasted it to the object-less silent-illumination practice, which generally led, he felt, to know-nothing quietism, a fixation upon a state of blankness or emptiness, rather than to a direct, personal experience of realization. Practitioners of silent-illumination, wrote Ta-hui, "think that enlightenment deceives people, that enlightenment is a fabrication. Since they've never awakened themselves, they don't believe anyone has awakened." He leveled this criticism not at Hung-chih in particular but at all who taught the *mo-chao* method, including two fellow monks who had earlier studied with him under Yüan-wu.

Furthermore—and not secondarily—Ta-hui advocated *k'an-hua* Ch'an as a corrective to superficial, intellectual study of the old cases. He saw evidence in all quarters of people dabbling in Ch'an as a literary pastime, contenting themselves with ill-founded explanations and imitations of Ch'an stories and discourse. This failure mirrored the problem that Ta-hui had identified in scholar-officials as a class, the problem of learning abstracted from experience and behavior, with the consequence of moral and institutional decline.

Believing that Ch'an, no less than China, was in danger of collapse, he took determined action to safeguard the tradition. His most dramatic step was to order suppression of his teacher's masterpiece, *The Blue Cliff Record.* Every retrievable copy was burned, along with the blocks used to print them, effectively removing the venerated text from circulation for the next two centuries. Ch'an and Zen historians have praised this extraordinary move as an act of loyalty to the Way and to Yüan-wu's own intentions. The old teacher himself had closed the text with a verse expressing doubt about its value: "Having brought up one hundred old public cases, / How much sand have I thrown in the eyes of people today?"

Ta-hui also took constructive steps to shore Ch'an up from within. Most importantly, he and his Dharma cousin Chu-an Shih-kuei (1083–1146) compiled a volume of inscriptions, letters, and other documents, forming a text titled *Precious Lessons from the Ch'an Schools.* This compendium goes far beyond Fa-yen's "Ten Guidelines" or Yüan-wu's letters in assessing the problems polluting the stream of Ts'ao-chi and also contains remedies put forward by past masters. It constitutes a frontal assault on love of finery, sloth, status-seeking, and other evils they saw afflicting the Ch'an institution.

Ta-hui's life was memorable right to the end. His efforts to relieve suffering in his plague-stricken place of exile won him a pardon in 1155, which permitted him to don his robes again, but for another year he rejected invitations to return to the Chinese heartland. Finally he accepted an appointment to head the major monastery at Mt. A-yü-wang in China's easternmost state, close to Hung-chih's T'ien-t'ung. En route to the new post, Ta-hui said later, he found the teaching of silent illumination prevalent, but when he paid Hung-chih a visit just one month after arriving, there was no sign of rancor or discord.

Ta-hui may have been grateful to his elder colleague for proposing that he receive the A-yü-wang abbacy, and he must have recognized then, if not before, that the accent fell on illumination—awakening—rather than on silence in Hung-chih's version of *mo-chao* Ch'an. Evidence of Hung-chih's wisdom was readily at hand, after all, in the manuscript of his poems for the later *Book of Equanimity*. Whatever the precise details, the two teachers had such a meeting of minds that, when he died the following year, Hung-chih saw fit to put his estate in Ta-hui's hands rather than in those of his own Dharma heirs.

By this time, Ta-hui himself had reached his late sixties and had only six years to live. He lived them in triumph. In 1158, an imperial directive restored to him the abbacy at Mt. Ching that he had lost seventeen years earlier, and a while afterward he even traveled to the barbarian-held north, lecturing by invitation at the T'ien-ning monastery where he had awakened under Yüan-wu's guidance. On his retirement in 1161 and his death two years later, the emperor showered him with honors and accolades. Though his own line of succession eventually gave out and never reached Japan, he continues to be revered, particularly in Rinzai Zen circles, for his role as defender of the Dharma and for his creative contributions to teaching. ⊗

SELECTED LETTERS OF TA-HUI TSUNG-KAO

Letter from Tseng Shih-lang to Ta-hui:[1]
Years ago when I was in Ch'ang-sha,[2] I received a letter from Master Yüan-wu. [In the letter] he said that you began to follow him in his later years. Nonetheless, in that short period of time, your attainment was outstanding. It has since been eight years, and I have often thought about you. I regret not having received your teaching, and I can only admire you from afar.

When I was young I decided to seek the Way, and I studied with good

---

1. Ta-hui received this letter when he was forty-seven. Tseng Shih-lang (n.d.) was a civil servant. Tseng's first name is Kai. Shih-lang is an official title translated as vice director. He held the second executive post in the Secretariat and Chancellery during the Sung dynasty.
2. Ch'ang-sha, a city in the Hunan province of China.

teachers, inquiring about the Great Matter. At twenty, I became busy with family and career, and no longer concentrated on practice. It is still the case today. I am old, yet I have learned nothing. I feel ashamed and I grieve about my situation all the time.

My determination and inspiration are not lacking. I do not seek shallow knowledge and understanding. For me, it is all or nothing. If I am to attain enlightenment, I must go directly to the point people of the past have reached. Only then would I be sure that I have reached the "great peaceful place." Although my determination has not wavered even for a single moment, I know that my practice has never been pure. I have great determination, but little strength.

In the past I requested instruction from Master Yüan-wu, and he gave me six personal Dharma talks. First he spoke directly about the Great Matter, and then he related two *kung-ans*: Yün-men's "Mt. Sumeru"[3] and Chao-chou's "Put It Down."[4] He told me to practice these vigorously, and said if I constantly raised them in my mind, eventually I would enter [the gate of enlightenment].

Although the Master was compassionate in his teaching, my stupidity was too severe. Fortunately my worldly obligations are over now, and I am living at my leisure, with no outside concerns. It is the right time to fulfill my initial aspiration. My only regret is that I have not been able to receive your teaching.

I have described my lifelong failure to you. I am sure you can see into my mind clearly. It is my hope that you will advise and caution me in my daily practice so that I will not digress onto other paths, but instead remain in accordance with the Original State.

I have filled this letter with my failures. It is because I am sincere in my intentions that I have concealed nothing from you. Please have pity on me.

Respectfully,

Tseng Shih-lang

Letter of Reply from Ta-hui:

. . . You were a civil servant, so you relied upon a salary for living expenses. As to marriage, civil service exams, and the official post, these things cannot be avoided in daily life. You are not at fault. It is precisely because you have, for countless *kalpas*, served true teachers and engaged yourself in the acquisition of profound wisdom that you have generated such great fear from such a small fault. Even sages cannot avoid what you regard as a great fault.

3. A monk asked Ch'an Master Yün-men, "Is one at fault to not give rise to a single thought?" Yünmen replied, "Mt. Sumeru."
4. Venerable Yen-yang asked Chao-chou, "What should one do when one does not take up a single thing?" Chao-chou replied, "Put it down." Yen-yang asked, "When you do not take anything, how can you put it down?" Chao-chou replied, "Then carry it with you."

As long as you know that illusions are not the ultimate Dharma, and you are able to turn your mind toward the gate [of enlightenment], that is enough. As long as you cleanse the defiled nature of worldly attachments with the water of wisdom and remain pure, that is sufficient. It is enough to cut [illusory thoughts] in half and never again give rise to a moving mind. There is no need to think about the past or future.

All things are illusory: when you create [karma] it is an illusion, and when you receive [karma] it is an illusion. When you are conscious it is an illusion, and when you are confused it is an illusion. Past, present and future are all illusions. If today you discover your faults, use the illusory medicine to cure the illusory sickness. When the sickness is gone and you no longer need the medicine, you will still be the same person. If, aside from this, there is still another person or Dharma, then it is the view of devils and heretics. Think deeply about this.

Simply pursue the following practice to its end. At all times stay in quietude, and do not forget the two *kung-ans*—"Mt. Sumeru" and "Put it Down." Do not fear or ponder what has already passed, for it will obstruct the Way. Make a great vow before the Buddhas: "This mind will be firm and will never regress. Relying on the blessings of the buddhas, I will meet a good teacher, cease the cycle of birth-and-death, and become enlightened to the ultimate wisdom. Afterward, I will continue, repaying the Buddha's grace by helping sentient beings develop the wisdom of the buddhas." If you make and follow such a vow, there is no reason to believe that you will not be awakened after a time. . . .

I hear that before you sent your letter, you burned incense before the buddhas and bowed toward my temple. Your sincerity is genuine. Although we do not live far apart, we have not yet had the opportunity to meet. I have been writing as thoughts come to me, and have only now become aware of this letter's length. Though the words seem trivial and complicated, they come from the heart. Trust that I have not deceived you with my words. To deceive you would be to deceive myself.

I recall that Sudhana visited the Brahman of Great Quiescence and obtained the Liberation of Sincere Words. Because of sincerity, all the buddhas and bodhisattvas of the past, present, and future have not regressed, do not regress, and will not regress from the unsurpassed wisdom. They fully accomplish whatever they seek. Your familiarity with bamboo chairs and meditation cushions is not different from Sudhana's seeing the Brahman of Great Quiescence.

Again, before you sent your letter, you paid respects to the sages and bowed to me from afar, hoping that you would gain my trust and acceptance. The intensity of your sincerity is evident. Trust my words. As long as you practice in this way, there is no doubt that in the future you will achieve the unsurpassed wisdom.

Second Letter from Ta-hui to Tseng Shih-lang:
Although you are well-to-do and work in a high position, it is clear that you are not affected by wealth and power. If you had not cultivated true wisdom in the past, how could you be like this now? What is to be feared, however, is that you may lose sight of your feelings and intentions during the process of practice and be obstructed by your keen capacity and intelligence. A person practicing with a mind that anticipates attainment is unable to cut his mind in half at the pivotal point, and cannot directly attain peace. He fails where men of old succeeded. Not only officials, but even Ch'an monks who have practiced a long time, have made such mistakes. A monk is often not willing to step back and practice the easy way. Instead, he uses his intelligent awareness to seek outward and contemplate with a discriminating mind. When a good teacher gives him a clue to enlightenment, a clue which goes beyond intelligent awareness and discriminative thinking, he will most likely miss it, even though it is right before his eyes. He thinks instead that the ancestors used concrete teachings when they preached, and that *kung-ans* such as Chao-chou's "Put it down" and Yün-men's "Mt. Sumeru" were examples of such teachings.

Master Yen-t'ou[5] once said, "It is superior to expel things and inferior to pursue things." He also said that one must know "the phrase" in order to govern the basic principles. What is "the phrase"? When no thought exists, that is called the True Phrase. It is also called "residing at the top," "abiding," "being vividly clear," "being aware," or "at this time." When the mind is "at this time," all distinctions of right and wrong are equally destroyed. As soon as something is deemed positive, it becomes negative. When you are "at this time," positive statement is cut away, negative statement is cut away. Like a fireball that burns anything it touches, there is no way it can be approached.

Most present-day officials dwell in thought and calculation, so when they hear criticisms such as this, they defend their own actions, arguing, "Wouldn't one fall into emptiness otherwise?" Such an attitude is like jumping into water before the boat capsizes. It is indeed pitiable.

I recently went to Chiang-hsi and met Lu Chu-jen (1084–1145). Chu-jen had worked on the One Causal Event for a long time, but was also seriously troubled by this problem I am speaking about. He is certainly intelligent. I asked him, "You are afraid of falling into emptiness. Is the person who senses fear empty, or is he not? Try to answer me."

Lu Chu-jen pondered for a moment, and intended to reply through calculation, but at that moment I shouted unexpectedly at him. Since then he has been confused and cannot grasp the Truth. It is because he possesses a mind that seeks enlightenment, and this creates an obstacle. There is no other reason.

5. Yen-t'ou Ch'üan-huo (828–887), Dharma descendant of Te-shan Hsüan-chien.

Please try to practice with my advice in mind. As time passes, your interactions with things will naturally become spontaneous. If, however, you expect to be enlightened and to obtain peace, even if you practice from now until the time when Maitreya Buddha descends to the world, you will not be enlightened. You will not obtain peace. You will become even more confused.

The monk P'ing-t'ien[6] said, "The clarity of the divine light is the splendid teaching of all times. Upon entering *this gate,* do not hold any views." An old worthy also said, "This Matter can neither be sought by the mind nor obtained by no-mind. It can neither be reached through words nor penetrated through silence." These are the finest examples of old woman's talk, in which one enters mud and water for the sake of saving sentient beings.

People who work on a Ch'an *kung-an* often do so in a casual way. They do not carefully examine the principle it contains. An upright person, upon hearing a *kung-an*, instantly cuts off entanglement from all directions with the precious sword of the Diamond King. Simultaneously, he removes the paths of birth-and-death, eliminates the paths of the profane and the sacred, stops discriminative thinking, and transcends gain and loss, right and wrong. Within him there is absolute purity and complete honesty. There is nothing to grasp onto. Isn't this pleasant? Isn't this satisfying?

As you know, the monk Kuan-hsi[7] sought instruction from Lin-chi. As Kuan-hsi entered the room for his initial meeting with the master, Lin-chi got up from his chair and suddenly grabbed him by the chest. Thereupon, Kuan-hsi said, "I understand, I understand." Lin-chi knew that he had been enlightened, and shoved him away, not bothering to test him further with words. At that moment, there was no way Kuan-hsi could have responded with thought and discrimination. We are fortunate to have such a model from the past. People today are unable to have such an experience because their minds are scattered. If Kuan-hsi had possessed even the slightest anticipation for enlightenment and peace, he would not have gotten enlightened when he was grabbed by Lin-chi. Even if he was pulled around the world with his hands and feet bound, he still would not have gotten enlightened and attained peace.

That which normally discriminates and calculates is consciousness. That which follows birth-and-death is consciousness. That which fears and panics is also consciousness. Practitioners today are not aware that consciousness is a disease, and that they fervently float and sink within it. In the sutras such people are said "to accord with consciousness rather than wisdom." Because of this, they obscure their original nature and original being.

When they discard everything and do not think or discriminate, when they

6. P'ing-t'ien P'u-an (770–843), Dharma descendant of Pai-chang Huai-hai.
7. Kuan-hsi Chih-hsien (?–895), Dharma descendant of Lin-chi I-hsüan. This is the monk whose story Yüan-wu tells in "Serene and Free," Chapter 25.

suddenly lose their footing and tread on their nostrils, consciousness transforms into the wonderful wisdom of true emptiness. Apart from this there is no other wisdom to be attained. If there is something else to be obtained or awakened to, it is not [true wisdom]. For example, when a person is confused, he sees east as west. When he is enlightened, west itself is east. There is no other east.

The wonderful wisdom of true emptiness has the same span of life as vast space. Is there anything within vast space which impedes it? Although space is not hindered by anything, it does not obstruct things from going back and forth in it. The wonderful wisdom of true emptiness is also like this. It does not adhere even to the slightest defilements of birth-and-death or the profane and sacred. However, it does not obstruct birth-and-death or the profane and sacred from coming and going within it. Only when you deeply believe and thoroughly perceive this will you be a man who attains freedom from birth-and-death, who attains great liberation. Only then will your mind accord with the *kung-ans* "Put it down," by Chao-chou, and "Mt. Sumeru," by Yün-men. If you do not have faith and cannot let go, then shoulder Mt. Sumeru in your pilgrimage. When you see a person with a bright mind, present the *kung-an* to him. Ha Ha!

INTERACTIONS WITH WOMEN

Since Fa-hen was widowed, she never used ornaments or makeup, and she always ate vegetarian food, not eating after noon. Once the Ch'an master Ta-hui sent a Ch'an adept to call on her son, Mr. Wei. Mr. Wei kept him [as a guest] at his house for a while, and the adept talked to him about Ch'an. One day the widow asked the adept about Ta-hui's method. He replied, "The master usually just has people observe the saying 'A dog has no Buddha-nature' and the saying about the bamboo rod.[8] He simply doesn't allow them to make comments or to think about them; he does not permit understanding at the bringing up of a saying or taking it at the mere mention of it. 'Does a dog have Buddha-nature or not? No'—he just makes people look at it just like this."

Fa-hen subsequently sat at night diligently investigating the saying. Suddenly one day her mind became clear, without any sticking points. The Ch'an adept then left, and Fa-hen sent a letter with him back to Ta-hui, telling of her entry into the Way, including several verses. The final verse read:

> All day long reading the words of the scriptures,
> It's like meeting an old acquaintance;

8. These sayings became well-known koans. This first originated in an exchange of Chao-chou's. See the introductory note for Chapter 18. The second appears as the forty-third case of the *Gateless Barrier:* "Master Shou-shan held his bamboo staff up before his assembly, saying, 'Oh monks! If you call this a staff, you're clinging to the fact. If you don't call it a staff, you're ignoring the fact. What do you call it?' "

Don't say doubts arise again and again—
Each time it's brought up, each time it's new.

Ta-hui was delighted; unconsciously she had accorded with Ta-hui's saying that, once one has mastered Ch'an, reading the scriptures is like going outside and running into an old friend.

Tsung had visited nearly all the well-known Ch'an masters of eastern China when she went along with her husband who was going to take up a new official post; she only regretted that she hadn't seen the great master Ta-hui. Then it happened that Ta-hui came to her city, and so she took this opportunity to go see him. When she met him, she just bowed in respect, that's all.

Ta-hui said to a companion, "The wayfarer who just came has seen spirits and ghosts, but has not yet had the opportunity for refinement by a forge and bellows. She's like a huge ship in a harbor with no outlet—she can't turn around and move, that's all."

Ping Kan-ch'u, another acquaintance of Ta-hui, said, "How can you say that so easily?"

Ta-hui said, "If she turned her head, she'd surely be otherwise."

The next day Tsung's husband, who was the local governor, had Ta-hui give a sermon. Ta-hui looked over the crowd and said, "Here today we have someone with some insight. I check people out like a customs officer—the minute I see them coming I can tell whether or not they have any dutiable goods." When he got down from the seat, Tsung finally came and asked him for an initiatory name; he named her Wu-cho, "No Attachments."

The next year, hearing that Ta-hui's teaching was flourishing at Mt. Ching, she went and spent the summer there. One night while she was sitting quietly, she suddenly had realization of enlightenment. She composed a verse:

Suddenly I came across my nose
And all my cleverness vanished.
Why should Bodhidharma have come from India?
The Second Ancestor needlessly bowed.
If you keep asking how and so what,
The whole bunch of you bandits are busted.

Ta-hui repeated the verse and said, "You have awakened to the living meaning of Buddhism, cutting all in two with one fell stroke. Dealing with situations, leave everything to natural reality. Whether in the world or beyond the world, there is no excess or lack. I make this verse as a testimony to your enlightenment:

The four ranks of sages and six types of ordinary beings are all shook up;
Stop being shook up—even Bodhidharma has not yet understood."

One day she paid her respects and took her leave, to return to her home town.

Ta-hui said, "When you leave this mountain, if someone asks about the teaching here, how will you answer?"

She said, "Before arriving at Mt. Ching, one couldn't help doubting."

Ta-hui said, "What about after arriving?"

She said, "As of old, early spring is still cold."

Ta-hui said, "Doesn't such an answer make me out to be a fool?" She covered her ears and left.

Henceforth she was much admired by the congregation and she became famous. After a long time in concealment, she finally became ordained as a nun. Though she was well advanced in years and virtue, she kept the precepts very strictly, and polished herself with austerity and frugality.

Because of her fame in the Way, she was eventually ordered by a governor to appear in the world and teach as Abbess of Ch'i-shou monastery, but before long she retired.

28

Shih-wu

(1272–1352)

China underwent profound change in the century between Ta-hui's death and the birth of Shih-wu. Early in the thirteenth century, Genghis Khan swept into China, and by mid-century, most of the north was in the hands of his grandson, Kublai Khan. The south fell to Mongol forces with scant resistance when Shih-wu was a boy, so he grew up in a nation reunited under foreign rule. Buddhism fared very well throughout the new regime, the Yüan dynasty, though Ch'an slipped to second place in imperial favor, behind the Vajrayāna tradition of Tibet, which Kublai Khan himself preferred.

In stark contrast to Ta-hui, Shih-wu is almost unknown today. He lived his entire life within a seventy-five mile radius of his birthplace in far eastern China, making his longest trip at seventeen, when he became a novice at a temple near Mt. Ching. After ordaining at twenty, he entered the mountains to study first with the important Yang-ch'i school teacher Kao-feng Yüan-miao (1238–1295) and then with Chi-an, another master in this branch of the Lin-chi lineage. After nine years of mountain practice, upset by a sharp reproach from Chi-an, Shih-wu set out to leave, but a glimpse of a rain shelter suddenly turned him around for good. He went back, received confirmation of his realization, and spent much of the next eleven years with Chi-an, accompanying him to the nearby city of Huchou when Chi-an was named abbot of a monastery there. At forty, rather than accepting a temple appointment himself, Shih-wu (lit., Stone House) headed back to the hills, resuming the hermit life so lovingly described in his poems.

The ancient Taoist themes of simplicity, naturalness, and ease resound in Shih-wu's writing, ringing out clearly within the Ch'an setting. Everything in his mountain life that might seem a hardship to others—very plain food, crude and cramped quarters, dearth of human contact—Shih-wu celebrates as an outright virtue or at least preferable to what a city dweller can know. Though he evokes Pai-chang's dictum that "A day without work is a day without eating" and obviously prided himself on his labors, he also exults in the leisureliness of his life, "relaxing all day on a peak." The unharried work that he did with his hoe he contrasts with the chase for fame and fortune going on in the dusty world below, even among Ch'an monks. "I wear myself out," he writes, "but not for the

State"—and not for the Dharma either, it seems. He represents himself as reluctant even to open his mouth if a visitor came seeking guidance.

Yet Shih-wu packed his verses with practice pointers and encouragements, enticements and goads, allusions to sutras and Ch'an stories. They seem casually tossed off, and perhaps were, but he clearly intended them to inspire and instruct his readers. While rejoicing over the wild pleasures of his home, he also cautions that "pine trees and strange rocks remain unknown / to those who look for mind with mind"—a warning that goes at least as far back as Seng-ts'an (Chapter 2): "To get hold of the mind by using the mind, / isn't that a gross error . . . ?" Other of his allusions are more current and less direct. When he confesses to idle thoughts during sitting meditation, he comments, "the dead wood I gather for my stove," and though he has not used the characters for *k'u-mu*, the silent-illumination debate echoes discernibly in the distance.

Two of Shih-wu's poems refer explicitly to Han-shan, inviting comparisons between these Ch'an hermit-poets. Given the blurred image we have of Han-shan, such comparisons cannot be very finely or assuredly drawn, but it seems safe to say that Shih-wu makes basically the same critique of society as Han-shan does and touts the same dual freedom of wild solitude and awakened mind. Yet Shih-wu seems more domestic and more serene in his choices than his forerunner was, both less anguished and less zany than Han-shan. He definitely was less isolated, better established, and more widely appreciated by people of his own day.

Shih-wu mentions "two or three fellow monks" on his mountaintop and an occasional visitor from the flatland, but like Po Chü-i and countless other Chinese poets, he tended to write from a more solitary spot than he occupied in actuality. His roost was only a day's walk from the temple where he lived in the latter years of his study with Chi-an, and its elevation was hardly forbidding—just 1350 feet. Enough people beat a path to his door during his forties and fifties that Shih-wu became famous, and in 1330, he reluctantly accepted the abbacy of an important temple that Kublai Khan had undertaken to restore. After seven years as abbot, at sixty-six, he retired again to his mountain home, and the poems that follow were written there, sometime in the fourteen years before he died. A few months prior to his death, the empress honored the elderly recluse with a golden robe.

Two anthologies of Shih-wu's work were published posthumously—his *Mountain Poems,* excerpted here, and a collection of *gāthās* and occasional verse. These have barely kept his name alive in Chinese poetry, and his reputation as a Ch'an master has faded even more. As a teacher, Shih-wu may have made his greatest, most lasting contribution through his Dharma heir Taego Pou (1301–1382), a Korean master who unified his country's nine schools of Sŏn (i.e., Ch'an) Buddhism into the Chogye order, which remains vigorous today not only in Korea but in the United States and elsewhere. ⊗

FROM MOUNTAIN POEMS

SHIH-WU'S INTRODUCTION

Here in the woods I have lots of free time. When I don't spend it sleeping, I enjoy composing chants. But with paper and ink so scarce, I haven't thought about
writing them down. Now some Zen monks have asked me to record what I find
of interest on this mountain. I've sat here quietly and let my brush fly. Suddenly
this volume is full. I close it and send it back down with the admonition not to
try singing these poems. Only if you sit on them will they do you any good.

1
I live far off in the wild
where moss and woods are thick and plants perfumed
I can see mountains rain or shine
and never hear market noise
I light a few leaves in my stove to heat tea
to patch my robe I cut off a cloud
lifetimes seldom fill a hundred years
why suffer for profit and fame

2
good and bad fortune never lose their way
success and failure both follow karma
just realize they're empty at heart
and what doesn't change is real

3
this body's existence is like a bubble's
may as well accept what happens
events and hopes seldom agree
but who can step back doesn't worry
we blossom and fade like flowers
gather and part like clouds
worldly thoughts I forgot long ago
relaxing all day on a peak.

LINE 1   The *Diamond Sutra* ends with this *gāthā:* "Everything dependent / is a
dream an illusion a bubble a shadow / it's dew or it's lightning / regard it like this."

4
my Ch'an hut leans at the summit
clouds sail back and forth
a waterfall hangs in front
a mountain ridge crests in back
on a rock wall I sketched three buddhas
for incense there's a plum branch in a jar
the fields below might be level
but can't match a mountain home free of dust

LINE 5   The images were probably those of Amitābha, Shākyamuni and
Maitreya, the buddhas of the past, present, and future.

5
I searched creation without success
then by chance found this forested ridge
my thatch hut cuts through heaven's blue
a moss-slick trail through dense bamboo
others are moved by profit and fame
I grow old living for Ch'an
pine trees and strange rocks remain unknown
to those who look for mind with mind

6
the sun rises east and falls west at night
the bell sounds at dusk the rooster at dawn
Yin and Yang have turned my head to snow
over the years I've used a hundred crocks of pickles
I plant pines for beams in the clearings
spit out peach pits for shade along the trails
tell the world's hunted birds
head for the mountains and choose any tree

LINE 4   Chinese eat pickles, especially in the morning, with steamed rice or rice
porridge. There are hundreds of varieties made from just about every kind of
vegetable.

7
the Way is so rare it can't be copied
but a well-hidden hut comes close
for cover I've grown bamboo in front
from the rocks led a spring to the kitchen

gibbons bring their young when cliff fruits turn ripe
cranes change their nests when gorge pines turn brown
lots of idle thoughts occur in *ch'an*
the dead wood I gather for my stove

8
a friend of seclusion arrives at my fence
we wave and pardon our lack of decorum
a white mane gathered back
patched robe loosely draped
embers of leaves at the end of the night
howl of a gibbon breaking the dawn
sitting on straw facing in quilts
language forgotten we finally meet

LINES 2–3   Some sort of headgear is called for in meeting someone outside.

9
cares disappeared when I entered the mountains
serene at heart I let them fly
the shade in front fades in fall
the stream roars after a rain
I offer tea and greens to a visiting farmer
a neighbor monk daisies in a pot from town
the jaded life of the gentry
can't match a hermit's with scenes like these

10
where did that gust come from
whistling through the heavens
shaking the whole forest
blowing open my bamboo door
without arms or legs
how does it move around
impossible to track
in the cliffs a tiger laughs

LINE 8   Some texts have "a tiger roars."

11
you're bound to become a buddha if you practice
if water drips long enough even rocks wear through

it's not true thick skulls can't be pierced
people just imagine their minds are hard

12
becoming a buddha is easy
but ending illusions is hard
so many frosted moonlit nights
I've sat and felt the cold before dawn

13
stripped of reason my mind is blank
emptied of being my nature is bare
at night my windows often breathe white
the moon and stream come right to the door

14
no one else sees what I see clearly
no one else knows what I know well
I recall one misty day last autumn
a gibbon came by and stole two pears

15
my hut isn't quite six feet across
surrounded by pines bamboos and mountains
an old monk hardly has room for himself
much less for a visiting cloud

LINE 3   A grown man in China was called a *six-footer,* and six feet was also the
dimension of a monk's cell.

16
a pot of parched wheat and pine meal
a dish of bamboo shoots and vine buds
completely worn out I've no other thought
let others become gods or buddhas

17
standing outside my pointed-roof hut
who'd guess how spacious it is inside
a galaxy of worlds is there
with room to spare for a zazen cushion

18
Cold Mountain has a line
my mind is like the autumn moon
I have a line of my own
my mind outshines the autumn moon
not that the autumn moon isn't bright
but once full it fades
no match for my mind
always full and bright
as to what the mind is like
why don't you tell me

19
forty-some years I've lived in the mountains
ignorant of the world's rise and fall
warmed at night by a stove full of pine needles
satisfied at noon by a bowl of wild plants
sitting on rocks watching clouds and empty thoughts
patching my robe in sunlight practicing silence
till someone asks why Bodhidharma came east
and I hang out my wash

LINE 7   Probably the most common of all koans is "Why did Bodhidharma come east?" (Or "from the west").

JAPAN

29

Dōgen

(1200–1253)

Slowed by geographical, sociopolitical, and linguistic barriers, Ch'an took half a millennium to reach Japan. Dōgen Kigen was by no means the first Japanese monk to travel to China or even to study Ch'an in depth with a Chinese master. Indeed, several others preceded him in receiving formal recognition as Dharma heirs in one or another Ch'an lineage, and history recognizes one of his early teachers, Myōan Eisai (1141–1215), as the founder of Japanese Zen. Yet Dōgen opened the country's first Zen monastery, produced its first Zen record, established its first enduring line of succession, and stood head and shoulders above near-contemporaries in his contribution to Zen literature.

Dōgen's early life, like his teaching, defies simple or certain exposition. He was born into a time of extraordinary upheaval, marked by bitter competition for power between the imperial court and the shogunate, within the nobility and the rising samurai class, and among the Buddhist sects that served and depended on these groups. Maneuvering in Kyoto court circles probably accounts for both the liaison that produced him and the doubt that surrounds his parents' identities; all this remains subject to scholarly conjecture. His ancestry was certainly aristocratic, however, and after his mother's death in 1207, he grew up in the household of a high-ranking courtier from the powerful Minamoto clan. His upbringing included extensive tutelage in literature and the arts, the lifeblood of Kyoto society, and he is said to have demonstrated an extreme precocity in reading the Chinese classics.

Legend depicts the boy Dōgen realizing the impermanence of all existence and resolving to pursue a religious vocation as he watched clouds of incense billow over his mother's ashes. Disastrous events of the previous century—earthquakes, fires, famines, and epidemics as well as war—had put many of his compatriots in an apocalyptic mood, eager to adopt new forms of religious expression, but guided by family connections, Dōgen began his religious career in the Tendai sect, which then predominated in the imperial capital. Many details elude us, but by the time he was seventeen, Dōgen's quest had carried him to Tendai headquarters on Mt. Hiei, where he formally entered the Way, and back to Kennin-ji, in Kyoto, where the eminent Eisai had established a beachhead for Zen study. Along the way, no doubt, he got a look at Mt. Hiei's warrior-monks, a conspicuous manifestation of the rivalry and violence that infected Japanese Buddhism in those tempestuous times.

Whether this young monk of privileged background arrived soon enough and had sufficient entrée to meet Eisai himself is another of the enigmas in Dōgen's biography, but within two years of the old man's death, Dōgen did embark on Zen studies with Eisai's successor, Myōzen (1184–1225). Eisai had twice made the trip to China, had succeeded to the Huang-lung school of Lin-chi Ch'an, and had passed this teaching on to Myōzen, all while remaining within the Tendai fold. Myōzen took the same course to avoid an affront to Mt. Hiei, but his heart plainly lay with Zen. He and Dōgen formed a close bond during the six years they spent studying in Kyoto, and they sailed together to China in 1223, a difficult venture to execute but one that would give them firsthand access to the vaunted Chinese tradition.

When they arrived, the fall of the Southern Sung dynasty lay yet a century and a half in the future. Disembarking in easternmost China, they found the Yang-ch'i branch of Lin-chi still holding sway and descendants of Ta-hui directing most of the prominent temples. These included the big T'ien-t'ung monastery that Hung-chih had restored, where Eisai had later practiced and which they themselves soon entered. Myōzen settled down to practice, but Dōgen who seems to have had no affinity with Wu-chi Liao-p'ai, the master there, spent part of his first two years in China visiting other monasteries, perhaps searching for a more suitable teacher. In 1225, he lost both the one he had—Myōzen, who suddenly died—and gained another, the man he later revered as "the old Buddha." This was the monastery's incoming abbot, a Ts'ao-tung master of exceptional repute, commonly known as T'ien-t'ung Ju-ching. (The final selection in Chapter 32 gives a portrait of Ju-ching.)

The fact that Dōgen hit it off with the new abbot had nothing to do with lineage. Ju-ching (1163–1228) is said to have concealed his dharma pedigree, never saying whose heir he was until shortly before he died, preferring to regard himself, by Dōgen's testimony, as "the total storehouse of the Buddha-Dharma." Dōgen also reports that Ju-ching rejected not only the practice of categorizing Ch'an into schools and houses but even the view that Ch'an was one of many Buddhist sects. It is not surprising that Dōgen, having witnessed sectarianism at its violent worst in Japan, adopted this stance on the indivisibility of the Dharma, maintaining in his later preaching and writing that he taught the way of buddhas and Ancestors, not merely Zen, much less Sōtō Zen. It appears that Dōgen absorbed as well Ju-ching's perspective that false teaching had become pandemic and his emphasis on long and fervent practice of zazen, an emphasis traceable to Hung-chih and K'u-mu.

After a powerful awakening experience but less than two years of study with Ju-ching, Dōgen sailed home, taking Myōzen's ashes and a transmission document acknowledging him as Ju-ching's successor. The next three years he spent at Kennin-ji, probably with the hope of preaching Ju-ching's brand of Zen there or of obtaining an appointment to direct another established temple. No such opportunity materialized, however, and his work as a Zen master did not take off until he moved outside Kyoto in 1230 and began developing an independent base of activity at a small temple made available by unidentified patrons, perhaps members of his extended family. Within six years, he had succeeded in getting a monk's hall built, a major step toward transplanting the Chinese monastic model to Japanese soil. The phenomenon of monks sitting immobile for long hours in a hall dedicated to that purpose so intrigued Kyoto residents that they flocked to see it for themselves.

No doubt such notoriety drew the ire of the Buddhist establishment, but it also brought Dōgen political and financial support that he sorely needed in lieu of the official sponsorship or estate revenues other temples enjoyed. Judging by his early writings, he geared much of his teaching at this time to religiously inclined aristocrats who might back his efforts—and who were, after all, his own people. Perhaps the first piece of writing he prepared for distribution was a meditation manual, patterned after a century-old Chinese text, providing zazen instruction in relatively straightforward manner. He chose to write another early piece not in Chinese, the language of learning, but in Japanese and employed a question-and-answer format as an engaging means of introducing the practice and dispelling common misunderstandings. A third, highly accessible product of this initial phase of his teaching, *The Record of Things Heard*, consists of brief, informal talks on a wide range of subjects.

In these contexts, Dōgen made strong statements about lay practice that he would subsequently set aside, asserting that what mattered was not one's standing in the world but simply one's eagerness for the Way:

> In Sung China, kings and ministers, officials and common people, men and women, kept their intention on the ancestors' way. Both warriors and literary people aroused the intention to practice Ch'an and study the way. Among them, many illuminated the mind-ground. From this you should know that worldly duties do not hinder the Buddha-Dharma.

Rejecting all other practices as secondary or worse, Dōgen promoted zazen as "the front gate" of the Dharma, the practice for one and all, irrespective of intelligence, education, rank, or gender.

Such universalism aligned him, nominally, with the Pure Land movement that had taken hold in a populace driven to despair by the era's continuing crises, but he mercilessly ridiculed the Pure Land (and Tendai) practice of repeating the Buddha's name: "People who chant all the time are just like frogs croaking day and night in the spring fields. Their effort will be of no use whatsoever." Dōgen's anti-sectarianism in no way restrained him from this sort of criticism; instead, it led to another kind of impartiality—a readiness to denounce everything as a deviation from true Buddhism except *shikantaza,* pure sitting.

As time wore on, perhaps to correct the ideas of some monks who came to his community after prior training in Zen, Dōgen turned his fire increasingly on Zen methods that he considered deleterious, chief among which was Ta-hui's technique of "contemplating sayings." In a real sense, however, what Dōgen did was simply go Ta-hui one better: now koan study rather than silent illumination had become the *idée fixe* and thus a serious obstacle to genuine practice and realization, so Dōgen set out to eliminate it. That he had no fundamental objection to the contemplation of sayings in a larger sense is readily apparent from his own formal lectures, later polished and gathered under the title *Eye Treasury of the True Dharma*—the same title Ta-hui had chosen for his investigation of koan.

These were lectures prepared for delivery either to his growing assembly of monks or to devoted lay students and patrons, and he gave increasing attention to them as his first decade of teaching progressed. Ultimately, he intended his text, like Ta-hui's and like Yüan-wu's *The Blue Cliff Record* before it, to contain an even one hundred chapters and to present its author's most penetrating insights in a very elegant form. Dōgen did not live long enough to complete the full complement of essays, but those he finished are inventive, consummately crafted explorations of public cases, persistently urging and challenging his students to examine the old sayings in detail and from diverse perspectives. Among the chapters are "The Sound of the Valley Stream," inspired by Su T'ung-po's enlightenment poem (Chapter 24), and "Dragon Howl," a meditation on the famous dead-tree metaphor (Chapter 26).

"One Bright Pearl," a chapter completed in 1238, the same year as *Record of Things Heard* exemplifies the prose of the *Eye Treasury.* Poetic almost to the point of mystery, it abounds in twists, reversals, unexpected juxtapositions, and questions designed to surprise and illumine an unguarded mind while foiling any attempt to extract merely logical meanings. Dōgen often took extreme liberties in achieving these effects, misquoting texts, lifting passages out of context, mixing Chinese and Japanese characters in a single sentence, playing with grammar and syntax, and so forth. How much he owes his style to his Dharma ancestor Hung-chih will be seen by looking back at Chapter 26, especially by comparing Dōgen's "Lancet of Seated Meditation" with Hung-chih's verse of the same name.

Abruptly, but obviously with forethought, Dōgen and most of his monks left the Kyoto area in 1243, relocating without explanation to the mountainous, rural province of Echizen. In the year or so prior to this move, he had twice twitted the religious hierarchy by lecturing in the capital under the protection of his most prominent patrons, and this may have provoked an attack from Mt. Hiei. Indeed, one Tendai document claims that the sect drove Dōgen off to Echizen, and though no other records bear out this report, it probably contains a germ of truth. His teaching had come under criticism in the imperial court, and growing weary of defending himself, he may well have opted to remove the community from the spotlight. The news that a Lin-chi master of Japanese descent had been tapped to open a large monastery nearby probably weighed heavily in his decision, too. (See Chapter 30.)

In leaving Kyoto, Dōgen abandoned not only his hometown but whatever hopes for prominence he may still have harbored. On the other hand, he fulfilled a perception he had expressed three years before in "The Mountains and Rivers Sutra," a celebrated chapter of the *Eye Treasury:* that mountains are the natural dwelling place of sages. Whatever else it may have meant, the move to Echizen constituted a change of Dōgen's economic base from the Kyoto nobility to the samurai class—and in particular to Hatano Yoshishige, who represented the shogunate in the capital and whose property became the site of Dōgen's new monastery, Eihei-ji. Hatano, a one-eyed veteran of many battles, was such a sincere disciple that he oversaw clearing for the new building himself and eventually joined the monkhood. Dependence of this sort had its consequences, however. In 1247, Dōgen was obliged to interrupt his work for seven months to answer Hatano's summons to Kamakura, the seat of the shogunate, and in decades to come, the direction of Sōtō Zen would be greatly affected by the line's historic tie to the Hatano family and other rural patrons.

Dōgen produced many new chapters of the *Eye Treasury* before his death in 1253, along with exacting regulations on how his monks should eat, wash, dress, interact, use the library, and otherwise comport themselves. Dōgen obviously saw these very different kinds of text as serving his long-term goal of establishing the Way in Japan, and they form the bulk of his literary remains. Dōgen lives on as well in his *Record*, a transcript of his remarks to the Eihei-ji monks, and in the Sōtō tradition that he established, the largest of the Zen schools in Japan. Though he is now regarded as a genius, his name and work fell largely into obscurity a few generations after his death, and six centuries passed before the government, in a fit of nationalist pride, honored him with the title *daishi,* great master. ⊗

FROM THE RECORD OF THINGS HEARD

One day a student asked: "I have spent months and years in earnest study, but I have yet to gain enlightenment. Many of the old Masters say that the Way does not depend on intelligence and cleverness and that there is no need for knowledge and talent. As I understand it, even though my capacity is inferior, I need not feel badly of myself. Are there not any old sayings or cautionary words that I should know about?"

Dōgen replied: "Yes, there are. True study of the Way does not rely on knowledge and genius or cleverness and brilliance. But it is a mistake to encourage people to be like blind men, deaf mutes, or imbeciles. Because study has no use for wide learning and high intelligence, even those with inferior capacities can participate. True study of the Way is an easy thing.

But even in the monasteries of China, only one or two out of several hundred, or even a thousand, disciples under a great Ch'an master actually gained true enlightenment. Therefore, old sayings and cautionary words are needed. As I see it now, it is a matter of gaining the desire to practice. A person who gives rise to a real desire and puts his utmost efforts into study under a teacher will surely gain enlightenment. Essentially, one must devote all attention to this effort and enter into practice with all due speed. More specifically, the following points must be kept in mind:

"In the first place, there must be a keen and sincere desire to seek the Way. For example, someone who wishes to steal a precious jewel, to attack a formidable enemy, or to make the acquaintance of a beautiful woman must, at all times, watch intently for the opportunity, adjusting to changing events and shifting circumstances. Anything sought for with such intensity will surely be gained. If the desire to search for the Way becomes as intense as this, whether you concentrate on doing zazen alone, investigate a koan by an old master, interview a Zen teacher, or practice with sincere devotion, you will succeed no matter how high you must shoot or no matter how deep you must plumb. Without arousing this wholehearted will for the Buddha Way, how can anyone succeed in this most important task of cutting the endless round of birth-and-death? Those who have this drive, even if they have little knowledge or are of inferior capacity, even if they are stupid or evil, will without fail gain enlightenment.

"Next, to arouse such a mind, one must be deeply aware of the impermanence of the world. This realization is not achieved by some temporary method of contemplation. It is not creating something out of nothing and then thinking about it. Impermanence is a fact before our eyes. Do not wait for the teachings from others, the words of the scriptures, and for the principles of enlightenment. We are born in the morning and die in the evening; the man we saw yesterday is no longer with us today. These are facts we see with our own eyes and hear with our own ears. You see and hear impermanence in terms of another person, but try weighing it with your own body. Even though you live to be seventy or eighty, you die in accordance with the inevitability of death. How will you ever come to terms with the worries, joys, intimacies, and conflicts that concern you in this life? With faith in Buddhism, seek the true happiness of nirvana. How can those who are old or who have passed the halfway mark in their lives relax in their studies when there is no way of telling how many years are left?"

Think of those who gained enlightenment upon hearing the sound of bamboo when struck by a tile or on seeing blossoms in bloom. Does the bamboo distinguish the clever or dull, the deluded or enlightened; does the flower differentiate between the shallow and deep, the wise and stupid? Though flowers bloom year after year, not everyone who sees them gains enlightenment. Bamboos always give off sounds, but not all who hear them become enlightened. It is only by the virtue of long study under a teacher and much practice that we gain an affinity with what we have labored for and gain enlightenment and clarity of mind.

The most important point in the study of the Way is zazen. Many people in China gained enlightenment solely through the strength of zazen. Some who were so ignorant that they could not answer a single question exceeded the learned who had studied many years solely through the efficacy of their single-minded devotion to zazen. Therefore, students must concentrate on zazen alone and not bother about other things. The Way of the Buddhas and Ancestors is zazen alone. Follow nothing else.

At that time Ejō asked: "When we combine zazen with the reading of the texts, we can understand about one point in a hundred or a thousand upon examining the Zen sayings and the koan. But in zazen alone there is no indication of even this much. Must we devote ourselves to zazen even then?"

Dōgen answered: "Although a slight understanding seems to emerge from examining the koan, it causes the Way of the Buddhas and the Ancestors to become even more distant. If you devote your time to doing zazen without wanting to know anything and without seeking enlightenment, this is itself the Ancestral Way. Although the old Masters urged both the reading of the scriptures and the practice of zazen, they clearly emphasized zazen. Some gained enlightenment through the koan, but the merit that brought enlightenment came from the zazen. Truly the merit is in the zazen."

The basic point to understand in the study of the Way is that you must cast aside your deep-rooted attachments. If you rectify the body in terms of the four attitudes of dignity, the mind rectifies itself. If at first you uphold the precepts, the mind reforms itself. In China it is the custom among laymen to show their filial gratitude towards a deceased parent by assembling at the ancestral mausoleum and pretending to weep so earnestly that eventually real tears of grief would fall. Students of the Way, even though they do not have the mind that seeks the Way at the outset, eventually arouse this mind merely by a steadfast love and study of Buddhism.

Students who have been moved to study the Way should merely follow the rest of the assembly in their conduct. Don't try to learn the essential points and the examples from the past right away. It is best, however, that they be fully grasped before you go alone to practice in the mountains or conceal yourself within a city. If you practice by doing what the assembly does, you should be able to attain the Way. It is like riding in a boat without knowing how to row. If you leave everything up to a competent sailor, you will reach the other shore, whether you know how to row or not. If you follow a good teacher and practice together with the assembly and have no concepts of the Self, you will naturally become a [person] of the Way.

Students, even if you gain enlightenment, do not stop practicing, thinking that you have attained the ultimate. The Buddha Way is endless. Once enlightened you must practice all the more.

Every action of a [person] well versed in Buddhism shows deep thought, whether that action seems good or bad. This, ordinary people do not understand. One day the Abbot Eshin[1] asked a man to beat and drive away a deer that was eating grass in the garden. At that time someone remarked: "You seem to have no compassion. Why have you begrudged the grass and tormented this animal?"

The Abbot replied: "You do not understand. If I did not chase the deer away, it would soon become accustomed to people. If it came near an evil person, it would surely be killed. That's why I chased it away."

Although chasing the deer seemed to show a lack of compassion, it was motivated by a deep compassion.

While the late Abbot Eisai was living at Kennin-ji, a poor man from the neighborhood came and said: "My home is so poor that my wife and I and our three children have had nothing to eat for several days. Have pity and help us out."

This was at a time when the monastery was completely without food, clothing, and money. Eisai racked his brains but could think of no solution. Then it occurred to him that just at this time a statue of Yakushi[2] was being built at the temple and that there was a bit of copper that had been hammered out to make the halo. Eisai broke it up with his own hands, made it into a ball, and gave it to the poor man. "Exchange this for food and save your family from starvation," he said. The poor man left overjoyed.

His disciples were critical: "You've given the halo of a Buddhist statue to a layman. Isn't it a crime to make personal use of what belongs to the Buddha?"

"You are right," the abbot replied, "but think of the will of the Buddha. He cut off his own flesh and limbs for the sake of all sentient beings. Certainly he would have sacrificed his entire body to save starving people. Even though I should fall into the evil realms for this crime, I will still have saved people from starvation." Students today would do well to reflect on the excellence of Eisai's attitude. Do not forget this.

LANCET OF SEATED MEDITATION

Essential function of all the Buddhas,
Functioning essence of all the Ancestors—
It is present without thinking,
It is completed without interacting.
Present without thinking.
Its presence is inherently intimate;
Completed without interacting,
Its completion is inherently verified.

1. Otherwise known as Genshin (941–1003). A famous priest of the Tendai Sect, he lived at Yokawa on Mt. Hiei, near Kyoto.
2. Bhaishajya, the Healing Buddha.

Its presence inherently intimate,
It is ever without any stain or defilement;
Its completion inherently verified,
It is ever without the upright or inclined.
Intimacy ever without stain or defilement,
Its intimacy sloughs off without discarding;
Verification ever without upright or inclined,
Its verification makes effort without figuring.
The water is clear right through the earth,
A fish goes along like a fish.
The sky is vast straight into the heavens,
A bird flies just like a bird.

ONE BRIGHT PEARL

Great Master Tsung-i of Mt. Hsüan-sha, in Fu-chou, in great Sung China, had the Buddhist name Shih-pei, and the family name Hsien.[3] Before he became a monk, he loved fishing, and floating along on the River Nan-t'ai in his boat, he learned how to fish from other fishermen. He never expected the Golden Fish, which is never hooked but jumps into the boat of itself. In the beginning of the Hsien-t'ung era, during the Tang dynasty,[4] he suddenly wished to leave the world [and seek the Dharma]. He abandoned his boat and went off into the mountains. He was thirty years old, awakened to the dangers of this impermanent world, and aware of the loftiness of the Buddha Way.

He finally ascended Mt. Hsüeh-feng and, practicing with Great Master Chen-chüeh [i.e., Hsüeh-feng I-ts'un], pursued the Way day and night. Once, in order to practice with other masters elsewhere and get to the bottom of the whole matter, he got together his traveling gear and was in the process of descending the mountain when his toe struck a rock and began to bleed. In pain, he had an awakening experience and said, "The body does not exist. Where does the pain come from?" Then he returned to Mt. Hsüeh-feng. Master Hsüeh-feng asked him, "What is this Ascetic Pei?"[5] Replied Hsüan-sha, "Henceforth, I shall not deceive people."[6] Hsüeh-feng was delighted with this answer and said, "Everyone has the capacity to utter those words, but no one expresses them [as Shih-pei does]." Hsüeh-feng asked, "Ascetic Pei, why aren't you going on the

---

3. Hsüan-sha Shih-pei, or Hsüan-sha Tsung-i (835–908) was a successor to Hsüeh-feng I-ts'un (822–908) and seventh in the Ancestral line of Ch'ing-yüan Hsing-ssu.
4. That is, soon after 860, the beginning of the Hsien-t'ung era.
5. "Ascetic" is the translation of the Japanese *zuta,* which originally is the Sanskrit *dhuta.*
6. Okada Gihō says . . . that this is an alternate form of "To say something is to miss the mark." Hsüan-sha is thus denying that he is really Shih-pei as far as the ultimate truth is concerned. Hsüeh-feng's question is an alternative for the classic "What is it that thus comes?"

pilgrimage?" Hsüan-sha answered, "Bodhidharma did not come East, the Second Ancestor [Hui-k'o] did not leave [for India]." This answer especially pleased Hsüeh-feng.

Having been a simple fisherman, Hsüan-sha had never encountered the many sutras and treatises even in his dreams, but when he put his determination foremost, he manifested a spirit that surpassed that of others. Hsüeh-feng considered him to be superior to others and praised him as an outstanding disciple. His clothes were of cloth, and because he always wore the same ones, they were covered with patches. His underclothes were of paper and he used mugwort [for padding]. Apart from his practice with Hsüeh-feng, he had no other teacher. However, he experienced the power of succeeding to his teacher's Dharma straightaway.

After attaining the Way, he would instruct others by saying, "The whole universe is one bright pearl."[7] Once a monk asked him, "You have a saying, 'the whole universe is one bright pearl.' How can a student [like me] understand that?" The master replied, "What is the use of understanding that the whole universe is one bright pearl?" The next day the master asked the monk, "What is your understanding of 'the whole universe is one bright pearl'?" The monk said, "What is the use of understanding that the whole universe is one bright pearl?" Hsüan-sha said, "I know that you are alive among the demons in the Dark Cave."[8]

This expression, "The whole universe is one bright pearl," originated with Hsüan-sha. Its deep meaning is that the whole universe is neither vast and expansive nor minute and small. It is not square or round, middle or true. [Its dynamic workings are] neither the lively darting of fish[9] nor the disclosure of forms distinct and clear. Moreover, because it is not birth-and-death or arrival-and-departure, just so it is birth-and-death, arrival-and-departure. Because this is the way it is, it is the past departing from here, the present appearing from here. If it is penetrated to the very bottom, who will see it as limited to being a movement from life to death? Who can see it as being nothing but stillness?

"The whole universe" is the unresting pursuit of things as the self and the pursuit of the self as things.[10] Answering "separated" to the question, "When

7. "One bright pearl" translated *ikka myōju,* the title of this piece. *Myō* is "bright," "brilliant," "clear," and so on. *Ju* means such things as "bead," "jewel," and so on. It is a round beadlike object such as those found on Buddhist rosaries (*juzu*). . . .

8. This is an old Zen expression denoting abysmal ignorance. It recurs in a number of Zen stories, *mondō,* and elsewhere. Hsüan-sha means that even here, in the Dark Cave inhabited by dreadfully ignorant beings, the bright light of the pearl exists.

9. "Lively darting of fish" is a translation of the Chinese *huo p'op'o(ti).* . . . It seems to be a pre-Sung colloquialism, used, for instance, by Lin-chi in his recorded sayings, where English translations such as "brisk and lively" and "vividly alive" can be found. . . .

10. "Unresting pursuit of things." The *Monge* commentary says, "When one pursues things as the self, the self becomes the standard and things are not established. This is the place apart from forms.

feeling arises, is one separated from understanding?" is a turning of the head and an alteration of facial expression, an expanding of the problem and a seizing of opportunity.[11] As a result of pursuing the self as things, it is an unresting "whole universe." Because of its priority over its functional manifestations, this principle remains as something ungraspable even in the midst of its functioning.

"One bright pearl" thoroughly expresses it even though it is not itself revealed in its name, and we can recognize it in its name. "One bright pearl" directly transcends the eons, and because in the eternal past it never ceased to be, it reaches up to the eternal present. Though there is one's mind now and one's body now, they are just the one bright pearl. This grass or that tree are not grass and tree, nor are the mountains and rivers of the world mountains and rivers; they are one bright pearl.

The expression, "How can a student understand that?" makes it seem as if [the question] originates in the student's deluded karmic consciousness, but in reality it is the Great Model itself manifesting as this functional appearance. Continuing, you can make a foot of water into a one-foot wave, which is to say, make a ten-foot pearl into a ten-foot brilliance.

In expressing what can be expressed, Hsüan-sha says, "The whole universe is one bright pearl. What is the use of understanding that?" This expression expresses the fact that Buddha succeeds Buddha, Ancestors succeed Ancestors, and Hsüan-sha succeeds Hsüan-sha. Even if you try to avoid succession, you can not do it, because even if you avoid it for a while, any expression [such as 'what is the use of understanding?'] is, after all, the occasion of its manifesting.

The next day, Hsüan-sha asked the monk, "What is your understanding of 'the whole universe is one bright pearl'?" This expresses "Yesterday I spoke the fixed Dharma [in asking, 'What is the use of understanding that?'], and today I use a different approach [and ask 'What do you understand?']. Today, I speak the unfixed Dharma, turning my back on yesterday with a smile."

The monk said, "What is the use of understanding that the whole universe is one bright pearl?" This is nothing but a mimicry of Hsüan-sha; that is, "riding the thief's horse in pursuit of the thief." In speaking as he did for the sake of the monk, Hsüan-sha was conducting himself in the form of a different species.[12] Reverse the light and illumine within yourselves; how many are there of "what is the

---

Also, pursuing the self as things is the situation in which things are the measure and the self is not established. This is great and vast, life and death."

11. "Expanding the problem" is a reference to the technique of the *mondō* exchange between Zen master and disciple. "Seizing the opportunity" refers to the teacher's intuitive grasp of the student's problem and responding accordingly. This is sometimes done by "expanding the problem," exemplified in the text by the teacher's response of "Separated" to a student's question.

12. Hsüan-sha's taking on the form of a different species is a reference to a bodhisattva's assumption of a nonhuman form, such as that of an animal, in order to conduct the compassionate activities of a bodhisattva.

use of understanding?" If I try to express it, there may be seven sugar cakes or eight herb cakes, but this is teaching and practice north of the Hsiang [River] and south of the T'an.[13]

Hsüan-sha says, "I know that you are alive among the demons in the Dark Cave." You should understand that the faces of the sun and moon have not changed since time began. Because the sun's face always appears as the sun's face and the moon's face always appears as the moon's face, even though I say that my name is "Exactly Now" while it is summer, this does not mean that my name is "Hot."[14]

Thus, the bright pearl, existing just so and being beginningless, transcends changes in time and place. The whole universe is one bright pearl. We do not speak of two or three pearls, and so the entirety is one True Dharma-eye, the Body of Reality, One Expression. The entirety is Brilliant Light, One Mind. When [the bright pearl] is the entirety, nothing hinders it. Round [like a pearl], it rolls around and around. The merits of the bright pearl being manifested in this way. Avalokiteshvara and Maitreya therefore exist now, and old Buddhas and new Buddhas appear in the world and preach the Dharma.

When it is just so, it hangs suspended in space, it is hidden in the linings of clothing, it is held under the chin [of a dragon], and it is worn in the hair top-knot.[15] All these are the one bright pearl as the whole universe. It is its nature to be attached to the lining of clothing, so never say that it is attached to the surface. It is its nature to be guarded under the chin [of a dragon] or kept in a top-knot, so do not think that it is found on the surface. When you are drunk, a friend will give you the pearl, and you must give the pearl to a friend. When you

13. This phrase refers to the omnipresence of buddha, in what is called the "one bright pearl" in the present essay. The expression can be found in [The Blue Cliff Record], case 18, and Dōgen has used the same expression in Eihei kōroku, section 1, where he says, "Yellow gold is found in the land south of the Hsiang and north of the T'an. Ordinary people beyond number are engulfed in it." . . .

14. An allusion to a mondō recorded in the Wu teng hui yüan. "Li-ao asked Yüeh-shan, 'What is your family name?' Replied Yüeh-shan, 'Right Now.' Li-ao did not understand and later asked the head monk, 'Recently I asked Yüeh-shan what his family name is and he said "Right Now." Just what is his name?' The temple master told him, 'His family name is Han' [i.e., "cold." Yüeh-shan's family name was "Han," but written with a different character and having a different meaning]. When Yüeh-shan heard about this, he said, 'The temple head does not understand the difference between good and bad' [or anything else]. When Li asked his question, it was cold, so the temple head said 'cold.' I suppose that had it been summer, he would have said 'hot.' " According to Okada, the reason Dōgen alludes to the mondō is Yüeh-shan's expression. "Right Now." Despite such phenomena as "hot," "cold," "summer," and "winter," all time is just one bright pearl. This is Dōgen's meaning in the essay. Okubo's text (Zenshū) has "nature" where I have "family name" in the translation.

15. The four images are allusions to four stories: (1) in the sutra named P'u-sa ying-lo ching a passage speaks of a jewel suspended in the air and emitting a brilliant light; (2) a story in the Lotus Sutra tells of a man placing a precious jewel in the lining of the clothing of his drunken friend, who, upon awakening, is unaware of his wealth; (3) Chuang-tzu, the Taoist, speaks of a jewel guarded beneath the chin of a dragon; and (4) the Lotus Sutra tells of a grateful king who rewarded his military commander with castles, gold, and other things but would not part with a jewel that he wore in his topknot.

receive the pearl from a friend, you surely will be drunk. Because this is so, it is the one bright pearl as the whole universe.

Thus, though on the surface there may seem to be change or no change [i.e., enlightenment or no enlightenment], it is the one bright pearl. Realizing it is so is itself the one bright pearl. The shapes and sounds of the bright pearl are seen in this way. Saying to yourself, "It is so," do not doubt that you, yourself, are the bright pearl by thinking, "I am not the bright pearl." Confusion and doubts, affirmations and negations, these are nothing but the ephemeral, small responses of ordinary folk; however, still, they are [the bright pearl] appearing as small, ephemeral responses.

Should we not appreciate it? The bright pearl's colors and brilliance are boundless. Color after color and every scintillation of light are the merit of the whole universe. Could anything ever snatch them away? Would anyone ever toss away even a simple roof tile in the marketplace [while looking for the pearl]? Do not be anxious about being reborn in one of the six realms of cause and effect. The bright pearl, which from beginning to end is essentially uninvolved [with cause and effect], is your original face, your enlightened nature.[16]

However, you and I, unaware of what the bright pearl is and is not, entertain countless doubts and nondoubts about it and turn them into indubitable fodder for the mind. But Hsüan-sha's expression has made it clear that our own minds and bodies are the one bright pearl, and so we realize that our minds are not "ours." Who can be anxious as to whether birth and death are or are not the bright pearl? Even if there is doubt and anxiety, they are the bright pearl. There is not a single activity or thought that is not the bright pearl, and, consequently, both advancing and retreating in the Black Mountain Cave of demons is nothing but the one bright pearl.

16. "Uninvolved" is *fu-i,* which is literally, "does not taste." Here it is an abbreviation for *fu-i inga,* "not involved in cause and effect." Hence, my interpolation in the translation. The one bright pearl does not experience cause and effect.

30

Enni Ben'en

(1202–1280)

The career of Enni Ben'en paralleled Dōgen's into early adulthood: both were drawn to religion as boys; both began in the Tendai tradition, becoming Tendai monks; both rapidly earned reputations for great intellect and learning; both acquired their taste for Zen, and received initial instruction in it, within the Tendai institution; and both thereafter sailed to China to pursue this interest. From that point on, however, Enni's life took a different turn, and when the two men's paths crossed in Kyoto in 1243, Dōgen was on the verge of departing for the hinterlands, while the two-year-younger master was starting a lifelong, immensely successful tenure in the center of Japanese wealth, culture, and power.

Having immersed himself more deeply than Dōgen did in Tendai studies, Enni did not reach eastern China until 1235, but he seems to have hit the ground running, soon finding his way to Mt. Ching and forming a close relationship with the abbot there, Wu-chun Shih-fan (1177–1249). Wu-chun belonged to the Yang-ch'i line of Lin-chi Ch'an and was descended from Yüan-wu not through Ta-hui but through another successor, Hu-chiu Shao-lung. As his position at top-ranked Mt. Ching indicates, he was highly regarded, and fortunately for Enni and the future of Zen, he took an active interest in the transmission of Buddhism to Japan. After seven years of study, having received full certification as his heir, Enni returned to Japan laden with symbols of his new authority and with a thousand-text library of Ch'an, Confucian, and other literature.

Since Enni's travels had been sponsored by a merchant from Japan's southern-most island of Kyushu, he returned there to begin teaching. Though he was far away from Kyoto, his name swiftly came to the attention of one of the most power-ful men in the capital, Kujō Michiie, who called him in 1243 to serve as the found-ing abbot of a large, Chinese-style monastery whose construction he was funding. The new institution, to be named Tōfuku-ji, would have halls for Tendai and Shin-gon ceremonies as well as for Zen practice, but that posed no problem for Enni, who maintained a lifelong interest in Tendai teachings and held the unitary view of Buddhism, Confucianism, and Taoism that Ta-hui and many other Lin-chi teach-ers espoused—but that Dōgen, like Ju-ching, staunchly rejected.

Enni's arrival to direct the imposing new edifice rising very near his own monastery may have precipitated Dōgen's move to Echizen. Though he does not mention Enni by name in his writings, shortly after arriving at his new location, Dōgen did sharply criticize those who "stress the unity of Confucianism, Taoism, and Buddhism. They argue that the three are like the legs of a tripod vessel, which cannot stand upright if it lacks even one leg. The folly of such views is beyond belief." Dōgen may well have taken Enni's advent as a slap in the face; despite his seniority and his fifteen years of work in Kyoto, he had been passed over in favor of an upstart Lin-chi master. At the least, Enni's appointment confirmed other signals that Dōgen lacked standing with the court's major figures. It also meant that his effort to promulgate the Way would be further complicated, for Enni could be counted on to preach the contending message of Lin-chi Ch'an. Even from his mountaintop at Echizen, Dōgen felt the need to step up his campaign against the Dharma of Ta-hui and the wider Lin-chi house.

In all likelihood, Enni never even got wind of his criticism, for Dōgen's voice did not reach far, and publication of the *Eye Treasury* would not occur for centuries. In any event, he had little cause for concern. Under Kujō's wing, Enni could go about his business free of interference even from the jealous priests of Mt. Hiei. This he did, exercising his extracurricular interests as he pleased but generally, it seems, conveying in a very straightforward manner the Dharma he inherited from Wu-chun. Eisai is customarily credited with founding Japanese Zen and its Rinzai sect in particular, but he could do no more than secure them a toehold. Enni, in contrast, carried Zen to the center of nation life.

The appointments and honors that accrued to him indicate the degree of acceptance Enni won for himself and for Rinzai Zen. After fire devastated Kennin-ji in 1256, he was named abbot there as well and is said to have strolled over from Tōfuku-ji at noon each day. Under his supervision, the old temple was rebuilt and a monks' hall added for Zen training. In the course of his long life, he also served as abbot of a great monastery in Kamakura, gave personal instruction in Zen to the leader of the Kamakura shogunate, and lectured about the Dharma before three emperors, reigning or retired. After his death, he was honored with the imperial title Shōitsu Kokushi, designating him a national teacher. Although he named thirty heirs, this line did not endure and, he is now remembered for his role in advancing Zen's standing, for introducing Chinese monastic practices, and for his many writings, the best of which are refreshingly clear and energetic. ⊗

FROM INSTRUCTIONS OF NATIONAL TEACHER SHŌITSU

TO EMINENT KUMYO

In the direct teachings of the ancestral masters, there are no special techniques, just to lay down all entanglements, put to rest all concerns, and watch the tip of your nose for six hours in the daytime and six hours at night; whenever you wander into distinctions among things, just raise a saying—don't think of it in terms of the way to enlightenment, don't think of it in terms of purification, don't consciously anticipate understanding, don't let feelings create doubt or despair, but go directly in like cutting through an iron bun with a single stroke, where there is no flavor, no path of reason, without getting involved in other thoughts. After a long time, you will naturally be like waking from a dream, like a lotus blossom opening. At this moment, the saying you have been observing is just a piece of tile to knock at the door—throw it over on the other side and then look instead at the sayings of the enlightened ancestors and buddhas expressing activity in the world of differentiation. All of these are just to stop children crying; the one road going beyond does not let a single thread through, but cuts off the essential crossing between ordinary and holy, while students toil over forms like monkeys grasping at the moon. We might say that if you forget your own body and go frantically searching outside, when can you ever find it? Sitting peacefully on a cushion, day and night seeking to become buddhas, rejecting life and death in hopes of realizing enlightenment, are all like the monkey's grasping at the moon. If you want some real help, it's just that not minding is the way; yet it's not the same as wood or stone—always aware and knowing, perfectly distinctly clear, seeing and hearing are normal; there are no further details.

Elder Kumyo sits facing a wall day and night and has asked for some words to urge him on. Not begrudging the way of my house, I have let my brush write this, 1267.

TO EMINENT CHIZEN

In the school of the ancestral teachers we point directly to the human mind; verbal explanations and illustrative devices actually miss the point. Not falling into seeing and hearing, not following sound or form, acting freely in the phenomenal world, sitting and lying in the heap of myriad forms, not involved with phenomena in breathing out, not bound to the clusters and elements of existence in breathing in, the whole world is the gate of liberation, all worlds are true reality. A universal master knows what it comes to the moment it is raised; how will beginners and latecomers come to grips with it? If you don't get it yet, for the time being we open up a pathway in the gateway of the secondary truth, speak out where there is nothing to say, manifest form in the midst of formlessness. How do we speak where there is nothing to say? "A mortar [sails] through the sky." How do we manifest form from formlessness? "The west river sports with a lion."

During your daily activities responding to circumstances in the realm of distinctions, don't think of getting rid of anything, don't understand it as a hidden marvel—with no road of reason, no flavor, day and night, forgetting sleep and food, keep those sayings in mind.

If you still don't get it, we go on to speak of the tertiary, expounding mind and nature, speaking of mystery and marvel; one atom contains the cosmos, one thought pervades everywhere. Thus an ancient said:

> Infinite lands and worlds
> With no distinctions between self and others

Ten ages past and present
Are never apart from this moment of thought

Chizen brought some paper seeking some words, so I dashed this off, senile and careless; after looking at it once, consign it to the fire.

TO ZEN MAN CHIMOKU

Since the buddhas and ancestors, there have been three general levels of dealing with people. On the uppermost level there are no further techniques, no meaning of principle; verbal understanding is impossible. If you can take it up directly at this, then there is no difference from "the cypress in the garden," "three pounds of hemp," "swallow the water of the west river in one gulp."

On the second level, it is just a matter of bringing out a question, going along to break through; this is like Lin-chi questioning Huang-po and getting hit sixty times.

On the third level, we enter the mud and water, setting down footnotes, blinding people's eyes, destroying the lineage of the Buddha.

But a true patch-robed—one must search out and investigate the living word, not go for the dead word. Eminent Chimoku, you are pure and true; if you can attain realization at the living word, you can be teacher of buddhas and ancestors. Not begrudging my family way, I have shown you three levels of device.

TO ELDER KAKUJITSU

The fundamental style of the ancestral teachers, the one expression of transcendence, plunging into the other side with a heroic spirit, then being free wherever you are, inconceivable activities unhindered. Wielding the jewel sword of the diamond king, cutting off difficulty and confusion, using the killing and reviving staff to eliminate affirmation and denial. Striking and shouting at appropriate times, sitting one, walking seven; by this that tawny-faced old teacher Shākyamuni assembled all kinds of people over three hundred and sixty times—able to act as king of the teaching, he was free in all respects. The blue-eyed First Ancestor sat for nine years facing a wall and offered instruction for later students—"outwardly ceasing all involvements, inwardly no sighing in the mind, mind like a wall, thereby one may enter the way." These and their like are elementary techniques; later you realize on your own—casting off all involvements, letting myriad things rest, is the foremost technique. If you stick to this technique, then it is not right. It cannot be helped, to give meticulous explanations, to mix with the mud and water, to use a stake to extract a stake, to use a state to take away a state; a thousand changes, myriad transformations, seven ways up and down, eight ways across. If you take the words as the rule, you will produce interpretations along with the words and fall into the clusters and elements of physical-mental existence, the world of shadows; if you don't even know techniques, how could you know the true source?

Elder Kakujitsu is extraordinary by nature, a completely pure person. He asked for some words of exhortation, so I wrote this.

TO A ZEN MAN

On the forehead, at the feet, it is necessary to realize here is a great road through the heavens. Without establishing the practice and vows of Samantabhadra or speaking of the active knowledge of Mañjushrī, hold Vairochana still so that all traces of ordinary or holy disappear—then afterward the great capacity and great function will come into being wherever you may be; on the hundred grasses speaking of the provisional and the true, in the heap of sound and form setting up illumination and function, giving helpful techniques, freely and independently. But if you have a clear-eyed person look at this, it is still only halfway—it is still wearing stocks presenting evidence of your crime.

However, even so, you must know there are methods of offering help and guidance; one is the technique of sitting meditation, the other is the technique of direct pointing. Sitting meditation is the great calm; direct pointing is the great wisdom. Before the empty eon, on the other side of the ancient buddhas, self-enlightenment without a teacher, without any such techniques—this is what Bodhidharma taught, the hidden transmission of personal experience. After the empty eon, there is enlightenment and delusion, there are questions and answers, there are teachers and students; all these are guiding techniques. . .

An ancient said, "In the community of the Fifth Ancestor, seven hundred eminent monks all understood Buddhism. There was only workman Lu who didn't understand Buddhism." This is the way of direct pointing; as for the technique of sitting meditation, you are already thoroughly familiar with this and don't need my instruction. As you come with some paper asking for a saying, I scribble this senile confusion.

Awakening on your own without a teacher before the empty eon and being awakened by a teacher after the appearance of the buddhas and ancestors, that is awakening and being awakened, are both techniques of guidance. All that has been communicated from buddhas to ancestors, inconceivable liberated activity, is all just the mutual accord of states and words.

Great Master Bodhidharma crossed the sea and crossed the river, sat upright for nine years facing a wall, and returned alone with one shoe—this, too, was in the sphere of accord of words and actions. Eminent, if you want to attain accord, you must cut off the root of birth-and-death, break up the nest of sage and sainthood, become clean and naked, bare and untrammeled, not relying on anything; only then will you have some realization. Now when I speak this way, is there any accord? Is there none? If you can search it out, don't say I didn't tell you.

31

Daikaku

(1213–1279)

By the mid–thirteenth century, so many Japanese monks had embarked for China that "longing for the Dharma, entering the land of Sung" became a stock phrase to express religious aspiration. The number and zeal of these visitors so impressed Chinese masters that more than a dozen of them, including Lan-ch'i Tao-lung, hatched the opposite dream—sailing to Japan to promote the Dharma. Lan-ch'i reached the island of Kyushu in 1246 and spent the next thirty-three years, exactly half of his life, devising ways to teach Zen across the language barrier. For his efforts, he received the posthumous title Daikaku Zenji, Zen master of Great Enlightenment.

Born in western China, Daikaku left home at thirteen and made his way east for the next two decades, visiting monasteries and studying with various Ch'an teachers, including Enni's master, Wu-chun. He eventually settled with Wu-chun's lesser-known Dharma cousin, Wu-ming Hui-hsing, and apparently received transmission in this branch of the Yang-ch'i school at an exceptionally early age. Though he seems to have lacked an official invitation to visit Japan and did not speak Japanese, he managed to negotiate entry and, after a brief stay in Kyushu, traveled north to Kyoto and then Kamakura. Within three years of his arrival in Japan, he was introduced to the most powerful person in the land, Hojo Tokiyori, who ruled as regent for the shogun and had long cultivated an interest in Zen.

His good karma did not stop there. Tokiyori, having already explored the Tendai-influenced Zen of Eisai's school and having received instruction from Enni, welcomed the unexpected opportunity to study with a Chinese master and quickly ensconced the newcomer in the abbot's quarters of a Kamakura temple. With the regent's backing, Daikaku promptly added a monk's hall to this temple complex and established Zen training along Chinese lines. In that same year, Tokiyori undertook to build a new monastery patterned on the great institution at Mt. Ching. Daikaku lent advice and was installed as founding abbot in 1253, when construction was completed. In Kyoto, work on Tofuku-ji had proceeded slowly, so Kamakura's Kencho-ji opened sooner, becoming the first fully functioning Rinzai monastery in Japan.

Tokiyori had political as well as personal reasons for so embracing Daikaku and Zen as a whole. This newfound, highly impressive form of Buddhism lent the shogunate an aura of religious and cultural authority that helped legitimate it in a world dominated by these concerns. The leading position that Ch'an held in Sung China, along with the access émigré masters provided to mainland intellectual and aesthetic trends, made Zen a viable, even attractive alternative to those Japanese institutions that had previously served as legitimators of power—and it was put to such use right away. When Kenchō-ji opened, it was dedicated, first and foremost, to "the longevity of the emperor" and "the welfare of the shogunal line," and later, when Kublai Khan mounted an invasion threat, Daikaku and the Kenchō-ji monks were called upon to perform ceremonies for protection of the nation. The Chinese master apparently had no scruples about serving power in this way, and indeed, he preached that "faithful observance of the laws of the [secular] world does not differ from faithful observance of the laws of the religious world."

However he catered to the shogunate's demands, Daikaku went earnestly about the business of teaching Zen, and monks lined up to train with him by the hundreds. One problem: though many had a good command of written Chinese, few could understand spoken Chinese, and very few, if any, could make sense of Daikaku's Szechwan accent. Kenchō-ji annals note instances of a laborious, three-step process by which Daikaku's verbal instructions were communicated to his monks: they were first recorded in Japanese phonetic syllables, then these were carried to another Szechwan native who rendered them into Chinese characters, and finally these were translated into Japanese. To expedite exchange, teacher and student took to "brush talk," as later described by another Chinese master:

> I express my mind
> > using a brush instead of my tongue,
> and you seize my meaning
> > hearing my words with your eyes.

Even this strategy failed if a student's grasp of written Chinese left something to be desired. Witness the final item in this chapter.

Under these circumstances, Daikaku and other émigré masters found it necessary to improvise new training methods. To offer koan instruction in the preferred Chinese manner would have demanded so much brush talk—and time—as to make teaching a large group impractical. Instead, the Chinese teachers came up with new koans that could be expediently given, recalled, and tested. Some of them were created impromptu, out of a situation or to suit the character and the experience of a particular student.

When one of Wu-chun's senior successors appeared on the scene in 1260, Tokiyori named him second abbot of Kenchō-ji, and Daikaku moved to Kyoto for a few years, following Enni in the abbacy of newly restored Kennin-ji. During his time in the imperial capital, he tutored the former emperor Go-Saga in Zen and succeeded in eradicating Tendai rites and other such practices from Kennin-ji, bringing monastery operations fully into line with Rinzai traditions. As he had in Kamakura, Daikaku imposed a strict, Chinese monastic code, emphasizing four daily intervals of zazen and assiduous around-the-clock practice: "Even on bath days and holidays do not allow your practice of Zen to relax for an instant."

Despite his loyalty to the power structure, Daikaku fell victim to a rumor that he was a Chinese spy and found himself banished to the provinces. He is said to have weathered this stunning reversal not just with equanimity but with cheer, taking the occasion to spread the Dharma in the countryside. Reinstatement came in due course, enabling him to end his career in his old post at Kencho-ji. Before his death in 1279, he and Tokiyori's successor drew up plans for a second, large Kamakura monastery, later built and named Engaku-ji.

Daikaku left his imprint on Japanese Zen and Kamakura culture in many ways. Besides building temples and implanting the Chinese monastic regimen, he made his mark as a poet and calligrapher, helping the warriors of the shogunate develop a cultural base to rival that of the old order in Kyoto. Also, like Dōgen and Enni before him, he wrote a question-and-answer meditation manual making the rudiments of Zen practice available to anyone who could read. In the decades that followed, his twenty-four Dharma successors continued this work in Kamakura and elsewhere, doing much to expedite the naturalization of Ch'an to Japan. ⊗

SAYINGS OF DAIKAKU

Zen practice is not clarifying conceptual distinctions, but throwing away one's preconceived views and notions and the sacred texts and all the rest, and piercing through the layers of coverings over the spring of self behind them. All the holy ones have turned within and sought in the self, and by this went beyond all doubt. To turn within means all the twenty-four hours and in every situation, to pierce one by one through the layers covering the self, deeper and deeper, to a place that cannot be described. It is when thinking comes to an end and making distinctions ceases, when wrong views and ideas disappear of themselves without having to be driven forth, when without being sought the true action and true impulse appear of themselves. It is when one can know what is the truth of the heart.

The man resolute in the way must from the beginning never lose sight of it, whether in a place of calm or in a place of strife, and he must not be clinging to quiet places and shunning those where there is disturbance. If he tries to take refuge from trouble by running to some quiet place, he will fall into dark regions.

If when he is trying to throw off delusions and discover truth everything is a whirl of possibilities, he must cut off the thousand impulses and go straight forward, having no thought at all about good or bad; not hating the passions, he must simply make his heart pure.

Illusion is dark, satori is bright. When the light of wisdom shines, the darkness of passion suddenly becomes bright, and to an awakened one they are not two separate things.

This is the main point of meditation. But an ordinary beginner cannot mount to the treasure in one step. He moves from shallow to profound, progresses from slow to quick. When in the meditation sitting there is agitation of thought, then with that very agitated mind seek to find where the agitated thought came from, and who it is that is aware of it. In this way pressing scrutiny as to the location of the disturbance further and further to the ultimate point, you will find that the agitation does not have any original location, and that the one who is aware of it also is void, and this is called taking the search back.

If the press of delusive thoughts is very heavy, one of the koan phrases should be taken up, for instance seeing where it is that life comes from. Keep on inquiring into this again and again. An ancient has said that while you do not yet know life, how should you know death? And if you have known life, you also know death, and then you will not be controlled by life-and-death, but will be able to rise or set as you will.

Hearing a sound, to take it simply as sound; seeing a form, to take it simply as form; how to turn the light back and control vision, and how to turn hearing within—these are the things that none of you understand. In hearing sounds as you do all day long, find out whether it is the sound that comes to the convolutions of the ear, or the ear that goes out to the location of the sound. If it is the sound that comes to the ear, there is no track of its coming; and if it is the ear that goes to the sound, there is no track of its going. The practicer of Zen should carefully go into this in his silent inquiry. In silent investigation, with great courage turn the hearing back till hearing comes to an end; purify awareness till awareness becomes empty. Then there will be a perception of things, which is immediate without any check to it, and after that, even in a welter of sounds and forms you will not be swept away by them, even in a state of darkness and confusion you will be able to find a way. Such is called a man of the great freedom, one who has attained.

Whether you are going or staying or sitting or lying down, the whole world is your own self. You must find out whether the mountains, rivers, grass, and forests exist in your own mind or exist outside it. Analyse the ten thousand things, dissect them minutely, and when you take this to the limit you will come to the limitless, when you search into it you come to the end of search, where thinking goes no further and distinctions vanish. When you smash the citadel of doubt, then the Buddha is simply yourself.

When you set out to look for the way of the buddhas and ancestors, at once it changes to something that is to be sought in your self. When sight becomes no-sight, you come to possess the jewel, but you have not yet fully penetrated into it. Suddenly one day everything is empty like space that has no inside or outside, no bottom or top, and you are aware of one principle (*ri*) pervading all the ten thousand things. You know then that your heart is so vast that it can never be measured. Seng-chao says, "Heaven and earth and I are of one root; the thousand things and I are one body." These words are of burning import and absolutely true.

The holy men and illumined ones who have this principle clear in them, find that past, present, and future are like dream-stuff. Wealth and rank, gain and fame are all an illusion; the mined gold and heaped-up jewels, the beautiful voices and fair forms, are illusion; joy and anger and sorrow and happiness are this illusion. But in all this illusion there is something that is not illusion. When even the universes crumble, how should that crumble? When at the end of the world cycle the universal fire blazes everywhere, how should that burn? That which is not illusion is the true being of each and every man. Every day go into the calm quiet where you really belong, face the other way and turn your gaze back; if you do this over the long years, that which is not illusion will of itself reveal itself before you. After that manifestation, wherever you stand Maitreya [the future Buddha] is there, and when you turn to the left or glance to the right, it is Shākyamuni everywhere.

Realization makes every place a temple; the absolute endows all beings with the true eye. When you come to grasp it, you find it was ever before your eyes. If you can see clear what is before your very eyes, it is what fills the ten directions; when you see what fills the ten directions, you find it is only what is before your eyes.

It is not, as some ancients and the Confucians taught, that you sweep away ordinary feelings and bring into existence some holy understanding. When ordinariness and holiness exist no more, how is that? An octagonal grindstone is turning in empty space; a diamond pestle grinds to dust the iron mountain.

ANECDOTES ABOUT DAIKAKU

THE SUTRA OF ONE WORD

A man came to [Daikaku] who was a believer in repetition of mantras like the Lotus mantra and the mantra of Amida, and said, "The *Heart Sutra* which is read in the Zen tradition, is long and difficult to read, whereas Nichiren teaches the mantra of the Lotus, which is only seven syllables, and Ippen teaches the mantra of Amida, which is only six. But the *Zen Sutra* is much longer and it's difficult to recite."

The teacher listened to this and said, "What would a follower of Zen want with a long text? If you want to recite the Zen scripture, do it with *one word*. It is the six- and seven-word ones that are too long."

ONE-ROBE ZEN

A priest from the headquarters of the regent Yasutoki visited Kencho-ji and remarked to Daikaku, "Eisai and Gyōyū began the propagation of Zen here in

Kamakura, but the two greatest teachers of the way of the ancestors have been Dōgen of the Sōtō sect and [Enni Ben'en]. Both of them came to Kamakura at the invitation of regent Tokiyori to teach Zen, but both of them left before a year was out. So there are not many among the warriors here who have much understanding of Zen. In fact some are so ignorant about it that they think the character for Zen—written as they think it is by combining the characters for "garment" and "single"—means just that. They believe that Zen monks of India in the mountains practiced special austerities, and even in winter wore only one cotton robe, and that the name of the sect arose from this."

Zen

"one-robe"

Daikaku listened to all this and laughed. "The people of Kamakura are right to say that Zen means wearing a single garment. They well understand what the sect stands for. An ordinary man is clad in layers of the three poisons and five desires, and though by repetition of the buddha-name and reading the scriptures he tries again and again to strip them off, he cannot get out of his layers of passions. Fundamentally Zen means having no layers of clothes but just one piece. Repeating the buddha-name—it is becoming just one piece with the buddha; reading the scriptures—it is 'apart from the Law no I, and without I no Law,' so that I and the Law are one piece. This is called 'knocking everything into one.' The warriors of Kamakura, when they say Zen means the sect of a single robe, have grasped its deepest essence.

"If you don't have those layers of clothes, you will be cultivating the field . . . in the Zen way. Here and now let a man strip off the eighty thousand robes of the Treasure of the Law and experience the simplicity of the one robe. How would that be?"

The priest bowed in reverence and left.

32

Keizan

(1264–1325)

Keizan Jōkin, fourth in the line of Sōtō succession, is often styled the sect's second founder. Next to Dōgen, its father and Eminent Ancestor, he is looked up to as its mother and Great Ancestor. Behind these metaphors and carefully weighed phrases lies a tangled history that more than once has split the sect into feuding factions and that is only now being sorted out through a reading of its early administrative history so close as to merit the adjective "microscopic." Whatever this research may yet turn up, unquestionably Keizan played a key role in the sect's establishment, and his contributions to its literature likewise stand beyond challenge.

If the first phase of Japanese Zen was characterized by pilgrimage to China and the second by the advent of émigrés like Daikaku, then Keizan belongs to its third phase—Japanese masters teaching Japanese students. Keizan's training could hardly have been more homegrown; all of it occurred right in his native province of Echizen. He became a novice monk at seven, taking the tonsure at Eihei-ji, then studied there with Dōgen's immediate successor, Koun Ejō. Later, both there and in other Echizen temples, he trained with teachers in the third generation of the line.

Conventional Sōtō histories speak of a schism in the sect's third generation, centering on Tettsū Gikai (1219–1309), the teacher from whom Keizan would later receive Dōgen's robe as a symbol of Dharma-transmission. The term schism seems too strong in light of current research, but apparently disciples of another third-generation teacher, twelve years senior to Gikai, felt that he had been slighted by Gikai or wrongly passed over for the abbacy, and they succeeded in making his tenure at Eihei-ji so uncomfortable that Gikai stepped down after fewer than five years. Four decades later, when Keizan himself missed appointment to the abbot's seat at Eihei-ji, he set his sights on founding another great monastery farther to the north. These events created factional wrangling for centuries to come but also brought a broadening of the Sōtō base that has made it the largest of the Japanese Zen sects by far.

As Eihei-ji's principal sponsor, the Hatano family had effectively controlled the naming of its abbots. Among Keizan's initial steps in developing the new monastery, Yōkō-ji, was ensuring its freedom from such patron interference. In 1317, his backers in this enterprise gave him a commitment in writing allowing him extraordinary latitude: "We will take absolutely no notice whether the temple thrives or decays. We are not concerned whether the master keeps the precepts or breaks the precept. Likewise, we will not interfere if [he] gives the land to a wife, child, or relative, or even to outcasts and beggars." Two years later, they signed another version of this pledge, expanded to guarantee that the Yōkō-ji abbacy would always remain in the hands of Keizan's Dharma heirs, passing in order of priestly seniority from one person to the next.

The successional squabbles at Eihei-ji and elsewhere gave Keizan all the motivation he needed to lock up the Yōkō-ji abbacy in this manner. In addition to preventing a patron from installing a representative of a rival line—even a Rinzai master, as had happened at another temple—it dramatically reduced chances of his descendants falling into discord. Furthermore, it promised the monastery a much-needed stream of economic support, in the form of offerings that incoming abbots, their followers, and other contributors would make for the accession ceremonies. This practice became the norm in the Sōtō sect and undoubtedly helped power its growth, but it probably also had the side effect of devaluing the abbacy, making it a nominal honor and ceremonial office, so that naming an abbot no longer served as a means to recognize exceptional insight or to secure superior leadership for the monastic community.

Keizan's new patrons occupied a more marginal social position than the Hatanos of Eihei-ji, with less power, less influence, less wealth. To develop the monastic complex at Yōkō-ji, therefore, he had to find—or invent—additional means of support, and here, as elsewhere, Keizan displayed considerable creativity. Under his guidance, Yōkō-ji began to offer area residents a range of opportunities to enter the Way through ceremonies and offerings, to associate themselves and their families with the monastery's spiritual power, and to participate in its life, at least vicariously. These included, during his lifetime, administration of Buddhist precepts and granting of a Buddhist name in what came to be regarded as a lay form of ordination.

Desire to build a first-rate monastery probably drove Keizan's decisions to some extent, but so did desire to serve the needs of laypeople. He had spent his early years with his maternal grandmother, a deeply religious woman said to have been among Dōgen's first supporters. Her daughter, his mother, was an ardent devotee of Kannon, the Bodhisattva of Compassion, and became the abbess of a Sōtō convent in later life. Having grown up in such a household, he undoubtedly knew the place that Zen could fill, if it deigned to do so, in less-than-elite Japanese society. Prayers for protection of the nation and longevity of its leaders had been offered in Zen monasteries at least since the Mongols' attempted invasions half a century before, so Keizan's step of introducing prayers for the welfare of his patrons—to relieve bad karma, attain worldly success, improve their deceased relatives chances of future enlightenment—was, in some ways, not a very big one.

He took this step clearly within the context of the monastic tradition he had inherited, and we have no reason to suppose he saw his work as anything other than a faithful extension of Dōgen's. On the contrary, he ran Yōkō-ji according to Dōgen's monastic codes, using the same handbooks followed at Eihei-ji. In a shrine erected on its grounds, he placed some of Dōgen's remains, along with a copy of Ju-ching's record, a sutra that Ejō had inscribed in his own blood, and other relics linking himself and the entire institution to Dōgen's lineage. His most renowned writing, the Denkōroku (Transmission of the Light), traces Dōgen's "bloodline" from Shākyamuni through Ejō, stopping short of Gikai and himself but creating a powerful impression of how the great tradition had come to them—as well as displaying his talent for Zen history, commentary, and poetry.

However strong Keizan's sense of identity with his Sōtō ancestors, he had not known Dōgen and felt no need to imitate him in his work, literary or otherwise. Indeed, his teaching betrays the influence of another vein of Zen that had passed to him through Gikai—the Yang-ch'i school of Rinzai Zen. Whereas Dōgen preached the utter identity of zazen and enlightenment, Keizan's writings, especially the two meditation manuals he authored, express a somewhat more instrumental view of zazen as a means of enlightenment and explicitly suggest (but do not stress) the very approach of "contemplating sayings" upon which his great-grandfather in the Dharma had heaped such scorn.

The Denkōroku, like Dōgen's Eye Treasury, went unpublished for five centuries or more, and Keizan today owes his fame mainly to the institutional expansion that resulted from his practical reforms. Adopting and adapting his policies, his Dharma heirs and their successors founded temples throughout the country. The Rinzai sect followed suit but never caught up, and its temples and adherents now number only about a third as many as belong to the Sōtō sect. ❈

FROM THE DENKŌROKU

SHĀNAVĀSA

Case: The Third Ancestor was Shānavāsa. He asked Ānanda, "What kind of thing is the original unborn nature of all things?" Ānanda pointed to a corner of Shānavāsa's robe. Again, he asked, "What kind of thing is the original nature of the Buddhas' awakening?" Ānanda then grasped a corner of Shānavāsa's robe and pulled it. At that time, Shānavāsa was greatly awakened.[1]

Circumstances: The master was a man of Mathurā. In India he was called Shānaka [-vāsa], which here [in Japan] means "Natural Clothing." Shānavāsa was born wearing clothes and, later, the clothes became cool in summer and warm in winter. When he aroused the thought [of enlightenment] and made his

[1]. His name is given in several alternate forms, some of which occur in the story following the case. The Japanese *shōnawashu* seems to indicate an original Shanavasa, hence my reconstitution. Monier-Williams records both Shanavasa and Shānavāsika ("name of an *arhat*") in his *Sanskrit-English Dictionary.* He also translates *śānaka* as "a hempen cloth or garment."

home departure, his layman's clothes were spontaneously transformed into [monk's] clothes, just like [an incident recounted concerning] the nun "Lotus Color," during the Buddha's lifetime. . . .

The Venerable Shānavāsa was originally a wizard who lived in the Himalaya Mountains. He joined with the Venerable Ānanda and so we have this story. This "What kind of thing is the original unborn nature of all things?" is truly a question no one had ever asked. Shānavāsa alone asked it. There is no one who is not born with this original unborn nature of all things, but no one knows it and no one asks about it. Why is it called "unborn nature"? Even though the myriad things are born from it, this nature is not something which is born, so it is called "unborn nature." It is wholly the original Unborn. Mountains are not mountains and rivers are not rivers. Therefore, Ānanda pointed to a corner of Shānavāsa's robe.

Commentary: Kesa [*i.e., kasāya,* the monk's robe] is an Indian word and it means "spoiled color" or "unborn color." Truly, you should not see it as a color. One way to see it is as the color of the mind and body and external environment of all things[2]—from buddhas above to the ants, mosquitoes, and horseflies below. However, they are not form and color. Therefore, there are no three realms to leave[3] and no fruit of the Way to acquire.

Though he understood in this manner, Shānavāsa asked a second time, "What kind of thing is the original nature of the Buddhas' awakening?" Even though we are not confused in this matter since ages ago, if we do not realize its existence one time, we will be vainly obstructed by our eyes. Therefore, [Shānavāsa] asked in this way in order to clarify the place whence Buddhas come. In order to let him know that [Buddhas] respond to calls and appear in accordance with knocking, [Ānanda] showed him by grasping the corner of the robe and tugging it. At that time, Shānavāsa was greatly awakened.

Truly, though we are not confused about this matter since ages ago, if we do not experience it one time, we will not realize that we are the mothers of the wisdom of all Buddhas. Therefore, Buddhas have appeared in the world one after another and ancestral teachers have pointed it out generation after generation. Although one thing [*i.e.,* original nature] is never given to another or received from another, it should be like touching your own nostrils by searching your face.

2. "Mind and body and external environment" translates the Japanese *shō e hō.* These are two forms of karmic result. *Shō* means one's own mind and body, and *e* refers to such things as native place, race, social class, economic circumstances, and so on. Both are understood to result from past karma.

3. The "three realms" (*trailokya*) are 1) realm of desire (*kāmaloka*), 2) realm of form (*rūpaloka*), and 3) formless realm (*arūpyaloka*). These are arranged vertically in that ascending order, cosmologically speaking, and all sentient beings dwell within these three realms. However, for the same reason, all three realms are also realms of suffering and rebirth and consequently are understood to be something to transcend in nirvana, which is not a place to begin with and is not within the three realms. Hence Keizan's remarks.

The practice of Zen must be one's own practice of enlightenment. When you are enlightened, you should meet a person [who is a true teacher]. If you do not meet a person, you will be [like a bodiless spirit] vainly dependent on grasses and adhering to trees. You should use this story to clarify the fact that you must not practice Zen aimlessly and spend your whole life in vain. Do not vainly express naturalistic views or put your own individual views first.

You may think, "The Way of the Buddha ancestors distinguishes individuals and capacities. We are not up to it." Such a view is truly the stupidest of stupid views. Who among the ancients was not a body born of a mother and father? Who did not have feelings of love and affection or thoughts of fame and fortune? However, once they practiced [Zen], they practiced thoroughly [and achieved enlightenment]. From India to Japan, throughout the different times of the True Dharma, Counterfeit Dharma, and Collapsed Dharma, enough holy and wise men to overflow the mountains and oceans have realized the result [of enlightenment]. Thus, you monks who possess sight and hearing are no different from the ancients. Wherever you go, it can be said that you are this [complete] person, and you are Kāshyapa and Ānanda. There is no difference in the four great elements and five aggregates, so how are you different from the ancients as far as the Way is concerned?

As a result of merely not penetrating this principle and making an effort in the Way, you will not only lose your human body [which is hard to obtain], but you will not realize that it is the [expression of the] Self. Realizing in this way that one should not be negligent, Ānanda again took Kāshyapa as his teacher and Ānanda also accepted Shānavāsa. Thus the way of teacher and disciple was transmitted. *The Treasury of the Eye of the True Dharma and Wondrous Mind of Nirvana*, which has come down to us in this way, is not different from when the Buddha was alive. Therefore, do not grieve because you were not born in the land where the Buddha was born, and do not regret not living in the time when the Buddha was alive. In ancient times you planted the roots of good abundantly and you deeply created auspicious conditions for [acquiring] *prajñā*. As a result, you are now assembled here at Daijō [Monastery]. Truly, it is as if you were shoulder to shoulder with Kāśyapa and knee to knee with Ānanda. Thus, while we are host and guest for this one time, in later lives you will be Buddha ancestors. Do not get blocked by feelings about past and present, and do not get attached to sounds and forms. Do not spend your days and nights in vain. Carefully make an effort in the Way, arrive at the ancients' ultimate realm, and receive the authenticating seal and prediction [to buddhahood] of the present [master of Daijō-ji, Tettsū Gikai].

Verse: I would like to clarify this story with a humble verse. Would you like to hear it?

Sourceless stream from a ten-thousand-foot cliff,
Washing out stones, scattering clouds, gushing forth,
Brushing away the snow, making the flowers fly wildly—
A length of pure white silk beyond the dust.[4]

TA-YANG CHING-HSÜAN

Case: The Forty-third Ancestor was Great Master Ta-yang Ming-an. Once, he asked Priest Liang-shan, "What is the formless site of enlightenment?"[5] Liang-shan pointed to a picture of [the bodhisattva] Kuan-yin and said, "This was painted by the scholar Wu." The master was about to speak, when Liang-shan suddenly grabbed him and said, "This is what has form; what is it that has no form?" With these words, the master comprehended.

Circumstances: The master's initiatory name was Ching-hsüan. . . . He was from the Chang family in Chiang-hsia. He made his home departure with Zen Master Chih-t'ung. When he was eighteen, he became a full monk. He heard [lectures on the] ultimate meaning in the *Scripture on Perfect Awakening*[6] and no one could equal him in classes. He went traveling. When he first visited Liang-shan, he asked. "What is the formless site of enlightenment?" [and] finally he comprehended.

Then, he bowed and stood in place. Liang-shan asked, "Why don't you say something?" The master answered, "I am not avoiding speaking, I just worry that it will end up in writing." Liang-shan smiled and said, "Those words will end up on a stone tablet." The master presented a verse, saying:

Long ago, as a beginner, I studied the Way in error,
Seeking knowledge over thousands of rivers and mountains.
Clarifying the present, discerning the past, in the end I could not understand.
They spoke directly of no-mind, but my doubt remained.
My teacher showed me the mirror of Ch'in,[7]
And it reflected what I was before my parents bore me.
Having understood thoroughly now, what did I obtain?
If you release a black bird at night, it flies clothed in snow.

4. The length of pure white silk is an image of the flowing water and symbolizes the inner buddha-nature as inherently pure.
5. "Site of enlightenment" is the Sanskirt *bodhimanda*. It originally referred to the place with Shākyamuni was enlightened. Keizan extends the term to refer to Mind as the true *bodhimanda*.
6. The *Scripture on Perfect Enlightenment* (*Yüan wu ching*) is not of Indian origin but is a work composed in China. However, it seems to have been widely read and respected in China and Japan, where it is cited frequently in other texts.
7. The "mirror of Ch'in" is explained further on in the text. "Ch'in" means the emperor of the Ch'in dynasty.

Liang-shan said, "Tung-shan's tradition will flourish because of you."

[Ta-yang's] reputation grew all at once. When Liang-shan died, [Ta-yang] left the city and went to Mt. Ta-yang and called on Zen Master Chien. Chien resigned his position and made him the head of the community. From then on, he made Tung-shan's tradition flourish and people got wind of it. The master's appearance was unusual and dignified. From the time he was a child, he ate only one meal a day. Because he put a great deal of importance on what he had inherited from his predecessors, he never left the monastery. He never lay down to sleep, and he did this until he was eighty-one. Finally, he gave up his position, bade farewell to the community, and died.

Commentary: The most essential thing in the study [of Zen] is this "formless site of enlightenment." It is not bound by form and has no name. Although it is therefore unrelated to words, it definitely turns out to be something clear. It is the meaning of "your face before you were born." Therefore, when he tried to indicate this realm, [Liang-shan] pointed to a painting of Kuan-yin that had been painted by the scholar Wu, as if he were pointing to a mirror. This is what is meant by having eyes but not seeing, having ears but not hearing, having hands but not holding, having a mind but not discriminating, having a nose but not smelling, having a tongue but not tasting, and having feet but not walking. It is as if none of the six faculties was being used and the entire body became useless furniture. One is like a wooden figure or an iron man; at such a time, seeing forms and hearing sounds quickly disappear. When [Ta-yang] started to speak at this point, [Liang-shan] in order to prevent him from saying something delusory suddenly grabbed him and asked, "This is what has form; what is it that has no form?" He got Ta-yang to understand the faceless by means of something that has no function. It was like knowing who he was by looking into a clear mirror. (There was a mirror long ago in the time of Emperor Ch'in. By looking into it, it seemed that all the body's internal organs, eighty-four thousand pores, and three hundred sixty bones could be seen.) Even though you have ears and eyes, when you do not use them, you see what is not bound by a body or mind. Not only do you break through the thousand mountains and ten thousand rivers of form, you quickly break through the darkness of no-mind and nondiscrimination, heaven and earth are no longer separated, none of the myriad forms sprouts, and everything is perfectly complete. It was not only [Ta-yang] who made Tung-shan's tradition flourish all at once in this way; all the ancestors saw it the same way.

After he was made to grasp this point, while he was at Ta-yang, a monk asked him, "What is the style of your tradition?" The master said, "The brimming container is turned upside down but is not emptied, and there are no famished people in all the world." Truly, though you tip this realm over, it does not empty; though you push on it, you cannot open it. Though you try to lift it, you cannot pick it up. Though you touch it, there is nothing there. You cannot get it with your ears and eyes and, although, it is accompanied by speech and silence, movement and stillness, it is not at all hindered by movement and stillness. It is not just Zen masters who possess this thing. There is not a single person in the whole world who does not have it. Therefore, [Ta-yang] said, "There are no famished people."

Zen worthies, you have fortunately become descendants in Tung-shan's family and have encountered the family style of enlightened predecessors. If you practice precisely and carefully and are personally awakened to the time prior to birth and the arising of form and emptiness, reach the realm where there is not a fragment of form, experience the realm where there is not the least atom of external stuff, you will not find the four great elements and five aggregates in countless eons. If you can clarify that which is never missing even for a second, then you are really a descendent of Tung-shan's family and one of Ch'ing-yüan's offshoots.

Verse: Now, how can I convey this principle? Would you like to hear?

> The mind mirror hangs high and reflects everything clearly;
> The vermilion boat is so beautiful that no painting can do it justice.

T'IEN-T'UNG JU-CHING

Case: The Fiftieth Ancestor was Priest T'ien-t'ung Ju-ching. He studied with Hsüeh-tou.[8] Hsüeh-tou asked him, "Disciple Ju-ching, how can something that has never been soiled be cleaned?" The master spent more than a year [on this question]. Suddenly, he was awakened, and said, "I have hit upon that which is not soiled."

Circumstances: The master was a native of Yüeh-chou. His initiatory name was Ju-ching. After the age of seventeen, he abandoned doctrinal studies and practiced Zen. He joined Hsüeh-tou's community and spent a year there. He always excelled in zazen. Once, he asked to be the sanitation officer. Hsüeh-tou asked him. "How can something that has never been soiled be cleaned? If you can answer that, then I will appoint you to be the sanitation officer." The master was at a loss. . . . Again, Hsüeh-tou asked, "How can something that has never been soiled be cleaned?" [The master] did not answer for more than a year. Again, Hsüeh-tou asked, "Can you answer?" The master still could not answer. Hsüeh-tou said, "If you can climb out of your old rut, you will be free. Then you will be able to answer." Hearing this, the master investigated with all his strength and determination. One day, he was suddenly awakened. He went to [Hsüeh-tou's] quarters and told him, "I can answer." Hsüeh-tou said, "This time, say it." The master said, "I have hit upon that which is not soiled." Even

8. [This is the Tsao-t'ung master Hsüeh-tou Chih-chieh, not to be confused with Hsüeh-tou Ch'ung-hsien (Chapter 23).—Eds.]

before he finished speaking, Hsüeh-tou hit him. The master broke out in sweat and bowed. Then, Hsüeh-tou gave him his approval.

Later, at Ching-tz'u Monastery, he became the toilet cleaner in order to repay the occasion of his awakening. Once, when he was passing the Hall of Arhats[9] a strange monk said to the master, "Cleaner of toilets at Ching-tz'u, Ju-ching; you repay the Way, repay the master, and repay all people." So saying, he disappeared. The prime minister of the country heard about it and interpreted it to be an omen that the sages approved of the master becoming the abbot of Ching-tz'u [Monastery]. Consequently, he became the abbot of Ching-tz'u. People everywhere said that the master's merits of repaying [his debt] were really supreme. Since arousing the determination [to be awakened] at the age of eighteen, he stayed in the monastery and never returned to his native home. Not only that, but he never associated with his countrymen or went to the rooms of others in the monastery. He did not speak with those who sat near him [in the meditation hall]. All he ever did was single-minded zazen. He vowed, "I will [sit so long that I will] crush a diamond seat." As a result of doing zazen like this, sometimes the flesh on his buttocks split open, but he would not stop sitting. From the time he first aroused this determination up to the age of sixty-four, while he was at [Mt.] T'ien-t'ung, there was not a single day or night when he did not do zazen.

From the time he first became abbot of Ch'ing-tz'u and during the time he was at [Mt.] Shui-yen and [Mt.] T'ien-t'ung, his conduct was outstanding. He vowed to be the same [as monks] in the monks hall. Therefore, even though he had the [symbolic] patched robe transmitted by Fu-jung, he did not wear it. Whether giving formal talks or in his own quarters, he wore only a black surplice and robe. Even though he was offered a purple robe and master's title by the emperor of the Chia-t'ing era,[10] he declined them. Furthermore, he kept secret the matter of who made him a successor, only revealing it at the end [when he was about to die] by offering incense [in recognition]. He not only kept far away from mundane desires and fame, but was also concerned for the good reputation of Zen. Truly, no one at the time equaled his virtue. His conduct was exemplary then and now.

He always said to himself, "In the last century or two, the Way of the ancestral teachers has declined. Therefore, no spiritual teacher like me has appeared." All [other teachers] were in awe of him. The master never praised them. He would say, "Since the age of nineteen when I made a strong resolve and went on pilgrimage [to visit teachers], I have not met anyone who is enlightened. Many masters just greet visiting officials and never concern themselves with the monks' hall. They always say, 'Each person must understand the Buddha-Dharma himself.' So saying, they do not guide the monks. What is more, the present abbots of the great

9. The Hall of Arhats was a building sometimes found on temple or monastery grounds that contained the images of a number of *arhats*, those perfected individuals of earlier Buddhism, such as Ánanda. There were special ceremonies in honor of the *arhats*.
10. The Chia-t'ing era lasted from 1208 to 1225. The emperor was Ning-tsung.

monasteries do the same. They think that not caring about anything is the Way,[11] and they never emphasize Zen practice. What is the Buddha-Dharma in this? If it is as they say, then why are there [still] sharp old gimlets seeking the Way? It is ridiculous. They do not see the Way of the Buddha ancestors even in a dream."

He always encouraged people to just sit in zazen. Persuading them to do nothing but sit, he would say, "There is no need for burning incense, bowing, invoking the Buddha, making repentance, or reciting the scriptures—just sit." He would also say, "The important thing is being committed to the Way when you practice Zen." Even though you have a little understanding, you cannot hold onto what you know without a commitment to the Way. You end up with false views, become indolent, and become a non-Buddhist within Buddhism. People, do not forget the most important matter, commitment to the Way. Utilize that commitment in everything you do. Make the truth foremost. Do not get caught up in the fashion of the times, but continue to investigate the ancient style.

Commentary: If you are like this, then even if you have not yet understood it yourself, you will be an originally unsoiled person. Since you are unsoiled, how can you not be an originally clean, pure person? [Hsüeh-tou] said, "It is originally unsoiled, so how can it be cleaned? If you climb out of your rut, you will be free." The former enlightened masters originally did not bring about partial understanding. Committed to the single truth, they got people to practice with one objective without selfconcern. If for the entire twenty-four hours of the day there is no view of purity and defilement, you are naturally undefiled.

However, [Ju-ching] still had not escaped the view of defilement. He held on to the idea of using a broom [to sweep it away]. After a year of not getting it clarified, once there was no more skin to shed, nor mind and body that needed to shed, he said, "I hit upon that which is unsoiled." Even though it was so, a spot [of dirt] suddenly appeared. Therefore, it says that [Hsüeh-tou] hit him even before he finished speaking. Then, sweat broke out all over his body. He abandoned his body at once, and he found the power. Truly, he realized that he was intrinsically clean and had never been subject to impurity. This is why he always said, "The practice of Zen is the dropping off of mind and body."

Verse: Now, tell me, what is "that which is unsoiled"?

> The wind of the Way, circulating everywhere, is harder than diamond;
> The whole earth is supported by it.

11. "Not caring about anything" translates *buji* (Ch., *wu-shih*). *Buji* Zen is a false Zen characterized by an "I-don't-care" attitude. Nothing matters, everything is false and empty, and there are no concerns, even for practice. It is a nihilistic attitude condemned by Keizan and other Zen masters.

33

Musō

(1275–1351)

Just eleven years separate the births of Keizan and Musō Soseki, and both made enormous contributions to the diffusion of Zen in Japan, but their paths carried them in opposite directions and to distant positions on the social spectrum. While Keizan labored out of sight among the rural gentry, the well-born Musō made his mark in the capital cities of Kamakura and Kyoto, brushing elbows with rulers and warlords, exercising his considerable abilities not only in Zen but in political affairs and the arts as well.

Musō trained initially in a temple of the Shingon sect, beginning at the age of nine and ending shortly after he ordained, at eighteen. Inspired, it is said, by the agonizing death of his Shingon mentor and by a vivid dream of T'ang-dynasty Ch'an sages, he set out to find a Zen master. He got his start at Kennin-ji in Kyoto, under one of Daikaku's successors, then circulated a while, visiting other temples and teachers before committing himself to protracted study with I-shan I-ning, in Kamakura. This Chinese master possessed such an outstanding reputation as a teacher of both Ch'an and literature that the shogunate installed him in one after another of the city's greatest monasteries, attracting so many would-be students that I-shan had the luxury of screening for the most talented. To select among them, he devised a test of competency in composing Chinese poems, a test Musō passed handily.

After three years with I-shan, unsatisfied with this intellectual approach or perhaps floundering in his practice, Musō moved on to study with Kōhō Kennichi (1241–1316). Kōhō was the son of an emperor and, like I-shan, a Dharma grandson of the Yang-ch'i teacher Wu-chun, the same man Enni had succeeded. Records show only one brief exchange between Kōhō and Musō at this juncture, but the young monk left it with a new perspective, and when he returned from pilgrimage two years later in 1305, he did so to report a deep experience of realization: after zazen outdoors one night, groping in the darkness, he had fallen, and the whole universe had fallen with him. "[I] saw that without a thought / I had smashed the bones / of the empty sky," he wrote afterward. These words moved Kōhō to confirm his awakening, and after three further years of focused study, Kōhō authorized him to teach.

Since both master and disciple were well-connected, Musō could easily have secured a good posting in the capital, but he took to the road instead, as was his wont. For the next seventeen years, he traveled about, establishing a country temple here and a hermitage there, half a dozen in all. However footloose he may have been during this period, Musō made a name for himself as a poet and a Zen teacher, and when Kōhō died, Musō had to take extreme evasive action to dodge a request to return and direct his former monastery. Finally in 1325, at age fifty, he got an offer he couldn't refuse—from the reigning emperor, Go-Daigo, who tapped him to head Nanzen-ji in Kyoto.

By this point, Rinzai Zen had grown to such prominence in the capitals that the shogunate had put in place a *gozan* (Five Mountains) system patterned on the Sung-dynasty regime for controlling Ch'an. Nanzen-ji, previously an imperial palace, ranked among the foremost *gozan* monasteries, and though he stepped down from its abbacy after only a year, Musō never recovered his status as a private citizen or a purely religious leader. Rinzai histories generally portray him as a genuinely reluctant player on the national stage, but reluctant or not, for the next quarter of a century, he wielded enormous influence with the shogunate as well as the imperial court. Balancing adroitly between these contending powers, he used his clout very effectively to disseminate Rinzai Zen.

The next decade brought war and major changes in the political landscape. Musō rode out these events and emerged in 1336 having founded four new temples, holding the title of national teacher, and enjoying the confidence of the Ashikaga shoguns, who now ruled the country from Kyoto. In 1337, the Ashikaga accepted his proposal for the construction of a pagoda and a temple in each province dedicated to the war dead and to a peaceful future. This scheme, completed thirteen years later, resulted in a national network of Zen monasteries, most of them affiliated either with Musō and his successors or with Enni's line. It assisted the Ashikaga, not coincidentally, in their efforts to consolidate control of the country.

When Go-Daigo died in 1339, Musō won the shoguns' approval for another major building project: conversion of a Kyoto palace into a grand monastery where the departed emperor's spirit could come to rest. Thus commenced the building of Tenryū-ji, which formally opened in 1345 with Musō its founding abbot. Tendai leaders, distressed to see their sect's influence and patronage slipping away, sent a contingent of warriors to Kyoto before the dedication, demanding destruction of the new monastery and banishment of the "evil monk" responsible for it, but the Ashikaga stood them down with a huge show of force, only too happy for a chance to embarrass a rival military. When the Tenryū-ji monks' hall was completed six years later, not long before he died, Musō gave a talk addressing the politics of the young institution in Zen terms— a fascinating glimpse into his view and handling of political issues. 🕱

REFLECTIONS UPON THE ENMITY BETWEEN EMPEROR GO-DAIGO AND THE SHOGUN, ASHIKAGA TAKAUJI

In the realm of True Purity there is no such thing as "I" or "he," nor can "friend" and "foe" be found there. But the slightest confusion of mind brings innumerable differences and complications. Peace and disorder in the world, the distinction between friend and foe in human relationships, follow upon one another as illusion begets delusion. A man of spiritual insight will immediately recognize what is wrong and before long rid himself of such an illusion, but the shallow-minded man will be ensnared by his own blindness so that he cannot put an end to it. In such a case one's true friend may seem a foe and one's implacable foe may appear a friend. Enmity and friendship have no permanent character; both of them are illusions.

During the disorders of the Genkō era (1331–1334), the shogun, acting promptly on the imperial command, swiftly subdued the foes of the state [the Hōjō regents], as a result of which he rose higher in the ranks of government day by day and his growing prestige brought a change in the attitude of others toward him. Ere long slander and defamation sprang up with the violence of a tiger, and this unavoidably drew upon him the imperial displeasure. Consider now why this should have happened. It was because he performed a meritorious task with such dispatch and to the entire satisfaction of his sovereign. There is an old saying that intimacy invites enmity. That is what it was. Thereupon amity and good will were scattered to the winds and the imperial authority was endangered. The emperor had to take refuge in the mountains to the south, where the music of the court was no longer heard and whence the imperial palanquin could never again return to the capital.

With a great sigh the military governor [Takauji] lamented, "Alas, due to slander and flattery by those close to the throne, I am consigned to the fate of an ignominious rebel without any chance to explain my innocence." Indeed his grief was no perfunctory display, but without nurturing any bitterness in his heart he devoutly gave himself over to spiritual reflection and pious works, fervently praying for the enlightenment of the emperor and eventually constructing [in the name of the emperor] this great monastery for the practice of Buddhism. . . .

The virtuous rule of Emperor Go-Daigo was in accord with heaven's will and his wisdom was equal to that of the ancient sage-kings. Therefore the imperial fortunes rose high and the whole country was brought under his sway. A new calendar was proclaimed and a new era of magnificence and splendor was inaugurated. The barbarian peoples showed themselves submissive and his subjects were well-disposed. This reign, men thought, would be like that of the Sage-Emperor Yao [in ancient China]; it would endure and never come to an end. Who would have thought that this sage-like sun would soon set and disappear into the shadows? And what are we to make of it—was it a mere trick of fate? No, I surmise that his late Majesty paid off all the debt of karma incurred in the world of defilement and straightway joined the happy assemblage of the Pure Land. It is not so much that His august reign was brought to an untimely end, but that the great mass of the people were caused so much suffering and distress. As a result from the time of His passing right up to the present there has been no peace, clergy and laity alike have become displaced, and there is no end to the complaints of the people.

What I have stated above is all a dream within a dream. Even if it were true, there is no use finding fault with what is past and done—how much less with what has happened in a dream! We must realize that the Throne, the highest position among men, is itself but something cherished in a dream. Even the kings of highest heaven know nothing but the pleasure of a dream. . . .

The energy not consumed by political affairs Musō expended generously in teaching Zen, writing poems, and designing gardens. Over the years, records indicate, he instructed an astonishing 13,145 students—to some degree, at least. Numbered among these were seven emperors and Tadayoshi, the younger of the two Ashikaga brothers. Though this strongman seems to have preferred Chinese masters, he sought Musō's perspective on Zen in an extensive written exchange published in 1344 as *Muchū mondō* (*Dialogues in a Dream*). In an addendum to the text, Musō expressed hope it would be of value to monks and laypeople both, and it was among the first texts ever published in which the Japanese phonetic symbols were mixed with Chinese characters to enhance accessibility. ⌘

FROM DIALOGUES IN A DREAM

JUDGING TEACHERS AND TEACHINGS

There are many false teachings current confusing authentic Buddhism. In sports and games, there are formally established criteria of winning and losing, so there is no confusion in judging them. In civil and criminal legal disputes, it may be hard to determine right and wrong, but they can be settled by appeal to higher authorities.

Buddhism, in contrast, has no such predetermined winning or losing. People all think, based on what they have individually understood, that the doctrine they follow is best, even though others do not agree. There is no authority to which to appeal; though the proofs people adduce may be the words of Buddha and Zen masters, since the interpretation of literature changes according to the views people hold to, it is not sufficient as a basis of proof. People also take the approval of the teachers they believe in as proof, but the testimony of an interested party is not trustworthy.

In any case, unenlightened people think that the beliefs they imagine to be true are fundamental, so once they come to believe in any doctrine of any school, they reject all other schools. Once they have come to believe in someone as their own [master], some people think everyone else's doctrine is inferior and even refuse to hear anything else. Such people are the stupidest of imbeciles.

There are also those who remain hesitant and indecisive because the teachings of various schools and teachers differ.

Foods have many flavors; which one could be defined as quintessential? As people's constitutions differ, so do their tastes. Some people like sweets, some like peppery foods. If you said the flavor *you* like is *the* quintessential flavor and the rest are useless, you would be an imbecile. So it is with Buddhist teachings: because people's natural inclinations differ, it may be that a particular teaching is especially valuable to a given individual, but it becomes false if one clings to it as the unique and only truth, to the exclusion of all other teachings.

ACTIVITY AND MEDITATION

People meditating on the fundamental carry out their ordinary tasks and activities in the midst of meditation and carry out meditation in the midst of ordinary tasks and activities. There is no disparity between meditation and activity.

It is for those as yet incapable of this, those weak in focusing their intent on the Way, that special meditation periods were set up. The practice of meditating four times a day in Zen communities began in this manner during the twelfth century.

In ancient times, Zen mendicants meditated twenty-four hours a day. In later times, however, there were those who became monks to avoid the trouble of making a living in the ordinary world. Their appetites distracted them from Buddhism, and when they participated in rituals their attention was taken away from the fundamental. Since these and other things inhibited them from work on the fundamental, they would have wasted their lives had not some other expedient been devised. This expedient was the rule of four daily periods of sitting meditation.

People who really have their minds on the Way, in contrast, do not forget work on the fundamental no matter what they are doing. Yet if they still distinguish this work from ordinary activities even as they do them together, they will naturally be concerned about being distracted by activities and forgetting the meditation work. This is because of viewing things as outside the mind.

An ancient master said, "The mountains, the rivers, the whole earth, the entire array of phenomena are all oneself." If you can absorb the essence of this message, there are no activities outside of meditation: you dress in meditation and eat in meditation; you walk, stand, sit, and lie down in meditation; you perceive and cognize in meditation; you experience joy, anger, sadness, and happiness in meditation.

Yet even this is still in the sphere of accomplishment and is not true merging with the source of Zen.

Apart from those he instructed in Zen, Musō has reached countless people with his art. As a poet, he helped launch the movement known as the Literature of the Five Mountains (Chapter 35). As a calligrapher and, in his final decade, as a creator of temple gardens of exquisite beauty and sensitivity, Musō helped forge an aesthetic that literally changed Japanese culture and that, since World War II, has won worldwide renown. Although his line of succession did not last, the configurations he left in ink and in rock, water, and moss have certainly stood the test of time, eloquently expressing the Way. ❧

FROM THE BEGINNING

From the beginning
  the crooked tree
    was no good for a lordly dwelling
how could anyone
  expect the nobles
    to use it for their gates
Now it's been thrown out
  onto the shore
    of this harbor village
handy for the fishermen
  to sit on
    while they're fishing

REPLY TO REIZAN OSHŌ

I don't go out
  to wander around
    I stay home here in Miura
while time flows
  on through
    the unbounded world
In the awakened eye
  mountains and rivers
    completely disappear
the eye of delusion
  looks out upon
    deep fog and clouds
Alone on my zazen mat
  I forget the days
    as they pass
The wisteria has grown
  thick over the eaves
    of my hut

The subtle Way
    of Bodhidharma—
        I never give it a thought
Does anyone know
    the truth of Zen
        or what to ask about it?

OLD CREEK

Since before anyone remembers
    it has been clear
        shining like silver
though the moonlight penetrates it
    and the wind ruffles it
        no trace of either remains
Today I would not dare
    to expound the secret
        of the stream bed
but I can tell you
    that the blue dragon
        is coiled there

LAMENTING THE CIVIL WAR

So many times since antiquity
    the human world
        has barely escaped destruction
yet ten thousand fortunes
    and a thousand misfortunes
        and in one void after all
Puppets squabbling
    back and forth
        across the stage
People brawling
    over a snail's horn
        winning or losing
The ferocity
    of a snipe and a clam
        glaring at each other
only to arrive after death
    before the tribunal

of Yama the Judge of Hell
When will the horses of war
   be turned loose
      on Flower Mountain
It would be best
   to throw their bits away
      to the east of the Buddha's Palace

TITLE   The civil war (1336–1392) refers to the war between the two Ashikaga
brothers, Takauji and Tadayoshi.

SŪZAN OSHŌ'S VISIT TO MY WEST MOUNTAIN HUT

A few puffs of white cloud
   drift around the mouth
      of the cave
without hindering
   my Dharma friend when he comes
      to knock at my door
I've never found a way
   to hide my doing nothing
      day after day
We join hands
   and walk back and forth
      back and forth

WANDERING

A runaway son
   will never come
      into his own
My treasure
   is the cloud on the peak
      the moon over the valley
Traveling east or west
   light and free
      on the one road
I don't know whether
   I'm on the way
      or at home

34

Daitō

(1282–1334)

Myōchō Shuhō was Musō's contemporary and a fellow giant in the history of Rinzai Zen. Better known as Daitō Kokushi, he achieved eminence and success during his own lifetime but not of nearly the same magnitude as his colleague's. In the centuries since his death, however, admiration for Daitō has elevated him to a semilegendary status in Rinzai Zen circles, and Musō's star has declined somewhat. While Musō still wins praise for his cultural accomplishments, it is the younger and shorter-lived Daitō who is acclaimed for his clear Dharma-eye and his role in perpetuating the Rinzai heritage.

Born into a samurai family in the country west of Kyoto, at ten Daitō was placed in a Tendai temple near his home, and he spent about the next nine years studying there. Not long after the turn of the century, he quit the Tendai path for reasons unknown, traveling to Kyoto and then Kamakura. There he soon entered the monastery of Kōhō Kennichi, the teacher of imperial blood whom Musō later succeeded. After a year or two with Kōhō, during which he may have gotten an initial glimmer of Mind, he returned to Kyoto and took a new teacher, the elderly Nanpō Jōmyō (1235–1308), more widely remembered under his posthumous title of Daiō Kokushi. Daiō had trained for a decade with Daikaku before heading to China and studying at length with Hsü-tang Chih-yü, another Yang-ch'i master and Dharma cousin of the influential Wu-chun. Upon succeeding Hsü-tang (J., Kidō), Daiō returned to Japan, trained with Daikaku a couple more years, then taught Zen in Kyushu for more than three decades.

Daitō could not have found a more seasoned master, and for his part, Daiō detected such talent in his new disciple that, in 1305, he made him his personal attendant. Daitō already had taken up koan study with Kōhō and continued it now at close quarters with Daiō, wrestling with a famous exchange that culminates in one of Yün-men's one-word sayings: "Barrier!" Still banging his head against this barrier, he moved back to Kamakura again two years later, when the Hōjō regency installed Daiō as the abbot of Kenchō-ji. One day, soon after they arrived, tossing down a key, Daitō had a dramatic turnabout experience that his master promptly and joyfully confirmed.

Daiō died less than a year later but not before arming his twenty-six-year-old heir with a written proof of transmission that includes a stern warning in the best tradition of Zen: "Before making this sanction public, you must continue your spiritual cultivation for twenty years." After a period of mourning, Daitō repaired to a small temple in Kyoto and spent the next decade more or less alone, in accord with this injunction. Evidence suggests that he occupied the bulk of his time in poring over Ch'an literature, at one point devoting forty consecutive days to copying the immense work, *The Transmission of the Lamp.*

This period of seclusion later proved fertile ground for legend. Much as Bodhidharma is said to have faced the wall for nine years and the illiterate Hui-neng to have bettered seven hundred monks in a one-time contest of insight, so Daitō is reputed to have spent twenty years among the beggars beneath a certain Kyoto bridge. There he hid his light, the great story goes, until Emperor Hanazono went in disguise and flushed him out by offering a fruit Daitō especially enjoyed:

> [The emperor gave] melons to the beggars one by one, carefully scanning each face as he did so. Noticing one with unusually brilliant eyes, the emperor said, as he offered the melon, "Take this without using your hands." The immediate response was, "Give it to me without using your hands."

This account serves Daitō's image by stressing his humility, his willingness to bear hardship, and his quickness and sureness in matters of the Dharma.

The other character in the tale comes out pretty well, too—and for good reason. The former emperor, fifteen years Daitō's junior, may not have dressed down and gone trolling for a teacher beneath the bridge, but he did seek Daitō out at a time when the master possessed scant resources, and they did engage in Zen dialogue. In fact, Hanazono had developed a keen interest in Rinzai Zen and from the time the two men met, about 1223, until Daitō's death—a period of fourteen years—he studied koans under him, reportedly with good result. Hanazono also doled out lots of "melon," becoming his teacher's most thoughtful and consistent patron.

Daitō emerged from his period of intensive study about four years before meeting the former emperor, moving to a half-wild area to the north of Kyoto that aristocrats favored as a site for poetry-writing parties. His most powerful kinsman, an uncle who had parlayed martial abilities into a provincial governorship, helped him acquire his first plot of land here, and it soon became the site for something quite different—Daitoku-ji, a monastery of relatively modest proportions, to begin with, but today one of the largest and most important in all of Japan. How Daitō managed to move in just seven years from "beneath the bridge" to the abbot's seat of a new monastic complex still begs explanation, but all of a sudden, he had rich backers, including the reigning emperor Go-Daigo. At the dedication ceremony in 1226, two years short of the twenty his master had stipulated, Daitō made public his sanction to teach, offered incense to both his imperial supporters, and entered the history books as the first entirely Japanese-trained monk to establish a major Zen monastery.

Like Daikaku, Daitō seems to have had no hesitation in committing himself or his institution to intimate service of the politically powerful. In ninth-century China, monks had waged a fierce campaign to ensure that the dharma remained above the throne, that they did not bow down to emperors, and Dōgen reasserted that position in his lectures, even before it became a moot point in his own case. Daitō may not have literally bowed down, but at his worst, he stretched deference to the verge of brown-nosing. For example, when Go-Daigo's son, a general, gave the Daitoku-ji monks a vegetarian feast, Daitō's message of gratitude equated the young warrior with the Bodhisattva of Compassion: "The bodhisattva Kannon has thirty-two manifestations. Among them, the general of the gods is the most true. He dissolves all obstacles, bestows joy, seizes a hundred blessings, and rescues the destitute." In truth, the largess received from Go-Daigo and his family had very little to do with religious interest and everything to do with political ambition.

During the year of that feast, 1333, Go-Daigo succeeded in reasserting imperial rule, and Daitoku-ji rode the imperial tide to new wealth and prominence, but the tide soon turned, and when the Ashikagas took control in 1336, ousting Go-Daigo from the throne, the monastery's fortunes plummeted. The shogunate selected a new emperor from Hanazono's side of the house, however, which enabled the ex-emperor and loyal Zen student to step in and make sure that retribution did not go too far. His two most significant gestures were to elevate his teacher personally by giving him the title Daitō Kokushi—Great Lamp, Teacher of the Nation—and by donating part of his country estate for a second monastery, Myōshin-ji.

When Daitō died the following year, he left his principal successors, Tettō Gikō and Kanzan Egen, in charge of the two monasteries. Tettō, who accompanied Daitō during his decade of seclusion and had served ever since as his head monk, established a line that produced Ikkyū and Takuan (Chapters 37 and 38). Kanzan had once been Daitō's fellow monk under Daiō and, though five years senior, had later entered Daitoku-ji to study with him, awakening through the same "Barrier!" koan that Daitō did. "Kanzan" means Barrier Mountain, and its first syllable has been added to the second syllables of Daiō and Daitō to form an acronym used to designate what became the main line of Rinzai Zen. This Ō-tō-kan line gave rise to five of the masters featured in the chapters that follow and is the source of all the continuing Rinzai lineages.

This spectacular outcome suggests that Daitō possessed unusual abilities as a teacher. A good eye for talent surely helped, as did close, long-term association with his senior students and the fact that he guided them in their own language. His training methods may have been the greatest factor in his success, however. Hanazono's detailed diaries provide a general sense of how Daitō worked, at least with a former emperor: he led his student through a lengthy course of koan study based on Wu-men's *Gateless Barrier, The Blue Cliff Record,* and other texts, and he complemented this with Dharma discussions and spontaneous challenges. Other records seem to indicate that Daitō employed a variety of initial koans, including "The original face," Chao-chou's *mu,* and Ma-tsu's "This very mind is the Buddha."

Daitō's literary output was considerable but consists chiefly of capping-phrase collections and, probably for that reason, remains largely unavailable in

English. "The Original Face," a brief introduction to zazen written for Hana-zono's consort Senkō, is among the most accessible of his writings, along with his poems. His capping-phrase anthologies inaugurated in Japan the practice that Yün-men is credited with pioneering—interjection of terse, piercing comments into scripts of other masters' exchanges. (Daitō's penchant for such phrases, to-gether with the fact that his awakening came on a word of Yün-men's gained him the nickname "the second Yün-men.") Inspired by his example, subsequent Ō-tō-kan teachers made selection of appropriate capping-phrases a required part of koan study. Of even greater consequence, perhaps, is that Daitō im-mersed himself deeply in the literature of Ch'an, appropriating it for Rinzai Zen as Dōgen had, quite differently, for the Sōtō sect. ❦

THE ORIGINAL FACE

All Zen students should devote themselves at the beginning to zazen (sitting in meditation). Sitting in either the fully locked position or the half-locked posi-tion, with the eyes half-shut, see the original face that was before father or mother was born. This means to see the state before the parents were born, be-fore heaven and earth were parted, before you received human form. What is called the original face will appear. That original face is something without color or form, like the empty sky in whose clarity there is no form.

The original face is really nameless, but it is indicated by such terms as original face, the Lord, the buddha-nature, and the true Buddha. It is as with man, who has no name at birth, but afterwards various names are attached to him. The sev-enteen hundred koan or themes to which Zen students devote themselves are all only for making them see their original face. The World-honoured One sat in meditation in the snowy mountains for six years, then saw the morning star and was enlightened, and this was seeing his original face. When it is said of others of the ancients that they had a great realization, or a great breaking-through, it means they saw the original face. The Second Ancestor stood in the snow and cut off his arm to get realization; the Sixth Ancestor heard the phrase from the *Dia-mond Sutra* and was enlightened. Ling-yün was enlightened when he saw the peach blossoms, Hsiang-yen on hearing the tile hit the bamboo, Lin-chi when struck by Huang-po, Tung-shan on seeing his own reflection in the water.

All this is what is called "meeting the lord and master." The body is a house, and it must have a master. It is the master of the house who is known as the origi-nal face. Experiencing heat and cold and so on, or feeling a lack, or having de-sires—these are all delusive thoughts and do not belong to the true master of the house. These delusive thoughts are something added. They are things that vanish with each breath. To be dragged along by them is to fall into hell, to circle in the six paths of reincarnation. By going deeper and deeper into zazen, find the source of the thoughts. A thought is something without any form or body, but owing to the conviction of those thoughts remaining even after death, man falls into hell with its many pains, or suffers in the round of this changing world.

Every time a thought arises, throw it away. Just devote yourself to sweeping away the thoughts. Sweeping away thoughts means performing zazen. When thought is put down, the original face appears. The thoughts are like clouds; when the clouds have cleared, the moon appears. That moon of eternal truth is the original face.

The heart itself is verily the Buddha. What is called "seeing one's nature" means to realize the heart Buddha. Again and again put down the thoughts, and then see the heart Buddha. It might be supposed from this that the true nature will not be visible except when sitting in meditation. That is a mistake. [Yung-chia] says: "Going too is Zen; sitting too is Zen. Speaking or silent, moving the body or still, he is at peace." This teaches that going and sitting and talking are all Zen. It is not only being in zazen and suppressing the thoughts. Whether rising or sitting, keep concentrated and watchful. All of a sudden, the original face will confront you.

KOANS WITH CAPPING PHRASES

EMPEROR WU QUESTIONS BODHIDHARMA

Emperor Wu of Liang asked the great master Bodhidharma, "What is the highest principle of the holy teachings?"

Didn't think he could ask.

Bodhidharma said, "Vast emptiness, nothing holy."

One slab of iron stretching ten thousand miles.
Thrust out right in front.
Stars in the sky, rivers on the earth.

The emperor said, "Who is facing me?"

What a pity!

Bodhidharma replied, "I don't know."

Completely fills emptiness.
The moon is bright, the wind is pure.

THE KALPA FIRE

A monk asked Ta-sui, "In the roar of the kalpa fire, the whole universe is destroyed."

Spilled his guts and disgorged his heart.

"Tell me, is this destroyed?"

Why don't you go right away?

Ta-sui said, "Destroyed."

Spilled his guts and disgorged his heart.

The monk said, "Then [this] will go along with [the destruction of the universe]?"

So pitiful and sad.

Ta-sui said, "It goes along with it."

A double koan.

FROM THE POEMS OF DAITŌ

PILGRIMAGE

The moon and the sun my sandals,
I'm journeying above heaven and earth.

RAIN

No umbrella, getting soaked,
I'll just use the rain as my raincoat.

ZAZEN

How boring to sit idly on the floor,
not meditating, not breaking through.
Look at the horses racing along the Kamo River!
That's zazen!

ENLIGHTENMENT

I've broken through Cloud Barrier—
    the living way is north south east and west.
Evenings I rest, mornings I play,
    no other no self.
With each step a pure breeze rises.

NO DHARMAS

Rain clears from distant peaks, dew glistens frostily.
Moonlight glazes the front of my ivied hut among the pines.
How can I tell you how I am, right now?
A swollen brook gushes in the valley darkened by clouds.

NOTE P'an-shan instructed, "There are no dharmas in the three realms; where can mind be sought?"

BUDDHAS

If he had known buddhas exist
   in the three worlds,
suddenly no spring flowers,
no full moon in the fall.

NOTE Nan-ch'üan said, "I don't know anything about buddhas in the three worlds."

RECOVERY

It's over, the "buddhas and ancestors" disease
that once gripped my chest.
Now I'm just an ordinary man
with a clean slate.

TATTERED SLEEVE

So many years of begging,
this robe's old and torn;
tattered sleeve chases a cloud.
Beyond the gate, just grass.

FACING DEATH

I cut aside all buddhas and ancestors,
my Mind-sword honed to a razor edge.
Activity's wheel begins to turn—
emptiness gnashes its teeth.

HERE I AM

No form, no sound—
here I am;
white clouds fringing the peaks,
river cutting through the valley.

35

Jakushitsu

(1290–1367)

Jakushitsu Genkō is considered the last great Japanese Zen master to train in China. By the time he traveled to the Asian mainland in 1320, the number of monks going there to study Ch'an had peaked; there were safer, less costly ways of encountering the authentic tradition than crossing the Japan Sea. Monks at home enjoyed access to many fine Chinese teachers as well as to lines of Japanese succession that boasted strong ties to mainland Ch'an.

Jakushitsu explored both of these avenues before setting sail. After ordaining at fifteen, he studied Zen with Yakuō Tokken, a Japanese heir of the émigré master Daikaku, and subsequently, like Musō, he spent several years practicing Zen—and absorbing Chinese aesthetics—under I-shan I-ning. Only after the death of these two did he make the journey to China, where he trained with the most celebrated Ch'an master of his day, Chung-feng Ming-pen (1263–1323), before he, too, died. All three of his teachers were products of the Yang-ch'i school, and when he returned from China, Jakushitsu joined Musō and Daitō among the school's leading lights, helping to cement its domination of the *gozan*.

Yet Jakushitsu took a very different route than his capital-city brethren—a route that led first to his native province west of Kyoto, then to thirty-four years of pilgrimages and short stays at small, rural temples. He clearly preferred the "drab and uneventful" life of the countryside, for he had both the qualifications and the opportunity to assume leadership in premier *gozan* monasteries if he had wished to do so. Of noble stock, impeccably educated, holding excellent credentials as a Zen teacher, he declined the abbacy of both Tenryū-ji and Kenchō-ji in his later years and had to be prevailed upon to settle, even at seventy-one, in a rural monastery built specifically for him.

Jakushitsu's poems leave no doubt that he loved mountains, rivers, and wild-to-rustic environs generally, but his avoidance of Kyoto and Kamakura almost certainly expressed as well a disdain for the politics and effete culture he had seen in urban Zen. His third teacher, Chung-feng, spent the last thirty-six years of his life moving from one remote hermitage to another and declined imperial requests to teach in the capital, precedents that must have impressed his young Japanese student. Criticisms of the *gozan* life that appear in Jakushitsu's writings typify the attitude that country masters held: ruing the decadence of the city temples, they viewed the stringent circumstances of their rural temples both as more faithful to ancient Ch'an and as more conducive to the preservation of true Zen.

Interestingly, Jakushitsu chose to follow Chung-feng in allowing the Pure Land practice of *nembutsu*—reciting the name of Amitābha Buddha (J., Amida). Texts from the formative stages of Ch'an display some sympathy for *nembutsu* (Ch., *nien-fo*) practice, and Fa-yen's Dharma grandson Yung-ming Yen-shou, among others, strongly asserted the harmony of Pure Land and Ch'an in the early Sung period. By the late Sung and Yüan dynasties, the recitation of the Buddha's name had become unexceptional among Ch'an monks, and both Chung-feng and Jakushitsu at least tolerated this development, taking pains to state that the Pure Land being sought was Mind itself, not somewhere over the rainbow. In China, Pure Land practices eventually were completely integrated into Ch'an, while Zen went no farther than approving *nembutsu* for those lacking the opportunity or capacity for Zen practice per se.

Jakushitsu made his most unique contribution to the zen tradition through his poetry. Along with Musō, he ranks among the finest authors of the *gozan bungaku,* or the Literature of the Five Mountains, a tradition of Chinese-language prose and poetry written by medieval Japanese monks. Their mutual teacher I-shan, sometimes called the "patriarch" of this movement, had given fresh impetus to the poetry craze Fa-yen had noticed—and tried to check—some three and a half centuries before. After I-shan, it seemed every man in the monastery turned his brush to poetry as an adjunct to Zen practice. It came to be reckoned almost essential to learn the fundamentals of Chinese prosody and be able to turn out a credible Chinese poem in short order.

While most such poems soon vanished to wind and fire, Jakushitsu's are still treasured, particularly for their spareness and energy. His record preserves some three hundred and fifty of these, along with brief instructions given orally to his students and a selection of letters. Unlike Musō and Daitō, he left no major prose works, no commentaries, no manuals. His poems were his presentation, and together with his good reputation, they gained him a large following during his own lifetime. Once he finally hung up his pilgrim's hat, students and admirers came from all directions, two thousand of them visiting his out-of-the-way monastery the year it opened.

NOTES FROM JAKUSHITSU

TO WAYFARER ZENTATSU

The Sixth Ancestor of Ch'an in China, in replying to a question from a government inspector, Mr. I, said, "Deluded people invoke a buddha's name seeking to be reborn in that buddha's land, but enlightened people purify their own minds. That is why the Buddha said that as the mind is pure, so is the Buddha land pure. Mr. Inspector, you are a man of the East; as long as your mind is pure, you are faultless. Even people of the West [in the direction of paradise], if their minds are not pure, still have something wrong with them. When people of the East commit crimes, they invoke Amitābha Buddha's name, seeking to be reborn in the western paradise; when people of the West commit crimes, what land should they seek to be born in by invoking Buddha's name? The ignorant don't comprehend their own nature and do not recognize the pure land within their bodies, but wish for the West, for the East," and so on.

Essentially invoking of buddha-names is for liberation from birth-and-death; investigation of Zen is for realizing the nature of Mind. We have never heard of anyone who awakened to the nature of Mind who was not liberated from birth-and-death; how could someone freed from birth-and-death misunderstand the nature of Mind? It should be realized that buddha-name remembrance and investigation of Zen have different names but are essentially the same.

Nevertheless, as an ancient said, "The slightest entanglement of thought is the basis of the most miserable types of behavior; if feelings arise for a moment, they lock you up for ten thousand eons." So even buddha-name remembrance is producing dust on a mirror, even investigating Zen is putting rubbish in the eye. If you can just trust completely in this way, then you will not be deceived.

Wayfarer Zentatsu has diligently practiced concentration on buddha-name remembrance for years, and has suddenly come to my house asking for a robe and bowl, and to receive the great precepts; as he needs some admonitions for his daily life, so I hurriedly wrote this and gave it to him.

TO BLIND TSUMEI

In ancient times Aniruddha used to indulge in sleeping, so the Buddha scolded him, "You're like a clam." So he didn't sleep for seven days and awakened the power of [clear-sightedness] whereby he could see the whole universe like looking at a fruit in his hand.

If you have real will regarding the great matter of birth-and-death, you should take the koan "Mind itself is Buddha" and bring it up time and again to awaken you, summoning it up wherever you are. One morning you will suddenly break through the lacquer bucket of ignorance—this is called "having the eye of the truth on your forehead." At that time, will you fly around seeing the worlds of the universe? Hundreds of millions of polar mountains, infinite Buddha fields, you see on the tip of a hair—there is nothing else. This is my ultimate bequest to you.

TO WAYFARER RYOSEI

A monk asked great master Ma-tsu, "What is Buddha?"

Ma-tsu said, "The mind itself is Buddha."

That monk was greatly enlightened at these words. It seems that what is so close that it is hard to see is the mind, and what is so far and yet easy to approach is buddhahood. If you misunderstand your mind, you are an ordinary man; if you realize your mind, you are a sage. There is no difference at all whether man, woman, old, young, wise, foolish, human, animal, whatever. Thus, in the Lotus of Truth assembly, was it not the eight-year-old Naga girl who went directly south to the undefiled world Amala, sat on a jewel lotus flower, and realized universal complete enlightenment?

In ancient times, master Yen-t'ou once was a boatman. A woman came with a child in her arms and asked, "I don't ask about plying the pole and rudder—what about the child in this woman's arms, where does it come from?" Yen-t'ou immediately hit her once. The woman said, "I have nursed seven children; six did not meet a real knower, and this one can't appreciate it." Then she threw the child in the river. This woman found out the way that mind itself is Buddha.

WRITTEN ON THE WALL OF A MOUNTAIN RETREAT IN SHII VILLAGE

Water in the ravine flows down to the world of men,
clouds from the scarps pass on to other mountains.
Listen a while to the hidden birds chattering,
as though they're extolling the idleness of this countryside monk!

SPENDING THE NIGHT AT KONGŌ-JI

Often I come visiting this nearby temple.
We talk all night, never breaking off.
In this mountain village there are no signal drums.
When the window whitens, then we know it's dawn.

NOTE There are several temples by the name Kongō-ji and it is uncertain which is intended here.

PUTTING UP FOR THE NIGHT AT SENKO-JI

Ten years ago I visited my friend.
At sight of each other, we clasped hands, talked on like spring.
Who'd have thought tonight I'd sleep in his old room,
moonlight piercing the cold window, wind rocking the bamboo.

NOTE Senkō-ji was a temple in Onomichi on the Inland Sea.

TWO POEMS WRITTEN ON THE WALL
AT MOUNT KONZŌ

Wind buffets the waterfall, sending me cold sounds.
From peaks in front, a moon rises, the bamboo window brightens.
Old now, I feel it more than ever—so good to be here in the mountains!
Die at the foot of the cliff and even your bones are clean.

NOTE At Konzōsan-ji temple in Tantō, Hyogo Prefecture; second of two poems.

UNTITLED

I cut reeds for a new hut in a crook of the empty mountain.
You must have cared, coming so far to see me in my distant retreat.
We've burned up all the dry sticks, run out of words as well;
together we listen to the sound of icy rain pelting against the window.

NOTE My former attendant Zaiō came to visit me at my new place in Nobe
[Shizuoka Prefecture]. We sat around the fire pit all night talking of worthwhile
matters. When he got ready to leave, I put together this little poem to express my
gratitude.

SPRING DAY, MOUNTAIN WALKING

Head covered with wispy hair, twisted in silvery tufts:
can't tell if I'll be around to welcome spring next year.
Bamboo staff, straw sandals, lots of delights in the country;
looking at mountain cherries—how many trees does this make?

TWO POEMS TO SHOW A MONK

This thing—I show it to you clear as can be!
No need to plot any special feats or exploits.
Breezes mild, sun warm, yellow warblers caroling;
spring at its height already there in the blossoming treetops.

NOTE First of two poems.

TO SHOW TO THE PRIEST NAMED SON

A man of the Way comes rapping at my brushwood gate,
wants to discuss the essentials of Zen experience.

Don't take it wrong if this mountain monk's too lazy to open his mouth:
late spring warblers singing their heart out, a village of drifting petals.

AT THE REQUEST OF THE WOMAN
LAY-BELIEVER JIGEN

Who took these splendid robes of purple and gold,
wrapped them around the old fool's lump of red flesh?
When bystanders see him, I'm afraid they'll laugh—
better send him back to stay in his old green mountain!

NOTE Written to accompany a formal portrait of Jakushitsu.

36

Bassui

(1327–1387)

Even more than Jakushitsu, whom he knew, Bassui Tokushō occupied a marginal position in the Zen world. Unlike his elder colleague, he never trained in the *gozan* monasteries, making only one trip to Kamakura and quickly leaving, unimpressed by his experience. Bassui avoided even country temples, entering them only for private instruction, otherwise spending his time in solitary practice. He came to study the Way, he explained when challenged, not to study the elaborate protocols of the monastic regimen.

As this suggests, Bassui had a questing, independent spirit, born in part, perhaps, of his samurai background. According to a biography prepared by one of his students soon after his death, Bassui's search began at the age of seven, when a Zen priest told him that offerings made to honor his deceased father would be consumed by his father's soul. Doubt about the soul, or later, about what it was in him that saw and heard, fueled an ardent meditation practice and led him, even as a teenager, to a taste of emptiness that freed his mind. When this faded, at about twenty, Bassui for the first time sought formal instruction in Zen, but not until eleven years later did he don monk's robes. By that time, his fierce inquiry into the fundamental mind had brought a second opening, triggered by the sound of a mountain stream, and his awakening had been certified by the abbot of Kenchō-ji.

All the same, Bassui was unsatisfied and sought further, eventually coming to meet the teacher Kōhō Kakumyō (1271–1361)—not the Kamakura master with whom Musō and Daitō studied but a different man, who had received Dharma-transmission from Keizan of the Sōtō sect as well as from Shinchi Kakushin (1207–1298), a well-known teacher who combined Rinzai-style koan study with Shingon practices. The aged Kōhō had also trained in China with Jakushitsu's last teacher, Chung-feng, and experienced as he was, he did not immediately sanction Bassui's realization. On the contrary, grilling him one day about Chao-chou's *mu,* Kōhō delivered a rebuff that burst the bottom of Bassui's bucket once and for all. The following day, Kōhō confirmed his awakening, and within two months, Bassui formally became his Dharma heir.

Still just thirty-two, Bassui set out on further travels, alternating trips to meet highly regarded masters with stretches of solitary practice and koan study in a sequence of hermitages. Among the teachers he visited was Jakushitsu, whose upright and unembellished way pleased him greatly, and the most prominent of

Keizan's successors, Gasan Jōseki (1276–1366). His encounter with this leading Sōtō master seems to have enhanced Bassui's appreciation of monastic discipline and to have opened his eyes to the potential for substantial lay participation in Zen. When, after eighteen years of post-transmission wandering, he finally let students gather around him, Bassui made ample room in his temple for laypeople and lectured at length on the importance of observing the Buddhist precepts as the ethical base of Zen practice.

Bassui's outsider status entailed more than just distance from the Buddhist establishment; he was, apparently by nature, a critic and chose to do his teaching in a manner entirely his own. Eschewing both the Rinzai approach to koan study, which he evidently found formulaic, and the Sōtō approach, which he deemed merely intellectual, Bassui counseled his students to dwell single-mindedly on the question "Who is the master of hearing this sound?"—a restatement of his own natural koan. In his writings and oral record, he returns again and again to this problem, pressing it on his audience with a fervency and creativity striking even in translation, six centuries later. Questions from his listeners betray incredulity and even skepticism that the Way could be so simple, so uniform for one and all, but Bassui staunchly defends his method. When he does allude to cases from the classic texts, he takes them up mainly to test his students and to drive them off of superficial understandings in the interest of achieving thoroughgoing realization. In the process, he demonstrates an impressive command of koans, leaving little doubt about the depth of own studies.

Though he always referred to his temple as a hermitage, Bassui spent his last ten years amidst a crowd of disciples—as many as a thousand at a time—and a strong populist streak is apparent in his words. Like the Pure Land and Nichiren teachers who had attracted a large public during the preceding two centuries, he preached a path of liberation accessible to all; demystifying enlightenment, he located it within the reach of anyone who undertook the practice earnestly and energetically. Gender, ordination, education, and social station mattered not at all.

Consistent with this view, he stipulated that his writings be published in *kana,* easy-to-read phonetic Japanese syllables. Though he established no line of succession, these texts extended his influence far beyond his immediate circle, his rural setting, and his own time. Bassui's lively interpretation of the Way and his emphasis on immediate, personal experience of buddha-nature (*kenshō*) won him the approval of later mainstream figures like Hakuin (Chapter 44) and make him an inspiration still for practitioners today. &

FROM MUD AND WATER

A layman asked: "Though Zen is said to be transmitted outside the scriptures and not through words, there are many more incidents of monks questioning teachers and inquiring of the Way than in the [doctrinal] sects. How can Zen be said to be outside the scriptures? And can reading the *Records* of the old masters and seeing how they dealt with kōans ever be considered outside the realm of words? What is the true meaning of the statement, 'Outside of the scriptures, not through words'?"

The master called to him at once: *"Koji"* [a term for lay students].

He responded immediately: "Yes?"

The master said: "From which teachings did that 'yes' come?"

The layman then lowered his head and bowed.

The master then said: "When you decide to come here, you do so by yourself. When you want to ask a question, you do it by yourself. You do not depend on another nor do you use the teachings of the Buddha. This mind that directs the self is the essence of 'the transmission outside the scriptures and not through words.' It is the pure Zen of the Tathāgata. Clever worldly statements, the written word, reason and duty, discrimination and understanding, cannot reach this Zen. One who looks penetratingly into his true self and does not get ensnared in words, nor stained by the teachings of the Buddhas and ancestors, one who goes beyond the singular road which advances toward enlightenment and does not let cleverness become his downfall, will, for the first time, attain the Way.

"This does not necessarily mean that one who studies the scriptures and revels in the words of the Buddhas and ancestors is a monk of the teaching sects, and one who lacks knowledge of the scriptures is a monk of Zen—which is independent of the teaching and makes no use of words. This doctrine of nondependence on the scriptures is not a way that was first set up by the Buddhas and ancestors. From the beginning everyone is complete and perfect. Buddhas and ordinary people alike are originally the Tathāgata. The leg-and-arm movement of a newborn baby is also the splendid work of its original nature. The bird flying, the hare running, the sun rising, the moon sinking, the wind blowing, the clouds moving, all things that shift and change are due to the spinning of the right dharma wheel of their own original nature. They depend neither on the teachings of others nor on the power of words. It is from the spinning of my right dharma wheel that I am now talking like this, and you are all listening likewise through the splendor of your buddha-nature. The substance of this buddha-nature is like a great burning fire. When you realize this, gain and loss, right and wrong will be destroyed, as will your own life functions. Life, death, and nirvana will be yesterday's dream. The countless worlds will be like foam on the sea. The teachings of the Buddhas and Ancestors will be like a drop of snow over a burning red furnace. Then you will not be restrained by dharma, nor will you rid yourself of dharma. You will be like a log thrown into a fire, your whole body ablaze, without being aware of the heat.

"Do you wish to penetrate directly and be free? When I am talking like this, many people are listening. Quickly! Look at the one who is listening to this talk. Who is he who is listening right now?

"If, for example, you were to conclude that it is the mind, nature, Buddha, or the Way; if you were to call it the principle, the matter, the nontransmitted teaching of the Buddhas and ancestors, the wonderful miracle, the occult, the mysterious, form, or emptiness; if you were to understand it to be existence and nothingness, nonexistence, non-nothingness, the absence of nonexistence, or the absence of non-nothingness; if you were to conclude that it is eons of emptiness before creation or consider it the understanding of koans, no-mind or noninterference, you would still be mixed-up ordinary people who haven't left the path of reason.

Questioner: "Master, you said earlier that the true teaching of the Buddhas and ancestors is nothing other than pointing directly to peoples' minds and showing them that seeing into their own nature is buddhahood. Now you talk neither of mind nor of nature. You just say we should look at that which listens to the dharma. What does this mean?"

Bassui: "This is the true key to seeing into your own nature directly."

Questioner: "Is this phrase 'that which hears the dharma' an expedient means created by you, Master, or is it from the sayings of the Buddhas and ancestors?"

Bassui: "It is neither my expedient means nor is it from the sayings of the Buddhas and ancestors. It is the innate perfection of all people, the exquisite gate of emancipation of the Buddhas and ancestors."

Questioner: "It has been said that what has not appeared in any of the texts since ancient times is no subject for discussion by wise men. If it has never appeared in the sayings of the Buddhas and ancestors, who would believe it unquestionably?"

Bassui: "There are no words for the Way. That's why it is independent of the sayings of the Buddhas and Ancestors. Though it is innate to all people, words are used to express it. So how could it be contrary to the writings of the Buddhas and ancestors?"

Questioner: "If that is so, then which sutra concurs with this teaching?"

Bassui: "At the Shūramgama meeting,[1] where many sages practiced and entered the gate, there were twenty-five perfections in all. The one gate—the so-called 'one who hears the dharma' just mentioned—was the perfection achieved by the bodhisattva Kannon. The bodhisattva Mañjushrī, asked by the World-honored One to comment on this gate, praised it and called it the primary gate. At this point Mañjushrī, said to Ānanda: 'Though you have heard all the secret teachings of Buddhas as countless as atoms, you have yet to eliminate the flow of

---

1. The Buddha met with twenty-five-hundred people and addressed the bodhisattva Drdhamati, describing the meditation named Shūramgama. The substance of the talk makes up the *Shūramgama Sūtra*.

desires and thus have been mistakenly holding onto all you have heard. Rather than entertaining what you have heard from the many Buddhas, why don't you listen to the listener?' "

Questioner: "All teachers everywhere give medicine in accord with the illness. You, Master, give this one medicine to everybody. Wouldn't this cause people to descend into a cave?"

Bassui: "There are an infinite variety of medicines that can be given in response to illnesses. The poisons that kill people do not discriminate between those of slight and considerable ability. If one actually consumes this poison and loses his life, who will have descended into a cave?"

Questioner: "When we listen to all kinds of sounds, we are supposed to look penetratingly into the one who is listening. What if there isn't even one sound?"

Bassui: "Who is it that doesn't hear?"

Questioner: "I have no doubt as to the one who is listening to the dharma."

Bassui: "What is your understanding?"

The monk was silent.

Bassui spoke reprovingly: "Don't spend your life sitting in a ghost cave."[2]

Questioner: "An ancient said:[3] 'If your understanding is based on living words, you will never forget. If your understanding is based on dead words, you will not be able to save yourself.' What does this mean?"

Bassui: "In understanding based on dead words, function does not exist apart from the context. If your understanding is based on living words, it is because you have exhausted the way of thinking."

Questioner: "Are the words 'the one who hears the dharma' dead words or live ones?"

Bassui: "Revered monk!"

Questioner: "Yes?"

Bassui: "Was that alive or dead?"

Questioner: "A buffalo passes by the window. His head, horns, and four legs all go by; why can't his tail go by?[4] Is this a dead phrase or a live one?"

Bassui: "For the present I will ask all of you what you see as the principle. Each one of you should state your own understanding."

One said: "Some beautiful fish pass through the net and remain in the water."

---

2. This is a quote from the first case of *The Blue Cliff Record.* It is a line from the master Yüan-wu's verse warning against dwelling on recollections.

3. Lung-ya Chü-tun (835–923), a disciple of Tung-shan Liang-chieh. The quote is from the twentieth case of *The Blue Cliff Record.*

4. This quote from Wu-tsu Fa-yen (?–1104) makes up the thirty-eighth case of the *Gateless Barrier.*

Another one said: "To experience liberation is quite easy, but to walk the path of the liberated is difficult."

Another said: "The buffalo is the dharma-body of the pure self. Since it is beyond past and present, both outside and inside, we can say that the tail can't go by."

Another said: "This is an enlightened student who still can't forget the traces from recognition of enlightenment."

Another said: "Though one clearly realizes the nature of the self, he still can't forget past habits."

The master lit into them in a loud voice: "Wrong! Wrong! Though this was originally a living phrase, when you interpret it with your ordinary mind, it becomes a dead phrase. This is no longer the gate of the ancestors but rather a parable of the dharma gate. When you look at a live phrase with the interpretation of an ordinary mind in this manner, you banish this true teaching of our sect to another land. . . .

"You should know that in the past as well as the present those who have not clarified the great dharma have all aroused these kinds of discriminating feelings, staining the living words of the ancestors. Though it may be a dead phrase, if a 'living being' were to work with it, it would immediately become a live phrase. This is what is meant when it is said: 'If you understand how to treat it, even a dead serpent will come to life again.' Do you understand?"

Questioner: "If the essence of all the Buddha's teachings were contained in the practice of looking directly into one's nature and attaining Buddhahood, wouldn't that make the formal practice of keeping the precepts meaningless?"

Bassui: "Keeping or violating the precepts is prior to the division of things and ideas [matter and mind]—when essence and form were part of One Vehicle. Having not yet seen into his own nature, a person sinks in the sea of passion and discrimination, killing his own buddha-mind. This is the murder of murders. That's why keeping the true precepts is the enlightened way of seeing into your own nature. When deluded thoughts arise, you damage the dharma treasure, destroy its merit, and hence become a thief. When you give rise to deluded thoughts, you cut off the seeds of buddhahood and continue the life, death, and rebirth-causing karmic activities. This is what is meant by adultery. When you are blinded by deluded thoughts, you forget your precious dharma body and, seeing only illusion, you call it your body. This is what is meant by lying. Isolated by deluded thoughts you lose sight of your inherent wisdom and become frantic. This is what is meant by being intoxicated. The other precepts should be understood similarly.

"Thus when your mind is deluded, you are breaking all the precepts, and when you see into your own nature, you are at once keeping all the precepts perfectly. The power from seeing into your own nature will extinguish all delusion and bring life to buddha-nature. This is the precept not to kill living things. If you put deluded thoughts out of your mind through the power from seeing into your own nature, you will purify the six sense organs and prevent the appearance of the six rebels.[5] This is the precept against stealing. If you see through deluded thoughts by means of this power, the ordinary world will no longer exist. This is the precept against lust. If you see through deluded thoughts by means of this power, you will be able to realize the manifestation of true sublime wisdom. You won't stop at expedient means, mistaking it for the true vehicle, or call the illusive physical body the real one. This is the precept against lying. When you are able to see into your own nature, you will have wisdom. You will not drink the wine of delusion and ignorance. This is the precept against drinking liquor.

"Hence buddha-nature is the body of the precepts and the precepts are the workings of buddha-nature. When this body is perfect, its activity lacks nothing. When you desire to mount the platform of the true precepts, you must tread upon the ground of the true self. This is the meaning behind the statement that a young monk having attained buddhahood need not receive the precepts."

"The precepts are a shortcut for entering the Buddha gate. They are the wall and moat that keep out the six rebels, the fortress that protects the jeweled dharma. If the fortress is not secure, it will be destroyed by the enemy: life-and-death. And you will be put to shame before the king of darkness while suffering limitless pain in the lowest chambers of hell. Moreover, the precepts set the standards for this world. When the rules for the Royal Way[6] are followed, there is peace in the four seas. When humanity and justice are disregarded, quarreling will take place. When wind and rain conform to their laws, the country will be calm and peaceful. When the rules for farming are not followed, the five grains will not grow. How much more is this so in the house of the Buddha. Even when, for example, there is no enlightenment, if you earnestly follow the precepts and do not create a great deal of bad karma while doing good deeds, you will have the good fortune to be born in the world of humans and heavenly bodies. It goes without saying that one who outwardly keeps the precepts while inwardly seeking his own true nature will attain the Buddha Way as surely as water combines with water."

5. The delusions caused by the six sense organs.
6. The laws governing the nation.

37

Ikkyū

(1394–1481)

Few Zen masters have been as deeply or fondly assimilated into Japanese culture as Ikkyū Sōjun. During his own lifetime, he endeared himself to his compatriots by his compassionate response to suffering, his blunt rejection of grandiosity and hypocrisy, his zany humor, and his unmonkish delight in the pleasures of the body, notably sex. After his death, his fame grew as new stories were attached to his name or old ones enlarged. Modern Japanese know him as a sort of cultural icon, somewhat the way Americans know Benjamin Franklin. Literati admire his poems, calligraphy, and ink paintings, while schoolchildren sing songs attributed to him, repeat his wordplays, and consume spurious tales of his wise sayings and curious doings.

Scholars have made some progress in sorting out the facts and fictions of his life, but questions abound. A biography prepared not long after Ikkyū's death by one of his students, the painter Bokusai, claims that he was the son of an emperor and a noblewoman whose service in the court abruptly ended before his birth, owing to jealousy on the part of the empress. Ikkyū himself held sternly to the ancient Ch'an ideal of the monkhood as a classless society, writing that "there should be no toleration of gossip among the clergy about who is of high or low birth," and in all his work there is just one passing mention of royal descent that can be taken to support Bokusai's contention. Despite the absence of documentary evidence, four centuries after his death, the imperial family honored Ikkyū as one of its own, decorating his grave with its chrysanthemum crest.

Ikkyū's relationships in the Zen world are easier to ascertain but in their own way problematic. Like most other masters of the time, he entered the temple as a boy and received his education there. At thirteen, after seven years in one of Kyoto's lesser monasteries, he moved to Kennin-ji, where a concentrated program in Chinese poetry gave him the grounding for the densely allusive verse that he wrote the rest of his life. Four years of this left him hungry to deepen his Zen practice, and he betook himself to an out-of-the-way temple and a little-known priest named Ken'ō Sōi who belonged to the Ō-tō-kan lineage but had declined the proof of transmission that would have enabled him to rise in the Zen world. Ikkyū took to this unprepossessing man and was so grief-stricken when his mentor died in 1414 that, Bokusai reports, he nearly committed suicide.

Instead, he mustered the resolve to join another of Daitō's descendants, Kasō Sōdon (1352–1428), whose small temple near beautiful Lake Biwa had gained a

reputation as a place of the strictest practice. After surviving a stiff test of his met-
tle, the young monk entered Kasō's community and began studying koans with
him. An initial opening was followed by a deep realization experience triggered
by the caw of a crow, and at twenty-seven, Ikkyū received from Kasō a certificate
of Dharma-transmission. This he spurned, according to his biographer, who re-
counts in detail the efforts that were made to preserve this precious document
from its owner. Finally Ikkyū burned it, we are told, and he himself never offered
such a certificate or otherwise publicly designated Dharma heir.

In early Ch'an, at least in legend, teachers handed down Bodhidharma's robe
and alms bowl as symbols of transmission, and later other items had served the
same purpose—a portrait, a bit of calligraphy, an armrest or fly whisk. The
awarding of formal transmission documents was a relatively recent development
but one that had assumed critical import as Japanese masters sought to establish
their own legitimacy and distinguish themselves from pretenders. Dōgen put especially great stock in these documents, venerating them as sacred objects, but
such high valuations were thrown into doubt by the liberality with which some
Chinese teachers dispensed them—even, in one famous instance, without ever
meeting the intended recipient.

Ikkyū is said to have come across one of these certificates in a pawnshop and,
in rejecting them as he did, associated himself with classical Ch'an tradition,
fresh and uncorrupted. According to the *Record of Lin-chi*, when Huang-po
moved to present him tokens of succession, Lin-chi immediately called for fire:
how could any special object represent the inexpressible, ordinary, and empty
Mind? Ikkyū referred to this incident in one of his poems, taking it as one of
many indications that Zen needed serious reform in order to recover the spirit of
its founders.

Nothing galled Ikkyū more than signs of degeneracy in his own lineage. He
had found rigorous teaching among the descendants of Daitō and was dismayed
when Yōsō Sōi, a fellow successor of Kasō, took what Ikkyū considered a too-
worldly course in restoring the line's fortunes. Daitoku-ji had held top place in
the *gozan* during the mid-1330s when Go-Daigo enjoyed his brief opportunity
to exercise full imperial power. Despite Hanazono's best efforts, however, afterwards the monastery had fallen on hard times, receiving sub-*gozan* ranking and
scant support. In 1431, giving up on prospects for government patronage, its
leaders successfully petitioned for removal from the *gozan* system and set out to
secure backing from other sources, particularly from merchants newly prosperous in the China trade.

They succeeded all too well in this pursuit, Ikkyū felt. Accusing them of giving away secrets of koan study in exchange for patronage, he directed a torrent
of particularly scathing criticism at Yōsō, who became abbot of Daitoku-ji in
1438. Yōsō and his colleagues worked to refurbish Daitō's public image as well
as his old monastery, and a biography one of them published inspired Ikkyū to
compose a sarcastic verse playing on the meaning of the old master's name,
Great Lamp:

Hold the Great Lamp high, let it light the heavens!
Imperial carriages vied outside the Dharma Hall
but no one recalls his eating mind, living on water—
twenty years spent begging beneath Gojō Bridge.

The pursuit of grandeur falsified Daitō's real legacy, Ikkyū felt, and he identified himself with Daitō's description of his rightful successor as a person "who leads an upright life in the open fields, dwelling in a simple thatched hut, eating vegetable roots boiled in a broken-legged pot, and devoting himself to single-minded investigation of himself. . . . "

Ikkyū's life in the decades after Kasō's death does bear some resemblance to Daitō's ideal. He spent much of his time on the road, taking shelter in modest temples and hermitages, eating food that was a cut above vegetable roots but not exactly a luxurious diet. When in 1440 Yōsō named him the abbot of a sub-temple within the Daitoku-ji compound, Ikkyū lasted only ten days, resigning with two poems, the first saying that the life of a wanderer suited him better than temple comforts and the second advising anyone seeking him to "look in a fish stall, a sake shop, or a brothel."

Besides scorning the taste for titles, finery, and vapid ceremony that he saw in the Zen establishment, Ikkyū charged it with gross hypocrisy in the question of sex. Homosexual love was common enough in the monasteries to find its place in *gozan* poetry and on the *Nō* stage, and heterosexual hankerings led some masters, Ikkyū believed, to go so far as to install lovers in private quarters on monastery grounds—yet monks maintained an elegant facade of abstinence. Ikkyū expressed misgivings about his own failure to abide by the precept that put sexual contact out of bounds, but he prided himself, at least, on not concealing his passions from himself or from others and spoke out for the fundamental purity of sex itself. Late in his life, an enduring relationship with a blind songstress named Mori seems to have brought him to a wholehearted acceptance of sexuality as a feature of the ordinary mind celebrated in Zen.

The Ashikagas never fully consolidated their rule, and in 1467, jockeying for power among the warlords under them touched off a furious and futile war that lay waste to the elaborately renovated Daitoku-ji, along with much of Kyoto. Even before the war was over, Ikkyū received a call to assume the abbacy and rebuild the monastery, and despite advanced age and all the vitriol that he had focused on similar efforts by the now-deceased Yōsō, he could not walk away from this assignment. Quite to the contrary, he set himself so energetically to the task that it was completed in short order.

That Ikkyū was tapped to lead the reconstruction and that he succeeded so splendidly in achieving it must be attributed to the force of his personality. Call it charisma, if you will, but records make it plain that he inspired love and loyalty, whatever his foibles. Some of his power sprang from his creative genius, present for all to see in his excellent ink paintings, in calligraphy that couples enormous vitality with balance and fluidity, and above all in his thousand-poem

Crazy Cloud Anthology. His brilliance attracted other highly talented people to his circle, and through them, more than through his own work, he exerted a lasting influence on the development of *Nō* drama, tea ceremony, poetry, and painting. The grateful artists pitched in substantially in raising the funds for Daitoku-ji's rebuilding.

Like so much else, Ikkyū's poetry sets him apart from the culture of Musō and the *gozan,* even from Jakushitsu, with whom he otherwise shares an outsider status. Ikkyū's poems differ from those of the *gozan* literary tradition in two key respects: they treat overtly Buddhist subjects (he classed most of them as *gāthās*) and exuberantly violate rules of Chinese prosody that *gozan* poets carefully kept. Most are also so layered with allusions that readers need a deep knowledge of Ch'an literature and Chinese verse in order to appreciate them fully. A conspicuous exception is his "Skeletons," a fanciful account, blending prose and poetry, of a meeting with the dead. This vivid, motivational text, written mainly in Japanese phonetic syllables and illustrated in his own hand, reveals another facet of Ikkyū's complex personality—the earnest Zen teacher concerned for the spiritual welfare of ordinary people. ⌘

FROM THE CRAZY CLOUD ANTHOLOGY

UNTITLED

Stilted koans and convoluted answers are all monks have,
Pandering endlessly to officials and rich patrons.
Good friends of the Dharma, so proud, let me tell you,
A brothel girl in gold brocade is worth more than any of you.

RAINCOAT AND STRAW HAT

Woodcutters and fishermen know just how to use things.
What would they do with fancy chairs and meditation platforms?
In straw sandals and with a bamboo staff, I roam three thousand worlds,
Dwelling by the water, feasting on the wind, year after year.

MY MOUNTAIN MONASTERY

A thatched hut of three rooms surpasses seven great halls.
Crazy Cloud is shut up here far removed from the vulgar world.
The night deepens, I remain within, all alone,
A single light illuminating the long autumn night.

A MEAL OF FRESH OCTOPUS

Lots of arms, just like Kannon the Goddess;
Sacrificed for me, garnished with citron, I revere it so!

The taste of the sea, just divine!
Sorry, Buddha, this is another precept I just cannot keep.

UNTITLED

(*Long ago, there was an old woman who had supported a hermit monk for
twenty years. She had a sixteen-year-old girl bring him meals. One day she instructed the girl to embrace the monk and ask, "How do you feel right now?"
The young girl did as told, and the monk's response was, "I'm an old withered
tree against a frigid cliff on the coldest day of winter." When the girl returned
and repeated the monk's words to the old woman, she exclaimed. "For twenty
years I've been supporting that base worldling!" The old woman chased the
monk out and put the hermitage to the torch.*)

The old woman was bighearted enough
To elevate the pure monk with a girl to wed.
Tonight if a beauty were to embrace me
My withered old willow branch would sprout a new shoot!

NOTE   The introduction to this poem relates one of the toughest koans for a
Zen practitioner to solve: "Why did the old woman drive the monk out?"

UNTITLED

Every night, Blind Mori accompanies me in song.
Under the covers, two mandarin ducks whisper to each other.
We promise to be together forever,
But right now this old fellow enjoys an eternal spring.

UPON BECOMING ABBOT OF DAITOKU-JI

Daitō's descendants have nearly extinguished his light;
After such a long, cold night, the chill will be hard to thaw even with my
     love songs.
For fifty years, a vagabond in a straw raincoat and hat—
Now I'm mortified as a purple-robed abbot.

UNTITLED

Every day, priests minutely examine the Dharma
And endlessly chant complicated sutras.
Before doing that, though, they should learn
How to read the love letters sent by the wind and rain, the snow and
     moon.

UNTITLED

Monks these days study hard in order to turn
A fine phrase and win fame as talented poets.
At Crazy Cloud's hut there is no such talent, but he serves up the taste of truth
As he boils rice in a wobbly old cauldron.

FROM SKELETONS

I came to a small lonely temple. It was evening, when dew and tears wet one's
sleeves, and I was looking here and there for a place to sleep, but there was none.
It was far from the highway, at the foot of a mountain, what seemed a Samādhi
Plain. Graves were many, and from behind the Buddha Hall there appeared a
most miserable-looking skeleton, which uttered the following words:

> The autumn wind
> Has begun to blow in this world;
> Should the pampas grass invite me,
> I will go to the moor,
> I will go to the mountain.

> What to do
> With the mind of a man
> Who should purify himself
> Within the black garment,
> But simply passes life by.

All things must at some time become nought, that is, return to their original reality. When we sit facing the wall doing zazen, we realize that none of the
thoughts that arise in our minds, as a result of karma, are real. The Buddha's fifty
years of teaching are meaningless. The mistake comes from not knowing what
the mind is. Musing that few indeed experience this agony, I entered the Buddha
Hall and spent the night there, feeling more lonely than usual, and being unable
to sleep. Towards dawn, I dozed off, and in my dream I went to the back of the
temple, where many skeletons were assembled, each moving in his own special
way just as they did in life. While I marveled at the sight, one of the skeletons approached me and said:

> Memories
> There are none:
> When they depart,
> All is a dream;
> My life—how sad!

If Buddhism
Is divided into Gods
And Buddhas;
How can one enter
The Way of Truth?

For as long as you breathe
A mere breath of air,
A dead body
At the side of the road
Seems something apart from you.

Well, we enjoyed ourselves together, the skeleton and I, and that illusive mind that generally separates us from others gradually left me. The skeleton that had accompanied me all this while possessed the mind that renounces the world and seeks for truth. Dwelling on the watershed of things, he passed from shallow to deep, and made me realize the origin of my own mind. What was in my ears was the sighing of the wind in the pine trees; what shone in my eyes was the moon that enlightened my pillow.

But when is it not a dream? Who is not a skeleton? It is just because human beings are covered with skins of varying colors that sexual passion between men and women comes to exist. When the breathing stops and the skin of the body is broken there is no more form, no higher and lower. You must realize that what we now have and touch as we stand here is the skin covering our skeleton. Think deeply about this fact. High and low, young and old—there is no difference whatever between them.

Give up the idea "I exist." Just let your body be blown along by the wind of the floating clouds; rely on this. To want to live forever is to wish for the impossible, the unreal, like the idea "I exist."

This world
Is a dream
Seen while awake;
How pitiful those
Who see it and are shocked!

It is useless to pray to the gods about your destiny. Think only of the One Great Matter.

38

Takuan

(1573–1645)

Among the Zen masters of old, none did more than Takuan Sōhō to forge the now-commonplace association of Zen with the martial arts, with the way of sword-fighting (*kendō*) in particular. Born into a samurai family in the year the Ashikaga shogunate finally crumbled, he was strongly intellectual by nature, artistic and retiring, but events conspired to thrust him onto the national stage. He wound up a counselor to the country's greatest sword-master, teacher of an emperor, and an intimate of the shogun Tokugawa Iemitsu. Though he never lifted a sword himself, his name still evokes images of martial prowess and not by coincidence was he honored with the title National Teacher in 1944, as Japan braced for the end of World War II.

As Daitoku-ji recovered its prominence through the efforts of Yōsō, Ikkyū, and others, it built a nationwide network of affiliated temples similar to those maintained by the *gozan* monasteries. It was such a temple in his native province that Takuan entered at the age of thirteen, after four years of study in the Pure Land tradition. Thus began, at long distance, a long and fateful relationship with the Kyoto institution. He moved to the head temple eight years later but broke off his training there in 1601, evidently dissatisfied. Setting concentrated practice aside for a while, Takuan decamped for the seaport city of Sakai, there devoting himself to study of Chinese poetry and Confucianism under a scholar-monk who specialized in these subjects. Both were abiding interests for Takuan and figure prominently in his collected writings.

In 1603, as Japan entered the calm and unity of the Tokugawa era, Takuan resumed his Zen training in a Sakai-area hermitage attached to yet another of the Daitoku-ji sub-temples, Nanshū-ji. The master of the hermitage, Ittō Shōteki, was a descendant of Daitō known for his uncompromising attitude, and just a year of his guidance produced dramatic results for Takuan. He emerged as Ittō's sole successor and did his teacher proud in the following decade, becoming abbot of Nanshū-ji and distinguishing himself in Dharma "combat" at Daitoku-ji. For a few days, indeed, he wore the purple robe as chief abbot of the great Kyoto monastery, and though this was largely an honorary matter, it had a measure of significance. Whereas *gozan* heads were named by the shogunate, since Daitoku-ji was founded under imperial sponsorship its abbots were always appointed by the emperor, so Takuan's tenure indicated, at the least, highly positive notice from the court.

In 1615, not long after Takuan served his brief term, Daitoku-ji's special tie to the imperial house was plunged into jeopardy when the Tokugawa religious and diplomatic affairs adviser Ishin Suden, a Rinzai master from the top-flight *gozan* monastery of Nanzen-ji, drafted new regulations to govern Daitoku-ji and its sister monastery, Myōshin-ji. Part of a larger program to bring all Buddhist institutions under the shogunate's control, these rules stipulated that "The chief priest must be someone who has completed thirty years of Zen training under an eminent master, who has mastered the 1,700 koans, who has traveled to all the high-ranking priests for instruction, who is capable of conducting both clerical and secular affairs, and whose name has been forwarded to the shogunate for approval."

These onerous requirements outraged leading monks of Daitō's line but went largely unenforced and uncontested for a dozen years. Takuan spent most of this time rebuilding temples damaged in the wars of unification or enjoying semi-seclusion at a hermitage in his home province west of Kyoto, but when push came to shove, he went to Kyoto and organized opposition to the regulations, thereby precipitating a national incident known as the "Purple Robe Affair." When the smoke cleared in 1629, Takuan and another leading master were exiled to remote reaches of the country, and the emperor abdicated to protest both this outcome and the loss of his power of appointment. In Takuan's eyes, the integrity of Daitō's entire Dharma legacy seemed to be at stake, and he felt so passionate on this point that he spent much of his later life working to obtain a reversal of the policy. His outrage stemmed in part from great reverence for Daitō; he had earlier written a biography of the esteemed founder and, like Ikkyū, identified keenly with him and his heritage.

In personal terms, however, exile posed no great problem for the studious, solitude-loving Takuan. Cared for by the lord who held him as solicitously "as if I were the lord's grandfather," he made use of his three-year banishment to write, among other things, two essays on swordsmanship that made his name among the samurai. "The Mysterious Record of Immovable Wisdom" and "Annals of the Sword Taia" were written for Yagyū Munemori and perhaps one other *kendō* master in the service of the shogun. In each, Takuan appropriates and develops a metaphor from the vast body of religious and cultural lore he had at his disposal, employing it as a means to address swordplay and original mind. The former essay builds on the image of Fudō Myō-ō, the Immovable Wisdom King, a sword-flourishing figure more closely linked with the tantric tradition of Shingon Buddhism than with Zen. The latter essay takes a sword from Chinese mythology as its principal metaphor, treating it an expression for Buddha-nature itself.

No one knows exactly how Takuan came into contact with the shogunal sword-masters or what prompted him to write the two pieces, but in retrospect, these turns seem almost inevitable. For nearly four centuries, Zen masters had consorted with, taught, and received the patronage of Japanese warriors, and it seems natural that Takuan, himself of samurai family, should feel a strong bond with them; few teachers would understand their needs better than he. Living in bloody times and under a stringent code of honor, Samurai faced the constant threat of sudden death either on the battlefield or by their own hands, in *seppuku,* if they breached even minor rules of etiquette.

Moreover, sword imagery had ancient roots in Ch'an tradition, going back at least as far as Yung-chia's *Song of Realizing the Way* and recurring frequently in the literature thereafter—in the letters, for example, of Yüan-wu and Enni. A well-worn phrase describes the Ch'an or Zen master himself as one who wielded "the sword that kills, the sword that gives life," the sword of wisdom that at once puts an end to delusion and initiates a new life of freedom.

His sword-fighting essays expose Takuan to criticism on two fronts. First, they dwell on issues of mental and physical condition that Ch'an and Zen masters classically have dismissed as, at best, secondary to awakening and, at worst, liable to preoccupy students, becoming a hindrance to true practice. Second, they may be read as encouragement to wield the blade with cool detachment, contravening the age-old Buddhist precept against killing and the bodhisattva ideal of universal compassion. Takuan may have accepted an explicit discussion of condition and of technique as the price of doing business with sword fighters, as a skillful means of teaching Yagyū and others in the field; he does not address the point. The ethical issues, however, loom too large to evade even if he had wanted to, and he treats them ingeniously, sometimes seeming to endorse the perfectly ruthless dispatch of opponents and at other times seeming to preach the reverse: though a person accomplished in the martial arts "does not use the sword to cut others down, when others are confronted by this principle [of nonduality], they cower and become as dead men of their own accord. There is no need to kill them."

In a subsequent passage from his essay on the Taia sword and in other of his writings, Takuan considered the larger topic of right and wrong from several perspectives. In counseling the swordsman, he advocates an intuitive approach: "Without looking at right and wrong, [the seasoned fighter] is able to see right and wrong; without attempting to discriminate, he is able to discriminate well." In one of his hundred poems on the dream of life, he took the fundamental view:

> Thirty-six thousand days, a hundred years,
> we talk about Maitreya and Avalokiteshvara, right and wrong.
> Right is a dream, wrong is too—
> the Buddha says to see it this way.

Elsewhere, he urges a moral sense grounded in the neo-Confucian philosophy that Japan adopted in the decades ahead to undergird the social structure and ensure peace and stability after two centuries that reminded the nation's historians of a phrase from the *I Ching:* "the overturning of those on top by those below."

As Takuan may have foreseen, his sword-fighting treatises gave him great cachet in the shogun's new capital of Edo, which has since become Tokyo. When his exile ended, he was obliged to reside there for two years before returning to Kyoto, and during this period, he so solidified relationships in ruling circles that in 1634, after the religious adviser Sūden died, Tokugawa Iemitsu recalled him from Daitoku-ji to fill the vacant position. Takuan spent the rest of his life in Edo (visiting Kyoto and his home province occasionally), but refused to assume as active a policy-making role as his nemesis Sūden had. Though he enjoyed his privileged exposure to Iemitsu, Takuan chafed at the demands of Edo life, likening himself to "a performing monkey pulled around at the end of a string." Perhaps it was to appease him that, the following year, Iemitsu had the new temple of Tokai-ji built for him on the outskirts of the capital.

Despite Takuan's move to this site, the Zen master and the ruler continued their close relationship, with Iemitsu visiting approximately once a month. In 1641, at last the shogun also took the step Takuan had advocated for thirteen years, scrapping the rules Sūden had imposed on Daitoku-ji and Myōshin-ji. No longer on a string—that string, anyway—Takuan might have gone elsewhere at this juncture, but now sixty-nine and well situated, he stayed put and died at Tokai-ji three years later.

Consumed as his life was with political affairs, scholarship, poetry, and other cultural activities—calligraphy, ink painting, tea ceremony, garden design—Takuan concerned himself unusually little with training of disciples and named no Dharma heirs. Indeed, he showed a strong inclination to efface all trace of himself. "Bury my body in the mountain behind the temple," he directed the monks who attended him at Tokai-ji, "cover it with dirt and go home. Read no sutras, hold no ceremony. Receive no gifts from either monk or laity. Let the monks wear their robes, eat their meals, and carry on as on normal days." Asked for a final poem, he brushed the single character for dream and then passed away. In the dreamworld of modern Japan, he is among the best-known Zen masters, his memory kept alive not only through his connection with swordsmanship but also because he is said to have invented a popular, dried-daikon pickle—*takuan zuke.* ⌘

FROM THE MYSTERIOUS RECORD OF IMMOVABLE WISDOM

THE RIGHT MIND AND THE CONFUSED MIND

The Right Mind is the mind that does not remain in one place. It is the mind that stretches throughout the entire body and self.

The Confused Mind is the mind that, thinking something over, congeals in one place.

When the Right Mind congeals and settles in one place, it becomes what is called the Confused Mind. When the Right Mind is lost, it is lacking in function here and there. For this reason, it is important not to lose it.

In not remaining in one place, the Right Mind is like water. The Confused Mind is like ice, and ice is unable to wash hands or head. When ice is melted, it becomes water and flows everywhere, and it can wash the hands, the feet, or anything else.

If the mind congeals in one place and remains with one thing, it is like frozen water and is unable to be used freely: ice that can wash neither hands nor feet. When the mind is melted and is used like water, extending throughout the body, it can be sent wherever one wants to send it.

This is the Right Mind.

THE MIND OF THE EXISTENT MIND
AND THE MIND OF NO-MIND

The Existent Mind is the same as the Confused Mind and is literally read as the "mind that exists." It is the mind that thinks in one direction, regardless of subject. When there is an object of thought in the mind, discrimination and thoughts will arise. Thus it is known as the Existent Mind.

The No-Mind is the same as the Right Mind. It neither congeals nor fixes itself in one place. It is called No-Mind when the mind has neither discrimination nor thought but wanders about the entire body and extends throughout the entire self.

The No-Mind is placed nowhere. Yet it is not like wood or stone. Where there is no stopping place, it is called No-Mind. When it stops, there is something in the mind. When there is nothing in the mind, it is called the mind of No-Mind. It is also called No-Mind-No-Thought.

When this No-Mind has been well developed, the mind does not stop with one thing nor does it lack any one thing. It is like water overflowing and exists within itself. It appears appropriately when facing a time of need.

The mind that becomes fixed and stops in one place does not function freely. Similarly, the wheels of a cart go around because they are not rigidly in place. If they were to stick tight, they would not go around. The mind is also something that does not function if it becomes attached to a single situation.

If there is some thought within the mind, though you listen to the words spoken by another, you will not really be able to hear him. This is because your mind has stopped with your own thoughts.

If your mind leans in the directions of these thoughts, though you listen, you will not hear; and though you look, you will not see. This is because there is something in your mind. What is there is thought. If you are able to remove this thing that is there, your mind will become No-Mind, it will function when needed, and it will be appropriate to its use.

The mind that thinks about removing what is within it will by the very act be occupied. If one will not think about it, the mind will remove these thoughts by itself and of itself become No-Mind.

If one always approaches his mind in this way, at a later date it will suddenly come to this condition by itself. If one tries to achieve this suddenly, it will never get there.

An old poem says:

To think, "I will not think"—
This, too, is something in one's thoughts.
Simply do not think
About not thinking at all.

ENGENDER THE MIND WITH NO PLACE TO ABIDE

If we put this in terms of your own martial art, the mind is not detained by the hand that brandishes the sword. Completely oblivious to the hand that wields the sword, one strikes and cuts his opponent down. He does not put his mind in his adversary. The opponent is emptiness. I am emptiness. The hand that holds the sword, the sword itself, is emptiness. Understand this, but do not let your mind be taken by emptiness.

When the Zen priest at Kamakura, Mugaku, was captured during the disturbances in China and was at the point of being cut down, he quoted the *gāthā,* "With the speed of a flash of lightning, / Cut through the spring breeze," and the soldier threw down his sword and fled.[1]

Mugaku meant that in wielding the sword, in the infinitesimal time it takes lightning to strike, there is neither mind nor thought. For the striking sword, there is no mind. For myself, who is about to be struck, there is no mind. The attacker is emptiness. His sword is emptiness. I, who am about to be struck, am emptiness.

If this is so, the man who strikes is not a man at all. The striking sword is not a sword. And for myself, the person who is about to be cut, in a flash of lightning, it will be like cutting through the breeze that blows across the spring sky. It is the mind that absolutely does not stop. And it is not likely that the sword will react to cutting through the wind.

Completely forget about the mind and you will do all things well.

When you dance, the hand holds the fan and the foot takes a step. When you do not forget everything, when you go on thinking about performing with the hands and the feet well and dancing accurately, you cannot be said to be skillful. When the mind stops in the hands and the feet, none of your acts will be singular. If you do not completely discard the mind, everything you do will be done poorly.

1. Mugaku (1226–86), a Chinese priest of the Lin-chi (Rinzai) sect, invited to Japan by Hōjō Tokimune in 1278. The above story refers to the invasion of the Southern Sung by the Mongols in 1275 [after Mugaku had returned to China].

The Mugaku quoted verse runs, "In all of heaven and earth, no place to stand up a single pole. / Happily I understand: Man is emptiness, the Buddhist Law is emptiness. / How wonderful is the three-foot sword of the Great Yuan. / With the speed of a flash of lightning, / Cut through the spring breeze."

FROM THE ANNALS OF THE SWORD TAIA[2]

Taia is the name of an [ancient Chinese] sword that has no equal under heaven. This famous jeweled sword can freely cut anything, from rigid metal and tempered steel to dense and hardened gems and stones. Under heaven there is nothing that can parry this blade. The person who obtains this uncreated mysterious ability will not be swayed by the commander of huge armies or an enemy force of hundreds of thousands. This is the same as there being nothing that can impede the blade of this famous sword. Thus I call the strength of this mysterious ability the Sword Taia.

All men are equipped with this sharp Sword Taia, and in each one it is perfectly complete. Those for whom this is clear are feared even by the Maras, but those for whom this is obscure are deceived even by the heretics.[3] On the one hand, when two of equal skill meet at swords' point, there is no conclusion to the match; it is like Shākyamuni 's holding the flower and Kāshyapa's subtle smile.[4] On the other hand, raising the one and understanding the other three, or distinguishing subtle differences in weight with the unaided eye are examples of ordinary cleverness.[5] If anyone has mastered this, he will quickly cut you into three pieces even before the one has been raised and the three understood. How much more so when you meet him face to face?

All men are equipped with this sharp Sword Taia, and in each one it is perfectly complete. This means that the famous Sword Taia, which no blade under heaven can parry, is not imparted just to other men. Everyone, without exception, is equipped with it, it is inadequate for no one, and it is perfectly entire.

This is a matter of the mind. This mind was not born with your birth and will not die with your death. This being true, it is said to be your Original Face.[6] Heaven is not able to cover it. Earth is not able to support it. Fire is not able to burn it, nor is water able to dampen it. Even the wind is unable to penetrate it. There is nothing under heaven that is able to obstruct it.

2. [In this essay, Takuan alternates passages in Chinese with his line-by-line explanations in Japanese.—Eds.]
3. *Mara* is a Demon, the Sanskrit literally meaning "Robber of Life." The reference here is to the *Deva Mara,* who from his position in the Sixth Heaven obstructs the practice of Buddhism.
4. Kāshyapa (Mahākāshyapa), foremost in ascetic practices of the ten chief disciples, became the leader of the disciples after the Buddha's death.
5. The text here is unclear. Grammatically, it would seem to equate the example of the "one and the three" with the reference to Shākyamuni and Kāshyapa, but this fits neither in terms of the total meaning nor with the development of the text.
   The reference to "the one and the three" is probably from the Confucian *Analects* (7:8): "The Master said, 'I do not enlighten those who are not enthusiastic or educate those who are not anxious to learn. I do not repeat myself to those who, when I raise one corner, do not return having raised the other three." The latter part of the sentence is from *The Blue Cliff Record*. "Raising the one and understanding the other three, distinguishing subtle differences in weight with the unaided eye—these are the ordinary tea and rice of the Buddhist monk."
6. Original Face is the pristine nature of the Mind, as yet unstained by human affairs or intentions.

Those for whom this is clear are feared even by the Maras, but those for whom this is obscure are deceived even by the heretics. For the person who is clearly enlightened concerning his Original Face, there is nothing in the universe that obscures or obstructs his vision. Thus there is no means of enacting the supernatural power of the Maras. Because such a person sees through to the bottom of his own intentions, the Maras fear and avoid him; they hesitate to draw near. Conversely, the person who is obscure and lost concerning his Original Face accumulates any number of confused thoughts and delusions, which then adhere to him. Heretics are easily able to deceive and swindle such a person.

When two of equal skill at this meet at swords' point, there is no conclusion to the match. The meaning of this is that if two men who had both penetrated their Original Face were to meet, each unsheathed the Sword Taia, and they faced off, it would be impossible to bring matters to a conclusion. If one were to ask about this, it might be likened to the meeting of Shākyamuni and Kāshyapa.

Shākyamuni's holding the flower and Kāshyapa's subtle smile. At the gathering at Gridhrakuta Peak when Shākyamuni was about to die, he held up a single red lotus. He showed this to eighty thousand monks and every one of them remained silent. Only Kāshyapa smiled. Knowing at that time that Kāshyapa had been enlightened, Shākyamuni entrusted him with the Correct Doctrine, which does not rely on the written word and is specially transmitted without instruction, and affirmed on him the Buddha-seal.[7]

The doctrine of "holding the flower . . . the subtle smile" is difficult to arrive at and is not easily unraveled by guesswork. One must drink in the breath of all the Buddhas while swallowing one's own voice.

Although there is really no way to express this principle, if pressed, one might summon up the example of taking water from one vessel and pouring it into another so that the waters become mixed and indistinguishable. This is the moment when the eyes of Shākyamuni and Kāshyapa meet and become one. Relativity is no longer there.

Among all martial artists of every discipline, there is not one in one hundred thousand who has grasped the purport of "holding the flower . . . the subtle smile." Nevertheless, if one did have the most steadfast of intentions and truly wanted to understand, he would have to discipline himself for another thirty years. Erring in this would not simply be a matter of not mastering martial arts; he would enter hell like an arrow shot from a bow. This is truly a frightening thing.

Raising the one and understanding the other three means that as soon as one part is shown, the other three are immediately understood.

Distinguishing subtle differences in weight with the unaided eye. Distinguishing . . . with the unaided eye means the eye's function, or measurement by the

---

7. Not relying on the written word and transmission without instruction are two points especially stressed in Zen. They underscore the principle that one is to look into his own nature rather than rely on texts or the teachings of others.

eye. Differences in weight are extremely subtle. The man who is able to measure out any weight of gold and silver by eye and not err by the slightest amount is a clever and skillful person.

These are examples of ordinary cleverness signifies that such clever people are ordinary and their number is legion, and thus there is nothing special about them.

If anyone has mastered this, he will quickly cut you into three pieces even before the one has been raised and the three understood. This pertains to the person who has been enlightened concerning the cause of the Buddha's appearance in the world. It is he who will quickly cut you into three parts before the one has been raised, the three understood, or before any indication whatsoever appears. Thus I suppose that, in meeting someone like this, there is nothing that could be done.

How much more so when you meet him face to face? A man who has gained such celerity and subtlety, when meeting another man face to face, will cut so easily that his opponent will never know that his head has fallen off.

In the end, a man like this never exposes the tip of his sword. Its speed—even lightning cannot keep up with it. Its brevity—it is gone even before the quick wind of the storm. Not having such a tactic, if one, in the end, becomes entangled or confused, he will damage his own blade or injure his own hand, and will fall short of adroitness. One does not divine this by impressions or knowledge. There is no transmitting it by words or speech, no learning it by any doctrine. This is the law of the special transmission beyond instruction.

39

Ishikawa Jōzan

(1583–1672)

Ishikawa Jōzan had much in common with the ten-years-older Takuan, including a samurai background, a deep interest in neo-Confucianism, and a love of both solitude and poetry. In most respects, however, the two men's lives played out very differently. Whereas Takuan's sword flashed only on paper, Ishikawa's saw action on the battlefield in service to Tokugawa Ieyasu, founder of the new shogunate. Whereas Takuan's passion for out-of-the-way scholarly and artistic endeavors was frustrated by his political involvement, Ishikawa succeeded in withdrawing to the hills outside Kyoto and devoting his final three decades to undisturbed pursuit of things literary. Whereas Takuan's wish for obscurity has, if anything, added to the luster of his reputation, Ishikawa's fame has dimmed considerably since his death, and he is today little known even in Japan.

Ishikawa's Zen practice began, it appears, with the abrupt termination of his samurai career. Despite a heroic performance in the 1615 siege of Osaka that dispatched the last major barrier to Ieyasu's power, Ishikawa was cashiered by the shogun for failure to execute orders precisely. His warrior topknot was shaved off soon thereafter, as he entered the great Myōshin-ji monastery at the age of thirty-two. His Confucian studies, which commenced a couple of years later, permanently turned his life in the direction of letters. To support his aged mother, he worked subsequently for twelve years as tutor to the family that ruled the Hiroshima area, then retired at fifty-eight to dwell on the lower slopes of Mt. Hiei and to exercise his literary faculties full time.

Zen Dust, an encyclopedic sourcebook on Rinzai tradition, makes only one passing reference to Ishikawa, calling him "a samurai who [became] an eminent Confucian scholar and poet." While his ties to Rinzai institutions were not strong, this description understates Ishikawa's commitment to Buddhism and to Zen, in particular. Abounding with Zen themes and phrases, his work continues in the direction of the Literature of the Five Mountains, bearing close relationship to the work of its more rural representatives like Jakushitsu. Among the Chinese poets who inspired Ishikawa, Wang Wei and Su T'ung-po stand out, and his life after retirement resembles Wang Wei's semi-monkhood. Though his home was not a Buddhist temple per se, it became one after his death.

The Tokugawa shogunate closed Japan to foreigners in the 1630s, in part to exclude firearms. Chinese influence was little diminished by this action, and indeed, the government's promotion of Confucian ideals as a social stabilizer so fueled study of Chinese language and literature that, in the next two centuries, an ever greater proportion of the population gained competency in written Chinese. Among well-educated people, ability to compose a proper Chinese poem came to be expected, but in Ishikawa's day, such ability was still rare, and even rarer was the grace, freshness, and intimacy of the verses he produced. While other writers adopted an aesthetic philosophy of emulating great eighth-century Chinese poets, Ishikawa put Chinese prosody to his own devices, in accord with a rival aesthetic urging expression of one's "innate sensibility." There is no doubt which of these philosophies produced the better results.

Since a command of Chinese is no longer considered essential academically or culturally, Jakushitsu, Ishikawa, and other poets who did their work exclusively or primarily in Chinese are now out of reach for a lot of highly literate Japanese—as Emily Dickinson and Walt Whitman would be for Americans if they had created in Latin instead of English. Lacking any other grip upon their compatriots' hearts and minds, as generations pass, the Chinese-language poets become increasingly ghostly presences in the national literary heritage. That has been Ishikawa's fate, though the Shisendō, his lovely house-cum-temple on Mt. Hiei remains intact and helps anchor his reputation in present realities. ⌘

WRITTEN AT THE WALL OF IMMOVABLE STONE

Evening mountains veiled in somber mist,
one path entering the wooded hill:
the monk has gone off, locking his pine door.
From a bamboo pipe a lonely trickle of water flows.

TITLE   The Wall of Immovable Stone, or Ishi Fudō no Heki, is in present-day Tokushima Prefecture, Shikoku.

HELL VALLEY

Beyond the village, an unpeopled region—
everyone calls it the citadel of Avichi.
When the sun sets, woodcutters grow fearful;
when clouds rise up, the angry thunder growls.
Mountain spirits weep in the gloomy rain,
night monkeys cry to the moon as it shines.
In this lonely, deserted valley
the voice of the cuckoo would frighten your soul.

TITLE   Hell Valley is in Arima hot spring near present-day Kobe. The mineral waters issuing in the area were thought to be poisonous, hence the evil reputation of the spot.

LINE 2   Avichi, or the hell of incessant suffering, is the most terrible of the eight
hot hells in the Buddhist concept of the underworld.

SUDDEN SHOWER

Darkness and light divide the tall sky,
the rumble of thunder passes over distant mountains.
The evening is cool, and beyond the slackening rain,
through broken clouds, a moon immaculate.

UP AFTER ILLNESS

Old and sick here in spring mountains,
but the warm sun's just right for a skinny body.
I sweep the bedroom, put the bedding out to air,
peer into the garden, leaning on a cane.
Birds scold, as though resenting visitors;
blossoms are late—it seems they've waited for me.
Trust to truth when you view the ten thousand phenomena
and heaven and earth become one bottle gourd.

RECORDING THOUGHTS

Years ago I retired to rest,
did some modest building in this crinkle of the mountain.
Here in the woods, no noise, no trash;
in front of my eaves, a stream of pure water.
In the past I hoped to profit by opening books;
now I'm used to playing games in the dirt.
What is there that's not a children's pastime?
Confucius, Lao-tzu—a handful of sand.

SPRING DAY, SINGING OF IDLE PLEASURES

The lingering cold, a burden, is still bearable,
but blossoms are late—spring is taking its time.
Mountain clouds billow out in dense masses;
from the rocks a stream of water gushes down.
In my distaste for wine, I remind myself of Vimalakīrti;
praising poetry, I emulate Pu Shang.
Though my wits have not deserted me completely,
of ten characters I've forgotten how to write two or three.

LINES 5–6   Vimalakīrti, a contemporary of Shākyamuni Buddha, was a wealthy layman who had a wife and family but nevertheless possessed a profound understanding of Buddhist doctrine and lived a life as pure as that of the Buddha's monk disciples. Pu Shang, better known by the name Tzu-hsia, was a disciple of Confucius and the reputed author of the "Great Preface" to the *Book of Odes*, which discusses the nature and function of poetry.

AUTUMN NIGHT: DEPICTING BUSYNESS IN THE MIDST OF SILENCE

White-haired, in clear autumn touched by scenes and emotions,
among hills, moon my companion, living out the last of my life:
night deepens, no lingering echoes from the ten thousand pipes;
all I hear is the sound of the *sozū* tapping the rock.

LINE 4   The *sozū* is a device made of a bamboo tube that periodically fills with water from a stream, tips to pour out the water, and then returns to its original position, striking a rock and producing a sharp rapping sound as it does so. It was intended to scare deer away from the garden. The device continues to thump away in the Shisendō garden today. The "ten thousand pipes" in the preceding line is a reference to the famous passage on the noises made by the wind in the forest in the second chapter of *Chuang-tzu*.

ON A SUCCESSION OF THEMES, FIVE POEMS

A hundred battles that were over in an instant,
ten thousand goods consigned like chips of tile:
through the reigns of four sovereigns I've come and gone,
nothing right, nothing not right.

LINE 3   Jōzan's long life actually touched on the reigns of seven emperors. But since this poem was written in 1663, he probably has in mind the reigns of the four previous rulers, Gomizunoo (1612–1628), Meishō (1629–1648), Gokōmyō (1649–1654), and Gosai (1655–1662).

THREE ENOUGHS: AN ORAL COMPOSITION (IN THE STYLE OF HAN-SHAN)
(*The years of my age—enough; the years of retirement—enough; the number of my poems—enough. So I have given myself the title Old Man Three Enoughs.*)

Stubbornly long-lived—eighty-three;
since entering retirement—thirty years;

assorted poems—more than a thousand:
enough of everything to finish off one lifetime.

LEANING ON A CANE, SINGING

Leaning on a cane by the wooded village,
trees rising thick all around:
a dog barks in the wake of a beggar;
in front of the farmer, the ox plowing.
A whole lifetime of cold stream waters,
in age and sickness, the evening sun sky—
I have tasted every pleasure of mist and sunset
in these ten-years-short-of-a-hundred.

NOTE   Jōzan's last recorded poem.

40

Shidō Munan

(1603–1676)

To appreciate the part Shidō Munan played in the unfolding of Rinzai Zen, consider the position the sect had reached by the middle of the seventeenth century. As part of a larger program to impose order on the country, the Tokugawa shogunate had promulgated strict regulations for all religious organizations, Shintō as well as Buddhist. (Christianity had been altogether suppressed.) Each Buddhist temple was required to have a clearly identified place within a hierarchy of larger and smaller temples to which it was related, and each of the various sects had to be licensed by the government and accountable to it. Further, the shogunate had decreed that each citizen must henceforth be registered at its family temple. On top of their existing problems—the pursuit of wealth and comfort that so ired Ikkyū, overemphasis on literary achievement, the neglect of practice—Zen temples had thus been thrust into service as cogs in the machine of government and had to cope with new bureaucratic demands.

Since Musō's time, the *gozan* monasteries had hit the skids, and leadership had clearly passed to the growing network of temples headquartered at Daitoku-ji and Myōshin-ji. Of the two streams flowing from Daitō, the Daitoku-ji line also had begun to fall off, with its chief abbacy not much more than a revolving door and talented masters like Ikkyū and Takuan dying without naming successors. Leading members of the Myōshin-ji, or Ō-tō-kan, line recognized that their strand of the tradition also stood in need of revival, and some went to extraordinary lengths to get a new infusion of red-blooded Ch'an from China (Chapter 43). That renewal of the Ō-tō-kan line actually came through Munan, a longtime layman of limited education, is perhaps the most delicious irony of modern Zen.

Though Munan wrote next to nothing and gave scant space to his personal life when he did, he provides a capsule history covering what he evidently considered the salient facts of his life:

> I was born in a poor neighborhood and when I was a child was awkward in appearance and weak in constitution. We lived in the village of Fujikawa in Sekigahara in Mino, and my usual occupation was tending the cattle. When I reached the age of fifteen, I traveled with my father to Kyoto and passed the time there until I was twenty. I saw the vicissitudes of this transient world, and pondered the teaching of the "special transmission" [i.e., Zen]. To attain it I shaved off my hair

and beard and dyed my robe, and visited teachers asking about the Way. I wandered east and west, sleeping in the dew and lodging in the grasses, and was growing older. Then I heard of a teacher in the mountains northwest of Mino who could "draw out the nails and pull out the wedges." I immediately went to him, and entered his room. For twenty or thirty years since I received his instruction, whether drinking tea or eating rice, I went on cultivating this matter.

Elsewhere he identifies this wedge-puller as Zen master Gudō Tōshoku (1577–1661), a Rinzai teacher who served an exceptional four terms as chief abbot of Myōshin-ji, and he associates their meeting with his work at a post station on the Tōkaidō road linking Kyoto and Edo:

I used to be a gatekeeper in the province of Mino. When I was in attendance on Master Gudō and accompanied him to Edo, he took pity on me and gave me the teaching of "From the beginning not one thing exists." Considering this to be a blessing, I practiced for thirty years, and directly became "not one thing." Thanks to my master, I know the precious blessings of Buddha; I teach the Buddha-Dharma to people and cherish it.

The earliest biography of Munan, by his great-grandson in the Dharma Tōrei (Chapter 45), fills in some of the gaps in this account but probably contains as much legend and invention as fact, since Tōrei prepared it in petitioning the government to issue Munan a posthumous title. One detail Tōrei had no incentive to fabricate is that gatekeeping fell to Munan as a familial obligation and entailed running an inn where Gudō often stayed. The biography places Munan's early instruction, practice, and opening to "not a single thing" at the inn, while it dates his ordination and receipt of Dharma-transmission to his mid-forties, after he had "accompanied [Gudō] to Edo." He received the name Munan on ordination, Shidō when authorized to teach. The latter event, Tōrei notes, was occasioned by a great breakthrough involving the second case of *The Blue Cliff Record* (Chapter 23), whose key phrase, quoted from Seng-ts'an's old poem *Relying on Mind*, is *shidō munan*—the Supreme Way is not difficult.

Thus the gatekeeper from Sekigahara became a living testament to the fact that the Way is open to all, indeed that all beings travel it, wittingly or not. Munan must have cut an unusual figure among masters of the capital city, a goose among its swans. Tōrei puts a positive face on the matter, writing that Munan "did not follow the currents of the time, did not rely upon words or letters or rules; he was sincere and humble throughout his lifetime; he did not seek name or glory and his words and deeds were marked by a simplicity and directness." Munan is said to have had nobles among his students but plainly did not receive the acclaim and patronage that came to better-born, better-educated masters. Neither the court nor the shogunate saw fit to appoint him to an abbacy, and he declined even the two small temple offers that came his way, always teaching from a hermitage in the precincts of Edo.

"Forgetting about the ridicule of other people," late in his life Munan wrote two brief tracts entitled *On Self-Nature* and *On This Mind*. Both are miscellanies set down in colloquial Japanese, as if he had swept up three decades of jottings and strung them together with little concern for coherence. Even his admirers acknowledge the elementary quality of Munan's words, and he himself went well beyond customary protestations of humility in introducing his work. Expressing hope that his writing might "be instructive at least for children," he compared himself unflatteringly to Ikkyū and other past masters: "How laughable they must think what is done by a person like me, without wisdom or learning. Still, I beg their forgiveness for the addition . . . of these words of mine. I used to be a gatekeeper at Sekigahara. . . . "

Munan did not write out of literary tradition as Ikkyū, Ishikawa, and others did, but what his work lacks in depth and subtlety is offset, at least in part, by its refreshing directness. Munan puts his thoughts so straightforwardly as to verge on bluntness at times. He is exceptionally self-revealing, confessing ignorance on certain points and going so far as to admit, "I abstain from contact with women because the mind of a beast still remains in me." That he wrote at all may result from confidence in his experience of the Supreme Way. When a samurai observed that people of the Way seemed very learned, Munan assured and challenged him, answering, "You need only know what the basis of everything is." Plainly, he knew where he stood.

This confidence carried over to questions of conduct. Munan's most famous dictum, one of many aphoristic verses interspersed in his writings—

> Die while you live!
> Be utterly dead,
> Then do what you please,
> All is good.

—has often been misconstrued as moral license for the awakened. Far from it. As Munan's stance on female contact indicates, he held himself and other monks to exacting, perhaps rigid, standards of behavior. Another verse, addressed "to one who is supposed to become a teacher," makes it clear that the freedom found in dying to oneself must not be conflated with freedom from ethical concerns:

> How foolish to consider,
> When you and nothingness are one,
> That you are beyond all sinfulness
> In whatever you may do.

Munan enjoyed sufficient freedom, by his own account, to instruct at least some women. Both nuns and elderly laywomen appear in anecdotes that he tells, and Tōrei lists several nuns among the master's most accomplished students. The biography reports, however, that only one person received Munan's full sanction as a successor—Dōkyō Etan (1642–1721). Though he had a much more privileged upbringing than Munan, this man revered Munan as his true teacher and went on, in his own career, to take a position even farther outside the mainstream of Zen. Such was the unpredictable way to Hakuin and the Rinzai renaissance. ⚭

FROM ON SELF-NATURE

Someone asked about the great Dharma. I taught him the attainment of original Mind. He then asked how he could cultivate it. I said, "Satori is a treasure not to be traded for Heaven and Earth. The cultivation of it is in your own mind."

Someone asked, "How can you teach satori to people?"

I said, "If you do not open your eyes, you will not see the myriad things. If you are not enlightened, Buddha-nature will not be manifested."

Someone asked, "In the past and now it has been said that satori is difficult to attain. How can we become enlightened?"

I said, "Under the Sixth Ancestor more than forty people and under Ma-tsu more than one hundred and thirty attained great enlightenment."

Then he asked, "What is satori?"

I said, "It is original Mind."

He asked, "What is this original Mind?"

I said, " 'Not one thing.' "

He asked again, "What is this 'not one thing'?"

I said nothing.

Someone said, "This country is the country of the gods. To stop practicing the Way of the gods [Shinto], which we have been blessed with since antiquity, and to practice the Way of Buddha is a great mistake."

I said, "That is foolish. What are called the gods of this country are also Mind. A poem—

If your mind is in accordance with the true Way,
Even if you don't pray, the gods will protect you.

There are many poems like this. Besides, the abode of the gods is a person's body. This abiding of the gods is what we call the illumination of the heart. This is Mind. The basis of Confucianism is also Mind. India's Buddha is also Mind. It is certain that it is Mind that has been passed down in the three countries. Confucianism and Shinto teach the rectification of the body and the illumination of the heart. India goes beyond the body and manifests Mind directly, so in India customarily the Buddha's Way is practiced. The sages of these Ways have been revered since antiquity, so if the Buddha's Way prospers, there is nothing wrong.

A certain old nun said she had doubts about the statement of the Tathāgata Shākyamuni in the *Verses of the Self:* "Should I depart taking with me this great assembly, even though I leave, I shall still be here."[1] I said, "If we speak about the manner of this mystery, we call it no-thought. This itself is the mystery that fills Heaven and Earth. It is the eternal abode of the World-honored One." The old nun joined her hands together in agreement and departed.

Someone asked, "The living beings in the world all have various forms. Are their species determined from the very beginning?"

I said, "There are species, but Mind is the one essence of Heaven and Earth."

He said, "What is the sign of one essence?"

I said, "We see the moon, we see flowers, we hear a bell. Who doesn't? This is the sign of the one essence. . . .

I met an old woman. I asked her, "What koan are you practicing?"

She said, *"Who."*

"I can tell you about it," I said. "There is something that utilizes everyone even Shākyamuni and Maitreya." I said, "Please come over here," and she came as I asked. Then I said, "What is the thing that has just now utilized your body?"

The old woman said, "Not one thing."

I said, "We give various names to the very 'not one thing' which utilizes you, and call it koan. Not knowing this, we search outside, and so there is delusion."

FROM ON THIS MIND

There was a disciple of a certain Buddhist priest who said that he practiced zazen day and night; that there was no distinction between himself and others, and that there was no birth-and-death. I asked him of his satori, and although he was extremely apprehensive about answering, he said, "It is beyond someone like me."

To be a Buddhist master is by no means a trifling matter. Above all, the practice of the Way of Buddha is difficult without a master. Those who practice zazen suffer acutely from the awareness that zazen and their everyday life are not in harmony. They say that right now there is no distinction between the things before their eyes and themselves. But that is absurd. People hate to eat *miso* (bean paste) that stinks of *miso.*[2]

---

1. From a verse section in Chapter 5 of the *Lotus Sutra.* This is not an exact quotation, but apparently a misquotation, misattribution or rough paraphrase of ideas occurring in the verses.
2. When *miso* is freshly made, it has a strong odor. As it ages this odor becomes more and more refined, until it eventually disappears. The best *miso* is that which is longest aged and most matured. The same, Munan suggests, is true of a student of Zen.

To my disciples I say, "If your practice of Zen cannot be accomplished successfully, you must return to lay life. Then your sin will not be so great. If you remain
as a Buddhist priest while you still have a sensuous mind you will assuredly become a beast (in your next life). Our life in this world is indeed short.

The teachings of Buddhism are greatly in error. How much more in error it is to
learn them. See directly. Hear directly. In direct seeing there is no seer. In direct
hearing there is no hearer.

> Why do you take
> What does not see, nor hear,
> Nor think, nor know,
> As something apart,
> And different from yourself?

People say that *kenshō* is difficult. It is neither difficult nor easy; no thing whatsoever can attach to it. It stands apart from the right and wrong of things, while
at the same time corresponding to them. It lives in desires and it is apart from
them; it dies and does not die; it lives and does not live; it sees and does not see;
it hears and does not hear; it moves and does not move; it seeks things and does
not seek them; it sins and does not sin. It is under the domination of causality,
and it is not. Ordinary people cannot reach it, and even bodhisattvas cannot ac-
tualize it. Therefore, it is called Buddha.

While one is deluded, one is used by one's body. When one gains awakening,
one uses one's body.

Everything has a time for ripeness. For instance, as a child, one learns *iroba*.[3] Then
as an adult in the busy world, there is nothing one is unable to write about, even
about things of China. This is the ripening of *iroba*. People who practice Buddhism
will suffer pain while they are washing the defilements from their bodies; but after
they have cleansed themselves and become Buddha, they no longer feel any suffering. So it is with compassion as well. While one is acting compassionately, one is
aware of his compassion. When compassion has ripened, one is not aware of his
compassion. When one is compassionate and unaware of it, he is Buddha.

To one who determined to retire to a mountain to live a Buddhist life, I said, "I
am glad for your resolve, and urge you to diligence. But even were you to hide in
the remotest mountain recess, you would still be a part of this floating world.
And if your mind remained the same as before, your mountain life would be
nothing but a change of residence."

3. *Iroba,* the Japanese syllabary. [Equivalent to the ABCs.]

You should enter not a mountain,
But your own mind—
Making your hiding place
In the unknown.

One day, accompanied by a friend, I walked past Kurodani towards Kyomizu.[4]
We followed a narrow path that led to the left and came upon a small dwelling
surrounded by a fallen-down fence. Pushing open the brushwood gate, we
peered inside. At the far end we could see a dust-covered floor, turned up from
long neglect. Wisps of smoke, all that remained of a breakfast fire, curled in the
air. An altar-shelf hung off at an angle, so there was no offering of flowers or incense. We saw what appeared to be a Buddha-image—although with its hands
and feet missing it was difficult to distinguish—and a figure reciting the *Nembutsu* in a hoarse voice. He was a distinguished-looking fellow, more than fifty
years old, perhaps of a noble family that had come on bad times. He asked me
where I had come from. I replied that, feeling something drawing me as I passed
nearby, I dropped in at his hermitage. I commented that it must have been the
work of profound causation. We talked much with each other; of people past
and present, praising good things and censuring the bad. Although we had
much to talk of, yet neither of us were attached to the world. He was so sorry
when it came time for me to leave that he recited the name of Amida. As we listened to the sound of a temple bell tolling the end of day, he said that he felt one
more day was now gone in the relentless passage of his life. Suddenly, I felt sad
myself for him.

When we listen,
Freed from the thoughts of this world,
The sound of the bell tolling the evening hour
Is the sound of the wind
Blowing through the seaside pine trees.

To one who seeks the Great Way.

The true body fills the universe,
Fills and overflows it;
But rain cannot wet it,
The sun's rays cannot reach it.

To someone sincerely seeking the Way.

Originally it cannot be taught or learned;
When you do not know it

4. Kiyomizu, Kurodani—places in the Higashiyama area of Kyoto.

It is unknown;
When you know it
It is still unknown.

A person asks the Way.

Patch the wind in the pines
To your hempen robes;
Use the moon as a pillow,
The ocean waves as your sheet.

Men are all perplexed
When asked what Buddha is;
No one knows
It is his own mind.

Those who seek the Dharma
In the depths,
Are those who leave it
Behind in the shallows.

41

Bankei

(1622–1693)

Aglob of black phlegm slipping down the wall of his meditation hut—that sight brought Bankei Yōtaku a sudden glimpse of the Unborn. Alone, sealed into the hut by his own hand, his buttocks raw from ceaseless zazen, and so sick that he was coughing blood, the twenty-five-year-old son of a samurai saw in a flash that all his suffering had been needless, that what he later called the "unborn buddha-mind of illuminative wisdom" is ours by birthright, never wanting. Not long thereafter, Bankei began to preach this Dharma far and wide, hoping to spare others such exertions as he had endured. So great was the passion and ingenuity of his teaching, so plain and welcome his message, that people of all backgrounds thronged to hear him, and late in his life, he became unquestionably the most popular Zen master of his day.

In many respects, Bankei's path paralleled that of Bassui, who preceded him in popularizing Zen by three hundred years, but he traveled that path from first to last with an even greater determination, bordering on ferocity. After the premature death of his father, ten-year-old Bankei encountered in school a Confucian passage that ignited his search. "The way of great learning lies in clarifying bright virtue," he read in an assigned text, yet no one could tell him what bright virtue was—not to his satisfaction, anyway. He pursued this question so obsessively that he gave little attention to anything else and was booted out of the family house for his disobedience at the age of eleven. Whatever other effects it had, banishment from home gave Bankei the liberty to intensify his inquiry, and during the next five years, besides puzzling over bright virtue on his own, he sought guidance at the local Pure Land and Shingon temples. At sixteen, he went twenty miles on foot to meet Umpo Zenjō, an elderly teacher of the Ō-tō-kan line, whom he promptly asked to ordain and instruct him.

Three years of close study with this fine master and four years of rigorous pilgrimage, visiting teachers from Kyoto to Kyushu, brought Bankei no peace. "It's your desire to find someone that keeps you from your goal," Umpo told him on his return, and this pointer prompted the two-year stretch of solitary, ascetic practice that culminated in his illness and initial experience of the Unborn. Though Umpo confirmed his fiery young student's opening, he sent him off for further testing, first to the premier Japanese master of the day—Shidō Munan's teacher, Gudō—and then, since Gudō proved unavailable, to a visiting Chinese master, Tao-che Ch'ao-yüan (1600?–1661?).

Although Japan remained closed to foreigners, the shogunate had permitted an exception for the southern port city of Nagasaki, making it a magnet not only for commerce but also for international contacts of other kinds, including religious study. Tao-che and other Ch'an masters and monks were drawn there from China, while enterprising students and patrons of Zen gravitated to Nagasaki's temples from other parts of Japan. Bankei entered the big leagues apparently unfazed. By both his own testimony and Tao-che's, within a year he had won the full approval of the Chinese master, the only Japanese monk reported to have done so. Rivalry subsequently made life in Nagasaki untenable first for Bankei and then for Tao-che as well, and though Bankei absented himself to reduce tensions and lobbied later on his teacher's behalf, the situation could not be salvaged. Both men quit the city, Tao-che ultimately returning to China just eight years after he had left it.

Meanwhile, Umpo had died, directing his immediate successor to equip Bankei with a document of Dharma-transmission and "push him out in the world" to carry the banner of Zen. This deathbed mandate was carried out in 1657, but Umpo need not have worried. Bankei does not seem to have been predisposed to self-concealment. He had, in fact, begun teaching shortly after getting Tao-che's sanction, and the formal seal of succession mainly had the effect of legitimating him with the Rinzai hierarchy. Shortly after he received transmission, Myōshin-ji summoned him to teach, and fifteen years later, he returned by imperial appointment to preside as the great monastery's chief abbot.

Bankei accepted these honors but manifested little patience for, or interest in, the traditional institutions and methods of his sect. He spent the latter half of his life traveling around the country—"I'll go anywhere I'm asked," he declared—building an association of some fifty temples where he taught a brand of Zen very much his own. Like Bassui, he developed a radically simplified form of practice, but his approach differed from Bassui's and from the koan study of mainstream Rinzai in stressing understanding and belief rather than a personal breakthrough to awakening. Deep and difficult inquiry into "Who hears?" or more conventional koan study was unnecessary, Bankei taught. "You can grasp your buddhaminds very easily, right where you sit, without that long, painstaking practice." Hearing him preach the truth of the Unborn even once, he crowed, was all it took for some people, changing their lives literally overnight.

Accordingly, the massive retreats that he conducted in his last decade and a half, centered on his lectures rather than on sitting in zazen or wrestling with a koan. Bankei allowed as much as six hours a day of zazen if participants elected it, but he flatly rejected a monastic-style regimen of group sitting: "Around here, if people have something to do while they're sitting, they're free to get up and do it. It's up to them, whatever they've a mind to do. . . . They aren't bound by any set rules." Further, he professed no concern about what practice retreat participants maintained—or whether they did any practice at all:

I won't tell you that you have to practice such and such, that you have to uphold certain rules or precepts or read certain sutras or other Zen writings, or that you have to do zazen. . . . If you want to recite sutras or do zazen, observe precepts, recite the *Nembutsu* or the *Daimoku* [the mantra of the Nichiren sect], you should do it. If you're a farmer or a tradesman and you want to work your farm or your business, then go ahead, do it; whatever it is, that will be your personal *samadhi*.

The extraordinary catholicity of Bankei's attitude attracted members of all the Buddhist sects active in Japan, Sōtō and Rinzai practitioners attending retreats alongside laypeople and clerics of the Tendai, Shingon, Nichiren, and Pure Land traditions.

Bankei prided himself on offering an unprecedented presentation of the Unborn, and though no one disputes his creativity, he seems to have developed an exaggerated sense of his own originality. Both Bassui and Umpo anticipated his teaching style, interacting with their students in what the latter called "the direct method of the buddhas and ancestors, without the indiscriminate use of koans." Bankei described his technique in similar but, characteristically, somewhat more extreme terms: "All I do is comment directly on people themselves. That takes care of everything. I don't have to quote other people. So you won't find me saying anything about either the 'Buddha-Dharma' or the 'Zen Dharma.'" In the same vein, he rejected use of Chinese, offering instruction strictly in the vernacular. He made no effort to set his teaching down on paper and forbade others to do so, but a few disciples found the will and means to make notes on his talks and exchanges, thus preserving a record of his vivid words.

Toward the end of his life, Bankei's fame had grown to such proportions that he was awarded an imperial title and drew several thousand people to open retreats, some coming from as far away as Okinawa. He named several successors but none, apparently, with a charisma equal to his, and his lineage did not last. Fifty years after his first imperial title, he was posthumously promoted to the status of national teacher, but thereafter he faded into obscurity. He would have no currency today except that in the 1940s, D.T. Suzuki rescued him from what translator Norman Waddell terms "two and a half centuries of near total neglect." ❈

FROM THE RECORDS OF BANKEI

What I teach everyone in these talks of mine is the unborn buddha-mind of illuminative wisdom, nothing else. Everyone is endowed with this buddha-mind, only they don't know it. My reason for coming and speaking to you like this is to make it known to you.

Well then, what does it mean, you're endowed with a buddha-mind? Each of you now present decided to come here from your home in the desire to hear what

I have to say. Now if a dog barked beyond the temple walls while you're listening to me, you'd hear it and know it was a dog barking. If a crow cawed, you'd hear it and know it was a crow. You'd hear an adult's voice as an adult's and a child's as a child's. You didn't come here in order to hear a dog bark, a crow caw, or any of the other sounds which might come from outside the temple during my talk. Yet while you're here, you'd hear those sounds. Your eyes see and distinguish reds and whites and other colors and your nose can tell good smells from bad. You could have had no way of knowing beforehand of any of the sights, sounds, or smells you might encounter at this meeting, yet you're able nevertheless to recognize these unforeseen sights and sounds as you encounter them, without premeditation. That's because you're seeing and hearing in the Unborn.

That you do see and hear and smell in this way without giving rise to the *thought* that you will is the proof that this inherent buddha-mind is unborn and possessed of a wonderful illuminative wisdom. The Unborn manifests itself in the thought "I want to see" or "I want to hear" not being born. When a dog howls, even if ten million people said in chorus that it was the sound of a crow crying, I doubt if you'd be convinced. It's highly unlikely there would be any way they could delude you into believing what they said. That's owing to the marvelous awareness and unbornness of your buddha-mind. The reason I say it's in the "Unborn" that you see and hear in this way is because the mind doesn't give "birth" to any thought or inclination to see or hear. Therefore it is *un-born*. Being Unborn, it's also undying: It's not possible for what is not born to perish. This is the sense in which I say that all people have an unborn buddha-mind.

Each and every Buddha and bodhisattva in the universe, and everyone in this world of humans as well, has been endowed with it. But being ignorant of the fact that you have a buddha-mind, you live in illusion. Why is it you're deluded? Because you're partial to yourself. What does that mean? Well, let's take something close to home. Suppose you heard that your next-door neighbor was whispering bad things about you. You'd get angry. Every time you saw his face, you'd immediately feel indignant. You'd think, oh, what an unreasonable, hateful person! And everything he said would appear to you in a bad light. All because you're wedded to your self. By becoming angry, losing your temper, you just transform your one buddha-mind into the sinful existence of the fighting spirits.

If your neighbor praised you instead, or said something that pleased you, you'd be immediately delighted, even if the praise was totally undeserving and the pleasure you felt unfounded, a product of your own wishful thinking. The delight you experience when this happens is due to that same obstinate, constitutional preference to yourself.

Just stop and look back to the origin of this self of yours. When you were born, your parents didn't give you any happy, evil, or bitter thoughts. There was only your buddha-mind. Afterwards, when your intelligence appeared, you saw and heard other people saying and doing bad things, and you learned them and made them yours. By the time you reached adulthood, deep-set habits, formed in this way of your own manufacture, emerged. Now, cherishing yourself and your own ideas, you turn your buddha-mind into the path of fighting spirits. If you covet what belongs to other people, kindling selfish desires for something that can never be yours, you create the path of hungry ghosts, and you change the buddha-mind into that kind of existence. This is what is known as [rebirth].

If you realize fully the meaning of what I've just said, and do not lose your temper, or think you must have this, or decide that you don't like that, or have feelings of bitterness or pity—that in itself is the unborn buddha-mind. You'll be a living Buddha.

Be sure, then, that you don't go brewing up a lot of unnecessary thoughts in your heads. Make up your minds that you're never going to revolve in the wheel of existence. Don't forget, if you miss the chance to become Buddhas in this life, you won't be born into the human world again, and get another chance, for millions of ages. By all means, then you want to confirm yourselves in the unborn buddha-mind now, and keep yourself free of illusion. When you've done that, the men will live undeluded in their men's buddha-minds, and the women in their women's buddha-minds—you'll all be Buddhas. Enlightened Buddhas.

And while we're on the subject of women's buddha-minds, I know there are many women who are deeply troubled by the people who say that they're cut off from buddhahood just because they're women.[1] Nothing could be farther from the truth. I'm addressing the women here now, so listen carefully. How could women be any different from men in this? Men are buddha-beings. Women are too. You needn't doubt it for a moment. Once you've got the principle of this Unborn fixed in your minds, you're Unborn whether you're a man or woman. Men and women are not the same in appearance. We all know that. But there's not a whisker of difference between them when it comes to their buddha-minds. So don't be deluded by outward appearances.

Here's something that will prove to you that the buddha-mind is the same in men and women. There are a lot of people gathered here. Now suppose that outside the temple walls someone started to beat on a drum or strike a bell. When you heard those sounds, would the women here mistake the drumbeat for the bell, or the bell for the drumbeat? No. As far as hearing those sounds is concerned, no difference exists between men and women. It's not only true of men and women, there are people of all kinds in this hall: old people and young,

1. This idea derives originally from Indian Buddhism. In India, where the social position of women was low, the idea developed that women were unable to attain salvation as women; they had first to assume the body of a man. Although later, the Mahāyāna teaching that all beings possess the buddha-nature allowed to women the possibility of attaining buddhahood, the earlier notion did not completely die out. It is even seen in parts of the written Buddhist canon, from which, perhaps, the idea found its way into Japan.

priests and laity, and so on. But there wouldn't be any difference in the way that a young person, or a monk, or a layman heard the sounds either. The place in which there's no difference in the hearing of those sounds is the Unborn, the buddha-mind, and it's perfectly equal and absolutely the same in each one of you. When we say "This is a man," or "This is a woman," those are designations that result from the arising of thought. They come afterward. At the place of the Unborn, before the thought arises, attributes such as "man" or "woman" don't even exist. That should make it clear that there's no distinction between men's buddha-minds and women's. There's no reason, then, to doubt about women having buddha-minds.

You see, you are always unborn. You go along living in the buddha-mind quite unconscious of being a man or woman. But while you are doing that, perhaps you'll happen to see or hear something that bothers you, perhaps someone will make a nasty remark about you, saying they don't like you, or whatever. You let your mind fasten onto that, you begin to fret over it, and thoughts crowd into your mind. You may feel that you want something, or you may feel unhappy, and yet if you don't allow this to lead you astray, into thinking that it can't be helped *because you're only a woman,* then you will be able to gain a strong confirmation of the Unborn. Then you yourself are a Buddha, of the same substance not only as other men and women but also as all Buddhas of the past and future.

While you're walking down a road, if you happen to encounter a crowd of people approaching from the opposite direction, none of you gives a thought to avoiding the others, yet you don't run into one another. You aren't pushed down or walked over. You thread your way through them by weaving this way and that, dodging and passing on, making no conscious decisions in this, yet you're able to continue along unhampered just the same. Now in the same way, the marvelous illumination of the unborn buddha-mind deals perfectly with every possible situation.

Suppose that the idea to step aside and make way for the others should arise spontaneously in your mind before you actually moved aside—that too would be due to the working of the buddha-mind's illuminative wisdom. You may step aside to the right or to the left because you have made up your mind to do that, but still, the movement of your feet, one step after another, doesn't occur because you think to do it. When you're walking along naturally, you're walking in the harmony of the Unborn.

A layman: Every time I clear a thought from my mind, another appears right away. Thoughts keep appearing like that without end. What can I do about them?

Bankei: Clearing thoughts from the mind as they arise is like washing away blood in blood. You may succeed in washing away the original blood, but you're still polluted by the blood you washed in. No matter how long you keep washing, the bloodstains never disappear. Since you don't know that your mind is originally unborn and undying and free of illusion, you think that your thoughts really exist, so you transmigrate in the wheel of existence. You have to realize that your thoughts are ephemeral and unreal and, without either clutching at them or rejecting them, just let them come and go of themselves. They're like images reflected in a mirror. A mirror is clear and bright and reflects whatever is placed before it. But the image doesn't remain in the mirror. The buddha-mind is ten thousand times brighter than any mirror and is marvelously illuminative besides. All thoughts vanish tracelessly into its light.

A monk: It took much hard practice for the great Zen masters of the past to penetrate great enlightenment so deeply. From what I have heard, your own realization also came only after many hardships. Someone like me, who hasn't engaged in any practice or arrived at any enlightenment, couldn't possibly achieve true peace of mind simply by perceiving the necessity of living in the unborn buddha-mind and staying just as I am.

Bankei: It's like this. A group of travelers, climbing through a stretch of high mountains, gets thirsty, and one of them strikes out and makes his way far down into the valley to fetch water. It's not easy, but he finally finds some and brings it back and gives his companions a drink. Don't those who drink without having exerted themselves quench their thirst the same as the one who did? Now, if a person refused to drink the water because he felt that doing it was wrong, there wouldn't be any way to quench his thirst.

My own struggle was undertaken mistakenly, because I didn't happen to meet up with a clear-eyed master. Eventually, though, I discovered the buddha-mind for myself; ever since, I have been telling others about theirs, so they'll know about it without going through that ordeal, just as those people drink water and quench their thirst without having to go and find it for themselves. So you see, everyone *can* use the innate buddha-mind just as it is and achieve a troublefree peace of mind, without resorting to any misguided austerities. Don't you think that is an invaluable teaching?

A layman: I don't question that there are no illusory thoughts in the primary mind, but just the same, there's no let-up to the thoughts that keep coming into my mind. I find it impossible to stay in the Unborn.

Bankei: Although you arrived in the world with nothing but the unborn buddha-mind, you fell into your present deluded ways as you were growing up, by watching and listening to other people in their delusion. You picked all this up gradually, over a long period of time, habituating your mind to it, until now your deluded mind has taken over completely and works its delusion unchecked. But none of those deluded thoughts of yours was inborn. They weren't there from the start. They cease to exist in a mind that's affirming the Unborn.

It's like a sake-lover who has contracted an illness that forces him to give up drinking. He still thinks about it. Thoughts about having a few drinks still enter his mind whenever he has a chance to get his hands on some sake. But since he abstains from drinking it, his illness isn't affected and he doesn't get drunk. He stays away from it despite the thoughts that arise in his mind, and eventually he becomes a healthy man, cured of his illness. Illusory thoughts are no different. If you just let them come and let them go away, and don't put them to work or try to avoid them, then one day you'll find that they've vanished completely into the Unborn mind.

A monk: I have great difficulty subduing all the desires and deluded thoughts in my mind. What should I do?

Bankei: The idea to subdue deluded thoughts is a deluded thought itself. None of those thoughts exist from the start. You conjure them up out of your own discriminations.

A monk: I've been working on "Pai-chang's Fox" for a long time.[2] I've concentrated on it as hard as I know how, but I still can't seem to grasp it. I think it's because I'm unable to achieve total concentration. If possible, I would like to receive your teaching.

Bankei: I don't make people here waste their time on worthless old documents like that. You don't know yet about your unborn buddha-mind and its illuminative wisdom, so I'll tell you about it. That will take care of everything. Pay careful attention.

Bankei then taught him about the Unborn. The monk was completely convinced. He is said to have developed into an exceptional priest.

Another monk (who had been listening to this): If that's true, what about all the old koans? Are they useless and unnecessary?

Bankei: When worthy Zen masters of the past dealt with those who came to them, every word and every movement was appropriate to the moment. It was a matter of responding to their students and their questions face to face. They had no other purpose in mind. Now there's no way for me to tell you whether that was necessary, or helpful, or not. If everyone just stays in the buddha-mind, that's all they have to do—that takes care of everything. Why do you want to go and think up other things to do? There's no need to. Just dwell in the Unborn. You're eager to make this extra work for yourself—but all you're doing is creating illusion. Stop doing that. Stay in the Unborn. The Unborn and its marvelous illumination are perfectly realized in the buddha-mind.

---

2. "Pai-chang's Fox" is a famous koan, found in the popular koan collection *Mumonkan* (Ch., *Wumen kuan*), case 2.

42

Bashō

(1644–1694)

In 1483, the Japanese monk and literatus Ten'in Ryūtaku characterized the relationship of Zen and poetry in the most definite terms, writing that "Outside
of poetry there is no Zen, outside of Zen there is no poetry." This formulation
was original only in its absoluteness, for poets and critics of both China and
Japan had observed and explored relationships between the two fields of endeavor centuries before Ten'in wrote. His words signal, however, that the energy
of the Zen-poetry fusion had not been exhausted and that it would carry Japanese writers to new horizons in centuries to come.

No one exemplifies these later developments better than Matsuo Bashō.
When Ishikawa Jozan retired, shortly before Bashō's birth, it was still uncom-
mon to do as he did—to devote oneself fulltime to composing poems and to
training disciples in that art. By the time Bashō reached maturity, however, poetry writing had come into its own as a "way," much like the other disciplines
with which Zen was associated. Taught by independent poetry masters, students
entered into it with great seriousness as a means not just of learning how to
churn out good verse but also of refining their characters and deepening their
understanding of the world. While Chinese-language poems continued to be
produced, the cultural momentum had long since shifted to Japanese, and a native form of light, linked verse known as *haikai* had become particularly popular.
Groups of people all over the country, from villagers in the hinterlands to
courtiers in the capital, wrote *haikai* as a social activity, taking turns at improvis-
ing lines in keeping with a set of formal requirements. The first verses of such poems had to have seventeen syllables and, written independently, developed into
the new form for which Bashō became famous, the haiku.

Bashō began his literary training under the guidance of his father, a samurai
by family background but a writing teacher by necessity or inclination. Perhaps
because he displayed an early talent, at nine Bashō was selected to enter the service of the local lord as a page and, more specifically, as companion to the family
heir, a boy just two years older than he who was passionately interested in literature. In those fortunate circumstances, Bashō received instruction in poetics
from a noted *haikai* master while still no more than a teenager. Both he and his
master became adept at the form and published their first work while they were
still in their early twenties. When the young lord died tragically in 1666, Bashō

abandoned both his position and his native province in favor of Kyoto, where for the next five years or so he broadened his education in literature and the ways of the world.

Not until his early thirties, after a move to Edo, did Bashō establish himself as a *haikai* master or, as far as we know, undertake formal Zen study. He rapidly achieved success as a professional poet, publishing very actively and attracting both students and patrons. In 1680, one of the latter built him a hermitage called Bashō-an in honor of a banana tree on its grounds, and the poetry master took his pen name from this plant, which he loved for its beauty and especially "for its very uselessness." He wrote, "the tree does bear flowers, but unlike other flowers, there is nothing gay about them," nor would the tree set fruit in such a northerly locale. Further, "the big trunk of the tree is untouched by the axe, for it is utterly useless as building wood." Ch'an had long before adopted this theme of perfect inutility from Taoism as an expression of the unconditioned—that which stands free of cause and effect. It was a quality he saw in his own writing, too: "My poetry is like a [heating] stove in summer or a fan in winter. It runs against the popular tastes and has no practical use."

As for Zen per se, by his own account Bashō studied with the Edo-area Rinzai master Butchō (1643–1715). How long this lasted or what results it had Bashō chose not to say, but many have conjectured that this turning point both in poetry and Zen came with his most famous haiku, written at the age of forty:

> The old pond,
> a frog jumps in—
> sound of the water!

A century later, Hakuin painted a portrait of Bashō doing zazen, inscribing it, "A linked-verse poet skilled at haiku heard a frog jump into a well and dropped off body and mind"—that is, awakened to emptiness. Zen master and painter Sengai Gibon (1750–1837) took the matter another turn, depicting a frog sitting beneath a banana tree and adding a haiku that, with his trademark humor, neatly seconds Hakuin's point:

> The old pond,
> Bashō jumped in—
> sound of the water!

Whether or not the old pond haiku was actually an enlightenment verse is less important than the fact that, from this time onward, he frequently referred to Zen in his work and plainly was deeply influenced by his training with Butchō. It is hard to imagine that without such meaningful exposure to Zen he would have stated his poetic method as he did:

> Go to the pine if you want to learn about the pine, or to the bamboo if you want
> to learn about the bamboo. And in doing so, you must leave your subjective pre-
> occupation with yourself. Otherwise you impose yourself on the object and do

not learn. Your poetry issues of its own accord when you and the object have become one—when you have plunged deep enough into the object to see something like a hidden glimmering there. However well-phrased your poetry may be,
if your feeling is not natural—if the object and yourself are separate—then your
poetry is not true poetry but merely your subjective counterfeit.

Though he wore black robes and looked the part of a monk, Bashō regarded
himself like his great forerunners among the Chinese poets as "neither priest nor
layman" and compared himself to a bat—neither "bird nor rat but something in
between." During his Kyoto years, he is said to have had a long-term liaison with
a woman named Juteini, but he never married or fathered children, either living
alone or in the company of his disciples and fellow poets.

In his fifth and final decade, spent largely on the road or in temporary quarters, he seems to have found an identity he could claim without reservation:

> Traveler
> you can call me—
> first rain of winter

Later, he noted that he had "considered entering the precincts of the Buddha and
the teaching room of the ancestors. Instead, I've worn out my body in journeys as
aimless as those of the winds and clouds, expending my feelings on flowers and
birds." Taking this purposeless path, he made clear, was following consciously in
the footsteps of other Buddhist pilgrim-poets, both Chinese and Japanese.

English readers have been taught to associate Bashō with haiku, which
grossly distorts his accomplishments. Though he perfected that form and
though many of his haiku succeed handily on their own merits, his mature work
consists mainly of considerably longer pieces, either linked verses written col-
laboratively with other poets or travelogues, in which he alternates prose passages with haiku. In both cases, the whole is much more than the sum of its parts.
A travelogue like his masterpiece the *Narrow Road to the Interior* treats readers
to an extended tour through a landscape simultaneously physical, emotional,
historical, and cultural, especially literary and religious. The journey proceeds
temporally from spring to fall, chronicling the weather, wildlife, and human activities associated with the seasons, but at the same time it roves back and forth
across the ages, evoking the transience of life but also the enormous vitality of
the ancient—the survival of the past in immediate phenomena.

In this and other works, Bashō probes and reveals his heart and mind—reveals them as at once particular to him and common to his people. Immersed in
his surroundings and in the Japanese heritage, in a very real sense he walked the
backcountry as the awareness of Japan itself, treading down illusory boundaries
of inside and outside, self and other. He evoked the national experience deliberately through extensive and artful placement of allusions, sometimes bending
the facts of his trip to touch on things, events, or places that he deemed important. In Bashō's work, as one of his translators observes, "Allusions are everywhere, often in single words" but unlike Ikkyū, he did not deal in obscure or

specialized knowledge. His allusions "were expected to be grasped at once by any likely reader of that time." With the help of explanatory notes, those of us coming to his words across a great gulf of time and culture have a chance to glimpse the richness of his writing, and to discover that his heart and mind are ours as well—ultimately timeless and universal.

Bashō undertook the journeys of his last years despite a chronic disease of unknown nature, so it was not mere hyperbole when he wrote, at the outset of one trip, that he had resolved to bleach his bones on the moors. As a celebrated poet, he received an enthusiastic welcome and ample hospitality in all except the most remote spots. Hard travel still took a heavy toll on him, and he died at fifty in Osaka, en route to southern Japan. His last poem reaps the harvest of illness itself:

> Sick in mid journey—
> my dreams keep meandering
> dry fields of fall

Bashō's condition worsened after he completed this haiku, and four days later, with death impending, the students attending him asked for a *yuige*, a deathbed poem. The non-monk, non-layman rose to the occasion, refusing brush and paper with the explanation—the teaching—that each poem he had written since the age of forty had been his *yuige*. 𐤀

FROM NARROW ROAD TO THE INTERIOR

In a mountain hermitage near Ungan Temple, my Dharma Master Butchō wrote:

> A five-foot thatched hut:
> I wouldn't even put it up
> but for the falling rain

He inscribed the poem on a rock with charcoal—he told me long ago. Curious, several young people joined in, walking sticks pointed toward Ungan Temple. We were so caught up in talking we arrived at the temple unexpectedly. Through the long valley, under dense cedar and pine with dripping moss, below a cold spring sky—through the viewing gardens, we crossed a bridge and entered the temple gate.

I searched out back for Butchō's hermitage and found it up the hill, near a cave on a rocky ridge—like the cave where Miao Ch'an-shih lived for fifteen years, like Ch'an master Fa-yün's retreat.[1]

> Even woodpeckers leave it alone:
> a hermitage
> in a summer grove

One small poem, quickly written, pinned to a post.

1. Miao Ch'an-shih [Kao-feng Yüan-miao] and Fa-yün were Ch'an masters famed for their asceticism.

Set out to see the Murder Stone, Sesshō-seki, on a borrowed horse, and the man leading it asked for a poem, "Something beautiful, please."

> The horse lifts his head:
> from across deep fields
> the cuckoo's cry

Sesshō-seki lies in dark mountain shadow near a hot springs emitting bad gases. Dead bees and butterflies cover the sand.

At Ashino, the willow Saigyō[2] praised, "beside the crystal stream," still grows along a path in fields of rice. A local official had offered to lead the way, and I had often wondered whether and where it remained. And now, today, that same willow:

> Girls' rice-planting done
> they depart:
> I emerge from willow-shade

A little anxious, thinking of the Shirakawa Barrier, thinking on it day by day, but calmed my mind by remembering the old poem, "somehow sending word home." I walked through heavy green summer forests. Many a poet inscribed a few words at one of the Three Barriers—"autumn winds" and "red maple leaves" come to mind.[3] Then, like fields of snow, innumerable white-flowered bushes, *unohana,* covered either side of the road. Here, Kiyosuke wrote,[4] people dressed their very best to pass through the mountain gate, men in small black formal hats as though dressed for the highest courts. Sora wrote:

> *Unohana*
> around my head
> dressed for ancient rites

Over the pass, we crossed the Abukuma River, Mount Aizu to the left, the villages of Iwaki, Sōma, and Miharu on the right, divided from the villages of Hitachi and Shimotsuke by two small mountain ranges. At Kagenuma, the Mirror Pond, a dark sky blurred every reflection.

We spent several days in Sukagawa with the poet Tōkyū, who asked about the Shirakawa Barrier. "With mind and body sorely tested," I answered, "busy with other poets' lines, engaged in splendid scenery, it's hardly surprising I didn't write much":

2. [Saigyō (1118–1190), a wandering poet-priest of the Shingon Sect, was an inspiration and fore-runner for Bashō.—Eds.]

3. The phrases "autumn winds" and "red maple leaves" refer to poems by Nōin and Yorimasa, both influences on Saigyō.

4. Kiyosuke (1104–1177) was a Heian-period poet.

Culture's beginnings:
from the heart of the country
rice-planting songs

"From this opening verse," I told him, "we wrote three linked-verse poems."

Staying the night in Iizuka, we bathed in a mineral hot springs before returning to thin straw sleeping mats on bare ground—a true country inn. Without a lamp, we made our beds by firelight, in flickering shadows, and closed our tired eyes. Suddenly a thunderous downpour and leaky roof aroused us, fleas and mosquitoes everywhere. Old infirmities tortured me throughout the long, sleepless night.

At first light, long before dawn, we packed our things and left, distracted, tired, but moving on. Sick and worried, we hired horses to ride to the town of Kori. I worried about my plans. With every pilgrimage one encounters the temporality of life. To die along the road is destiny. Or so I told myself. I stiffened my will and, once resolute, crossed Ōkido Barrier in Date Province.

Through narrow Abumizuri Pass and on, passing Shiroishi Castle, we entered Kasashima Province. We asked for directions to the gravemound of Lord Sanekata, Sei Shonagon's exiled poet-lover,[5] and were told to turn right on the hills near the villages of Minowa and Kasashima when we came to the Shrine of Dōsojin. It lies nearly hidden in sedge grass Saigyō remembered in a poem. May rains turned the trail to mud. We stopped, sick and worn out, and looked at the two aptly named villages in the distance: Straw Raincoat Village and Umbrella Island.

Where's Kasashima?
Lost on a muddy road
in the rainy season

The night was spent in Iwanuma.

Deeply touched by the famous pine at Takekuma, twin trunks just as long ago. The poet-priest Nōin came to mind. Before he came, Lord Fujiwara-no-Takayoshi cut down the tree for lumber, building a bridge across the Natori-gawa. Nōin wrote: "No sign here now of that famous pine." Reported to have been cut down and replaced several times, it stood like a relic of a thousand years, impossibly perfect. The poet Kyohaku had given me a poem at my departure:

Remember to show my master
the famous Takekuma pine,
O northern blossoming cherries

5. The story of Lord Sanekata is told in *The Pillow Book of Sei Shonagon.*

To which I now reply:

> Ever since cherry blossom time
> I longed to visit two-trunked pine:
> three long months have passed

Rose at dawn to pay respects at Myōjin Shrine in Shiogama. The former governor rebuilt it with huge, stately pillars, bright-painted rafters, and a long stone walkway rising steeply under a morning sun that danced and flashed along the red lacquered fence. I thought, "As long as the road is, even if it ends in dust, the gods come with us, keeping a watchful eye. This is our culture's greatest gift." Kneeling at the shrine, I noticed a fine old lantern with this inscribed on its iron grate:

> In the Third Year of the Bunji Era [1187]
> Dedicated by Izumi Saburō

Suddenly, five long centuries passed before my eyes. A trusted, loyal man martyred by his brother; today there's not a man alive who doesn't revere his name. As he himself would say, a man must follow the Confucian model—renown will inevitably result.

Sun high overhead before we left the shrine, we hired a boat to cross to Matsushima, a mile or more away. We disembarked on Ojima Beach.

As many others often observed, the views of Matsushima take one's breath away. It may be—along with Lake Tung-t'ing and West Lake in China—the most beautiful place in the world. Islands in a three-mile bay, the sea to the southeast entering like floodtide on the Ch'ien-t'ang River in Chekiang. Small islands, tall islands pointing at the sky, islands on top of islands, islands like mothers with baby islands on their backs, islands cradling islands in the bay. All covered with deep green pines shaped by salty winds, trained into sea-wind bonsai. Here one is almost overcome by the sense of intense feminine beauty in a shining world. It must have been the mountain god Ōyamazumi who made this place. And whose words or brush could adequately describe a world so divinely inspired?

Ojima beach is not—as its name implies—an island, but a strand projected into the bay. Here one finds the ruins of Ungo Zenji's hermitage and the rock where he sat zazen.[6] And still a few tiny thatched huts under pines where religious hermits live in tranquillity. Smoke of burning leaves and pine cones drew me on, touching something deep inside. Then the moon rose, shining on the sea, day turned suddenly to night. We stayed at an inn on the shore, our second-story windows opening on the bay. Drifting with winds and clouds, it was almost like a dream. Sora wrote:

6. Ungo Zenji (1583–1659) was a famous monk.

In Matsushima
you'll need the wings of a crane
little cuckoo

On the eleventh day, fifth moon, we visited Zuigan Temple and were met by the
thirty-second-generation descendant of the founder. Established by Makabe-no-
Heishiro at the time he returned from religious studies in T'ang China, the temple was enlarged under Ungo Zenji into seven main structures with new blue tile
roofs, walls of gold, a jeweled Buddha-land. But my mind wandered, wondering
if the priest Kembutsu's tiny temple might be found.[7]

Early morning of the twelfth day, fifth moon. We started out for Hiraizumi, intending to go by way of the famous Aneha Pine and the Odae Bridge. The trail
was narrow and little-traveled—only the occasional woodcutter or hunter. We
took a wrong road and ended up in the port town of Ishinomaki on a broad bay
with Mount Kinka in the distance. Yakamochi has a poem for the emperor in the
Man'yōshū saying Kinka's "where gold blossoms."[8] It rises across water cluttered
with cargo boats and fishing boats, shoreline packed with houses, smoke rising
from their stoves. Our unplanned visit prompted an immediate search for lodging. No one made an offer. Spent the night in a cold shack and left again at day-
break, following unknown paths. We passed near the Sode Ferry, Obuchi
Meadow, and the Mano Moor—all made famous in poems. After crossing a long
miserable marsh, we stayed at Toima, pushing on to Hiraizumi in the morning.
An arduous trek of more than forty difficult miles in two days.

Here three generations of the Fujiwara clan passed as though in a dream.
The great outer gates lay in ruins. Where Hidehira's manor stood, rice fields
grew. Only Mount Kinkei remained. I climbed the hill where Yoshitsune died; I
saw the Kitakami, a broad stream flowing down through the Nambu Plain, the
Koromo River circling Izumi Castle below the hill before joining the Kitakami.
The ancient ruins of Yasuhira—from the end of the Golden Era—lie out beyond
the Koromo Barrier where they stood guard against the Ainu people. The faithful elite remained bound to the castle, for all their valor, reduced to ordinary
grass. Tu Fu wrote:

The whole country devastated,
only mountains and rivers remain.
In springtime, at the ruined castle,
the grass is always green.

We sat awhile, our hats for a seat, seeing it all through tears.

7. Kembutsu was a famous twelfth-century priest whom Saigyō visited in Matsushima.
8. The *Man'yōshū* (*Collection of Ten Thousand Leaves*) is the first imperial anthology of poetry and
was compiled in the eighth century.

> Summer grasses:
> all that remains of great soldiers'
> imperial dreams

Two temple halls I longed to see were finally opened at Chuson Temple. In the Sutra Library, Kyōdō, statues of the three generals of Hiraizumi; and in the Hall of Light, Hikaridō, their coffins and images of three buddhas. It would have all fallen down, jeweled doors battered by winds, gold pillars cracked by cold, all would have gone to grass, but added outer roof and walls protect it. Through the endless winds and rains of a thousand years, this great hall remains.

> Fifth-month rains hammer
> and blow but never quite touch
> Hikaridō

The road through the Nambu Plain visible in the distance, we stayed the night in Iwate, then trudged on past Cape Oguro and Mizu Island, both along the river. Beyond Narugo Hot Springs, we crossed Shitomae Barrier and entered Dewa Province. Almost no one comes this way, and the barrier guards were suspicious, slow, and thorough. Delayed, we climbed a steep mountain in falling dark and took refuge in a guard shack. A heavy storm pounded the shack with wind and rain for three miserable days.

> Eaten alive by lice and fleas
> now the horse
> beside my pillow pees

Today we came through places with names like Children-Desert-Parents, Lost Children, Send-Back-the-Dog, and Turn-Back-the-Horse—some of the most fearsomely dangerous places in all the North Country. And well named. Weakened and exhausted, I went to bed early but was roused by the voices of two young women in the room next door. Then an old man's voice joined theirs. They were prostitutes from Niigata in Echigo Province and were on their way to Ise Shrine in the south, the old man seeing them off at this barrier, Ichiburi. He would turn back to Niigata in the morning, carrying their letters home. One girl quoted the *Shinkokinshū* poem, "On the beach where white waves fall, / we all wander like children into every circumstance, / carried forward every day. . . . "[9] And as they bemoaned their fate in life, I fell asleep.

In the morning, preparing to leave, they came to ask directions. "May we follow along behind?" they asked. "We're lost and not a little fearful. Your robes bring the spirit of the Buddha to our journey." They had mistaken us for priests.

9. The *Shinkokinshū* is the eighth imperial anthology of "new and old poems," and the primary source for Bashō's study of Saigyō's poetry.

"Our way includes detours and retreats," I told them. "But follow anyone on this road, and the gods will see you through." I hated to leave them in tears and thought about them hard for a long time after we left. I told Sora, and he wrote down:

> Under one roof, prostitute and priest,
> we all sleep together:
> moon in a field of clover

43

Baisaō

(1675–1763)

Like Bashō, Baisaō described himself as a bat, but they were bats of different species. For sixty of his eighty-eight years, Baisaō was a monk of the Ōbaku sect, the third and last of the Ch'an traditions successfully established in Japan. Not until he quit the monkhood at seventy could he make the claim Bashō did—that he belonged neither to the secular world nor to the religious—and even then, by preference or habit, he seems to have remained at heart a monk. To the end, his poems were patently Zen poems, written mostly in Chinese and tightly linked to the Ch'an literary corpus.

The order that Baisaō entered as a boy of eleven was founded by Yin-yüan Lung-ch'i (1592–1673), an eminent master in the Yang-ch'i line of Lin-chi Ch'an. Landing in Nagasaki in 1654 with an entourage of twenty disciples and ten temple craftsmen, Yin-yüan effectively displaced his junior Dharma cousin Tao-che, Bankei's teacher, and eventually succeeded in winning warm enough support in shogunal circles to build Mampuku-ji, a major, Chinese-style monastery, near Kyoto. Some Ō-tō-kan higher-ups had hoped that this master—Ingen, as he was called in Japan—would provide the impetus to revitalize their line, but the orientations of Lin-chi Ch'an and Rinzai Zen had so diverged that neither Ingen and his party nor Gudō and other influential Rinzai masters could see their way to unity. Thus, going its own way, Ingen's line emerged as a separate sect, absorbing dissatisfied Sōtō and Rinzai monks, among others.

Apart from one visit to Mampuku-ji shortly after joining the monkhood, Baisaō trained for his first decade in a small Ōbaku temple on the southern island of Kyushu, where he had been raised. At twenty-one, he left on a pilgrimage that lasted fourteen years altogether, counting several years in an Ōbaku monastery, a stretch of concentrated precept study, and one or two long periods of seclusion. He subsequently returned to serve and study with his original teacher in Kyushu and might well have become his successor, but Baisaō actively avoided that role. A friend quoted him as saying:

> In the past, when Zen master Fo-yen asked his chief monk Shih-ch'i to succeed him as head priest, Shih-ch'i refused. "It is like a physician piercing a patient's eye with his golden needle," he explained. "If his hand errs by even a hair breadth, he will blind the patient. It is better that I remain as a student and continue my training." I

always keep that story in my thoughts by way of admonishment. If I were really capable of responding freely to all students with the spontaneous means of a real Zen teacher, then I should go out into the world to help other people. But just to arm myself with a smattering of learning and strut around with my nose in the air, calling myself a Zen teacher—I would be ashamed to do that.

The death of his master left Baisaō free, at the age of forty-nine, to follow his own nose. What he did for the next eleven years remains unknown except that he headed north once again. Perhaps he studied poetry and tea, for when finally he settled in Kyoto at sixty, those were the two interests that occupied and sustained him. Though the standards of monkhood prohibited engaging in a trade, he had stepped outside the institutional structures of his sect, and to support himself, he brewed and served tea at beautiful spots around the capital city, often on temple premises. Next to his mobile teashop, which he called Tsūsentei—the shop that leads straight to the immortal sages—he set out a slotted bamboo tube and a sign requesting donations: "You may give me any amount you like for my tea, from a hundred in gold to half a *mon*. It's up to you. Have it free if you wish. I'm sorry I can't let you have it for less."

Both his sign and shop name hint that Baisaō was dispensing something else with his tea, and his poems confirm that impression. In his verses, he plays endless variations on the theme of tea and Zen, taking tea, its preparation, and its consumption as metaphors for the nature and activity of Mind. The association of tea and Zen has a lengthy pedigree of its own, going back to Bodhidharma, who is credited with introducing it into China, and to the Rinzai founder Eisai, believed to have carried it on to Japan. Ceremonially consumed in Zen monasteries as a meditation aid, tea appears in a number of Ch'an and Zen dialogues, probably the most renowned example being these flavorless words of old Chao-chou:

Once Chao-chou asked a freshly arrived monk, "Have you been here before?"

"No, I haven't," the monk answered.

"Have a cup of tea," said Chao-chou. Then he asked another monk, "Have you been here before?"

"Yes, I have," replied the monk.

"Have a cup of tea," said Chao-chou.

The head monk asked the master, "You instructed the monk who hasn't been here before to have a cup of tea; I say nothing about that. But why did you tell the monk who's been here before to have a cup of tea?"

"Head monk!" cried Chao-chou.

"Yes, master?"

"Have a cup of tea!"

Several laywomen who figure in the annals of Ch'an sold tea by the wayside, and like them, Baisaō evidently felt at liberty in this humble setting to show the Way to passersby. No question here of strutting about with his nose in the air. The tea that he poured must have been tasty, though, for his clients and friends came to include some of the nation's finest poets, painters, calligraphers, and thinkers, as well as leading Zen masters.

After a decade of this life, Baisaō arranged to continue it as a layman, and until he hit eighty, he persisted in packing his plaited-bamboo tea caddy all over town. "With a white head of hair and a beard so long it seems to reach his knees," he became a Kyoto fixture, referred to simply as the Old Tea Seller—Baisaō. A vivid, contemporary report gives a sense of his impact:

> . . . where the pebbled streams run pure and clear, he simmers his tea to offer to the people who come to enjoy these scenic places. Social rank whether high or low means nothing to him. He does not care if people pay him for his tea or not. . . . His name is now known everywhere. But no one has ever seen an expression of displeasure cross his face. He is regarded by one and all as a truly great and wonderful man.

In 1675, too decrepit to heft his equipment any longer, Baisaō retired to a stationary tea stall. When he did so, he fondly and ritually immolated his large tea caddy, which he had always called *Senka*, the Den of Sages: "I hate to think that after I die you might be defiled by falling into worldly hands. So I am eulogizing you and committing you to the Fire Samadhi. Enter forthwith amidst the flames, and undergo the Great Change." Eight years later he followed Senka into the fire, but the month before he died, ninety-eight of his Chinese-language poems were published, among them the following verses. ꕤ

IMPROMPTU

I'm confirmed in my zany ways,
Out of step with the world.
Peddling tea for a living
Goes with the natural grain.
A quiet mind and a plain life
Excels the finest luxury;
A content mind and tattered robe,
Better far than finest silk.
At dawn I dip from the well,
When I leave I carry the moon;
I shoulder my brazier at evening
And come back trailing the clouds.
This is how I've learned to live—
The life of an old tea seller—
Rambling free of material things
Beyond the clash of "pro" and "con."

FROM TEN IMPROMPTU VERSES

II

I've opened shop this time
On the banks of the Kamo.
Customers, sitting idly,
Forget host and guest.
They drink a cup of tea,
Their long sleep is over;
Awake, they then realize
They're the same as before.

LINE 2   The Kamo River runs from north to south through the center of Kyoto.

LINE 4   The Zen meaning of host and guest is also intended here.

III

I emulate old Chao-chou:
"Have a cup of tea!"
I've stock for a thousand years,
But no one's buying.
If only you would come
And take one good drink
The ancient mental craving
Would instantly cease.

FROM THREE VERSES ON CHOOSING
A LOCATION FOR A DWELLING

This aimless shifting east and west,
I even have to laugh myself.
But how else can I make
The whole world my home?
If any of my old friends
Come round asking for me,
Say I'm down at the river
By the second Fushimi Bridge.

LINE 8   This was the second of three bridges located on the busy Fushimi
Highway, near the Tofuku-ji Temple.

SETTING UP MY SHOP IN A GROVE OF TREES IN FRONT OF THE HŌJŪ-JI

In a grove of tall bamboo
Beside an ancient temple
Steam rolls from the brazier
In fragrant white clouds;
I show you the path of Sages
Beyond this floating world,
But will you understand
The lasting taste of spring?

TITLE   The Hōjū-ji was located about half a kilometer southeast of the Rengeō-in. Its wells were noted for their fine water.

IMPROMPTU, AT THE END OF THE YEAR

The years of a man's life
Spin like the wheels of a cart;
Beyond the cave of immortals
Is a world of timeless spring.
Chin-deep in the city dust
I leave no tracks or traces;
But even when I'm traceless
My presence is never concealed.

LINES 3–4   Refers to a Taoist fairyland inhabited by immortals, reached by passing through a cave.

THREE VERSES ON A TEA-SELLING LIFE

I

I'm no Buddhist or Taoist
Nor Confucianist either,
I'm a black-faced white-haired
Hard-up old man.
You think I just prowl
The streets selling tea?
I've got the whole universe
In this tea caddy of mine.

I I

When I left home at ten,
I turned from worldly fame,
Now I'm in my dotage,
A layman once again.
A black bat of a man,
A joke even to myself,
But still the old tea seller
I always was.

I I I

Seventy years of Zen—
I got nowhere at all
I shed my black robe
Became a shaggy crank.
I have no business with
The sacred or profane,
Selling tea is all I do—
It holds starvation off.

VERSE II, LINES 5–6   I suppose he means that it is hard to tell whether he is a
priest or layman; like a bat, which was thought to be neither beast nor bird but
something in between.

SETTING UP SHOP ON A SUMMER NIGHT BESIDE THE IRIS POND AT THE HALL OF A THOUSAND BUDDHAS

The iris pond has flowered
Before the old temple;
I sell tea this evening
By the water's edge.
It is steeped in the cups
With the moon and stars;
Drink and wake forever
From your worldly sleep.

FROM THREE VERSES IN PRAISE OF MYSELF

What's the tea seller
Got in his basket?

Bottomless teacups.
A two-spouted pot.
He moseys around town
Earning what he can,
Toiling very hard
For next to nothing.
Blinkered old drudge
Just plodding ahead—
     BAH!

44

Hakuin

(1685–1768)

Shidō Munan's Dharma grandson, Hakuin Ekaku, had enough talent for three people—three rather different people—and he exercised it with an abandon that seems reckless, sometimes damaging his own health. Above all, he was a follower, lover, teacher, and protector of the Way, blazing with ardor, demanding that fellow monks and masters pursue the Dharma strictly, purely, to the limit. To the folk of his province, he presented another face: warm, brimming with humor, he ministered to their needs with great empathy and flexibility. The rich and powerful experienced a third Hakuin, a man with a deep concern, more typically Confucian than Buddhist, for peaceful maintenance of the social order. In all three roles, he displayed sharp intelligence, a sensitive and passionate nature, and a wild streak of creative genius that lent sparkle to his teaching and made him a brilliant calligrapher, painter, and writer.

Like Munan's, Hakuin's family operated a post station on the Tōkaidō highway, theirs being located near Mt. Fuji, about halfway between the capitals of Kyoto and Edo. Accounts of his early years depict a boy struck by the ephemerality of clouds, terrified of falling into hell, wondrous in his powers of recall, and much taken with religious ritual. At fourteen, he began reading Buddhist texts at a Zen temple that his family had long helped support and there received, as his first Zen book, an anthology of capping phrases still used today in Rinzai koan study. His long and eventful career formally commenced some months later, when his head was shaved in a ceremony at this same temple, Shōin-ji. For most of the ensuing eighteen years, he would be occupied elsewhere—training in other temples, on pilgrimage, studying Chinese literature, in seclusion—but he always returned to Shōin-ji. It was his home temple and, quite exceptionally, remained so; he did most of his teaching at this rural site and died there, the most famous master of his day and the greatest in modern Rinzai history.

Hakuin's biography abounds with dramatic episodes, a fact attributable probably in equal parts to the headlong, do-or-die quality of his practice and to the uses he made of his story, citing it for inspirational value in his writings and lectures. We have little information from other sources about his first fifty years and thus have little choice but to accept Hakuin's, judiciously. He describes an initial breakthrough at age twenty-three, after two lesser openings and several days of such profound absorption in the koan *mu* that he "forgot both to eat and rest." Thus immersed, he felt sometimes as though he "were frozen solid in the midst of an ice sheet extending tens of thousands of miles," other times as though he "were floating through the air." Suddenly the booming of the temple bell brought him to, "as if a sheet of ice had been smashed or a jade tower had fallen with a crash." But with the dissolution of his doubt came another challenge, recognized on reflection: "My pride soared up like a majestic mountain, my arrogance surged forward like the tide. Smugly I thought to myself: 'In the past two or three hundred years no one could have accomplished such a marvelous breakthrough as this.' "

At this juncture, "shouldering my glorious enlightenment," he went off to meet a master of whom he had heard great things—Munan's lone heir, Dōkyō Etan (1642–1721), better known as Shōju Rōjin, the Old Man of Shōju. This eccentric teacher, who lived in the mountains with his aged mother and a few dedicated students, swiftly let the air out of Hakuin's balloon:

> "How do you understand Chao-chou's *mu?*" the master asked him.
> "Where is *mu* such that one could put arms or legs on it?" he replied.
> The Old Man abruptly twisted Hakuin's nose, declaring, "Here's somewhere to put arms and legs!" Getting no response, he guffawed and exclaimed, "You poor, pit-dwelling devil! Do you suppose somehow you have sufficient understanding?"

From that time on, Shōju Rōjin hounded Hakuin, calling him a pit-dwelling devil whenever they met, much as T'ou-tzu had berated Hsüeh-feng for being a black lacquer bucket almost a millennium before. Hakuin redoubled his efforts, and one day, as he sought alms in a nearby town, an attack by a broom-wielding madman precipitated a realization that the Old Man found persuasive. The two continued rigorous studies together for another six months or so, and though no ceremony of transmission is recorded, Hakuin has always been counted as Shōju Rōjin's heir.

In later years, Hakuin quoted his master's counsel on many things, among them the necessity for stringent, extended post-enlightenment practice. He went about this period of maturation with his customary zeal and, in the process, fell into an illness that one Rinzai authority termed "a severe nervous breakdown." Hakuin later described acute burning sensations in his head and chest, chills in his legs, and in his ears "a rushing sound as of a stream in a valley. My courage failed and I was in an attitude of constant fear. I felt spiritually exhausted, night and day seeing dreams, my armpits always wet with sweat and my eyes full of tears." When conventional remedies proved fruitless, he consulted a cave-dwelling practitioner of Chinese medicine (formerly a disciple of Ishikawa Jōzan), who taught him meditative techniques by which he eventually cured himself of this "Zen sickness."

Further pilgrimage and a nearly two-year seclusion ended in 1717, when Hakuin's father called him home, urging that he restore now-deserted Shōin-ji. He accepted this request in the spirit of filial piety, installing himself as the temple's abbot and fixing it up with the help of a few disciples. Yet he pushed himself as relentlessly as ever in his practice:

> When darkness fell he would climb inside a derelict old palanquin and seat himself on a cushion he placed on the floorboard. One of the young boys studying at the temple would come, wrap the master's body in a futon, and cinch him up tightly into this position with ropes. There he would remain motionless . . . until the following day when the boy would come to untie him so that he could relieve his bowels and take some food. The same routine was repeated nightly.

In 1726, these draconian measures paid off in an experience, triggered by the hum of a cricket, that caused tears to spill down his cheeks "like beans pouring from a ruptured sack." This time Hakuin found lasting peace and turned his energies to teaching for the next forty years.

Not long after reopening Shōin-ji, Hakuin had been honored with a three-month appointment as head monk at Myōshin-ji, but his reputation took time to develop, even when teaching became his first priority. As late as 1736, records show, only eight resident monks and twenty-two visitors attended a series of talks he delivered at Shōin-ji. The following year, for the first time, he was invited to speak elsewhere—at a temple in a neighboring province—and the curve of his fame steepened thereafter. A turning point appears to have come in 1740, when four hundred monks from all across Japan congregated at Shōin-ji to hear such blistering lectures as "Licking Up Hsi-keng's Fox Slobber" and "The True and Untransmittable Dharma."

During this special gathering of 1740 and in his subsequent work, Hakuin fulminated against the laxity in Zen training that he had witnessed in his years of roaming and inveighed against specific errors that he found evident in latter-day Ch'an writings as well as in Japanese monasteries. Integration of the Pure Land *nembutsu* practice into Zen training, as promoted by the Ōbaku sect, came in for especially scathing criticism. Quoting texts and naming names, Hakuin excoriated teachers who expressed a literalistic understanding of rebirth in the Pure Land, likening them to "a troop of blind Persians who stumble upon a parchment leaf inscribed with Sanskrit letters . . . and attempt to decipher the meaning of the text, but not having the faintest idea of what it says, they fail to get even a single word right, and turn themselves into laughingstocks in the bargain." Adopting Pure Land recitation, he warned, would sap the vitality of their already imperiled tradition, reducing even the most promising Zen students to "sitting in the shade next to the pond with listless old grannies, dropping their heads and closing their eyes in broad daylight and intoning endless choruses of *nembutsu*."

Contradictory as it may seem, Hakuin elsewhere recommended *nembutsu* practice. He viewed it as good and useful in its own right for those who lacked the aspiration or the ability to undertake Zen training. In making his criticisms of Pure Land Buddhism, he said, "I am not referring to those wise saints, motivated by the working of the universal vow of great compassion, who wish to extend the benefits of salvation to people of lesser capabilities." He enthusiastically quotes Tenkei Denson, a highly regarded Sōtō master of the previous generation, on the undesirability of crossing the sects: "Adding Pure Land to Zen is like depriving a cat of its eyes. Adding Zen to Pure Land is like raising a sail on the back of a cow."

Hakuin also revived Ta-hui's old campaign against the evils of "silent illumination," which he considered less a matter of adherence to a specific method than a crucial and common failure of insight. He identifies it as a fixation upon emptiness, the "one-sided view" that "there is absolutely no birth, no death, no nirvana, no passions, no enlightenment. All the scriptures are but paper fit only to wipe off excrement, the bodhisattvas and the *arhats* are but corrupted corpses. Studying Zen under a teacher is an empty delusion. The koans are but a film that clouds the eye." He himself, he implies, was rescued from such misunderstanding of Shōju Rōjin's timely intervention, while those less fortunate are condemned to waste their lives: "Every day these people seek a place of peace and quiet; today they end up like dead dogs and tomorrow it will be the same thing. Even if they continue in this way for endless *kalpas,* they will still be nothing more than dead dogs."

The high voltage of Hakuin's lectures must have moved his audiences, and it remains striking even today, as does his command of Ch'an and Zen history. He gives the impression of firsthand knowledge of bygone masters, speaking of them as if of old friends, giving them nicknames, alluding in an offhand manner to their experiences and peculiarities. He obviously felt a particular affinity and affection for several of them—Shih-shuang, who jabbed himself with an awl in desperation to stay alert; the fiery Lin-chi and Ta-hui; and Hsü-t'ang Chih-yü, the Sung master who gave rise to the Ō-tō-kan line. Hakuin also had favorites among his Japanese predecessors, notably the three Ō-tō-kan founders as well as Ikkyū, Munan's teacher Gudō, and Shōju Rōjin. He lectured extensively on Daitō's record, singling him out for tribute as one who had been to the bottom of the Great Matter and as the greatest of the Japanese forebears.

Hakuin's words and example had an indisputably galvanizing effect on the Rinzai world, rejuvenating a tradition that had lost much of its verve, maybe even its sense of purpose. Zazen! he emphasized. Koan study! Awakening! More and deeper practice, more and deeper awakening! Genuine enlightenment, tested in the forge of a genuine master! Though he might lecture on Han-shan's verses and publish poems of his own, no one could suppose that Hakuin's interests centered on literature. Nor could they suppose, given the humble facilities at Shōin-ji, that he cared much for comfort or grandeur or nicety. His message was clear, and it carried well above the buzz of other masters, attracting students—both men and women, ordained and lay—that Hakuin himself considered "the finest flowers of the Zen groves, dauntless heroes to all the world."

By the time he died in 1768, some fifty of these heroes are known to have received his sanction as Dharma heirs, and an equal number of other successors suspected. The best and brightest of the Rinzai world, these disciples went on to have enormous impact on the future of Zen. Fanning out from Shōin-ji and from Ryūtaku-ji, the monastery Hakuin founded late in life, they and their descendants rose to take leadership at more and more Rinzai monasteries until finally Hakuin's teaching lineage overwhelmed all others; today's Rinzai masters universally trace their Dharma ancestry to him. Accordingly, the Rinzai curriculum and teaching methods also bear his imprint. The two sub-lineages established by his Dharma grandsons Inzan Ien (1751–1814) and Takujū Kosen (1760–1833) differ to some degree in temper and details, but they maintain Hakuin's focus on zazen and koan study, cover the same body of koans, and employ the capping phrases so favored by Daitō. Just one of Hakuin's indelible contributions to the Rinzai curriculum is his perpetually misquoted koan "the sound of a single hand" (no clapping), which is usually assigned as one of the first barriers in a student's course.

If Hakuin's lectures alone had been preserved, we would know him in his most noteworthy aspect—the one of greatest importance to him and to history— but we would have a terribly pinched perception of his character. Fortunately, the ink paintings, calligraphy, letters, and other writings that represent his dealings with the laity enrich and humanize our image of him. The master who otherwise might be mistaken for a hissing, fuming fanatic here appears gentle, charming, eager to accommodate others, and as genuinely concerned for the welfare of geishas and farmers as for the perpetuation of the Buddha Way. In a lengthy letter offered to a provincial lord "as an aid to benevolent government," he deferentially but passionately criticizes luxury and waste. For merchants or villagers, he was quite prepared to put the Dharma into the comic form of a salesman's spiel or to brush a talisman for fertility, long life, good fortune, protection from fire, or the like. The breadth of his sympathies and the multiplicity of his talents mark Hakuin as a great human being no less than a great Zen teacher. ❦

FROM THE TRUE AND UNTRANSMITTABLE DHARMA

Zen people today, being unable to tell slave from master, common stones from jades, can only prattle. They say things like: "Priest So-and-so treats his monks as solicitously as nurslings." "Priest B regards prostrations before Buddhist images as the very heart of Buddhist practice." "Priest C takes only one meal each day." "Priest D sits long periods at a stretch without ever lying down—he's a living buddha."

What has the Zen school come to!

Long ago during the Southern Sung dynasty, Zen master Mi-an Hsien-chieh, a native of the state of Min, was crossing the mountains into Wu-chou to visit the reacher Chih-che Yüan-an. One day, as he was sitting warming himself in the sun, he was approached by an elderly monk who was obviously a veteran of the Dharma wars. "Where will you go when you leave here?" the monk asked him.

"I'm going to Ssu-mei to visit Fo-chih T'uan-yü at the monastery at Mount

A-yü-wang," Mi-an replied. "When the country falls into spiritual decline, even young monks on pilgrimage are affected," said the monk. "They pay attention to what they hear, but neglect what they see."

"What do you mean?" demanded Mi-an. The monk replied, "There are currently a thousand monks residing at Mount A-yü-wang. The abbot can't possibly give personal instruction to each one. Do you think he's going to find time to work with someone like you, who's making out all right on his own?"

"Then where am I to go?" said Mi-an, tears appearing in his eyes. "There's a priest named Ying-an T'an-hua in Mei-kuo, Ch'u-chou. He's young but his discernment is second to none. Go see him."

Mi-an followed the monk's advice. He studied under Ying-an for four years, in the course of which he was able to break through and grasp the vital life-source of the buddha-ancestors.

Practicers today move around from temple to temple looking for a place that offers them comfortable living conditions and serves them bowls of thick gruel at mealtimes. They don't give much thought to the problem of birth-and-death, or to penetrating the secret depths. They come wandering into temples like herds of deer; they come filing in like a swarm of ants. There is a world of difference between practitioners like them and a true seeker like Mi-an.

Priest Wu-tsu Fa-yen once addressed the following remarks to his pupils:

> Back twenty or thirty years ago, I traveled around the country looking for a teacher. After I had spent some time practicing under several experienced masters, I thought my study was over. But when I reached Mt. Fu and joined the assembly under master Yüan-chien, I found that I couldn't even open my mouth. After that, while I was practicing under Master Pai-yün, I got my teeth into an iron bun. When I was finally able to chew it, I discovered it possessed hundreds of marvelous flavors. How would I express that? I'd say:
>   The flowers on the cockscomb crown the early autumn;
>   Who dyed the purple in their splendid silken heads?
>   Soon winds will come, their combs will brush together,
>   An endless struggle will unfold before the temple stairs.

Did you hear him? "I thought my training was over." Now if Fa-yen,[1] when he believed his practice was at an end, had not entered Yüan-chien's chambers, and had not come under Pai-yün's wing, he might have carried his mistakes around with him to the grave. What a precious thing a Zen teacher is whose eyes are truly open. A priceless treasure not only for men, but for *devas* as well. But even that remains unknown to those today who throw their lives away by supposing prematurely they have concluded their training.

1. [Here Hakuin continues to discuss the life of Wu-tsu Fa-yen, teacher of Yüan-wu (Chapter 25), not to be confused with Fa-yen Wen-i, founder of the Fa-yen house (Chapter 22).—Eds.]

One day early in Fa-yen's career, when he was studying under Yüan-chien, Yüan-chien told him, "I'm not getting any younger. By staying here with me, you may be wasting valuable time. I want you to go to Pai-yün Shou-tuan. He's young in years, and I've never actually met him, but judging from the verse comment he made on the three blows Lin-chi received from Huang-po, he's an exceptional monk.[2] If you study with him, I'm sure you'll be able to bring your Great Matter to completion."

Fa-yen knew in his heart the truth of his teacher's words. He bade him farewell and set out for Mt. Pai-yün.

What magnanimity! Yüan-chien's total selflessness deserves our deepest respect. How different from the Zen teachers today! When they certify a student, they hand him a piece of paper containing a line or two of some lifeless words they have written on it, telling him, "You are like this. I am like this too. Preserve it carefully. Never change or deviate from it."

Students receive these certificates with deep bows of gratitude, raise them over their heads in attitudes of reverence. They guard them religiously all their sleeping and waking hours until the day they die—and in the process they make a total waste of their lives. Their own true face remains forever unknown to them. The reason why Yüan-chien chose Pai-yün's temple to send Fa-yen to is because he was suspicious of prosperous training halls that were filled with monks, and because his sole concern was to keep the true Zen wind from dying out.

One day, when Fa-yen was working as head of the milling shed, one of the monks suddenly pointed to the turning millstone and said, "Does that move by supernatural power? Or does it move naturally?" Fa-yen hitched up his robe and made a circumambulation of the stone. The monk said nothing.

Later, Master Pai-yün came into the shed and spoke to Fa-yen. "I had some monks here visiting from Mt. Lu. They had all experienced enlightenment. When I asked them to express their understanding, they did it very well, with words of substance. When I questioned them about episodes involving Zen masters of the past, they were able to clarify them. When I requested comments on Zen sayings, the comments they supplied were perfectly acceptable. In spite of all that, they still weren't there yet."[3]

Pai-yün's words brought deep doubts to Fa-yen's mind. "They had achieved enlightenment," he pondered. "They were able to express their understanding. They could clarify the stories the master gave them. Why did he say they still

2. When Lin-chi was studying with Huang-po, he asked him three times about the meaning of the Buddha-Dharma, and each time Huang-po struck him. Pai-yün Shou-tuan's verse comment is: "With one blow, he demolishes the Yellow Crane Tower; / With one kick, he turns Parrot Island on its back. / When the spirit is there, fuel it with more spirit. / Where there is no elegance, there too is elegance." The first two lines are taken from a celebrated verse by the poet Ts'uei Hao.

3. Hakuin includes this koan, Pai-yün's "Not Yet There," among the [most difficult] koans.

lacked something?" After struggling with this for several days, he suddenly broke through into enlightenment. Everything that had seemed so precious to him was now cast aside, as he raced to Pai-yün's chambers. When Pai-yün saw him, he got up and began dancing about for him, waving his arms and stamping his feet. Fa-yen just looked on and laughed.

Afterward, Fa-yen said, "I broke into great beads of sweat . . . then suddenly I experienced for myself 'the fresh breeze that rises up when the great burden is laid down.' "[4]

We must prize Fa-yen's example. After only a few days of intense effort, he transcended in one leap all the gradual stages of attainment—the Three Wisdoms and the Four Fruits—and penetrated directly the hearts of all the twenty-eight Indian and the six Chinese Ancestors. After that, he spoke with effortless freedom whenever he opened his mouth, taking students completely unaware when he responded to their questions, and cutting the ground from under them with his own questions. Reflect deeply, and you will see that this is the very point at which men of great stature surpass the countless ranks of average men; and it is at this same point that the lax and indolent lose hope.

Long ago, Emperor Yü saved a hundred provinces from the ravages of flood by having a passage cut open for the Yellow River at the Dragon Gates. But the project took years, required the forced labor of countless men and women, and cost many of them their lives. Emperor Kao-tsung struggled through a period of great upheaval to establish the foundations for a dynasty of Han rulers that endured for four centuries. But the policies he initiated during the forty years of his reign resulted in death and suffering for untold millions of his subjects. What these two emperors accomplished has made their names known throughout the world. Yet their achievements were defiled by the illusory passions that engendered them. The difference between such worldly achievements and the spiritual exploits of a Zen teacher like Fa-yen, which were utterly free of the defiling passions, is vaster than the difference between sky and sea.

Unfortunately, however, we have another species of teacher in our Zen school. The kind who puffs up self-importantly when he's able to round up seven or eight monks. He stalks like a tiger with a mean glint in his eye. Parades around like an elephant with his nose stuck proudly in the air. He delivers smug judgments:

> Master So-and-so is an excellent priest. His poems are reminiscent of Li Yu-lin. Writes prose like Yüan Chung-lang. And the ample fare you get in his temple cannot be matched anywhere else in the country. There is a morning meal, a mid-day meal, tea and cakes three times a day. Before the afternoon tea-break is even over, the board sounds announcing the evening meal. The master teaches the Dharma of "direct pointing" itself, and ushers students into enlightenment with

4. A saying of Chao-chou.

no more effort than it takes to pick up a clod of dirt at the roadside. Mr. Kobayashi's third son went to him and was immediately enlightened. Mr. Suzuki's fourth son went and grasped the Dharma right off. Samurais and farmers, artisans and merchants, even butchers, innkeepers, peddlers, and everyone else who passes through the gates of his temple—he leads them all straight into the realm of truth. I don't know of a training hall in the world to compare with it. Any monk on pilgrimage who fails to enter So-and-so's gate is making the mistake of a lifetime; he is throwing his search for satori right out the window.

Phffmp! What graveyard did you pillage for those old leftover offerings? Who did you get that line about "direct pointing" from? How can you say that enlightenment comes as effortlessly as "picking up a clod of dirt"? Are you really talking about the "secret transmission" of the Sixth Ancestor? The "essential matter" Lin-chi transmitted? If it was as easy as you say it is, and it was enough for a student merely to receive and accept a teaching after his teacher explained it to him, why do Zen people speak of the "wondrous Dharma that the buddhas and ancestors do not transmit"?

FROM A LETTER TO LORD NABESHIMA

Do not say that worldly affairs and pressures of business leave you no time to study Zen under a master, and that the confusions of daily life make it difficult for you to continue your meditation. Everyone must realize that for the true practicing monk there are no worldly cares or worries. Supposing a man accidentally drops two or three gold coins in a crowded street swarming with people. Does he forget about the money because all eyes are upon him? Does he stop looking for it because it will create a disturbance? Most people will push others out of the way, not resting until they get the money back into their own hands. Are not people who neglect the study of Zen because the press of mundane circumstances is too severe, or stop their meditation because they are troubled by worldly affairs, putting more value on two or three pieces of gold than on the unsurpassed mysterious way of the Buddhas? A person who concentrates solely on meditation amid the press and worries of everyday life will be like the man who has dropped the gold coins and devotes himself to seeking them. Who will not rejoice in such a person?

This is why Myōchō[5] has said:

> See the horses competing at the Kamo racegrounds;
> Back and forth they run—yet this is sitting in meditation.

---

5. Shūhō Myōchō (1282–1338). More commonly known by his posthumous title, Daitō Kokushi. [See Chapter 34 re Daitō for author translation of this poem.]

The Priest of Shinjū-an[6] has explained it in this way: "Don't read the sutras, practice meditation; don't take up the broom, practice meditation; don't plant the tea seeds, practice meditation; don't ride a horse, practice meditation." This is the attitude of the men of old to true Zen study.

Shōju Rōjin always used to say: "The man who practices meditation without interruption, even though he may be in a street teeming with violence and murder, even though he may enter a room filled with wailing and mourning, even though he attends wrestling matches and the theatre, even though he is present at musical and dance performances, is not distracted or troubled by minutiae, but conscientiously fixes his mind on his koan, proceeds single-mindedly, and does not lose ground. Even if a powerful *asura* demon were to seize him by the arm and lead him through innumerable rounds of the great chiliocosm,[7] his true meditation would not be cut off even for an instant. One who continues in this way without interruption can be called a monk who practices the true Zen. At all times maintain an unconcerned expression on your face, steady your eyes, and never for a moment bother yourself with the affairs of man." This statement is truly worthy of respect. Don't we also find in the military laws the instructions: "Fight and cultivate the fields; this is by far the safest method"? Studying Zen is just the same. Meditation is the true practice of fighting; introspection is the ultimate of cultivation. They are what two wings are to a bird; what two wheels are to a cart. . . .

If you think that dead sitting and silent illumination are sufficient, then you spend your whole life in error and transgress greatly against the Buddha Way. Not only do you set yourself against the Buddha Way, but you reject the lay world as well. Why is this so? If the various lords and high officials were to neglect their visits to court and to cast aside their governmental duties and practice dead sitting and silent illumination; if the warriors were to neglect their archery and charioteering, forget the martial arts, and practice dead sitting and silent illumination; if the merchants were to lock their shops and smash their abacuses, and practice dead sitting and silent illumination; if the farmers were to throw away their ploughs and hoes, cease their cultivation, and practice dead sitting and silent illumination; if craftsmen were to cast away their measures and discard their axes and adzes, and practice dead sitting and silent illumination, the country would collapse and the people drop with exhaustion. Bandits would arise everywhere and the nation would be in grievous danger. Then the people, in their anger and resentment, would be sure to say that Zen was an evil and an ill-omened thing.

6. Ikkyū Sōjun (1396–1481). Shinjū-an is a sub-temple within the grounds of Daitōku-ji [with which Ikkyū was associated]. [See Chapter 37.]
7. A billion Buddha worlds in the Tendai cosmology.

But it should be known that at the time that the ancient monasteries flourished, old sages . . . heaved stones, moved earth, drew water, cut firewood, and grew vegetables. When the drum for the work period sounded, they tried to make progress in the midst of their activity. That is why Pai-chang said: "A day without work, a day without eating." This practice is known as meditation in the midst of activity, the uninterrupted practice of meditation sitting. This style of Zen practice no longer exists today.

I do not mean to say, however, that sitting in meditation should be despised or contemplation damned. Of all the sages, the men of wisdom of the past and of today, there is not one that perfected the Buddha Way who did not depend on Zen meditation. The three essentials, precepts, meditation, and wisdom, have always been the very center of Buddhism. Who would dare to take them lightly? But if anyone should have attempted to approach such men as the great Zen sages mentioned above, men who transcend both sect and rank, while they were engaged in the true, unsurpassed, great Zen meditation, lightning would have flashed and the stars would have leapt about in the sky.

How then can someone with the eye of a sheep or the wisdom of foxes and badgers expect to judge such men? Even should there be such a thing as attaining the status of a Buddha or reaching a state where the great illumination is released by means of dead sitting and silent illumination, the various lords, high stewards, and common people are so involved in the numerous duties of their household affairs that they have scarcely a moment in which to practice concentrated meditation. What they do then is to plead illness and, neglecting their duties and casting aside responsibilities for their family affairs, they shut themselves up in a room for several days, lock the door, arrange several cushions in a pile, set up a stick of incense, and proceed to sit. Yet, because they are exhausted by ordinary worldly cares, they sit in meditation for one minute and fall asleep for a hundred, and during the little bit of meditation that they manage to accomplish, their minds are beset by countless delusions. As soon as they set their eyes, grit their teeth, clench their fists, adjust their posture, and start to sit, ten thousand evil circumstances begin to race about in their minds. Thereupon they furrow their brows, draw together their eyebrows, and before one knows it they are crying out: "Our official duties interfere with our practice of the Way; our careers prevent out Zen meditation. It would be better to resign from office, discard our seals, go to some place beside the water or under the trees where all is peaceful and quiet and no one is about, there in our own way to practice *dhyāna* contemplation, and escape from the endless cycle of suffering." How mistaken these people are!

For this reason the Ancestors with great compassion were kind enough to point out the correct way of true meditation and uninterrupted meditation sitting. If all possessed this true meditation, the lords in their attendance at court and their conduct of governmental affairs, the warriors in their study of the works on archery and charioteering, the farmers in their cultivation, hoeing, and ploughing, the artisans in their measuring and cutting, women in their spinning and weaving, this then would at once accord with the great Zen meditation of the various Ancestors. This is why the sūtra says: "The necessities of life and the production of goods do not transgress against True Reality."[8] If you do not have this true meditation it is like sleeping in an empty hole abandoned by some old badger. How regrettable it is that people today "cast aside this Way as if it were a clump of dirt."[9]

INTERACTIONS WITH WOMEN

One of the first persons to join the community was a sixteen-year-old girl named Satsu. She was awakened soon after studying with Hakuin. One day she was sitting zazen on a box when her father approached and asked, "What do you think you're doing? Buddha's image is in that box." She replied, "If there is any place where Buddha does not exist, I ask you to take me there." Her father was shocked. On another occasion a monk asked her, "What is the meaning of breaking the white rock within the rubbish heap?" She immediately threw down and shattered the tea bowl she was holding.

Explaining a koan to Satsu in a private interview, Hakuin once said, "Now do you understand?" She responded, "Would you please explain it again?" Just as he opened his mouth to speak she interrupted him with, "Thank you for your trouble," and bowed her way out of the room. Hakuin, looking crestfallen, exclaimed, "I've been overthrown by this terrible little woman!"

There was also an older woman of Hara who heard Hakuin say in a lecture: "Mind is the Pure Land, and the body itself is Amitābha Buddha. When Amitābha Buddha appears, mountains, rivers, grasses, and trees radiate a great light." The old woman thought this was a difficult matter to comprehend; she pondered it day and night. One day, as she was washing a pot, a great insight flashed through her mind. She threw down the pot and ran to Hakuin. "Amitābha Buddha has crashed into my body. Mountains, rivers, grasses, and trees all shine greatly. Splendid! How marvelous!" She jumped up and down for joy. "What's that?" Hakuin remarked. "Nothing can shine in your asshole." She pushed him aside and cried, "Hey, you aren't enlightened yet!" Hakuin burst into laughter.

8. *Lotus Sūtra*; Hakuin does not quote accurately.
9. Line from Tu Fu's *Song of Poverty.*

PRESCRIPTION FOR THE PENETRATING-ONE'S-NATURE-AND-BECOMING-A-BUDDHA PILL[10]

My name is Yūsuke Odawara.
I've been a pharmacist since before my parents were born.
Although soliciting is prohibited in this country,
listen to me for a second about the effects
of a certain medicine.
The pill I'm talking about is called
Penetrating-One's-Nature-and-Becoming-a-Buddha.
It's got Direct-Pointing-at-Human-Mind in it.
If you take this pill, you'll get rid of the diseases
of four sufferings and eight sufferings.
You can rest easy, far from the drifting and sinking
of the three worlds,
and get relief from the aches of going round
in the six realms.

The medicine is Prince Siddhārtha's.
He's the son of King Shuddhodana from Kapilavastu, India.
At birth, the prince walked seven steps and said,
"Alone above and below the heavens,
I am the honored one."
As you all know, one day he suddenly left home and went to Mt. Dandaka
    seeking special herbs.

He had a difficult, painful time.
Out of this there later came four kinds of pharmacological texts
with more than five thousand and forty volumes.
At about that time he had sixteen apprentices and five hundred students.
They transmitted the Becoming-a-Buddha Pill, which is the essential cure for
    the suffering of sentient beings.
There were four times seven, count them, twenty-eight masters in India.
The twenty-eighth, great master Bodhidharma, transmitted it scrupulously.
There were two times three, that is, six unique masters in China.
The school split into five and then seven houses, while this and that were going on.
For instance, Shen-kuang's arm-ache was cured.[11]

10. This chant, in its language and tone, echoes the cries of Japanese street vendors. The colloquialism and slang of the translation reflect the style of the original.
11. According to legend, Shen-kuang [Hui-k'o] cut off his arm and gave it to Bodhidharma as a sign of his sincerity. . . . (See Chapter 1.) [In the following lines, Hakuin alludes off handedly to other injuries incurred by Ch'an masters of old.—Eds.]

So was Hsüan-sha's sore foot, Yün-men's limp, and Pai-chang's nosebleed.
Lots of other things happened—too many to talk about.
National Teacher Senkō first brought this pill to Japan.[12]
Twenty-four branches of pharmacists were started.
Later, Daitō of Murasakino got an imperial appointment.
Pharmacists peddling the Exoteric Pill and the Esoteric Pill came along to
    challenge and compete with the Becoming-a-Buddha Pill.
The emperor ordered a contest between Daitō, and the pharmacists of Mii
    Monastery in Nara, and of Hiei.[13]
Daitō won.
The Cloistered Emperor Hanazono sent a messenger to Ibuka, Mino Province,
    summoning Daitō's heir, National Teacher Kanzan.
The emperor took the pill and rewarded Kanzan with an imperial cup.
Now I run that Hanazono Company, the Original Family Store.
I'll tell you the recipe for the pill:
First, cut Chao-chou's cypress with an axe and pound it in the Sixth Ancestor's
    mortar.
Then add Ma-tsu's West River Water,
knead it on Daitō's octagonal board,
put it on Hakuin's one hand,
shape it into a ball with Chü-chih's finger,
wrap it with Hsüan-sha's white paper,
and write on it:
"Penetrating-One's-Nature-and-Becoming-a-Buddha Pill,
Manufactured by Hanazono Company,
Rinzai County, Zen School."
When you swallow this pill, you'll throw up swollen knowledge,
and the cathartic effect won't fade.
Chew it well, chew it well—it will stay with you coming, going, standing, or
    sitting.
Gulp it down, let it rest below your navel.
Then even in heaven, pleasure won't matter to you.
Even in hell, you won't have pain.

---

12. National Teacher Senkō: Myōan Eisai, founder of the Rinzai School.
13. [Refers to the Shōchin Debate, in which Daitō representing Zen, defeated masters of other Japanese sects in a formal contest of religious insight.—Eds.]
14. Six-Character: The Japanese words *Namu Amida Butsu* (I take refuge in Amitābha Buddha) consist of six ideograms, *na-mu-a-mi-da-butsu*. Chanting these words is the central practice of the Pure Land schools. [It was taught that intoning this phrase at the brink of death would occasion re-birth in Amitābha's Pure Land.—Eds.]

I don't mean to slander, but recently something called the Six-Character Pill
    has come onto the market.[14]
Now if the common, everyday person takes that pill before breakfast or after
    supper, it might give him a little boost,
but it's no good against the agony of death.
Even so, people in the world call it the "Chanting-Buddha's-Name-at-the-
    Moment-of-Death Pill."
The price of that pill is three pennies, but my Becoming-a-Buddha Pill doesn't
    cost a cent.

Well, that's my little pitch.
I can't keep myself from saying, "Won't you take my pill?"

45

Tōrei

(1721–1792)

Tōrei Enji stands in the long shadow cast by his teacher, Hakuin. Having entered a temple of the Daitoku-ji line at nine, by the time he met Hakuin, he had studied with two other Rinzai masters, had made a three-year pilgrimage on the island of Kyushu, had spent the better part of two years in seclusion—and was still just twenty-two. This fine, young flower of the Zen forest had experienced an awakening during his tenure as a hermit, but upon entering Hakuin's lair, he reported later, "I could not utter a single word." Awestruck, he settled in among the other monks, nuns, and laypeople who had jammed Shōin-ji and its environs since Hakuin's celebrated lecture series of 1740.

One day in the room for private instruction, Hakuin demanded, "If all of a sudden a monstrous demon king grabbed you from behind and thrust you into a cavern of raging fire, how would you find a way out?" Again, Tōrei says, he had no answer whatsoever; he burst into a cold sweat and, attempting to rise, found that he could not stand. Thereafter, at every meeting the master pressed the question, asking, "Is there a way out?" Try as he might, Tōrei could not find one. "From then on, whether walking or standing, I had no peace at all. Heaven and earth shrunk and seemed narrow, sun and moon darkened. The following year I begged to be allowed to retire into solitude and there applied myself ceaselessly day and night." Hakuin counseled him then not to fear the fiery cavern but to walk straight into it, and with this encouragement, several days later Tōrei found his freedom.

No sooner had he done so, however, than Hakuin set another barrier in his path, then another and another. These included the koan of Chao-chou's meeting the crone who tripped up monks on their way to Mt. Wu-tai (Chapter 15), Huang-lung's question "How does my hand resemble the Buddha's hand?" and the story that Ikkyū so relished about an old woman sending a teenage girl to test a hermit with her embrace (Chapter 37). When Tōrei responded inadequately to the third of these koans, "the Master, unleashing all his power, roared at me. That sound penetrated into my very marrow. My chest ached for days, my mind was stunned as if in a daze, and my body seemed to be enveloped in foggy clouds." Dismayed by this setback, Tōrei again threw himself into zazen but months passed without release.

Ultimately, in 1746 he left Shōin-ji and holed up alone in Kyoto, practicing day and night "like a condemned man" whose execution was swiftly approaching. Borrowing a leaf from Hakuin's hero Shih-shuang, he poked himself with a needle to stay alert and applied himself so energetically, he tells us, that his clothes were clammy with sweat even on the coldest mornings. After more than a hundred days of this—and eighty-nine "small" awakenings!—Tōrei at last got the big laugh that he had long awaited. He got something else, too: a life-threatening illness (some say pneumonia) that took three years to cure. Apparently Tōrei immersed himself in Ch'an and Zen literature during his recuperation and, fearing that he would die without fulfilling the vow to liberate others, wrote *The Inexhaustible Lamp of Our School* as an offering and "incentive for later students."

When his health permitted, Tōrei returned to Shōin-ji and there, at twenty-nine, became the first of Hakuin's Dharma heirs. Kindred spirits in temperament and experience, the two men maintained a very close working relationship for the rest of Hakuin's life, often collaborating. In 1750, with the master's assent, Tōrei published *The Inexhaustible Lamp,* which helped to establish his own reputation and, more importantly, provided the first comprehensive description of Hakuin's training methods. In 1755, when Tōrei was called to Myōshin-ji for a stint as head monk—the same honor accorded to Hakuin three and a half decades earlier—he took along a magnificent self-portrait that Hakuin painted for him as a testament of succession.

That same year, Tōrei published "The Spur for a Good Horse," a primer on Zen practice addressed to an interested samurai. Here again, he was following in Hakuin's footsteps rather than striking off in another direction. "The Spur" recalls the elder master's letters of instruction to his upper-crust inquirers, though a bit more coolly and systematically presented. In this case as well, Tōrei sought Hakuin's approval before the text was printed. Perhaps this was purely a gesture of respect, but he may also have felt that the mantle of chief interpreter and custodian of Hakuin's Dharma had fallen on his shoulders. In years to come, he would prepare biographies not only of Shidō Munan, as already noted, but also of Shōju Rōjin and of Hakuin himself.

Owing to these and other writings, Tōrei has gained a reputation as a "Zen historian and literary man of eminence"—an accurate characterization, as far as it goes, but one that belies his importance as a Zen master in his own right. In 1760, Hakuin's community acquired Ryūtaku-ji, a dilapidated temple seven miles east of Shōin-ji that would become the principal platform for Tōrei's teaching. Under his guidance, it was reopened, refurbished, relocated, and expanded into one of the country's most beautiful and important monasteries. His greatest disciple, Gasan Jitō (1727–1797), initially studied with Hakuin and is usually placed on lineage charts as a successor of the old master, yet Tōrei worked longer with him and gave him Dharma-transmission nine years after Hakuin's death. Through Gasan, Tōrei contributed significantly to the flowering of Hakuin's Zen, for it was Gasan's heirs Inzan and Takujū who gave rise to the two Rinzai sub-lineages that have come down to the present day.

Unlike Hakuin, Tōrei was not a man of the people. Just as well probably, as he never fully regained the vitality sacrificed in his all-out pursuit of the Way and could not have matched the pace his teacher sustained in late life. Also, though he produced some ink paintings and a good deal of powerful calligraphy, he lacked the light touch that so endeared Hakuin to lay followers. The masterwork of Tōrei's final decade was his massive *Detailed Study of the Fundamental Principles of the Five Ch'an Houses,* a skilled and even-handed assessment of the Ch'an tradition that he produced at Gasan's request. Tōrei's importance was recognized with the granting of an imperial title after he died in 1792. ⊗

FROM THE SPUR

In what Zen calls the ascent from the state of the ordinary vulgar man to the state of Buddha, there are five requirements. First is the principle that they have the same nature. Second is the teaching that they are dyed different colors. Third is the necessity for furious effort. Fourth is the principle of continuity of training. Fifth is the principle of returning to the origin. These five are taught as the main elements of the path.

The true nature with which people are endowed, and the fundamental nature of the buddhas of the three worlds, are not two. They are equal in their virtue and majesty; the same light and glory are there. The wisdom and wonderful powers are the same. It is like the radiance of the sun illuminating mountains and rivers and the whole wide earth, lighting up the despised manure just as much as gold and jewels. But a blind man may stand pathetically in that very light, without seeing it or knowing anything about it.

Though the fundamental nature of all the buddhas and of living beings is the same and not distinct, their minds are looking in quite different directions. The Buddha faces inward and makes the heart-essence (*hon-shin*) shine forth. The ordinary man faces outward, and is concerned with the ten thousand things.

For what he likes, he develops strong desire; for what he does not like, he develops hatred; when his thinking becomes rigid, he is stupefied. Bewildered by one of these Three Poisons, he turns into a clutching ghost, or a fighting demon ablaze with fury, or an animal. When they are equally mixed in him, he falls into hell, where he suffers in so many ways. . . .

If one wants to get out of the worlds of suffering, first of all one has to realize how they are all the time passing away. What is born, inevitably dies. Youth cannot be depended on, power is precarious, wealth and honor crumble away. High status requires constant vigilance to preserve it. The longest life hardly gets beyond eighty years. Since therefore it is all melting away, there is nothing enjoyable about it. The badly off suffer from not having things; the well-off suffer from having them. The high suffer from being highly placed, and the despised suffer from being lowly placed. There is suffering connected with clothes and food, suffering with the family, suffering from wealth and possessions, suffering from official rank.

So long as the nature is not freed from passions, and the path of seeking release has not been found, then even supposing there were some king and his ministers, glorious like a god among living sages, it would all be insubstantial like a lightning flash or a dewdrop under the morning sun—gone in a moment.

When karma happens to be favorable, these things appear solid enough, but as the favorable karma dissipates, it turns out that there was never anything there at all. By favor of the karma of our parents we have got this body, and by favor of the earth, the skin and flesh and sinew and bone grow. By favor of water, the blood and body fluids come, and by favor of fire, warmth, harmony, softness, and order come to be. By favor of winds, vitality, breath, movement, and change come about. If these four favorable karmas suddenly become exhausted, then breathing ceases, the body is cold, and there is nothing to be called "I." At that time this body is no true "I." It was only ever a rented accommodation.

However clingingly attached to this temporary abode, one cannot expect it to last forever. To realize the Four Noble Truths, that all this is passing, painful, empty, and without a self, and to seek the way of *bodhi*-intelligence, is what we call the Dharma of Hearing the Noble Truths.

If you would grasp the nature of the universal body of all the buddhas, first you must be clear about, and then you must enlighten, the root of ignorance in you. How is it to be made clear? You must search after your true nature. How to search? In the eye, seeing of colors; in the ear, hearing of sounds; in the body, feeling distinctions of heat and cold; in the consciousness, feelings of wrong and right: all these must be seen clearly as they are. This seeing and hearing and knowing is at the root of the practice. The ordinary man sees colors and is deluded by colors, hears voices and is deluded by voices, feels heat and cold and is deluded by heat and cold, knows right and wrong and is deluded by right and wrong. This is what is meant by the saying: "The ordinary man looks outward."

The training of a bodhisattva is: when looking at some color, to ask himself what it is that is being seen; when hearing some sound, to ask himself what it is that is being heard; when feeling hot or cold, to ask himself what it is that is being felt; when distinguishing wrong from right, to ask himself what it is that is being known. This is called the "facing inward of the buddhas." Practicing it is different from facing in the direction in which the ordinary man looks. At first, though facing the same way as the buddha, the buddha power and wisdom are not manifest in him. But still, he is a baby bodhisattva, and he must realize that he has come into that company. If he always keeps to his great vow to the Buddhas, praying to the spiritual lights and being loyal to the teacher, then one day the Great Thing comes about, and he is set free in the ocean of Own-good is Others' good.

When you get up in the morning, however much business there may be wait-ing, first affirm this one thought, first turn to this meditation on seeing and hear-ing. After that, engage in the activities of the day. When going to have a meal or a drink, first of all you must try to bring this one thought to the fore, and make a meditation on it. When you go to wash your hands, first you should try to bring this thought uppermost in your mind and meditate on it. When last thing at night you are going to lie down, sit for a little bit on the bedclothes and try to bring this thought to the fore and meditate; then lie down to sleep. This is prac-ticing the true path of buddhas and bodhisattvas. Whip up your enthusiasm for it by realizing how if you fail to grasp your true nature as one with the nature of Buddha, you will be lost in the wheel of continual rebirth, circling endlessly in the Four Births and Six Worlds.

From the beginning, you must learn to put your whole heart into this basic meditation, going ahead with each thought and practicing on each occasion as it comes up. Keep up the right line of the meditation: when you walk, practice while walking; when you sit still, practice while sitting; when talking to people, practice while talking. When there is no talking and things are quiet, then you can meditate more intensely. When you look at things, ask yourself what it is that you see; when you hear things, ask yourself what it is that you hear. When things get very rushed so that you easily get swept away by them, ask yourself what this is, that you should get swept away by it. And even if you do get swept away, don't give up your meditation. If you get ill, use the pain as the seed-subject for your meditation.

In every circumstance, the meditation must go forward in a straight line, how-ever much business there may be. It is not allowable that the meditation should be vivid and clear only when the surroundings are familiar and quiet. Unless the meditation is bright and clear at all times, it cannot be said to have power. If there is an outbreak of armed strife in a country that has to be stopped, at the critical time it is a question of taking the field, confronting the dangers, and fighting fear-lessly without ever thinking of turning back—that is the way to victory. The med-itation-fight is the same. It is just when you are caught up in situations where your thoughts are disturbed, that there is a chance to win a decisive victory.

Be aware of this heart of yours. See that it does not weaken, and go forward. In fact when things are quiet, it corresponds to the time when warriors are safe within the castle, when they must train themselves in tactics and strategy. They practice with courage and sincerity. When the country is disturbed by armed up-risings, they know that this is the time to go out to the field of battle and decide the issue. You must meditate with just such a strong resolve. You may not have the power of the buddhas yet, but you are one of those who are on the Way of all the buddhas.

It is a fact that little enlightenment obstructs great enlightenment. If you give up any little enlightenment you may have, and do not clutch it to yourself, then you are sure to get great enlightenment. If you stick at the little enlightenment and will not give it up, you are sure to miss the great enlightenment. It is like someone who sticks to little profits, and so misses the big ones. But if he does not hang on to little profits, he will surely be able to get big ones. When the little profits are not clung to, but invested bit by bit, it does end in a big profit. Similarly, if you stick to the little profit of little enlightenment, so that the whole life is a succession of experiences of little enlightenments, you will never be able to reach the great freedom, the great release. . . .

Now when you have penetrated into the truth wholly, all the powers of the Way are brought to fulfillment, all beings everywhere are blessed whenever any opening presents itself. Though you may indeed preach and teach, really there is nothing lacking: "I" and the others all attain the shore of the fourfold nirvana.

Through the great operation of the great vow, beings and worlds benefit themselves as well as others, and you must resolve never to turn away from it in the future. In the present meantime, there may be mistakes and lapses; legs are weak and the path slippery. If you don't get up when you've fallen down, surely you'll be destroyed. You will die where you've fallen. But if, though falling, you pull yourself up, and falling again, pull yourself up again, and so go ahead further and further, finally you do reach the goal. The sutra says: "If you have broken a commandment, make your repentance before the Buddha at once: then go forward along the Way."

The Zen realization [kenshō] is the very crown of all buddhahood. He who has his heart set on this is already a baby buddha. Thought after thought, he steps out toward the gate of peerless merit, along the way of holy perfection. Wonderful is the merit even of reading about such perfection, what to say of practicing it? Even to get another to read it aloud will save one from disaster of fire, so what shall we say of one who practices it himself? The buddhas bless him, the bodhisattvas stretch out their hands to him, the gods in their heavens applaud him. At a glimpse of his shadow, demons and evil spirits are routed. Spirits imprisoned in the depths, by contact with him realize the opportunity of release. This is called the highest, noblest, and very first dharma. Step by step it must be faithfully followed out.

46

Ryōkan

(1758–1831)

"The Child is father of the Man," wrote Wordsworth, looking back on his youth. Half the world away, his Japanese contemporary and fellow poet Ryōkan appears to have reached the same conclusion:

> As a boy I left my father, ran off to other lands,
> tried hard to become a tiger—didn't even make it to cat!
> If you ask what kind of man I am now,
> just the same old Eizō I've always been.

Eldest son of a village headman in the northerly, coastal province of Echigo, Eizō was groomed for his father's hereditary position, but shy and awkward, he was mocked by neighbors as a "lamp at noon" (i.e., worthless). At seventeen he bolted for the local Sōtō temple and became Ryōkan, a tiger-in-training. Talented as he was, in years ahead he would often be called upon to lead and would consistently decline; young or old, Eizō or Ryōkan, he took no pleasure in self-assertion or public attention.

After nearly four years as a monk, Ryōkan "ran off to other lands" to study at a monastery in southern Japan under Kokusen, a prominent Sōtō abbot of the day. Reflecting many years later on his decade there, he expressed regret that his "way was such a solitary one." Rather than enjoying the companionship of fellow monks, "Hauling firewood, I thought of Layman P'ang; / treading the rice pounder, I recalled old Lu"—that is, Hui-neng, the Sixth Ancestor. Though Ryōkan received Dharma-transmission from Kokusen in 1790, after the master's death a year later he quit the monastery and rejected all invitations to teach. Instead, there followed a five-year period of pilgrimage, return to his home province, and retirement, at about the turn of the century, to a one-room mountain hut.

Ryōkan lived as a hermit for three decades, until age and illness forced him to accept the shelter of a disciple in town. His choice may be ascribed to a solitary nature or to trauma in his youth, but he himself evidently viewed it as the only true option for a man of the Way:

> In general, to remove oneself from the doting involved with kin and family, to sit upright in a grass hut, to circle about beneath the trees, to be a friend to the voice

of the brook and the hue of the hills—these are the practices adopted by the ancient sages and the model for ages to come.

Su T'ung-po's enlightenment poem echoes in this passage, placing him among the ancient sages whose example lent Ryōkan strength and inspiration, but judging by Ryōkan's poems, the person most often in his thoughts at night or when snow kept him housebound was the old man of Cold Mountain, Han-shan.

Ryōkan's training in Chinese language and literature began early. As part of his preparation to become village head, his father had sent him to a Confucian scholar for tutoring in these subjects. Probably at the local temple and definitely at Kokusen's monastery, he had continued these studies along with his Zen training. The first of his surviving poems, written in Chinese, date from the latter period. Ryōkan wrote in his native tongue as well—and more prolifically, it seems, given the body of work that remains: some fourteen hundred poems in Japanese, about a third that many in Chinese. Ryōkan turned out his work in a dashing, spidery-fine calligraphy that is admired almost as much as his poetry itself.

Besides reading and writing, Ryōkan's daily activities were simple and few. He sat in zazen, maintained his hut and household, foraged for wild foods, chatted with the occasional visitor, and went down the mountain to offer his begging bowl in nearby villages. These trips afforded most of his social contact as well as most of his sustenance, and he plainly relished the opportunities they gave him to frolic with the children or quaff a cup of wine with farmers after work. Especially in his romps with young friends, Ryōkan seems to have felt very keenly the uninhibited function of no-mind, and poems arising from these encounters, flush with joyful abandon, furnish our best evidence that he deserved the name that he selected for himself—Daigu, Great Fool.

The image of Ryōkan as a blithe-hearted friend of one and all took hold and grew with such energy that today the recluse of Echigo ranks among the Japanese masters most celebrated in their homeland, on a par with the more public figures Ikkyū and Takuan. A lively folklore developed after his death, swelling details of his poems and anecdotes from his life to legendary proportions. Generation after generation has told, for instance, about the time his little playmates deliberately left him unfound in a game of hide-and-seek and Ryōkan remained crouching in his outhouse hiding-place all night. "Ssssh!" he said, when discovered there the next morning by an adult, "The children will find me!" Other famous tales depict him sawing holes in the floor of his hermitage to give bamboo shoots room to grow and delousing his robe only to sun the lice on a sheet of paper and restore them to the robe, where they could bite him happily ever after.

Like Ikkyū and Takuan, Ryōkan never produced a Dharma heir, but that is not to say that he slackened in his efforts at the Way or avoided teaching. By every indication, he maintained his practice devotedly, fortified by readings from Sōtō founder Dōgen. He gave instruction to at least a few people who sought him out and grieved deeply when one of them, an especially promising lay student (*koji*) named Miwa Saicho, died unexpectedly:

Ah—my *koji!*
studied Zen with me twenty years.
You were the one who understood—
things I couldn't pass on to others.

In a broader sense, Ryōkan taught with his presence and his poems. Sometimes he addressed the Dharma explicitly in his writing, as his friend Han-shan had before him, but most of his poems are simply lit with his realization, presenting everyday wonders on their own terms. Having no limit, these wonders arrive in every form. The empty begging bowl, memories of his long-dead mother, the theft of his zazen cushions, gut-gripping cold—these too have their own light.

One of Ryōkan's best-known verses asks:

Who says my poems are poems?
My poems aren't poems!
Once you get that my poems aren't poems,
then we can start talking about poems.

Burton Watson posits that Ryōkan intended these lines to fend off criticism for his repeated failure to abide by the forms of Chinese and Japanese prosody. Maybe so, but it seems more likely he meant them as part of a campaign he waged against pretense of any kind, whether it was "speaking Edo dialect like a country hick" or "talk that smacks of satori" or "poet's poetry." The poem invites us to set aside all categories and expectations when we pick up Ryōkan's poems, to read them with the reliable mind that precludes picking and choosing.

However solitarily Ryōkan spent his days and pursued his Zen practice, however much he went his own way as a poet, there is no mistaking his profound affection for others. Beyond the fond ties he had with his *koji* Saicho and village supporters, he kept up with members of his family and a handful of close literary friends by exchanging poems and making occasional visits. His most intimate relationships were with his younger brother Yoshiyuki, who had taken the role of village headman in his stead, and the nun Teishin, whom he met at sixty-eight, when he finally gave up the hermit life and moved into a renovated storehouse offered by one of his supporters. Forty years Ryōkan's junior, widowed young, Teishin too was a poet, and their acquaintance soon ripened into a powerful, if platonic, love:

Chanting old poems,
Making our own verses,
Playing with a cloth ball,
Together in the fields—
Two people, one heart.

Still the same old Eizō.

Teishin was on hand in 1731, five years after their meeting, when Ryōkan died, and she tended his memory until her own death four decades later. True to his nature, the Great Fool had handed poems out freely to friends and benefactors, never making an effort to publish them. Teishin took it as her task to gather what she could and succeeded in bringing out the first edition of his poems in 1735. Scholars continue to retrieve examples of his work from Echigo attics, each one a treasure, but they add nothing to the bequest Ryōkan brushed on his deathbed:

> My legacy, what will it be?
> The flowers of springtime,
> A cuckoo in the summer,
> The scarlet leaves of fall.

What a shame it would be to call this "Zen." ⊗

FROM THE COLLECTED POEMS OF RYŌKAN

1

In the still night by the vacant window,
wrapped in monk's robe I sit in meditation,
navel and nostrils lined up straight,
ears paired to the slope of shoulders.
Window whitens—the moon comes up;
rain's stopped, but drops go on dripping.
Wonderful—the mood of this moment—
distant, vast, known to me only!

LINES 3–4   This is the posture one is instructed to assume when practicing zazen.

2

Dark of winter, eleventh month,
rain and snow slushing down;
a thousand hills all one color,
ten thousand paths where almost no one goes.
Past wanderings all turned to dreams;
grass gate, its leaves latched tight;
through the night I burn chips of wood,
quietly reading poems by men of long ago.

3

WAKING FROM A DREAM OF YOSHIYUKI

Where did you come from,
following dream paths
through the night to reach me,
these deep mountains
still heaped high with snow?

TITLE   Yoshiyuki was the poet's younger brother.

4

Green spring, start of the second month,
colors of things turning fresh and new.
At this time I take my begging bowl,
in high spirits tramp the streets of town.
Little boys suddenly spot me,
delightedly come crowding around,
descend on me at the temple gate,
dragging on my arms, making steps slow.
I set my bowl on top of a white stone,
hang my alms bag on a green tree limb;
here we fight a hundred grasses,
here we hit the *temari* ball—
I'll hit, you do the singing!
Now I'll sing, your turn to hit!
We hit it going, hit it coming,
never knowing how the hours fly.
Passersby turn, look at me and laugh,
"What makes you act like this?"
I duck my head, don't answer them—
I could speak but what's the use?
You want to know what's in my heart?
From the beginning, just this! just this!

5

Done begging in a rundown village,
I make my way home past green boulders.
Late sun hides behind western peaks;
pale moonlight shines on the stream before me.
I wash my feet, climb up on a rock,

light incense, sit in meditation.
After all, I wear a monk's robe—
how could I spend the years doing nothing?

6
When even *I* haven't had
enough to eat,
at the bottom of my bowl
of rice gruel
my shadow hogging in!

7
First month of summer, Grain in Ear season
with a metal-ringed staff, alone I come and go.
Old farmers suddenly spy me,
drag me over to join their fun.
Woven rushes serve for our seats,
paulownia leaves take the place of plates.
A couple of rounds of wine in the field
and drunk, I doze off, head pillowed on the bank.

LINE 1   One of the divisions of the solar year, around June 6–20.

8
Time: first day of the eighth month;
with begging bowl I enter the city streets.
A thousand gates unbolted in the dawn;
ten thousand homes where cooking smoke slants up.
Last night's rain washed the road clean;
autumn wind shakes the metal rings of my staff.
Taking my time, I go begging for food—
how wide, how boundless this Dharma world!

LINE 1   Under the lunar calendar New Year came in early February and autumn comprised the seventh, eighth, and ninth lunar months.

9
Fleas, lice
any autumn bug that
wants to sing—
the breast of my robe
is Musashino moor!

LINE 5   Ryōkan is famous for taking the lice out of the breast of his robe, sunning them on a piece of paper on the veranda, and then carefully replacing them in his robe. [Musashino was a Kyoto beautyspot favored for elegant music and poetry parties.—Eds.]

10
Done with a long day's begging,
I head home, close the wicker door,
in the stove burn branches with the leaves still on them,
quietly reading Cold Mountain poems.
West wind blasts the night rain,
gust on gust drenching the thatch.
Now and then I stick out my legs, lie down—
what's there to think about, what's the worry?

Line 4   [I.e., the poems of Han-shan.—Eds.]

11

READING THE *RECORD OF EIHEI DŌGEN*

On a somber spring evening around midnight,
rain mixed with snow sprinkled on the bamboos in the garden.
I wanted to ease my loneliness but it was quite impossible.
My hand reached behind me for the *Record of Eihei Dōgen*.
Beneath the open window at my desk,
I offered incense, lit a lamp, and quietly read.
Body and mind dropping away is simply the upright truth.
In one thousand postures, ten thousand appearances, a dragon toys with the
      jewel.
His understanding beyond conditioned patterns cleans up the current
      corruptions;
the ancient great master's style reflects the image of India.

I remember the old days when I lived at Entsū Monastery
and my late teacher lectured on the *True Dharma-eye.*
At that time there was an occasion to turn myself around,
so I requested permission to read it, and studied it intimately.
I keenly felt that until then I had depended merely on my own ability.
After that I left my teacher and wandered all over.
Between Dōgen and myself what relationship is there?
Everywhere I went I devotedly practiced the true dharma-eye.
Arriving at the depths and arriving at the vehicle—how many times?

Inside this teaching, there's never any shortcoming.
Thus I thoroughly studied the master of all things.
Now when I take the *Record of Eihei Dōgen* and examine it,
the tone does not harmonize well with usual beliefs.
Nobody has asked whether it is a jewel or a pebble.
For five hundred years it's been covered with dust
just because no one has had an eye for recognizing dharma.
For whom was all his eloquence expounded?
Longing for ancient times and grieving for the present, my heart is exhausted.

One evening sitting by the lamp my tears wouldn't stop,
and soaked into the records of the ancient buddha Eihei.
In the morning the old man next door came to my thatched hut.
He asked me why the book was damp.
I wanted to speak but didn't as I was deeply embarrassed;
my mind deeply distressed, it was impossible to give an explanation.
I dropped my head for a while, then found some words.
"Last night's rain leaked in and drenched my bookcase."

12

TO INSCRIBE ON A PICTURE OF A SKULL I PAINTED

All things born of causes end when causes run out;
but causes, what are they born of?
That very first cause—where did it come from?
At this point words fail me, workings of my mind go dead.
I took these words to the old woman in the house to the east;
the old woman in the house to the east was not pleased.
I questioned the old man in the house to the west;
the old man in the house to the west puckered his brow and walked away.
I tried writing the question on a biscuit, fed it to the dogs,
but even the dogs refused to bite.
Concluding that these must be unlucky words, a mere jumble of a query,
I rolled life and death into a pill, kneading them together,
and gave it to the skull in the meadowside.
Suddenly the skull came leaping up,
began to sing and dance for me,
a long song, ballad of the Three Ages,
a wonderful dance, postures of the Three Worlds.
Three worlds, three ages, three times danced over—
"the moon sets on Ch'ang-an and its midnight bells."

LINES 16–17   The three ages of past, present, and future; the three worlds of
desire, form, and formlessness.

LINE 19   Taken verbatim from a poem entitled "For the Monk San-tsang on
His Return to the Western Regions," by the ninth-century Chinese poet Li Tung.

13
All my life too lazy to try to get ahead,
I leave everything to the truth of Heaven.
In my sack three measures of rice,
by the stove one bundle of sticks—
why ask who's got satori, who hasn't?
What would I know about that dust, fame and gain?
Rainy nights here in my thatched hut
I stick out my two legs any old way I please.

Sources and Resources

Our goal here is fourfold: to give credit to sources utilized for each chapter; to acknowledge such emendations as we have made in the texts; to offer access to further resources about each of the masters and poets featured; and to suggest books for those who care to read more about the history or practice of Ch'an and Zen. We have confined ourselves to materials in English. For information about original Chinese and Japanese texts, please consult the English sources cited.

All poetry selections appear in their entirety; that is, this anthology may contain only two poems of a ten-poem cycle, but those two poems are complete. In the case of prose selections and selections that combine prose and poetry, space limitations and other editorial factors have usually required excerption. Where we have omitted a relatively brief section from a work, a section a few words to a few sentences in length, we indicate that omission in the customary fashion, with ellipses. Where we have pruned a paragraph or more, we signal this serious interruption of the text with white space. While we have sought throughout to preserve all the contextual elements vital to understanding the selections, excerption inevitably causes at least some loss of context and thus of nuance. For this and other reasons, we encourage readers to investigate the original sources listed below.

As the following, detailed notes will indicate, in early chapters of the book we have drawn repeatedly upon the compendium of Ch'an biographies known as *The Transmission of the Lamp*. Two translations, both unfortunately just partial, are available in English. Chang Chung-yüan's *Original Teachings of Ch'an Buddhism* (New York: Pantheon, 1966) furnishes records of nineteen important masters; it is introduced and helpfully annotated by Dr. Chang and has the virtue of a good index. Sohaku Ogata's *The Transmission of the Lamp: Early Masters* (Wakefield, NH: Longview Academic, 1990) is a complete, though often awkward, translation of the first third of the original text; a gold mine of early Ch'an material, it has an index of personal and place names and includes interpolated comments that Chang omits. We will refer to these books simply as Chang and Ogata.

Chapter 1. This version of Bodhidharma's "Two Entrances and Four Practices" is by Nelson Foster. For alternative translations, see J. C. Cleary, *Zen Dawn: Early Zen Texts from Tun Huang* (Boston: Shambhala, 1986), pp. 33–36; John R. McRae, *The Northern School and the Formation of Early Ch'an Buddhism* (Honolulu: University of Hawaii Press, 1986), pp. 103–05; Red Pine [Bill Porter], *The Zen Teaching of Bodhidharma* (Port Townsend, WA: Empty Bowl, 1987), pp. 1–3; and D. T. Suzuki, *Essays in Zen Buddhism,* 1st ser. (New York: Grove

Press, 1949), pp. 180–83. The material excerpted from *The Transmission of the Lamp* appears in Ogata, pp. 68–71. McRae's book (cited above) is the best single source in English on the formative period of Ch'an, and we relied on it heavily in preparing the introductions to our first three chapters.

Chapter 2. This translation of Seng-ts'an's *Hsin hsin ming* is by Nelson Foster. Several other translations are available, including Ch'an Master Sheng-yen's, in *The Poetry of Enlightenment: Poems by Ancient Ch'an Masters* (Elmhurst, NY: Dharma Drum Publications, 1987), pp. 23–29; Arthur Waley's, in Edward Conze, *Buddhist Texts through the Ages* (New York: Harper & Row, 1964), pp. 295–98; Thomas Cleary's, published as an appendix to *Instant Zen: Waking Up in the Present* (Berkeley, CA: North Atlantic Books, 1994); D. T. Suzuki's, from *Manual of Zen Buddhism* (New York: Grove Press, 1978), pp. 76–82; and Richard B. Clarke's chapbook, *hsin hsin ming* (Buffalo, NY: White Pine Press, 1984). Master Sheng-yen has also published an extended commentary on this text under the title *Faith in Mind: A Guide to Ch'an Practice* (Elmhurst, NY: Dharma Drum Publications, 1987). The passage from the *Tao Te Ching* that concludes the introduction occurs in Chapter 48 of that text; this is our version.

Chapter 3. The Hui-neng selections are excerpted from Philip B. Yampolsky's authoritative *Platform Sutra of the Sixth Patriarch* (New York: Columbia University Press, 1967), pp. 137–39, 140–41, and 159–62. We have omitted many of Dr. Yampolsky's detailed footnotes, which serve a more scholarly purpose than this book does. For an unraveling of the Hui-neng legends, see his introduction and John McRae's indispensable guide to the early history of Ch'an, *The Northern School and the Formation of Early Ch'an Buddhism,* cited in our notes to Chapter 1, above.

Chapter 4. Yung-chia's *Cheng-tao ke* is published here in a new version by Nelson Foster. Previous translations are found in D. T. Suzuki, *Manual of Zen Buddhism* (New York: Grove Press, 1978), pp. 89–103; Ch'an Master Sheng-yen, *The Poetry of Enlightenment: Poems by Ancient Ch'an Masters* (Elmhurst, NY: Dharma Drum Publications, 1987), pp. 49–64; Nyogen Senzaki and Ruth Strout McCandless, *Buddhism and Zen* (San Francisco: North Point Press, 1987), pp. 21–58; and Lu K'uan Yü [Chas. Luk], *Ch'an and Zen Teaching,* ser. 3 (London: Rider & Company, 1962), pp. 116–45. The latter two translations are accompanied by detailed commentaries. In our biographical note, we have retold Yung-chia's meeting with Hui-neng, drawing on several sources, including Ogata, p. 165; Chang, pp. 27–28; and Suzuki, *Essays in Zen Buddhism,* 1st ser. (New York: Grove Press, 1949), p. 223.

Chapter 5. The Wang Wei poems are new translations by Nelson Foster. Pauline Yu's *The Poetry of Wang Wei: New Translations and Commentary* (Bloomington, IN: Indiana University Press, 1980) is a penetrating critical study of the poet and his work, containing a very informative chapter on his Buddhist poems. Barnstone et al., *Laughing Lost in the Mountains* (Hanover, NH: University Press of New England, 1991), offer the best contemporary translations of Wang's poems; their selection is generous and their translations generally musical and reliable. Wai-lim Yip's *Hiding the Universe* (New York: Grossman, 1972) is valuable because he preserves much of the structure and ambiguity of the original poems. Bill Porter includes an amusing chapter on Wang Wei in his *Road to Heaven: Encounters with Chinese Hermits* (San Francisco: Mercury House, 1993). The brief quotation from Wang's memorial for Tao-kuang that appears in the introductory note is from Yu, p. 44.

Chapter 6. The Shih-t'ou selections come from three sources. The excerpts from *The Transmission of the Lamp* appear in D. T. Suzuki, *Manual of Zen Buddhism* (New York: Grove Press, 1978), pp. 105–07. "Song of the Grass-Roof Hermitage" is found as an appendix to *Cultivating the Empty Field: The Silent Illumination of Zen Master Hongzhi* (San Francisco: North Point Press, 1987), translated by Daniel Leighton with Yi Wu. The *Ts'an tung chi* was newly translated for this book by Nelson Foster. For alternate translations of this last text, consult R. H. Blyth, *Zen and Zen Classics,* vol. 1 (Rutland, VT: Charles E. Tuttle, 1988), pp. 146–51; Thomas Cleary, *Timeless Spring: A Sōtō Zen Anthology* (Tokyo: Weatherhill, 1980), pp. 36–39; and again, Sheng-yen's *The Poetry of Enlightenment: Poems by Ancient Ch'an Masters* (Elmhurst, NY: Dharma Drum Publications, 1987), pp. 69–70. In our introduction, we retell Shih-t'ou's first encounter with Ch'ing-yüan, drawing on several sources, including Ogata, pp. 159–60; Chang, pp. 27–28; and Suzuki, *Essays in Zen Buddhism,* 1st ser. (New York: Grove Press, 1949), p. 223.

Chapter 7. The best single source for Ma-tsu is Cheng Chien Bhikshu's *Sun Face Buddha: The Teachings of Ma-tsu and the Hung-chou School of Ch'an* (Berkeley: Asian Humanities Press, 1992). This scholarly but approachable book contains brief records for a dozen of Ma-tsu's most renowned students as well as the great master's own record. We have selected excerpts from pp. 65–67, 69–77, and 80, omitting notes that exceed the needs of this book. Variant forms of Ma-tsu's record also appear in Chang, pp. 148–52, and in Ogata, pp. 187–91.

Chapter 8. There are more and better translations available for Han-shan than for anyone else in this book. Rather than selecting from several sources, each stylistically distinctive, we elected to draw exclusively upon Burton Watson's *Cold Mountain: 101 Chinese Poems,* rev. 2nd ed. (Boston: Shambhala, 1992) and to supplement Watson's graceful work with, we hope, harmonious renderings of a few poems that he did not translate. The Watson poems are nos. 1–7, 9–14, and 16 in this sequence; in his own book, they are numbered 40, 96, 49, 95, 68, 97, 98, 75, 88, 43, 62, 37, 63, and 67. The remainder of the poems (nos. 8, 15, 17, and 18) were translated by Nelson Foster. Gary Snyder's inimitable translation of two dozen Han-shan poems remains in print; see *Riprap and Cold Mountain Poems* (San Francisco: North Point Press, 1990). His book also includes a full translation of the wonderful classic account of Han-shan's life. Red Pine [Bill Porter] published a spare, well-annotated translation of the complete poems entitled *The Collected Songs of Cold Mountain* (Port Townsend, WA: Copper Canyon, 1983). A second complete edition is Robert G. Henricks's scholarly *The Poetry of Han-shan* (Albany: State University of New York Press, 1990). Like Red Pine, Henricks has annotated each poem and provides an index to prior English translations; he furnishes many other useful tools and helps as well, including a thorough review and analysis of theses about Han-shan's life. We have utilized Henricks's work extensively in making selections and preparing our biographical note.

Chapter 9. Pai-chang's record is translated and carefully annotated in Thomas Cleary, *Sayings and Doings of Pai-chang* (Los Angeles: Center Publications, 1978), by far the best source on this master. We have excerpted from pp. 17–20, 34–35, 46–48, 67, and 71–72, as elsewhere omitting notes more scholarly than this book demands. Another version of Pai-chang's record appears in Ogata, pp. 210–20. In our introductory note, we quote P'ei Hsiu from J. C. Cleary's *Zen Dawn* (Boston: Shambhala, 1986), pp. 10–11, and Pai-chang's monastic code from Ogata, p. 218. For Ch'en's statement, see p. 151 of *Chinese Transformation of Buddhism* (Princeton: Princeton University Press, 1973), a fascinating source on the political, economic, and cultural factors that worked to shape Ch'an.

Chapter 10. The complete record of Layman P'ang appears in Ruth Fuller Sasaki et al., *The Recorded Sayings of Layman P'ang: A Ninth-Century Zen Classic* (New York: Weatherhill, 1971); this book was recently reissued by the same publisher under the title *A Man of Zen.* The translators complement the record with an excellent introduction and abundant notes. We have excerpted passages from the 1971 edition, pp. 45–47, 51–52, 71, and 72–76. A briefer record of the P'angs is given in Chang, pp. 174–77, while scattered anecdotes from the Layman's wanderings appear in Ogata.

Chapter 11. We have drawn Nan-chüan's biography from Chang, excerpting pp. 153–63 and removing those notes unnecessary in the present context. The encounter with Governor Lu retold in the introductory note appears somewhat differently in Chang, p. 160, and Thomas and J. C. Cleary, *The Blue Cliff Record* (Boulder, CO: Shambhala, 1977), vol. 2, p. 292. See also Yüan-wu's comments on the interaction and on Nan-chüan's abilities, pp. 293–94. The story about Nan-chüan and his sickle is our own version; for a slightly different telling, see p. 312 of Kazuaki Tanahashi's *Moon in a Dewdrop: Writings of Zen Master Dōgen* (San Francisco: North Point Press, 1985).

Chapter 12. Kuei-shan's record appears in *The Transmission of the Lamp.* We have used the version in Chang, pp. 202–08, with emendations as indicated; we have also removed notes that exceed the requirements of this book. The only English translation of the "Admonitions of Kuei-shan" we are aware of is a chapbook by that title, uncredited, published in a limited edition by Nanyang Books in 1977.

Chapter 13. Most of the Po Chü-i selections come from the eminent British scholar of Chinese language and literature Arthur Waley and from his *Chinese Poems* (London: George Allen & Unwin, 1983), pp. 114, 140, 145, 157, 158, 160, 164, 169, and 172. One exception, "The Chancellor's Gravel-Drive," is from his *Translations from the Chinese* (New York: Knopf, 1941), p. 178. Since Waley made these translations early in the twentieth century, some of their language now feels archaic, and we have slightly emended several of them to soften this effect. The two final poems in the chapter are translated by Burton Watson in "Buddhism in the Poetry of Po Chü-i," *The Eastern Buddhist,* new ser., vol. XXI, no. 1 (spring, 1988), pp. 1–22, which offers an illuminating assessment of Po's Ch'an connections, practice, and understanding. We found Ch'en's chapter on "Literary Life" in *Chinese Transformation of Buddhism* (Princeton: Princeton University Press, 1973) a useful source as well. The poem about semi-reclusive living mentioned in the introductory note is translated by Waley in *Chinese Poems,* pp. 63–64, as are the lines that we quote from "Madly Singing in the Mountains," p. 145. Po's riposte to Lao-tzu also appears there, p. 173, but we have prepared our own version both of this verse and of his tribute to Tsung-mi, which is found in Peter N. Gregory's *Tsung-mi and the Sinification of Buddhism* (Princeton: Princeton University Press, 1991), p. 78. Ch'en discusses the "Biography of a Master of Wine and Song," pp. 218, 221–22, while Ogata, pp. 108–09, 368–69, is our source for the passages quoted or paraphrased from *The Transmission of the Lamp.* Burton Watson recently republished his translation of Po's "Record of the Thatched Hut on Mt. Lu" in his *Four Huts: Asian Writings on the Simple Life* (Boston: Shambhala, 1994).

Chapter 14. The Huang-po selections are from John Blofeld's translation of P'ei Hsiu's text, *The Zen Teaching of Huang-po* (New York: Grove Weidenfeld, 1958), pp. 29–30, 34–36, 57–59, 123–24, 96–97, 100–01, and 63–64. We have omitted some of Blofeld's many scholarly and explanatory notes. The introductory note draws heavily on Blofeld's translation as well, quoting pp. 28, 102, 96, 94, and 27. Both *The Blue Cliff Record* passages are from case 11; for a complete translation, refer to Thomas and J. C. Cleary, *The Blue Cliff Record* (Boulder, CO: Shambhala, 1977), vol. 1, pp. 72–80. Pai-chang's injunction appears in Chapter 9, above, and in somewhat different forms in Ogata, p. 211, and Isshū Miura and Ruth Fuller Sasaki, *Zen Dust* (New York: Harcourt, Brace & World, 1966), p. 231.

Chapter 15. We have chosen to adapt Chao-chou's biography in *The Transmission of the Lamp* from Ogata, pp. 346–59; it is also in Chang, pp. 164–73. The dialogues in the introductory note, like the biography itself, have their ultimate source in his voluminous record, most of which has been translated by Yoel Hoffman in *Radical Zen: The Sayings of Jōshū* (Brookline, MA: Autumn Press, 1978). See items no. 294, 67, and 445 for the dialogues we cite; we have rendered the first somewhat differently than Hoffman does. For another version of the exchange about the log bridge, with classical commentary, see Thomas and J. C. Cleary, *The Blue Cliff Record* (Boulder, CO: Shambhala, 1977), vol. 2, pp. 353–56.

Chapter 16. Both Te-shan selections are from Thomas and J. C. Cleary, *The Blue Cliff Record* (Boulder, CO: Shambhala, 1977), vol. 1, pp. 24–27, 231–32. The first is excerpted from a commentary by Yüan-wu that is integral to *The Blue Cliff Record*. The second is a portion of Te-shan's biography from *The Transmission of the Lamp*, which the Clearys have translated and appended to their book as a biographical supplement to the classic text.

Chapter 17. All selections are from Burton Watson, *The Zen Teachings of Master Lin-chi* (Boston: Shambhala, 1993), a complete translation of Lin-chi's record that manages to be both lively and scholarly. We have excerpted from pp. 38–39, 67–71, 31–32, 76–81, 99, 94, 93, 122–23, and 21–22. Earlier translations of the record are Ruth Fuller Sasaki, *The Recorded Sayings of Ch'an Master Lin-chi Hui-chao of Chen Prefecture* (Kyoto: Institute for Zen Studies, n.d.), and Irmgard Schloegl, *The Zen Teaching of Rinzai* (Berkeley: Shambhala, 1976). Lin-chi's biography as given by *The Transmission of the Lamp* is translated in Chang, pp. 116–23. Thomas and J. C. Cleary offer another version thereof in *The Blue Cliff Record* (Boulder, CO: Shambhala, 1977), vol. 1, pp. 253–55; they also translate some of his important teaching formulae, pp. 255–57. Passages from the record in the introductory note are either our own versions (the "true person" passage and foot-washing episode) or quoted from Watson, p. 109 (the altercation with Te-shan). The "true person" passage is especially famous, appearing in case 38 of the *Book of Equanimity*, among other places. For that text, see Thomas Cleary, *Book of Serenity* (Hudson, NY: Lindisfarne Press, 1990).

Chapter 18. William F. Powell's exemplary *The Record of Tung-shan* (Honolulu: University of Hawaii Press, 1986) furnished the text for this chapter and is, by far, the best single source of information about Tung-shan. The selection is excerpted from Powell, pp. 23–26, 27–28, 29, 33, 35, 39, 55, 56, 57, and 62–63. As in other selections, we have omitted notes that seem unnecessary in the current context. The master's record from *The Transmission of the Lamp* is translated in Chang, pp. 58–70, and from another old source in Thomas and J. C. Cleary, *The Blue Cliff Record* (Boulder, CO: Shambhala, 1977), vol. 2, pp. 449–52. Both verses quoted in the introductory note are from Miura and Sasaki, *Zen Dust* (New York: Harcourt, Brace & World, 1966), pp. 292 and 287. Porter's *Road to Heaven* (San Francisco: Mercury House, 1993), pp. 70–71, provides a recent photograph of stone chambers akin to Yün-yen's hermitage.

Chapter 19. The anecdotes about Hsüeh-feng are excerpted from three sources. The first three are from William F. Powell, *The Record of Tung-shan* (Honolulu: University of Hawaii Press, 1986), pp. 36–37. The next seven appear in Nyogen Senzaki and Ruth Strout McCandless, *The Iron Flute* (Rutland, VT: Tuttle, 1964), pp. 49, 120–23, 59, 64, 47–48, 136, and 77; we have omitted interlinear comments in two instances. The remainder are excerpted from Chang, pp. 277–282. The lacquer bucket incident discussed in the introductory note is translated in Thomas and J. C. Cleary, *The Blue Cliff Record* (Boulder, CO: Shambhala, 1977), vol. 2, p. 317 (note a). Slightly different versions of Hsüeh-feng's enlightenment story, poem, and "grain of millet" speech are found in vol. 1 of the same source, pp. 32–33, 145–46, and 31. Hsüeh-feng's advice to Ch'ang-ch'ing is found, otherwise rendered, both in Miura and Sasaki, *Zen Dust* (New York: Harcourt, Brace & World, 1966), p. 292, and in Cleary and Cleary, *The Blue Cliff Record* vol. 1, p. 241.

Chapter 20. We have excerpted Ts'ao-shan's record from Wm. Theodore de Bary, *The Buddhist Tradition in India, China, and Japan* (New York: Modern Library, 1969), pp. 232–240. Another translation is available in Chang, pp. 58–70. The story of Su-shan's adventures beneath the seat is found in Miura and Sasaki, *Zen Dust* (New York: Harcourt, Brace & World, 1966), pp. 286–87; names have been converted from the Japanese to the Chinese form. Several of Ts'ao-shan's writings are translated by Thomas and J. C. Cleary in their *The Blue Cliff Record* (Boulder, CO: Shambhala, 1977), vol. 2, pp. 464–67, and in Thomas Cleary, *Timeless Spring: A Sōtō Zen Anthology* (Tokyo: Weatherhill, 1980), pp. 50–53.

Chapter 21. Urs App's wonderful *Master Yunmen: From the Record of the Chan Teacher "Gate of the Clouds"* (New York: Kodansha, 1994) furnished virtually all of the material for this chapter. The selections are excerpted from pp. 83–85, 103–05, 137, 182–83, 134, 214, 116, 147, 113, 167, 168, 169, 92, 139, 96, 163, 161, 105, 106, 91, 121, and 203. App's excellent introduction and appendices provided much of the information we have used in the introductory note. See pp. 26–27 for Yün-men's audience with the emperor. The story and reference regarding horse medicine are given above, in Chapter 19, while the "hammer and tongs" quotation comes from Thomas and J. C. Cleary, *The Blue Cliff Record* (Boulder, CO: Shambhala, 1977), vol. 1, p. 39. Chang, pp. 283–95, provides the relatively brief *The Transmission of the Lamp* biography of Yün-men.

Chapter 22. The selections from Fa-yen's "Ten Guidelines" derive from two sources. The final three paragraphs come from Thomas Cleary's "Introduction to the History of Zen Practice" in Kōun Yamada, *The Gateless Gate,* 2nd ed. (Tucson: University of Arizona Press, 1990), p. 253. The remainder will be found in Cleary's *Zen Essence: The Science of Freedom* (Boston: Shambhala, 1989), pp. 12–14. Fa-yen's poem appears twice, in differing translations, in Thomas and J. C. Cleary, *The Blue Cliff Record* (Boulder, CO: Shambhala, 1977), vol. 1, p. 214, and vol. 3, p. 581; we have chosen to use our own version. Fa-yen's *The Transmission of the Lamp* biography is excerpted from Chang, pp. 238–45. In the introductory note, we have quoted passages from "Ten Guidelines" that, to the best of our knowledge, have so far been published only in *Ten Guidelines for Chan Schools,* mimeo (Nanyang Books, n.d.).

Chapter 23. As a source of Hsüeh-tou's writing, the only good book in English is *The Blue Cliff Record,* translated in its entirety by Thomas and J. C. Cleary (Boulder, CO: Shambhala, 1977). The Clearys have done extraordinary service in providing readers of English access to the original literature of Ch'an and Zen, but none has been a greater gift than their translation of this immense work. In our selections, we have paired the Clearys' translations of the poems with our own versions of the cases. Their poems appear in vol. 1, pp. 12–13, 19–20, 168–69, and 213; vol. 2, pp. 271–72, 276, 383–84, and 403; and vol. 3, pp. 533–34. We took the liberty of altering the initial line of the poem for case 2 to bring it into conformity with our rendering of the same words in the case and, more important, in the text being quoted (see Chapter 2). The comment on Chih-men's teaching style is Yüan-wu's, from *The Blue Cliff Record,* vol. 1, p. 141.

Chapter 24. For Su T'ung-po, as for so many other classical writers of China and Japan, Burton Watson has been our best source. He recently reissued *Selected Poems of Su T'ung-po* (Port Townsend, WA: Copper Canyon Press, 1994), offers 116 poems well translated, well annotated, and well introduced. Watson orders the poems chronologically, and we have done likewise, using poems no. 8, 17, 34, 38, 39, 41, 42, 62–63, 84, 87, 115, and 116. In our biographical note, we have supplied our own version of the valley stream verse and have quoted seven lines from Kenneth Rexroth's "The Weaker the Wine," which appears, along with two dozen more of Su's poems, in Rexroth's *One Hundred Poems from the Chinese* (New York: New Directions, 1971), p. 72–73. The Hakuin quotation is from Philip B. Yampolsky, *Zen Master Hakuin: Selected Writings* (New York: Columbia Univ. Press, 1971), pp. 56–57, while Su's statement about his literary wellsprings is translated by Bernard Faure in *Chan Insights and Oversights: An Epistemological Critique of the Chan Tradition* (Princeton: Princeton University Press, 1993), p. 206. A book-length treatment of Su's Buddhism is now available in Beata Grant, *Mount Lu Revisited: Buddhism in the Life and Writings of Su Shih* (Honolulu: University of Hawaii Press, 1994), which we discovered, unfortunately, too late to consult.

Chapter 25. We have drawn the Yüan-wu selections from three sources. His *The Blue Cliff Record* commentaries are from the Clearys' translation by that title (Boulder, CO: Shambhala, 1977), vol. 1, pp. 159–61; vol. 2, pp. 338–40; and vol. 3, pp. 571–73. For purposes of accessibility, we have omitted much of the text; to appreciate its scope and intricacy, consult the complete translation provided by the Clearys. The accounts of Yüan-wu's dealings with women are Thomas Cleary translations originally published in *Kahawai: Journal of Women and Zen,* vol. VI, no. 2, p. 16; vol. III, no. 3, p. 19; and vol. IV, no. 1, p. 14; we have replaced names rendered phonetically with conjectual Wade-Giles spellings. Finally, the passages excerpted from his correspondence appear in J. C. and Thomas Cleary, *Zen Letters: Teachings of Yuanwu* (Boston: Shambhala, 1993), pp. 54–55, 48–50, and 51–52. In preparing our introduction, we culled biographical information from many sources. The story of Yüan-wu's training and awakening has been variously rendered and retold; for two versions, see D. T. Suzuki, *The Zen Koan as a Means of Attaining Enlightenment,* new ed. (Boston: Tuttle, 1994), pp. 200–01, and Norman Waddell, *Essential Teachings of Zen Master Hakuin* (Boston: Shambhala, 1994), pp. 129–30 (n. 13). The publishing history of *The Blue Cliff Record* is detailed in Miura and Sasaki, *Zen Dust* (New York: Harcourt, Brace & World, 1966), pp. 356–58. Yüan-wu's statements concerning ancient precedents are quoted from Thomas Cleary, *Zen Lessons: The Art of Leadership* (Boston: Shambhala, 1994), p. 56, as is his dictum on life in the realm of demons, p. 105.

Chapter 26. The initial selections from Hung-chih—all the prose statements and the first two of his poems—come from Daniel Leighton's translations with Yi Wu in *Cultivating the Empty Field: The Silent Illumination of Zen Master Hongzhi* (San Francisco: North Point Press, 1981), pp. 18–19, 24—25, 36–37, 7, 46, and 47. His "Lancet of Seated Meditation" appears in Carl Bielefeldt, *Dōgen's Manuals of Zen Meditation* (Berkeley: University of California Press), pp. 199–200. Hung-chih's poems from the *Book of Equanimity,* with the corresponding cases, are excerpted from Thomas Cleary's *Book of Serenity: One Hun-

dred Zen Dialogues (Hudson, NY: Lindisfarne Press, 1990), pp. 167–68, 248, 250, 316–17, 356, and 358. We have omitted the bulk of the text here, but Cleary translates it in full, including original commentaries on both the cases and the poems. Leighton's introduction to his book is the best source in English on Hung-chih's life and work; we relied on it in preparing our own introduction. The entire "dead tree" exchange from *The Transmission of the Lamp* is given in the selection for Chapter 20 and translated in Chang, pp. 77–78; this is our version. Hung-chih's final poem is from Miura and Sasaki, *Zen Dust* (New York: Harcourt, Brace & World, 1966), p. 171.

Chapter 27.   Christopher Cleary's *Swampland Flowers: The Letters and Lectures of Zen Master Ta Hui* (New York: Grove Press, 1977) contains a large selection of Ta-hui's correspondence, but we elected to use the careful translations of Piegwang Dowiat, in part because they give us a taste of Ta-hui's incoming mail. Dowiat's translations were originally published in *Ch'an Magazine* (the journal of the Institute of Chung-Hwa Buddhist culture), vol. 8, no. 1, pp. 6–10, and vol. 8, no. 3, pp. 7–9; additional letters appeared in vol. 9 and 10 of the same journal. We have omitted notes unnecessary in this context. The stories of Ta-hui's interactions with women are drawn from translations by Thomas Cleary published in *Kahawai: Journal of Women and Zen,* vol. VI, no. 2, pp. 16–17 and 21–22; as elsewhere, we have replaced the names rendered phonetically with conjectural Wade-Giles spellings. In preparing our introduction, we relied on biographical materials in *Swampland Flowers,* pp. xiii–xx; in Takashi James Kodera, *Dōgen's Formative Years in China* (Boulder, CO: Prajna Press, 1980), pp. 85–95; and in Miura and Sasaki, *Zen Dust* (New York: Harcourt, Brace & World, 1966), pp. 163–65. Ta-hui's criticism of government officials is from Kodera, pp. 93–94. The passage quoting Assembly Chief Yin appears in Thomas Cleary. *Zen Lessons: The Art of Leadership* (Boston: Shambhala, 1994), pp. 95–96. This last text is a translation of Ta-hui's *Precious Lessons from the Ch'an Schools,* as edited (and supplemented) by one of his Dharma descendants; thus it offers an excellent overview of Ta-hui's concerns for the future of Ch'an. The lines of verse with which Yüan-wu closes *The Blue Cliff Record* are rendered a little differently in Thomas and J. C. Cleary's translation of that text (Boulder, CO: Shambhala, 1977), vol. 3, p. 640.

Chapter 28.   Shih-wu owes his English readership to Red Pine (Bill Porter), who has published a translation of all 185 poems in his main verse collection under the title *The Mountain Poems of Stonehouse* (Port Townsend, WA: Empty Bowl, 1986). Unfortunately, the book was issued only in a small edition, which is now out of print, but is soon to be revised by Mercury House of San Francisco. For our selection, we have used Shih-wu's introduction and poems no. 13, 159, 31, 18, 44, 54, 55, 28, 30, 64, 156, 108, 109, 116, 129, 142, 145, 174, and 37. We have emended poems 18, 44, 55, and 174 very slightly for consistency or readability. Lines from an additional poem, no. 180, appear in our introduction, along with a large quantity of information about Shih-wu borrowed from Red Pine's preface. Our source regarding Shih-wu's Korean disciple is Mu Soeng Sunim, *Thousand Peaks: Korean Zen—Tradition and Teachers* (Berkeley: Parallax Press, 1987), pp. 110–12.

Chapter 29. The selections from Dōgen's *Shōbōgenzō zuimonki,* or *Record of Things Heard,* are excerpted from Reihō Masunaga's *A Primer of Sōtō Zen* (Honolulu: University of Hawaii Press, 1971), pp. 38–39, 63–64, 96–97, 103, 106–07, and 27–28. His "Lancet of Seated Meditation" appears in Carl Bielefeldt, *Dōgen's Manuals of Zen Meditation* (Berkeley: University of California Press), p. 204, while "One Bright Pearl" is from Francis H. Cook's *Sounds of Valley Streams* (Albany: State University of New York, 1989), pp. 71–75. More English-language studies and translations are available for Dōgen than for any other Japanese master. Besides the Bielefeldt volume just cited, outstanding book-length studies include Takashi James Kodera, *Dōgen's Formative Years in China* (Boulder, CO: Prajna Press, 1980), and Hee-Jin Kim, *Dōgen Kigen: Mystical Realist,* rev. ed. (Tucson: University of Arizona Press, 1987). We examined all three of these closely in preparing our introduction and benefited as well from William Bodiford's treatment of Dōgen in his excellent study, *Sōtō Zen in Medieval Japan* (Honolulu: University of Hawaii, 1993). We quote Ju-ching via Dōgen from Kodera, p. 123, and Dōgen himself from Kazuaki Tanahashi's rich harvest of translations, *Moon in a Dewdrop: Writings of Zen Master Dōgen* (San Francisco: North Point Press, 1985), pp. 156, 148, and 105. In addition to sources already mentioned, for further translations, see Cook's *How to Raise an Ox: Zen Practice as Taught in Zen Master Dōgen's Shobogenzo* (Los Angeles: Center Publications, 1978) and a pair of books from Thomas Cleary, *Rational Zen: the Mind of Dōgen Zenji* (Boston: Shambhala, 1993) and *Shōbōgenzō: Zen Essays by Dōgen* (Honolulu: University of Hawaii, 1986).

Chapter 30. Enni Ben'en has not been published much in English. Our selections are drawn from Thomas Cleary's *The Original Face: An Anthology of Rinzai Zen* (New York: Grove Press, 1978), pp. 50–51 and 52–57. The principal sources of biographical information in our introduction are Martin Collcutt's fine study, *Five Mountains: The Rinzai Zen Monastic Institution in Medieval Japan* (Cambridge: Harvard University Press, 1981), pp. 41–48, and Heinrich Dumoulin's thorough *Zen Buddhism: A History,* vol. 2 (New York: Macmillan Publishing Company, 1988), pp. 24–29. The quotation from Dōgen appears in Collcutt, p. 52.

Chapter 31. Our selections from Daikaku are drawn from Trevor Leggett, *Zen and the Ways* (Rutland, VT: Charles E. Tuttle Company, 1987), pp. 58–61, 77, and 78–79. Leggett provided some of the information for our introductory note; we relied also on Collcutt, *Five Mountains: The Rinzai Zen Monastic Institution in Medieval Japan* (Cambridge: Harvard University Press, 1981), pp. 65–68, and Dumoulin, *Zen Buddhism: A History,* vol. 2 (New York: Macmillan Publishing Company, 1988), pp. 32–34. The passages quoted in the introduction are from Collcutt, pp. 66–68, except for the poem on brush-talk, which is translated by Kenneth Kraft in his *Eloquent Zen: Daitō and Early Japanese Zen* (Honolulu: University of Hawaii, 1992), p. 53. For more of Daikaku's writing, see his Zen manual in question-and-answer format, the *Zazenron,* in both Leggett, pp. 43–57, and Thomas Cleary, *The Original Face: An Anthology of Rinzai Zen* (New York: Grove Press, 1978), pp. 19–41.

Chapter 32. Two complete translations of Keizan's *Denkōroku* are available. We have used Francis H. Cook's *The Record of Transmitting the Light* (Los Angeles: Center Publications, 1991), in part because it is so thoroughly annotated. The selections are from pp. 39–42, 194–96, and 223–26. Thomas Cleary's alternative translation is *Transmission of Light* (San Francisco: North Point Press, 1990). The introductions of both these books provided material for our biographical note. For details about Keizan's part in development of the Sōtō sect, however, we relied on Bodiford's *Sōtō Zen in Medieval Japan* (Honolulu: University of Hawaii, 1993), especially the chapter that he devotes to Keizan, pp. 81–92. The passage specifying the terms at Yōkō-ji is quoted from Bodiford, p. 86. For more of Keizan's writing, see Thomas Cleary's *Timeless Spring: A Sōtō Zen Anthology* (Tokyo: Weatherhill, 1980), pp. 112–37.

Chapter 33. Musō's "Reflections upon the Enmity between Emperor Go-Daigo and the Shogun, Ashikaga Takauji" comes from Wm. Theodore De Bary, ed., *Sources of Japanese Tradition,* vol. 1 (New York: Columbia University Press, 1967), pp. 250–52. The subsequent prose passages are from Thomas Cleary, *Dream Conversations on Buddhism and Zen* (Boston: Shambhala, 1994), which offers a generous sample from the contents of the *Muchū mondō;* our selections are from pp. 182–85, and 103–06. A smaller sample from the same text, giving a fuller sense of the original, is Kenneth Kraft's "Musō Kokushi's *Dialogues in a Dream,*" *The Eastern Buddhist,* new ser., vol. XIV, no. 1 (Spring, 1981), pp. 75–93. The best and largest English translation of Musō's poetry is W. S. Merwin and Soiku Shigematsu's *Sun at Midnight: Poems and Sermons by Musō Soseki* (San Francisco: North Point Press, 1989); we have used poems no. 14, 7, 23, 130, 114, and 1. As Merwin notes in his introduction to the book, Musō wrote his poems as quatrains, but each of the lines is broken into three parts here, to represent the way the poems have been chanted, for centuries, in Japanese. For our biographical sketch, we turned to all the above sources and to Collcutt, *Five Mountains: The Rinzai Zen Monastic Insti-*

tution in Medieval Japan (Cambridge: Harvard University Press, 1981); Kraft, *Eloquent Zen: Daitō and Early Japanese Zen* (Honolulu: University of Hawaii, 1992); and Dumoulin, *Zen Buddhism: A History,* vol. 2 (New York: Macmillan Publishing Company, 1988). The lines we quote from Musō's enlightenment poem are in Merwin and Shigematsu, poem no. 110.

Chapter 34. Daitō's "The Original Face" is translated by Trevor Leggett in his *A First Zen Reader* (Rutland, VT: Charles E. Tuttle Company, 1960), pp. 21–22. By far the best general source on Daitō, however, is Kenneth Kraft's *Eloquent Zen: Daitō and Early Japanese Zen* (Honolulu: University of Hawaii, 1992). This latter volume has furnished our selection of his capping-phrase commentaries and poems (pp. 196, 186–87, 189, and 191–92), as well as all the quotations (pp. 41, 42, and 78) and much of the biographical material in our introductory note. For a briefer, less critical account of Daitō's life, see Dumoulin, *Zen Buddhism: A History,* vol. 2 (New York: Macmillan Publishing Company, 1988), pp. 186–92.

Chapter 35. Our selection of Jakushitsu's letters comes from Thomas Cleary's *Original Face: An Anthology of Rinzai Zen* (New York: Grove Press, 1978), pp. 76–78, while we owe Jakushitsu's poems to Burton Watson's little-known *The Rainbow World: Japan in Essays and Translations* (Seattle: Broken Moon Press, 1990), pp. 124–29. In preparing our introduction, we also consulted Dumoulin, *Zen Buddhism: A History,* vol. 2 (New York: Macmillan Publishing Company, 1988), principally pp. 203–06, as well as David Pollack's *Zen Poems of the Five Mountains* (New York: Crossroad Publishing Company, 1985). Very little of Jakushitsu's work has yet made its way into English, but fifteen more poems appear, in rather unpolished English, in Eido Shimano, ed., *Like a Dream, Like a Fantasy: The Zen Writings and Translations of Nyogen Senzaki* (Tokyo: Japan Publications, Inc., 1978), pp. 79–83, and another eight are scattered throughout Pollack's *Five Mountains* anthology. A brief piece of prose, "Ten Warnings to the Congregation," may be found in Lucien Stryk and Takashi Ikemoto's *Zen: Poems, Prayers, Sermons, Anecdotes, Interviews* (Garden City, NY: Doubleday & Company, 1965), pp. 59–60.

Chapter 36. Arthur Braverman's wonderful *Mud and Water: A Collection of Talks by the Zen Master Bassui* (San Francisco: North Point Press, 1989) is the source of all the selections in this chapter and most of the biographical information in our note. Our selections are from pp. 3–4, 98–100, 102, 105–06, 107–08, and 19–23. For additional translations from Bassui, look to Philip Kapleau, ed., *Three Pillars of Zen: Teaching, Practice, and Enlightenment* (Boston: Beacon Press, 1967), pp. 155–86, and to Thomas Cleary, *Original Face: An Anthology of Rinzai Zen* (New York: Grove Press, 1978), pp. 94–98.

Chapter 37. We have taken this selection of Ikkyū's poems from John Stevens, *Wild Ways: Zen Poems of Ikkyū* (Boston: Shambhala, 1995), pp. 56, 16, 21, 45, 64–65, 77, 91, 6, and 7. Though Stevens's anthology also contains Ikkyū's "Skeletons," we have chosen to excerpt another translation, begun by R. H. Blyth, completed by Norman Waddell, and published in Frederick Franck, *The Buddha Eye* (New York: Crossroad Publishing Company, 1991), pp. 77–79. In her scholarly *Ikkyū and the Crazy Cloud Anthology: A Zen Poet of Medieval Japan* (Tokyo: University of Tokyo Press, 1986), Sonja Arntzen has translated and painstakingly annotated a large, diverse assortment of Ikkyū's poems. While her translations fall short musically, the book is immensely informative and the best guide to the complexities of his verse; we relied upon it heavily as a source of our introductory note. Ikkyū's statement rejecting gossip about family background comes from Yusen Kashiwahara and Koyu Sonoda, eds., *Shapers of Japanese Buddhism* (Tokyo: Kosei Publishing Co., 1994), p. 147. His tribute to Daitō appears here in our own version; variations are found in Kraft, *Eloquent Zen: Daitō and Early Japanese Zen* (Honolulu: University of Hawaii, 1992), p. 43, and in Stevens, p. 13. Daitō's description of his rightful successor occurs in his "Final Admonitions," quoted from Kraft, p. 117, while Stevens, p. 10, furnishes Ikkyū's scornful line regarding his likely whereabouts after his retirement from Daitoku-ji.

Chapter 38. We have excerpted Takuan's essays from translations by William Scott Wilson in his *The Unfettered Mind: Writings of the Zen Master to the Sword Master* (Tokyo: Kodansha International, 1986), pp. 32–34, 37–38, and 85–89. Our biographical sketch draws from Wilson but also, more heavily, from Y. Kashiwahara and K. Sonoda, eds., *Shapers of Japanese Buddhism* (Tokyo: Kosei Publishing Co., 1994), pp. 172–84, and H. Dumoulin, *Zen Buddhism: A History,* vol. 2 (New York: Macmillan Publishing Company, 1988), pp. 274–88. Kashiwahara and Sonoda, pp. 177 and 183, supply the quotations we have used regarding Suden's regulations and Takuan's sense of being a performing monkey. Takuan's comments on not using the sword to kill and intuitively knowing right from wrong are in Wilson, pp. 81 and 82. The subsequent poem we have adapted from Zenkei Shibayama, *Zen Comments on the Mumonkan* (New York: Harper & Row, 1974), p. 187, while Takuan's instructions about the disposition of his remains appear in Dumoulin, pp. 278–79.

Chapter 39. The poems of Ishikawa Jōzan and much of the information in our introduction are drawn from Burton Watson's *Kanshi: The Poetry of Ishikawa Jōzan and Other Edo-Period Poets* (San Francisco: North Point Press, 1990); the verses that we have selected appear on pp. 15, 11, 13, 20, 21, 27, 25, and 31–33 of that book. The description of Ishikawa we quote from Miura and Sasaki's *Zen Dust* (New York: Harcourt, Brace & World, 1966), is on p. 216.

Chapter 40. The only English-language source that has published much either by or about Shidō Munan is the excellent, Kyoto-based, scholarly journal *The Eastern Buddhist.* Our excerpts of "On Self-Nature" come from a translation by Kusumita Priscella Pedersen, "Jishō-ki," *The Eastern Buddhist,* new ser., vol. VIII, no. 1, pp. 101–02, 111, 116, 122, and 129. "On This Mind" is excerpted from a translation by Kobori Sōhaku and Norman A. Waddell, published in three parts: "Sokushin-ki," *The Eastern Buddhist,* new ser., vol. III, no. 2, pp. 92, 93–94, 96, 101–02, 113, and 117–18. In preparing our introductory note, we have referenced and relied extensively on Kobori Sōhaku's translation of "The Biography of Shidō Munan Zenji" by Tōrei in *The Eastern Buddhist,* new ser., vol. III, no. 1. Quotations in our note appeared in "Jishō-ki," pp. 131–32, 98–99; the biography, p. 136; "Jishō-ki," p. 98; "Sokushin-ki," part 2, p. 122; and "Sokushin-ki," part 1, pp. 100, 112. We have provided our own version of Munan's famous "Die while alive" verse; for another rendering and to examine its context, consult "Sokushin-ki," part 2, p. 116.

Chapter 41. *The* great source for Bankei, from which we have drawn all our selections, is Norman Waddell's *The Unborn: The Life and Teaching of Zen Master Bankei, 1622–1693* (San Francisco: North Point Press, 1984). We have excerpted from pp. 77–79, 87–88, 40, 117, 118–19, and 69–70. In recounting Bankei's life, we quote Waddell's introduction as well as his translations: pp. 77, 5, 8–9, 16, 107, 80, 57, 107, 25 (n. 8), and 37.

Chapter 42. Bashō's famous *Oku no hosomichi* has been translated many times and published under many titles. For present purposes, we chose Sam Hamill's graceful and accessible *Narrow Road to the Interior* (Boston: Shambhala, 1991), pp. 15–21, 28–31, 40–44, 47–53, and 74–75. To get closer to the Japanese text and to plumb its allusive depths, we recommend Cid Corman and Kamaike Susumu's translation, *Back Roads to Far Towns* (Hopewell, NJ: The Ecco Press, 1996). In our introduction, we quote Ten'in Ryūtaku from Burton Watson's "Zen Poetry," in Kenneth Kraft, ed., *Zen: Tradition and Transition* (New York: Grove Press, 1988), p. 115. Bashō's reflections on the banana tree are from Nobuyuki Yuasa's collection of travel diaries by Bashō, *The Narrow Road to the Deep North and Other Travel Sketches* (Middlesex, England: Penguin Books, 1966), p. 26. Bashō's statements about the uselessness of his poetry and his bat-like status are from Wm. Theodore de Bary, ed., *Sources of Japanese Tradition,* vol. 1 (New York: Columbia University Press, 1967), pp. 449 and 447. Hakuin's painting is reproduced in Kazuaki Tanahashi's *Penetrating Laughter: Hakuin's Zen and Art* (Woodstock, NY: Overlook Press, 1984), p. 104; that is the source of the inscription quoted, too. Sengai's painting is in D. T. Suzuki's *Sengai the Zen Master* (Greenwich, CT: New York Graphic Society, 1971), pp. 176–77.

Bashō's directive to "Go to the pine" is from Yuasa, p. 33, while his comment about taking to the road rather than "entering the precincts of the Buddha" is adapted from his "Record of the Hut of Phantom Dwelling," translated by Burton Watson in *Four Huts: Asian Writings on the Simple Life* (Boston: Shambhala, 1994), p. 129. Corman and Kamaike's "Notes" is the source of both quotations concerning Bashō's allusions. R. H. Blyth reports Bashō's deathbed remarks in *Zen in English Literature and Oriental Classics* (Tokyo: Hokuseido Press, 1942), p. 247. We have devised our own versions of the four haiku incorporated in our biographical sketch. For a fuller introduction to Bashō and an illuminating examination of his poetry from the perspective of Zen, consult Robert Aitken's *A Zen Wave: Bashō's Haiku and Zen* (New York: Weatherhill, 1978), recently issued in a new edition.

Chapter 43. Like Shidō Munan, Baisaō is available in English thanks to *The Eastern Buddhist.* Our selections are from Norman Waddell's "The Old Tea Seller: The Life and Poetry of Baisaō," *Eastern Buddhist,* new ser., vol. XVII, no. 2, pp. 117, 100–01, 104, 106, 118, 114, 108, and 122. For biographical information, we have also relied upon Waddell, quoting from his introduction, pp. 97, 94, 93, and 122–23. Chao-chou's exchange may be found in his record, as translated by Yoel Hoffman, *Radical Zen: The Sayings of Jōshū* (Brookline, MA: Autumn Press, 1978), p. 140. Dōgen ends his essay "Everyday Activity" with a variant; see Kazuaki Tanahashi's *Moon in a Dewdrop: Writings of Zen Master Dōgen* (San Francisco: North Point Press, 1985), p. 128. Our version is based mainly on Hoffman.

Chapter 44. The Hakuin selections begin with excerpts from two sources: "The True and Untransmittable Dharma," translated by Norman Waddell in *The Essential Teachings of Zen Master Hakuin* (Boston: Shambhala, 1994), pp. 88–92, and "Orategama I," from Philip B. Yampolsky's *Zen Master Hakuin: Selected Writings* (New York: Columbia University Press, 1971), pp. 49–53 and 54. Next come stories about his interactions with women, as retold by Kazuaki Tanahashi in *Penetrating Laughter: Hakuin's Zen and Art* (Woodstock, NY: Overlook Press, 1984), pp. 14–15. Tanahashi's delightful book is also the source of the final selection, Hakuin's "Prescription," pp. 125–27, and it provides many of the details in our biographical note. Hakuin's story of his initial breakthrough and ensuing study with Shōju Rōjin is found in Yampolsky, pp. 118–19; we have adapted the account given there of his first interview with Shōju Rōjin. Miura and Sasaki describe Hakuin's illness as a nervous breakdown in *Zen Dust* (New York: Harcourt, Brace & World, 1966), p. 24; his own interpretation appears in his "Yasenkanna," which we quote from Trevor Leggett's *The Tiger's Cave and*

Translations of Other Zen Writings (Rutland, VT: Charles E. Tuttle Company, 1994), p. 142. Waddell's superb book is the source of the quotations concerning Hakuin's practice in the old palanquin (p. xvii), his tearful awakening (p. 33), and his position regarding recitation of the *nembutsu* (pp. 53, 57, 44, and 45). Passages expressing his position on "silent illumination" are from Yampolsky, pp. 114–15, while his paean to his students as "finest flowers" is again from Waddell, p. xix. The letter described as an "aid to benevolent government" is "Hebiichigo," translated by Yampolsky, pp. 181–222; that particular phrase occurs on p. 182.

Chapter 45. Tōrei's "The Spur" is translated by Trevor Leggett in *Three Ages of Zen* (Rutland, VT: Charles E. Tuttle Company, 1993), pp. 77–86. Our introductory note borrows heavily from Tōrei's *The Inexhaustible Lamp of Our School* as published, with commentary by the later master Daibi Zenji, under the title *Discourse on the Inexhaustible Lamp* (London: Zen Centre, 1989). All of the passages quoted from Tōrei describing his practice with Hakuin are from this source, pp. 390, 391, 392, and 399 (slightly modified); he calls his volume "an incentive to later students" on p. 28. The self-portrait that Hakuin painted for Tōrei is reproduced by Tanahashi in his *Penetrating Laughter: Hakuin's Zen and Art* (Woodstock, NY: Overlook Press, 1984), p. 109. Miura and Sasaki class Tōrei as a "Zen historian and literary man of eminence" in *Zen Dust* (New York: Harcourt, Brace & World, 1966), p. 367; they discuss his *Detailed Study* on pp. 359–60.

Chapter 46. All except one of our Ryōkan selections come from Burton Watson's *Ryōkan: Zen Monk-Poet of Japan* (New York: Columbia University Press, 1977), pp. 82, 85, 23, 74, 81, 55, 95, 77,54, 94, 104, and 89. The exception is "Reading the *Record of Eihei Dōgen*" from Tanahashi's *Moon in a Dewdrop: Writings of Zen Master Dōgen* (San Francisco: North Point Press, 1982), pp. 223–24. In addition, in our account of Ryōkan's life we quote from Watson the poem ending "just the same old Eizō" (p. 87), the lines about his isolation at Entsu-ji (p. 110), his statement on the hermit life (p. 120), the lament of his layman Saichi (p. 106), and phrases on his disdain for pretense (pp. 115–16). John Stevens also has published two worthwhile volumes of translations, *One Robe, One Bowl: The Zen Poetry of Ryōkan* (New York: Weatherhill, 1977) and *Dewdrops on a Lotus Leaf: Zen Poems of Ryōkan* (Boston: Shambhala, 1993). The former includes a substantial introduction where some of the best-known folktales about Ryōkan are summarized (pp. 13–15), and the latter presents a series of love poems for Teishin, including the one we quote (p. 140). We devised our own versions of Ryōkan's not-poem poem and deathbed verse.

FURTHER RESOURCES ON CH'AN AND ZEN

PRACTICAL INTRODUCTIONS

Philip Kapleau, ed., *Three Pillars of Zen: Teaching, Practice, and Enlightenment* (Boston: Beacon Press, 1967) combines modern teachings, personal accounts of practice, historic texts, and other materials to furnish an inspiring orientation to Zen as it has developed in the influential Harada-Yasutani line of Zen. Another perennial favorite is Shunryu Suzuki's *Zen Mind, Beginner's Mind* (New York: Weatherhill, 1973), in which the late founder of San Francisco Zen Center conveys the atmosphere and substance of practice in the Sōtō tradition. Robert Aitken's *Taking the Path of Zen* (San Francisco: North Point Press, 1982) offers clear, practical guidance to Zen as taught by Aitken Roshi, a successor to the Harada-Yasutani lineage and one of the first native-born Zen masters in the United States. In *A Flower Does Not Talk: Zen Essays* (Rutland, VT: Tuttle, 1970), Zenkei Shibayama, the late abbot of a great Rinzai monastery who also did some teaching in the United States, lays out the fundamentals of Zen practice from his perspective, in part through a sparkling commentary on Hakuin's "Song of Zazen." Nyogen Senzaki and Ruth Strout McCandless, *Buddhism and Zen* (San Francisco: North Point Press, 1987) is a collection of spirited, helpful essays for beginners, first published in 1953; Senzaki Sensei was among the first masters to settle and teach in America. See also Thomas Cleary's anthology of Chinese and Japanese instruction manuals, *Minding Mind: A Course in Basic Meditation* (Boston: Shambhala, 1995).

HISTORY AND CULTURE

Heinrich Dumoulin, *Zen Buddhism: A History,* vol 1. India and China, vol. 2 Japan (New York: Macmillan Publishing Company, 1988) is the best general history of Ch'an and Zen yet available in English. The work of a German Jesuit priest who spent many years in Japan, it basically ends with Hakuin, only touching upon 19th- and 20th-century developments. In *How the Swans Came to the Lake: A Narrative History of Buddhism in America,* 3rd ed. (Boston: Shambhala, 1993) Rick Fields covers many Buddhist ways other than Ch'an and Zen but manages to give the most complete historical treatment to date of the tradition's first century in the United States. For perspectives on Ch'an and Zen past, present, and future, see Kenneth Kraft's thoughtful anthology of essays *Zen: Tradition and Transition* (New York: Grove Press, 1988) and Helen Tworkov's *Zen in America: Five Teachers & the Search for an American Buddhism,* 2nd ed. (New York: Kodansha, 1994). A handy and reliable, if strangely titled, reference book is *The Shambhala Dictionary of Buddhism and Zen* (Boston: Shambhala, 1991).

Copyright Acknowledgments

About the Editors

As a writer and editor, Nelson Foster has published books in the fields of history and natural science as well as poems and essays. On religious subjects, his recent credits include *The Ground We Share: Everyday Practice Buddhist and Christian*, which he adapted from conversations between Zen master Robert Aitken and Benedictine brother David Steindl-Rast. He has studied Zen for twenty-five years and teaches it, as a layman, at Diamond Sangha centers in California and Hawai'i.

A native Californian, Jack Shoemaker has been a bookseller and publisher for more than thirty years. His Buddhist practice was initially inspired by the work of Kenneth Rexroth and Gary Snyder. He has published more than four hundred titles over the years under several imprints, including books by Robert Aitken, Gary Snyder, Helen Tworkov, Bankei, Bassui, Bodidharma, Dōgen, Hongzhi, Keizan, Musō, Nanao Sakaki, Nyogen Senzaki, Chang Chuan-Yuan, Miyazawa Kenji, Shuntaro Tanikawa, and Lu Yu in translations by Arthur Braverman, Thomas Cleary, David Gordon, Daniel Leighton, W. S. Merwin, Red Pine, Soiku Shigematsu, Kazuaki Tanahashi, Norman Waddell, and Burton Watson.